WOMEN IN ENGLAND IN THE MIDDLE AGES

Women in England
in the Middle Ages

Jennifer Ward

hambledon
continuum

Hambledon Continuum
A Continuum imprint

The Tower Building
11 York Road
London, SE1 7NX

80 Maiden Lane
Suite 704
New York, NY 10038

First Published 2006

ISBN 1 85285 346 8

A description of this book is available from the
British Library and from the Library of Congress.

Typeset by Carnegie Publishing, Lancaster,
and printed in Great Britain by MPG Books Ltd, Cornwall.

Contents

Illustrations

Text Figures

Preface

There is a growing interest in women of the past. Much more can be found out about them in the records than used to be thought. This results from work done by archaeologists on settlements, churches and houses, and from studies of medieval literature, as well as from research into historical documents. Although the middle ages seem distant from the present day, enough evidence survives to show that medieval women did not always conform to the models laid down by the church or crown. We can find as many varieties of women in the middle ages as we see around us in the modern world. Women appeared outwardly submissive and obedient but were capable of making their wishes felt, whether in peasant protest or as noblewomen making their views known to the king.

In writing the book, I have made use of imperial measurements, the units of money before decimalisation and the county structure as it existed before the local government reorganisation of 1974. £1 was made up of twenty shillings; one shilling comprised twelve pence; the penny was divided into two halfpennies or four farthings. The mark was a unit of account, worth 13s. 4d. A librate of land was a piece of land worth £1.

I would like to thank Lindy Grant, Tony Morris, Nigel Saul, Martin Sheppard and Anne Sutton for their help with the book; and Martin Stuchfield and the Conway Library, Courtauld Institute of Art, London, for permission to reproduce illustrations. Any remaining mistakes are mine. I would also like to thank family and friends for their readiness to discuss questions relating to medieval women and to visit the churches and sites associated with them.

To Joe

1

Women's Worlds

The women of the middle ages, living in England in the thousand years before 1500, seem remote from the twenty-first-century world, and, notwithstanding the amount of historical research over the past thirty years, it takes considerable imagination to grasp what their lives were like. Their world was one of limited technology and poor communications, of insecurity, war and high levels of mortality. Yet there are parallels with modern times in their concern to make a living for their families and in the bonds between husband and wife and parents and children. They lived very much in the present, aware that they might experience good fortune or disaster and that death might strike at any age.

Women's lives can only be understood against their overall background. Between about 500 and 1500, the face of England underwent great change. Early Anglo-Saxon settlements were often small and temporary and there were wide tracts of woodland and waste. With the growth of population between the tenth and thirteenth centuries, settlements grew and in many parts of England nucleated villages were established, encouraged by the unification of England under the West Saxon, Norman and Plantagenet kings and their emphasis on the importance of lordship. The Norman Conquest saw the arrival of new lords but did not interrupt the long-term economic expansion. Towns developed, so that by about 1300 England was covered by a network of market towns and larger centres, with London expanding to a population of about 80,000 before the Black Death of 1348–49.

The majority of people lived on the land, where husband and wife divided the responsibilities for the farm, household and children. The growth of marketing and industry provided opportunities for women to use their skills to earn extra cash for the family through brewing, working on textiles and marketing surplus produce. Life, however, remained harsh, with malnutrition, and even starvation, presenting a real threat to survival into the early fourteenth century.

The Black Death marks a watershed. Between one-third and one-half of the population died and outbreaks of plague continued until the mid seventeenth century. For many families that survived, conditions slowly improved, with more land being available at a lower rent, serfdom gradually disappearing and wages rising in both country and town. Some families accumulated land and rose to yeoman status, with larger and more comfortable houses, a better diet and more possessions. Others migrated to the towns, often finding openings in industry, the crafts and trade. By the later fifteenth century, the effects of the fall in population were to be seen in deserted villages and urban decline, but the population was to rise again in the Tudor period.

Women also have to be seen in a social and cultural context. Throughout the middle ages, they belonged to a complex hierarchical society. As members of different social groups, they lived in different worlds from each other, although subject to many of the same cultural attitudes. The life of a peasant woman, facing a constant daily round of toil, but enjoying the occasional celebration, stands in strong contrast to the noblewoman with her servants, leisured lifestyle and plenty to eat. The division of society into those who fought, those who laboured and those who prayed applied primarily to men, but the divisions between the women of the nobility, peasantry, the towns and religious houses were deeply rooted in society throughout the middle ages.

It was taken for granted that women were weaker than men and subordinate to them. These ideas were derived from the classical, Jewish and Christian past and continued to flourish in the middle ages. The classical belief in the four elements – fire, water, earth and air – and the four humours derived from them influenced, it was thought, the qualities displayed by men and women. Usually one or two qualities were dominant, but whereas men were considered choleric and sanguine, deriving their heat from fire and air, women, it was thought, tended to be cold and moist (as derived from the elements of water and earth) and to be phlegmatic and melancholic. Even in the womb, the girl foetus on the left side of the uterus was believed to be in a colder place than the boy foetus on the right. A woman's sexual organs developed inside their bodies and this was regarded as inferior to the male. Despite this, women were thought to be sexually voracious and had to be kept in check.[1]

Women were regarded as weak, irrational and subject to temptation, just as Eve in the Garden of Eden succumbed to the serpent's wiles, picked the fruit of the Tree of Knowledge of Good and Evil and gave it to her husband to eat. As a result of their disobedience to God's command, she and Adam were expelled from the Garden.[2] According to the Book of Genesis, the pains of childbirth suffered by women were part of the Fall. St Paul laid down that women should be subject to their husbands and this was reiterated by many later churchmen.

The idea of women's frailty appears in numerous medieval writings. In a sermon of c. 1200, Jacques de Vitry, who was in many respects sympathetic to women, stressed the need for female obedience, and described women as a slippery, weak and untrustworthy sex, devious and deceitful; women were stubborn and contrary. He told the story of a man who entertained guests in his garden and seated his sulky wife with her back to the river. She pushed her seat back and fell in. Her husband searched for her upstream because, he said, she never went the right way and would not have been swept down the river.[3]

Women were vulnerable because of their weakness. In this context, the laws on rape throw further light on male attitudes. Rape was seen in the early middle ages as a crime against father or husband, a violation of the protection they exercised over their households. Glanvill and 'Bracton' in the late twelfth and thirteenth centuries considered rape a felony, but there were few convictions. The statutes from 1275 conflated rape and the abduction of a woman; with the prosecution in the hands of male relatives or the king, the female victim of the assault was overlooked and her sexuality regarded as belonging to her father or husband.[4]

Because Jesus Christ was born of the Virgin Mary to redeem mankind, Mary could be taken to show a different side of womanhood. This is certainly true and was emphasised as interest in the Virgin grew from about 1100.[5] For medieval women, however, the Virgin Mary was an ideal to aspire to, not someone whose qualities could be copied by women on earth; no one else could be both virgin and mother. She was the supreme intercessor on behalf of women and a special protectress in pregnancy and childbirth. The female saints, however, served as better models for women's lives.

All these ideas, taken together, imply considerable ambiguity and ambivalence of attitudes towards women. The lives of most women encompassed the cycle of birth, marriage, motherhood and death. The woman's identity in the eyes of the church and the law was for most if not all of her life bound up with that of her father and husband. The way she was often referred to as the daughter or wife of a named man confirmed this lack of individual identity. Yet, in spite of the general emphasis on incapacity, the situation in reality was more complex. The church saw husband and wife as complementing each other and stressed a relationship of love and mutual counselling. From at least the twelfth century, the church saw marriage as based on the consent of both parties to the union. It set its face against divorce, and aimed at preventing the husband from simply abandoning his wife. The evidence from the twelfth century onwards shows women being treated as people in their own right, although they had to accept a subordinate role.

Moreover, for the woman who was left a widow and did not remarry, there was greater independence, since she was regarded as a *femme sole*, a woman on her own, able to make her own decisions about property and business and to plead in the courts. A few women became *femmes soles* in their husbands' lifetimes. Widows from Anglo-Saxon times to the fifteenth century ran estates and made grants to the church, but they usually acted with the agreement and in the interests of their families. On the whole, the legal position of widows improved during the middle ages. The rights of free and unfree women to dower were enshrined in the common and customary law of England in the late twelfth and thirteenth centuries. Widows also gained a much greater say over their remarriage. Women of the gentry and nobility often enjoyed a wealthy and comfortable old age, although problems remained for poorer women.

The family was at the centre of life for most medieval women but for those who adopted the religious life as nuns and anchoresses the focus was on the convent or cell. The religious life was highly regarded by lay society but the influence exerted by religious women varied over the middle ages. A high point was reached soon after the conversion of England to Christianity, when nuns, some of whom came to be regarded as saints, played a prominent role in the conversion and had close contact with royal families. During the eighth century, nuns joined St Boniface's mission to Germany. From the late Anglo-Saxon period, there was much greater emphasis on enclosure, a factor which dominated the rest of the middle ages. Women took part in the great European expansion of monasticism in the twelfth century. This was the period when St Gilbert of Sempringham devised the only English order, with double houses for nuns and canons, although they were rigorously separated from each other. Although nuns rejected the lay world in their professional lives, their families remained important and a mutual relationship between family and religious house frequently existed.

Looking at nuns and married women together, there was both continuity and change during the middle ages. The time of greatest change came in the twelfth and thirteenth centuries, not at the popular dividing date of 1066. That year saw William the Conqueror's victory at Hastings and the establishment of a new royal dynasty and aristocracy; for the Anglo-Saxon nobility it was a time of defeat and loss, the second defeat endured in the eleventh century. Yet for the majority of the population's life and its obligations continued with only temporary disruption, and economic expansion spanned the Conquest.

It was primarily in the twelfth century that changes in church and kingdom had a major impact on the lives of men and women. The church developed its teaching on the mass, marriage and the other sacraments, a movement culminating in the Fourth Lateran Council of 1215, and this brought home to all people how they should live their lives. The teaching was propagated in dioceses and parish churches after 1215, as well as by the preaching of the friars. The growth of canon law and ecclesiastical jurisdiction across Europe enabled the church to enforce its teaching and the expansion of the religious orders made for an additional church presence in the locality. The rise of parish churches also meant that local life was punctuated by the seasons of the church's year with its great festivals and times of fasting, with saints' days and local festivities.

At the same time, the growth of the English common law and of manorial custom dealt with matters directly affecting women's lives. Rules were laid down for allocating dower, and changes in arrangements in the guardianship of children increasingly involved the mother. Although girls who were unfree were expected to pay merchet to the lord before they married, most were allowed to choose their own partners in consultation with their families. Thirteenth-century changes over land tenure had an important effect on women, especially through the growing practice of husband and wife holding land jointly. This happened at all social levels and meant that if the husband died, the wife had the resources to bring up the children and run the family farm or business until the heir was old enough to take over. All these changes are reflected in the records of the time, as both church and kingdom adopted a more professional and bureaucratic approach to administration.

There have long been arguments as to whether the position of women improved during the middle ages. Anglo-Saxon women used to be thought more independent and powerful than Norman women, but neither group had free disposition of property and they conformed to family arrangements concerning marriage and land. The long-term decline in population after the Black Death undoubtedly benefited many men and their families. Greater employment opportunities in the towns by 1400 encouraged teenage boys and girls to enter apprenticeship and service and so gain greater independence of their families and a wider choice of marriage partners. Yet the number of women who benefited was probably comparatively small. There were relatively few opportunities for well-paid employment for women in the countryside and much of the work for women was of low status and poorly paid. Economic slumps, as in the mid fifteenth century, led to insecurity and unemployment, and by the end of the fifteenth century a preference for male workers was growing.

How wide were women's horizons in the middle ages? Queens were likely to have the widest knowledge of the world around them, particularly if they came from a foreign royal family. Eleanor of Castile, the queen of Edward I, was possibly the best informed; her travels took her from Castile to France and England and to the eastern Mediterranean when she accompanied her husband on crusade in 1270. Her travels within the British Isles took in England, Wales and Scotland; her lordship over widespread estates and constant travelling meant that she got to know the kingdom and was seen by many of her subjects. Women of the nobility had interests and contacts in many parts of the realm, as well as some knowledge of continental Europe. In the seventh century, Anglo-Saxon royal nuns entered Frankish houses, while a hundred years later English nuns were working in Germany and going on pilgrimage to Rome. Interests overseas after the Norman Conquest stemmed from birthplace, landholding and pilgrimage. As late as the Hundred Years War, Marie de St-Pol, countess of Pembroke, travelled both in England and France, supervising her estates. Friendships and letter-writing spread news of what was going on. Alice de Bryene and her circle, living in the early fifteenth century in the village of Acton in Suffolk, probably heard about the Mediterranean at first hand from the knight and traveller Sir Richard Waldegrave, who lived nearby.

It is more difficult to evaluate the horizons of peasant and urban women, but it would be a mistake to assume that they spent all their lives in one place and rarely journeyed. In addition to the migrants of the Anglo-Saxon and Viking invasions, there were always some immigrants from continental Europe, settling mainly in large towns and sometimes proving unpopular, as in the London of 1381. Much more usual was migration within England itself, to new settlements in the wake of agricultural colonisation and the conquest of Wales, and from country to town in the era of urban expansion. Migration often took place over relatively short distances, although the incomer was always termed a foreigner. Women moved on marriage and marriage partners were not only found in the villages or towns where they lived. Wherever a woman settled, she was likely to frequent the local markets and fairs.

What of the world of Christendom? The parish church brought women face to face with Christian faith and culture. They would hear of petitions being sent to the bishop or pope. At some time in their lives, they probably visited a local or more distant shrine, performing the pilgrimage on their own behalf or for someone else. Some women, like Margery Kempe, visited Rome and Jerusalem, as well as Santiago de Compostela and shrines in Germany; of these, the pilgrimage to Santiago was very popular in the later middle ages.

In thinking about women's sense of identity, it is likely that they saw themselves primarily as others saw them, in the context of their families and households. Judging by their actions, they accepted their identity as wives and mothers and concentrated on their family and household responsibilities. This is found among women at all social levels. They took a pride in their homes and enhanced the reputation of their households, working alongside their husbands and on their own to make as good a living as they could to provide for the future of their children, and taking responsibility for servants and apprentices as well.

Women also saw themselves as belonging to their community and this gave them an added measure of protection and security, especially in old age. They rarely held public office but played their part in carrying out their obligations to the lord or town government. They were expected to get on with their neighbours and keep the peace. In view of contemporary ideas on their frailties, and their propensity to gossip, it is hardly surprising to find them appearing in the courts as victims of sexual defamation, and they were most often summoned for sexually defaming others, notably other women. It was ordained at a manor court in Durham in 1378 that all the women should refrain from slander. Women were subject to the community's by-laws. At another manor court held by the prior of Durham in 1365, it was decided that one pool was to be reserved for watering the animals and for domestic use, so no washing was to take place there. A few years later it was decided that no one was to wash clothes in the ditch next to the chapel.[6]

Women for the most part were law-abiding but on occasion were ready to protest. The 1330s at Thornbury, Gloucestershire, saw organised protest against the lordship of Hugh Audley. In the early stages, this took the form of refusing labour services, doing them badly and not attending the manor court. Over two-thirds of the villeins took part, including almost every independent active widow. During the second phase, only about one-fifth of the tenants took part but the leaders continued to receive strong support from the women. Altogether, women made up 19 per cent of the protesters in the first phase and 26 per cent in the second. A somewhat different protest took place at Painswick in 1442. John Talbot, earl of Shrewsbury, had taken sixteen of the tenants to the French war but only five returned. The widows complained of losing their land as well as their husbands. An inquiry was held into grievances and the women were given the right to hold their husbands' lands for life and to make their own choice of second husbands.[7]

Relatively little is heard of the women themselves as individuals, although a few women, mainly from the elite, stand out. There are some indications of personal preferences in the wills of the later middle ages; by the fifteenth century, wills are found for yeomen and 'middling' townspeople as well as for the elite. From the early thirteenth century, wills were enforced by the church courts and were mainly concerned with the distribution of possessions.[8] Widows had the right to make wills, but wives had to have the consent of their husbands. The great majority of wills were concerned with the fate of the testator's soul and the future of her family. Alongside the concern for self went a concern for children, parents and ancestors, friends and benefactors.

Women's worlds show continuity and change, stemming from ideas about the nature of women, their place in society, economic and political circumstances, and religious and cultural developments. For the majority of women, marriage was the principal formative event in their lives, leading to their roles as wives and mothers. Girls were brought up in the expectation that they would marry and their mothers provided them with a practical training in housewifely skills and childcare, as well as inculcating religious and moral principles. By the time they were in their teens or early twenties, girls passed from their mother's care to embark on married life.

2

Marriage

Marriage was the most significant rite of passage in young women's lives, most women marrying at least once, unless they entered religious life as a nun. In many respects, it was very different from modern marriage, far more being involved than the personal bond between the couple. In fact, marriage based only on love and attraction was regarded as deplorable and short-sighted. Since marriage usually entailed the establishment of a new household, property arrangements made by the family of the bride and bridegroom, and sometimes by the couple themselves, were essential. Throughout the middle ages, an arranged marriage, supervised by parents and kindred, and sometimes by lord and king, was viewed as necessary for the long-term interests of the family, as well as of the couple. The formation of marriage was based on careful, sometimes lengthy (and sometimes abortive) negotiations which centred on the property brought to the marriage.

The eleventh and twelfth centuries can be seen as marking a watershed in the history of marriage. Before that period, the husband had made the major contribution, made up of the dower and morning-gift. Later, however, the bride's dowry came to be of great importance to the economic foundation of the new household. Changing practices over inheritance and the growth of primogeniture made it more likely that girls would become heiresses, and this inevitably had an impact on marriage plans. These changes coincided with the growth of the church's legislation over marriage. The church always held strong views over the nature of Christian marriage, and especially during the twelfth century these became the basis for the formation of marriage at all levels of society, and were enforced through church teaching and jurisdiction.

The evidence for marriage in the Anglo-Saxon period is much sparser than that available for the later middle ages, and much of it applies only to the royal families and nobility. More is heard of property arrangements than of any personal reasons underlying marriage. It is apparent from the time of the Conversion that the church aimed at encouraging Christian marriage, and that its ideas became more influential in the tenth and eleventh centuries. Royal law codes show a concern from early on to promote a stable society and to protect women within the family structure. Kings and churchmen can be seen to be working together to establish a framework for marriage.[1]

The earliest description of Germanic marriage comes in the account by Tacitus of the peoples of Germany, written in the first century AD. Tacitus described it as a strict and sacred bond. Although there were a few instances of polygamy (in cases where an advantageous alliance with a noble chief was desired), the Germans were on the whole monogamous. Wealth was given by the husband to the bride in the presence of her parents and relations, while she made a present of arms. Neither men nor women were married too young. The wife was treated as her husband's partner, and was faithful to him, and each showed affection to the other. If the wife committed adultery, she was driven from the house naked.[2] Much of this picture is idealised, as Tacitus was using the Germans to criticise the Romans of his own time. Yet the points that he made about monogamy and about the husband's gift of wealth to the bride apply to the Anglo-Saxons.

In the years after the Conversion, churchmen attempted to enforce their ideas on marriage, but this was achieved only slowly. Churchmen had to take account not only of earlier practice but also of constant wars and disorder which militated against stable relationships. Christian concepts had to be modified to take account of political and social circumstances, as seen in the questions posed to Gregory the Great by St Augustine about 600, and in Archbishop Theodore's Penitential. Augustine's questions concerned sexual relations after childbirth, the church's attitude to women before and after the baby was born, and incest, which proved to be an especially intractable problem. Gregory disapproved of marriages between close relations since he argued that they would be childless; he therefore forbade marriage between first cousins, and also with a stepmother or sister-in-law.[3] Such marriages, however, were long found in Anglo-Saxon royal families, and probably occurred in other social groups. Eadbald, son and successor of Æthelberht of Kent, temporarily reverted to paganism and married his father's wife. In the mid ninth century, on the death of Æthelwulf of Wessex, his son and heir Æthelbald married his stepmother, the Frankish princess Judith.[4] Doubtless they considered that their marriage had political advantages.

The Penitential of Theodore archbishop of Canterbury (668–90) discussed these questions and others in a thorough examination of marriage and family life. Theodore, however, was pragmatic in his approach, and realistic over the question of remarriage. If the husband had been sentenced to penal slavery for theft or fornication, his wife might remarry after a year, provided that she had only been married once. The same time had to elapse for remarriage after the husband's death, although, if the wife died, the husband might remarry after a month. The husband was allowed to remarry if he was deserted by his wife, and there was no reconciliation after five years, or if she was taken into captivity. If she was carried away by an enemy and returned to her husband after he had remarried, she was permitted to take another husband if she had been married only once before.[5] These passages in Theodore's Penitential underline the vulnerability of women on their own.

Penitential legislation was mirrored in the royal law codes. Theodore paid considerable attention to adultery and fornication, and both were condemned and punished according to the codes of Æthelberht, Alfred and Cnut. Rape was also condemned.[6] It is likely that much of this legislation represented wishful thinking, as adultery remained a problem frequently encountered in the church courts of the later middle ages. Wihtred of Kent, in his code of 695, was the first king to attempt to abolish illicit unions.[7] By the tenth century, there are signs that the church was exerting greater influence, with faithfulness between husband and wife being emphasised. The Northumbrian Priests' Law, probably dating from the early 1020s, forbade a man to have more than one wife; she was to be lawfully betrothed and married to him, and they were not to be related within four degrees. Marriage was to last for life.[8] Marriages within the four prohibited degrees of relationship were condemned within the royal family, as seen in the separation by St Dunstan of Eadwig from the noblewoman Ælfgifu after he left his coronation banquet.[9]

Divorce continued to be accepted in lay Anglo-Saxon society, although condemned by the church.[10] Many of the kings of the tenth century had a series of wives and this probably happened more widely in society. For kings, political advantage, physical attraction or the need for sons might well appear good reasons for a change of wife. Cnut found it advantageous to marry his predecessor's widow, Emma of Normandy, although Ælfgifu of Northampton, Cnut's previous wife, retained political power. Such a situation gave rise to tension and faction, especially at times of royal succession, as Emma found at the death of Cnut in 1035. [11]

Similarly, the church was unable to stamp out concubinage. This was prevalent in both Anglo-Saxon and Viking societies, although there is no means of knowing its actual extent. Much of the information relates to royalty and nobility, but it is likely that it was widespread among lower social groups as well. There are indications that men took concubines in their youth and only embarked on a full marriage as they grew older and presumably had the property with which to endow a wife. Although not all illegitimate children were acknowledged, concubines enjoyed certain rights, and, in contrast to the situation in the later middle ages, their children could inherit from their fathers. [12] Churchmen fulminated against kings who failed to marry lawfully, as in the letter of St Boniface and seven other bishops to Æthelbald of Mercia, but they made little headway before the tenth century. Cnut's second law code placed men who had a lawful wife and also a concubine outside the pale of the church. [13]

By the early eleventh century, priestly celibacy was also advocated, although it was not until the twelfth century that this policy was widely enforced and clergy wives were referred to as concubines. Twelfth-century cases in the church courts point to the complex family problems resulting from priestly celibacy. Theobald, archbishop of Canterbury, heard a case in 1158–60 concerning a woman who had been deserted by her husband, a clerk who was presumably in lower orders, and had married another man with whom she had had children. [14] The clerk was ordained priest while living abroad; on his return to England he embarked on priestly ministry and took no notice of his wife. The archbishop decided that he should not minister as a priest. His marriage was valid, but husband and wife should in future live apart. The woman was not to blame for the situation, although she should not have stayed with her second husband when she knew that her first husband was alive. The second husband was permitted to remarry, possibly thought to be the best plan for the sake of the children. The first husband was to hand back her dowry to the wife, but nothing is known of her later life. It may well have been bleak.

Lawful marriage was expected to be celebrated publicly with a ceremony and feasting. Theodore's Penitential referred to a priestly blessing of the couple at mass, and King Harthacnut's death in 1042 occurred at a marriage feast.[15] The negotiations were completed before the wedding, and the settlement of property on the bride gave her a measure of protection in the event of early widowhood or divorce. This recognition of the need to provide for the woman's future is found throughout the middle ages. Late Anglo-Saxon marriage arrangements can be traced in a document, probably of the early eleventh century, describing the betrothal of a woman, with the bridegroom negotiating with the woman's kindred. He offered remuneration to those who had brought her up, made a gift to the bride, and granted the dower she would hold if widowed. She was entitled to half the goods of the household if a child was born, unless she married again. Special protection was expected if she was taken away to another lordship, and care was also taken that bride and groom were not too closely related. Once the negotiations were finalised, a priest should marry the couple with God's blessing.[16]

A number of conclusions can be drawn from this text. Negotiation between the families was to remain normal practice for elite marriages during the rest of the middle ages, and it is likely that a measure of bargaining often took place at other social levels. The grant of dower for the widow remained universal; although there were changes in the amount conferred, it always came from the resources of the husband's family. The widow usually held the dower for her lifetime; it then reverted to her marital family, or, according to some late Anglo-Saxon wills, passed to the church as part of the overall family arrangements. What was unusual in the document in the light of later history was the emphasis on all the property coming from the bridegroom. In addition to dower, the husband also made a morning-gift to the bride, celebrating the consummation of the marriage.[17]

Two Anglo-Saxon marriage agreements survive, both of the early eleventh century. When he married the sister of Archbishop Wulfstan of York in 1014–16, Wulfric promised his bride several estates in Worcestershire, some for life, presumably representing her dower, one leasehold estate, and one which she was allowed to grant or bequeath to whom she pleased; this may well have been her morning-gift. He also promised her fifty mancuses of gold, thirty men and thirty horses. The witnesses to the agreement would be able to attest to its validity in the event of a dispute. The second agreement, made in the presence of Cnut in 1016–20, also had faith in widespread publicity. A man named God-wine married the daughter of Brihtric of Kent, giving her a pound's weight of gold in return for her acceptance of him, and also land, live-stock, horses and slaves. Three copies were made of the agreement, one of them remaining in the hands of Brihtric, the other two being deposited at Christ Church and St Augustine's, Canterbury. [18]

The fact that all the property came from the husband is typical not only of Anglo-Saxon England but also of pre-eleventh-century Europe. The bride's contribution of a dowry begins to be found in the eleventh century, but it was not until the twelfth that the morning-gift disap-peared and marriage became based economically on the bride's dowry and the dower from the bridegroom, a situation which lasted for many centuries to come. Early dowries usually took the form of land, the term *maritagium* being used under the Normans and Angevins. The *maritagium* was for the benefit of the couple and their children, and it reverted to the wife's family if the marriage was childless. [19] The will of Thurketel of Palgrave, dated before 1038, refers to the estate which he received when he married his wife Leofwyn; he left this estate to her, together with other land. [20] Further evidence is provided by the Domesday Survey. Edmund the priest held land in Suffolk that he received with his wife, and she consented to a subsequent agreement with the abbey of Ely concerning the land. Ansfrid de Cormeilles was granted six estates in Gloucestershire when he married the niece of Wal-ter de Lacy. The land was sometimes held of the father-in-law; Faderlin held two dowry estates in Hampshire of William Bellet. [21] Women in the eleventh century might therefore hold land as part of their dowry or dower, as well as by inheritance. Azelina, widow of Ralph Taillebois, held land in 1086 in ten places in Bedfordshire, several of the estates being described as belonging to her *maritagium* or dower. [22]

The two conquests of England in the eleventh century, by Cnut and William the Conqueror, had an impact on women of both great and small landowning families as the invaders settled in England. The marriage of an invader to an Anglo-Saxon woman of a landed family helped to validate the husband's land tenure. It is likely that many more of these marriages occurred than are found in the sources, and that some at least involved a measure of force. One of these marriages may lie behind the Herefordshire lawsuit of 1016–35 when Edwin, son of Enniaun, claimed land from his mother. The mother was not in court, and so was visited by Thurkil the White and three thegns, who asked her about the land. She asserted that she had no land belonging to her son, and announced that she was leaving all her land and goods to her kinswoman, Leofflaed. This statement was taken back to the shire court, where Thurkil the White, husband of Leofflaed, asked the court to validate the grant to his wife, and subsequently had the proceedings entered in a gospel-book at Hereford Cathedral.[23] Although this is nowhere stated in the record, Thurkil was probably a companion of Cnut who had married an Anglo-Saxon wife and was accumulating land.

The Domesday Book throws light on similar marriages in the wake of the Norman Conquest. Archbishop Lanfranc, in a letter to Gundulf, bishop of Rochester, referred to women who fled to nunneries for fear of the French. At Pickenham in Norfolk after 1066, one of Wihenoc's men loved a certain woman and married her, and took over her thirty acres of land without the king's grant. Robert d'Oilly married the daughter of Wigod of Wallingford, Wigod's lands subsequently passing to Miles Crispin, who married Robert's daughter.[24] Such marriages were to have long-term implications for landholding in England and have been taken as evidence of the long-held view that the position of women deteriorated after the Norman Conquest. In reality, women benefited from the long-term changes in the years between 1000 and 1200 over inheritance to land and the church's growing jurisdiction over the formation of marriage. Research carried out over the past twenty years has revealed the situation of women to be much more complex than used to be thought, and the idea of a Golden Age for late Anglo-Saxon women has been vigorously contested. Developments relating to dowry and royal interference in marriage formation which used to be dated to the Norman period have been found to have earlier origins.[25] The twelfth and early thirteenth centuries marked greater changes than the Norman Conquest for women at all social levels.

Changes in the law concerning inheritance in the eleventh and twelfth centuries inevitably had an impact on the formation of marriage and family fortunes, and in the long run increased the desirability of women as marriage partners. Anglo-Saxon inheritance was usually a matter for arrangement within the family, although bookland could be left outside the kin. Women are found inheriting and bequeathing land, but often only had a lifetime interest. The reeve Abba, making his will in 835, hoped for a child so that his land could pass to his direct descendants. If no child was born, however, the land was to pass to his wife, as long as she did not remarry. In that case, the land was to pass to his kinsmen, who were to restore her own property to his wife.[26] King and lord might have had a role in the succession to land, as wills often ask for the king's goodwill in carrying out the bequests, and Cnut's laws provided for the lord to divide an intestate man's property between his wife, children and close kin, once the lawful heriot had been taken.[27]

The eleventh and twelfth centuries saw inheritance rights among the kindred becoming restricted, as stress was placed on agnatic kinship (descent in the male line of the conjugal family), and increasingly on primogeniture (inheritance by the eldest son) so as to safeguard the identity of the family estate.[28] Male heirs were preferred, but in their absence daughters were not excluded, and many became heiresses. This long-term change was found in many parts of Europe, but it took a long time to implement, a factor of which the Norman kings, notably Henry I, took full advantage. From women's point of view, the change enhanced their landed and therefore marriageable value: although some families produced large numbers of sons, others were not as fortunate, and sons might well die before they grew up. By 1150, thirty baronies had descended via an heiress.[29] Marriage to an heiress gave many medieval men the opportunity to rise in the social scale.

In the twelfth century, moves were made to define the heiress's position in law. Before the 1130s, in the absence of a male heir, estates generally descended to one female heir, usually the eldest daughter. The division of an estate among co-heiresses, which gradually became usual in English common law and was described as the 'statutum decretum', probably represents a royal decision dating from the last years of Henry I's reign. Referred to in a charter issued by Roger de Valognes about 1145, it provided that 'where there is no son the daughters divide the father's land by the distaffs, and the elder by birth cannot take away half of the inheritance from the younger except by force and wrongdoing'.[30] In spite of this decision, however, female inheritance remained fluid during the twelfth century, and for the rest of the middle ages the king retained the right to overrule the division of land among co-heiresses if he so desired.

Of great significance for women were the twelfth-century changes in the formation of marriage spearheaded by the church through its legis-lation and its jurisdiction in its courts. Although the church's influence over marriage grew in the tenth and eleventh centuries, its overall supremacy was largely achieved during the twelfth and early thirteenth centuries through the growth and enforcement of canon law, with the latter's dissemination through councils, sermons and confessional man-uals to the whole of Western Christendom. Many of the ideas had a long history, but they had never previously become universally known or put into action. Lay society largely accepted the church's position and adapted itself to it, since it wanted to ensure valid marriage and legiti-macy of children in order to secure the future of the family and its property.[31] Families continued to arrange marriages, but within the parameters set by the church, and both kings and lords found ways of profiting from the situation.

The church defined marriage as one of the seven sacraments, and as a relationship to be encouraged at all levels of lay society. Peasant mar-riage posed problems for the church because so many peasants were unfree. The concept that two slaves might marry only developed slowly. In the case of serfdom, which was far more widespread than slavery, the church admitted in the mid twelfth century an element of seigneurial control, while at the same time stressing the necessity of the free con-sent of the couple to the marriage. It was only in the Decretals of 1234 that the necessity of the lord's consent was dropped, but intervention by the lord remained in the case of English villeins.[32]

The central issue in the formation of marriage was the consent of the couple, expressed in the present tense at the marriage ceremony (con-sent *de praesenti*). Marriage could take place at puberty, at the age of fourteen for boys and twelve for girls, and some young couples are found living with parents in their early years of marriage. Conditional or future consent (consent *de futuro*) did not make a marriage, although consent to marry in the future took place at betrothal, and betrothal followed by consummation constituted marriage. Betrothal might take place at the age of seven, but consent to the marriage had to be reiterated at puberty. In his *Decretum* of about 1130–40, the lawyer Gratian considered both consent and consummation as essential to the formation of the marriage, but Peter Lombard put all his emphasis on present consent, and this was reiterated by Popes Alexander III and Innocent III. Consummation of the marriage appears to have been taken for granted, non-consummation being a reason accepted by the church for annulment. The legislation was virtually complete when the Decretals of Gregory IX, known as the *Liber Extra*, were published in 1234.[33]

The church saw it as vital that marriage should take place in the presence of witnesses in a public setting. The publication of banns, announcing the marriage and asking for the declaration of any impediments, is first found in England about 1200, and was extended in Christendom by the Fourth Lateran Council of 1215. The church preferred marriage to take place at the church door, but it proved impossible to ensure that all marriages took place in public. The church courts handled numerous cases of clandestine marriages in which it proved difficult to discover when, where and in what form the words of consent had been spoken. Even when the correct words had been spoken, difficulties might arise. Alice Dolling brought a case against William Smith in 1271–2, alleging a marriage denied by William. One of Alice's witnesses, Cecilia Long, gave a vivid description of the couple plighting their troth in the house of John le Ankere in Winterbourne Stoke, Wiltshire. William and his witnesses claimed, however, that he was four miles away at Bulford, serving at a feast of the parish guild.[34]

The church frowned on the marriage of close kin, but the ban on marriage within seven degrees of relationship of the late eleventh century proved impossible to enforce. The Fourth Lateran Council forbade marriage within four degrees of relationship, so it was not permitted if the parties had a common great-great-grandparent. The ban applied to consanguinity (kindred relationships), to affinity (marital kin) and to relationships with godparents.[35] The elite in society got round the ban by securing papal dispensations to marry,[36] but it posed difficulties for members of small communities where there was a considerable amount of endogamous marriage (marriage within the community).

This legislation had a considerable impact on women. With attention focused on the couple, the parties had greater freedom to assent to or refuse marriage, and this may have applied particularly if they were older. In the later middle ages, women, especially in the towns, probably had considerable freedom in marriage formation.[37] The stress on publicity gave women greater security that the marriage would last, the danger with clandestine marriage being that one of the parties would change his (or her) mind, or that parents would intervene. However, although consent *de praesenti* constituted a safeguard to the parties, parental pressure is an imponderable and largely undocumented factor. Christina of Markyate was able to withstand it, as much later did the young Margery Paston. In view of the strength of ideas on family and lineage, however, and the importance attached to family strategies, it is likely that at least some young people succumbed to parental persuasion.[38] This is often assumed to have been the case with the elite, but it quite probably happened lower down the social scale as well.

The church employed a variety of means to ensure that the canon law of marriage became widely known. By about 1200, when the system of parish churches in England was virtually complete, men and women had greater access to church services and teaching than before. The decrees of the Fourth Lateran Council took advantage of this situation by laying down that four sermons should be preached in church each year. Parishioners were also expected to make their confession before their Easter communion. Manuals, such as that by Thomas of Chobham, guided the parish priest as to the canon law, and confession was used as an occasion for teaching parishioners.[39] Thomas was writing soon after the Fourth Lateran Council; he had studied for several years at the University of Paris, before becoming sub-dean of Salisbury Cathedral.

Diocesan statutes were designed in the first instance to guide the parish priest. They are found before the Fourth Lateran Council and became more common in the thirteenth century. Hubert Walter's Council at Westminster in 1200 laid down regulations about the prohibited degrees of relationship, the publication of banns and the marriage ceremony which was to take place in public in the presence of a priest. The public ceremony and the regulations about consanguinity were included in Stephen Langton's statutes for the diocese of Canterbury of 1213–14.

The statutes of Richard Poore of 1217–28 for the diocese of Salisbury were comprehensive and influential. They covered all the sacraments of the church, and viewed marriage as a public ceremony, preceded by the banns and celebrated with reverence. The correct form of the words of consent were given, as were the rules about consanguinity. Sorcery at any wedding was condemned. Clandestine marriages were forbidden, with the priest officiating to be suspended, but this provision could never be enforced during the middle ages.[40]

The foundation of the orders of friars in the thirteenth century provided a great incentive for preaching, and placed the church's teaching in the context of everyday life. Marriage sermons were commonly preached on the second Sunday after Epiphany when the appointed Gospel reading recounted Christ's first miracle at the marriage feast at Cana in Galilee. They portrayed marriage as a holy and indissoluble unit, based on love between husband and wife. The couple were urged to be faithful to each other, adultery being condemned in both partners. The theme of human marriage led to the concept of spiritual marriage, the marriage of the individual soul and of the church with Jesus Christ. Guibert de Tournai, for instance, divided a sermon into the themes of sacramental, bodily, spiritual and eternal marriage. Gerard de Mailly drew parallels between the ideal qualities of the bridegroom and of Christ. These teachings were illustrated with everyday anecdotes and moral tales. Such sermons by the great preachers associated with the University of Paris were copied and distributed across Europe. In all probability they reached a mass audience of men and women, clergy and laity.[41]

Jurisdiction over marriage was exercised by the church courts, although the royal courts dealt with issues of property. Litigants were anxious to ensure that their marriages were valid and their children legitimate. Surviving records of marital cases cover a wide range of problems, including under-age marriage, bigamy and desertion. Some decisions were pragmatic, showing compassion for the family. In a Lincolnshire case of 1174–81, rumours grew, after the banns and marriage ceremony, that the couple were too closely related. The matter having been referred to Pope Alexander III on appeal, it was decided that, if the report was true, the witnesses to the rumours were to be silenced and the couple absolved.[42] A more complex case of 1174–78, also sent on appeal to Alexander III, turned on a change of mind by one of the parties, something which the church courts often had to tackle. R. (his full name is unknown) and Mary, daughter of Gilbert de St Leger, were said to have been married by consent *de praesenti* during Lent, a season when marriage ceremonies in church were not supposed to take place. R. subsequently decided that he wanted to marry someone else, and, although forbidden by the archbishop, married Matilda, daughter of Hugh de Polstead. He owned up to both marriages; Mary claimed that she had only been betrothed to him while Matilda stated that he was her husband. Mary appealed to the pope when the issue arose of the two women's relationship. She was forbidden to remarry during the appeal, but married W. Alexander III upheld R.'s second marriage, probably on the grounds that the first marriage was not carried out in face of the church.[43] It might be argued in this case that the parties were simply doing what they wanted and ignoring the archbishop's pronouncements, yet the fact that the case was brought to the church courts shows that they wanted ecclesiastical endorsement for their marriage, presumably in the interest of their own peace of mind and the legitimacy of their children and heirs.

This issue of legitimacy and therefore of inheritance was at the heart of the best-known twelfth-century case, concerning Richard de Anesty, and dating from 1158–63. Richard claimed to be the heir of his uncle, William de Sackville, on the grounds that William's only child, Mabel de Francheville, was illegitimate. If Mabel had been legitimate, she would probably have inherited her father's land. Richard alleged that William had broken his marriage contract with Albereda de Tresgoz and married Mabel's mother, Adelicia, daughter of Amfrid the sheriff. William and Albereda were said to have expressed present consent, and, according to Richard's account, Albereda asserted that she was William's lawful wife at his wedding to Adelicia, but failed to be heard because of the crowd and because William turned a deaf ear. She was later granted a decree by the bishop of Winchester and Pope Innocent II that William should return to her as her husband. Mabel argued, however, that the marriage contract with Albereda only amounted to betrothal, and that both Albereda and William had agreed to end it; the relationship had never been consummated and William had returned Albereda's dowry. William and Adelicia's marriage had been carried out in the face of the church, and Albereda's father had been present at the wedding feast. The annulment of the marriage by the bishop was null and void. For Alexander III the annulment was the crucial issue, and Mabel was adjudged illegitimate.[44]

From the twelfth century, men and women made use of the church courts to sort out their marital problems, but the surviving records cover only a small proportion of the cases actually brought. Although people of rank normally took their problems directly to the bishop or pope, and cases were not brought by people at the bottom of the social scale, an analysis of marital pleas indicates that a wide social range of men and women made use of the church courts.[45] The church's views on marriage were generally accepted, although it failed to make good its view that subsequent marriage legitimised children already born to a couple. This had been the case in England in the twelfth century but was forbidden in the Statute of Merton of 1236. The church's insistence on present consent as the basis of marriage was widely understood, but the wording of that consent was often at the root of the cases which came to the church courts, particularly when the marriage had been clandestine and not celebrated publicly, with witnesses in attendance. It was probably not until the fifteenth century that the number of clandestine marriages declined.[46]

The church was therefore not completely successful in ensuring that all marriages accorded with its views but, compared with the situation in earlier centuries, its achievement in the twelfth century was remarkable. There was widespread knowledge of the church's rules on marriage. From 1200 until the end of the middle ages and beyond, the formation of marriage was dependent on the prescriptions of canon law. Society as a whole accepted that present consent between a couple who were not closely related to each other constituted marriage. The church was concerned with the personal tie between the couple, but marriage was an economic, social and sometimes political tie as well. Parents continued to negotiate the property arrangements of marriage, taking into consideration the political and social advantages of the alliance. Moreover, kings and lords had their say in the marriages of vassals, and lords' intervention in peasant marriage is apparent at least from the thirteenth century. All these aspects of marriage between the twelfth and fifteenth centuries can be traced in considerable detail as documentary evidence becomes more abundant, and as lay society became more reliant on the written word. [47]

The intervention of kings in marriage dates back to late Anglo-Saxon times, but is much more noticeable in the Norman and Angevin periods. As a result of the Norman settlement, those who held in chief of the king owed him knight service and counsel, and the king had the right of guardianship when the heir was a minor, gaining control over his marriage. [48] The fluid law of inheritance in the twelfth century gave the king further opportunities to intervene. Such royal rights were important for the security of the realm (no king would want one of his enemies married to a great heiress), and were a valuable source of reward and patronage for *curiales* (courtiers). Rights of wardship were lucrative for king and *curiales*, affecting not only the great nobles but lesser families also. Wardship continued into the Tudor period, but royal manipulation of marriage and inheritance was most marked in the twelfth and thirteenth centuries.

According to the charter of liberties issued at Henry I's coronation in 1100, consultation with the king had to take place if a tenant-in-chief wished to marry off a female relative, to ensure that she was not married to an enemy of the king. [49] The king was not to receive money for the marriage licence. An heiress of a tenant-in-chief was to be married with the advice of the barons, and a widow was not to be married against her will. The barons were to adopt a similar policy in relation to their own vassals. In fact, Henry I made extensive use of the marriage of heiresses and widows in rewarding his *curiales*, sometimes even passing over male heirs. Miles of Gloucester became a great lord in 1121 through his marriage to Sibyl de Neufmarché. Sibyl was assigned Brecon as her *maritagium*, to hold either after the deaths of her parents, or during their lifetimes if they so wished. The charter stated that Henry I was acting at the request of Bernard de Neufmarché, his wife and barons, but since the rights of Sibyl's brother were passed over (the claim that he was illegitimate came later), it is probable that pressure was brought to bear on the family by the king. [50] Provision was made for Henry's illegitimate son, Robert, earl of Gloucester, by marriage. He married the daughter, and received the inheritance, of Robert fitz Haimon, and in this case the two other daughters were placed in nunneries. The Basset family also benefited from marriage, this time from the marriage of Richard Basset to the daughter of Geoffrey Ridel, as did the future King Stephen, married to Matilda, heiress of Count Eustace of Boulogne.[51]

The vigorous exploitation of royal rights over marriage ceased at Henry's death, but the Angevin kings saw the advantages of marriage for purposes of reward and for financial gain. Henry II's general concern is highlighted in the *Rotuli de Dominabus et Pueris et Puellis de XII Comitatibus* (Rolls of Ladies and Boys and Girls of Twelve Counties) of 1185.[52] These comprised a royal inquiry into ladies and wards in the king's gift, and the information, provided by local juries, includes the names and ages of widows and a valuation of their lands. Their ages and landed status varied widely, and by no means all would be in demand as brides. Alice of Essex was described as sixty years old in one entry and eighty in another, had a grown-up family, and held land worth £67 in Northamptonshire and Essex.[53] In another case, at the beginning of Richard I's reign, William Marshal's service was rewarded when he married the heiress of Richard Strongbow, Isabella de Clare, who inherited extensive estates in Striguil and Leinster.[54]

Marriage to heiresses also benefited the royal family. Henry II's youngest son John gained the extensive estates of the honour of Gloucester through his marriage to Isabella, youngest daughter of Earl William. Little land was allocated to the two elder daughters who were already married, Henry II not applying the rule that an inheritance should be equally divided among co-heiresses. Isabella's marriage was childless and she was subsequently divorced. Her marriage in 1214 to Geoffrey de Mandeville, earl of Essex, who promised to pay a fine of 20,000 marks, reflects not only the financial gains to be made through marriage but also the way in which the king could use it as a financial weapon to secure loyalty.[55] Royal intervention in marriage continued under Henry III, Edward I and Edward II in the interests of the royal family, their kinsmen and the *curiales*.[56] From the time of Edward III, however, there was much less intervention in the marriages of the nobility, and parents were usually able to make their own arrangements.

Royal wardship, however, continued. Grievances over wardship and marriage led to attempts at regulation in the Magna Carta,[57] and changes in methods of landholding meant that fewer estates came into royal hands when a minor inherited. The practice of joint tenure by husband and wife, found from the late thirteenth century, meant that on the death of a husband, the wife continued to hold and administer the estates. Enfeoffment to use, found widely in the late middle ages, put the estate in the hands of trustees and precluded a royal takeover. Wardship remained a source of financial gain for the crown, and the right of marriage usually remained with the king or his grantee, but it was possible for minors to choose their own marriage partners on payment of a fine. [58]

Barons had similar rights to the king over their own vassals and heard cases of marriage in their honour courts. In the mid twelfth century, Roger de Mowbray was probably instrumental in marrying two of the four daughters and co-heiresses of William Tison to members of his household. The Clare earls of Hertford appear to have been using marriage of heiresses for patronage purposes in the twelfth century, when one of their stewards, Stephen de Danmartin, married the heiress of the vassal Alured de Bendeville. [59] By the time the honour court rolls begin, early in the fourteenth century, there was a set procedure for dealing with dower, wardship and marriage, which brought in the occasional financial windfall to the lord. In 1309, on the death of Thomas Auger, his land was taken into the earl's hand. His two granddaughters, Joan and Margaret, came to the court. The jury reported that Thomas held one messuage and twelve acres of arable land in two Norfolk villages. Joan and Margaret were his heirs, Joan aged twenty and Margaret thirteen. Thomas's wife Alice was to receive one-third of the tenement as her dower, and the two girls paid a fine of £4 for their marriage. [60]

Royal interventions in marriage give the impression, often rightly, that the heiress was treated as a pawn, valued more for her inheritance than for her personal qualities. Where marriages were arranged by parents of the nobility, gentry and elite townspeople, the girl was sometimes, although not invariably, similarly regarded. Although parents were mindful of their family interests, they wanted to achieve for their daughters an establishment where they would be secure. They also wanted their daughters to marry within their own social rank or possibly above. Margery Paston's marriage to the family bailiff, Richard Calle, angered her mother because the marriage was beneath her and a mark of disgrace to her upwardly mobile and ambitious family. The couple's love for each other was no excuse. [61] Marriages to fortune-hunters, and, still worse, elopements, were deplored, although parents often had to accept them. John Pelham, a member of the lesser Sussex gentry, made a raid one night in 1387 on the house of Sir John Shardelowe, and carried off and married Shardelowe's widowed daughter-in-law who was co-heiress of Sir Roger Grey of East Anglia. Unfortunately for him, his wife died childless three years later.[62]

Parents in these social groups made early plans for the marriages of their children. Marriage entailed careful and sometimes prolonged negotiation, and there was no guarantee that the outcome would be successful. The Paston letters throw light on how family and friends were on the lookout for likely marriage partners, but early hopes did not always lead to a successful conclusion.[63] In marrying daughters, parents had to bear in mind the cost of dowries, and a father dying before his children grew up was likely to make provision for the dowries in his will. In his will of 1393, Richard earl of Arundel (d. 1397) arranged for his daughter Margaret to have 100 marks a year for her support until she married, and he bequeathed 1000 marks towards her dowry, noting that the sum could be increased to 1500 marks. Thomas Stonor's will of 1431 provided for the marriage of his son and heir Thomas to be sold, and the money used for the dowries of his five daughters, who were to have at least 200 marks each. The girls were to marry in order of age, and if any daughter died unmarried, her portion was to be divided equally among the others. In the event of the deaths of both his sons and inheritance by the daughters, no cash dowry payments were to be made.[64]

In negotiating marriage, parents took account of property, status and the advantages of the alliance. Heiresses were always in demand, and many families rose in the social scale as a result of a series of fortunate marriages, as well as by successful royal or noble service or a career such as the law. Yet parents were aware that marriage was a gamble, that the heiress might die before succeeding to her inheritance, that the marriage might be childless, and that the demands made by her parents for jointure might be excessive. Such parents in the fifteenth century expected substantial settlements for their daughters, with the result that many heiresses were married to younger sons rather than to the heirs of the higher nobility.[65] Of possibly greater advantage to the bridegroom's family was the widowed bride with her dower and jointure, or the wife who only became an heiress during the course of her marriage. Even then there might be problems if her inheritance was subject to an entail in the

male line, as became increasingly common in the fourteenth and fifteenth centuries. Richard Beauchamp, earl of Warwick (d. 1439), married
as his first wife Elizabeth, the only child of Thomas Lord Berkeley.
Although there was no difficulty over Elizabeth's succession to the Lisle
lands, inherited through her mother, the Berkeley inheritance was subject to an entail and passed to her cousin James, despite the vigorous
opposition of Elizabeth, her husband and their descendants. The lawsuit
ended only in 1609. [66]

Many parents looked for advantageous alliances at court or locally.
Kinship between the couple was not a disadvantage, as a dispensation to
marry could be obtained from the church. Sometimes marriage was
used as a means of making peace between families. William de Bohun,
earl of Northampton (d. 1360), married Elizabeth de Badlesmere, widowed daughter-in-law of Roger Mortimer, whom William had been
closely involved in seizing when Edward III took power in 1330. The
marriage was arranged to end hostility between the families. [67] Alliances
might also increase a family's prestige and status. The later medieval
nobility was a closely interrelated group, and the higher nobility often
had ties with the royal family. In the Norman period, marriages were
concluded with French or Norman families; by the fourteenth century,
there were few continental alliances, although Aymer de Valence, earl
of Pembroke, married first Beatrice de Clermont, and then Marie de
St-Pol. On a county level, the gentry pursued a policy of local alliances,
some of them marrying into the peerage or the urban elite. The marriages of the knightly Conyers and Strangways families in the North
Riding of Yorkshire in two generations to the daughters and heiresses of
Philip, Lord Darcy, and William Neville, Lord Fauconberg, reflected
alliances found elsewhere in England. The daughter of Philip Mede,
merchant and mayor of Bristol, married into the Berkeley family, while
the wives of the London vintner Lewis John belonged to the families of
the de Vere earls of Oxford and Montagu earls of Salisbury. The
strengthening of the county network in Essex is seen in the marriages of
three of the daughters of William Coggeshale (d. 1426) to William Bate-
man, John Doreward and John Tyrell, all of them leading members of
the local gentry. Incomers entered the county gentry by marriage, and
in this way men such as lawyers rose in the social scale. Thomas Kebell,
whose ancestors were probably Coventry artisans, benefited from his

father's upward mobility; Walter Kebell served Joan Beauchamp, lady of Abergavenny, and married a Leicestershire heiress. Thomas, a younger son, pursued a career in the law and also made advantageous marriages.[68]

The marriage settlement itself centred on the legal, property and financial terms of the marriage. For the future benefit of their daughter, parents wanted a settlement which would match her dowry and ensure her future security, and from the fourteenth century contracts were imposing restrictions on the bridegroom's father's power to alienate land. Margery Brewes knew that, however much she wanted to marry John Paston III, her father would never consent without what he regarded as an adequate landed settlement.[69] The bride's dowry had to be matched to the dower and, from the late thirteenth century, jointure. This comprised land settled on husband and wife, to be held by the latter for life if she was widowed. Before about 1200, there was no set definition of dower, but it was usually assigned to the bride by her husband at the wedding ceremony at the church door. This custom survived into the fourteenth century, as at the wedding of Edmund Mortimer and Elizabeth de Badlesmere in 1316. From the time of the 1217 and 1225 issues of the Magna Carta, however, dower was standardised as one-third of the lands held by the husband during his lifetime. By the late fifteenth century, when there was a feeling that widows with dower and jointure held too much land, the development of the entailed use precluded the allocation of dower.[70]

The arrangements are clearly set out in the contract of 1268 for the marriage of Robert de Vere and Margaret Mortimer, set in the aftermath of the Barons' Wars. By then, the *maritagium* was giving way to a cash dowry. The bridegroom's father, Robert de Vere, earl of Oxford, had adhered to Simon de Montfort, was taken prisoner at Kenilworth in 1265, and his lands granted to Roger Mortimer. He recovered his estates under the Dictum of Kenilworth on payment of a fine of 4,000 marks, of which 1,000 marks were remitted in return for the marriage of his son and heir to Roger's daughter Margaret. In view of this remission, Roger paid no dowry. The contract provided for the marriage to take place when the couple reached puberty. The bridegroom was to dower Margaret with 100 librates of land at the wedding, and the estates were specified in the contract. If Robert junior died before the wedding,

Margaret was to marry his brother Hugh. Margaret was to receive a 100 librates of land for life if the marriage failed to take place because of obstruction by the de Veres, and the earl was to pay the 1,000 marks which Roger Mortimer had remitted; no payment was to be made if an impediment was raised by the Mortimers. The 1,000 marks also had to be paid if Robert, Hugh or Margaret died before the marriage.[71] In fact, the marriage went ahead.

Such a document makes marriage appear a cold-blooded affair, and there are cases where the parties appear little better than pawns. Ralph Neville, earl of Westmorland, appears to have been primarily concerned with wealth and connection when marrying off the children of his second marriage to Joan Beaufort.[72] Yet it has to be borne in mind that, while evidence often survives of the property arrangements, it is only rarely that there is information on the personal side. It is likely that many couples knew of each other before marriage. Noble and gentry society was close-knit, hospitality was widely exercised and visiting was frequent. Moreover, girls and boys often spent their teenage years in other households, and some betrothed children got to know each other before marriage by living in the same household. People became known by reputation if not personally, and Margery Brewes was in no doubt that she wanted to marry John Paston III. Margaret Mautby's marriage to John Paston I was carefully arranged, and the couple got on with each other when they first met.[73] It cannot be assumed that all children of the elite knew nothing of their marriage partners and were pressurised into marriage, although undoubtedly this happened in some cases.

It might be expected that the peasantry had greater freedom in the choice of marriage partners. In a village, people lived very much under the public gaze and children grew up, played and worked together. The leyrwite fines, levied for sexual relationships before marriage, point to young people's freedom to be together.[74] Yet dowry and dower were needed for peasant as for elite marriages, and in both cases marriage was subject to the requirements of canon law. In addition, the peasant bride might have to pay a fine to the lord for her marriage. Peasants were therefore likely to be influenced by parental wishes and their landed position, although it is possible that a couple's liking for each other often coincided with parental agreement. Negotiations had to be undertaken, sometimes with the help of a go-between, and fathers are found settling land on their children prior to marriage. At Brigstock, Northamptonshire, the agreement for the marriage of Beatrice Helkok and Henry Cocus specified that Beatrice's parents would give money, a cow and clothing, and would also pay for the marriage feast, while Henry's parents agreed that he would inherit half a virgate.[75] Some young men and women already had possessions and land to bring to the marriage as a result of inheritance or grant.

Age of bride and bridegroom is difficult to calculate because of the paucity of evidence. It is possible that before the Black Death couples married in their late teens or early twenties, as evidence at Brigstock and Halesowen suggests. Members of well-off families may have been younger when they married than poorer peasants. This may have continued after the Black Death as more land and work became available. Some women, however, may have delayed marriage until their mid-twenties, often after a period in service, as research on Yorkshire and Essex has indicated. Both bride and bridegroom were usually about the same age, making for a companionate marriage.[76]

In many villages, the lord of the manor had a say in peasant marriage. While the agricultural economy was expanding in the thirteenth century, it was in the lord's interests to encourage marriage and the establishment of new households, and some lords brought pressure to bear on villagers to marry. At Horsham St Faith in Norfolk, in the late thirteenth century, tenants were ordered to marry partners chosen by a village jury, but most preferred to pay a fine, presumably to make their own choices. The lord was especially interested in orphaned heirs and reserved the right to their marriage, although this could be remitted on payment of a fine. The manor of Park in Hertfordshire, on the St Albans Abbey estates, had a few cases of tenants being compelled to marry unless they paid a fine, and the ejection of a tenant for unlicensed marriage.[77]

On many manors, the lord insisted on the purchase of a licence to marry. This usually applied to the woman, and more often to the unfree than to the free. Merchet, as this due was called, was regarded in the thirteenth century and later as a mark of serfdom. There has been considerable discussion as to how it originated and what it stood for. It was probably connected with the transfer of the dowry to the husband, and payment of the fine marked the lord's acceptance of the marriage and the new tenant. The licence could be purchased at the time of the marriage or bought in advance. Merchet tended to be levied at a higher rate if the girl married a man from elsewhere and moved to another manor, and it was generally paid by the better-off villeins.[78]

Manorial customs over the payment of merchet varied. At Park before 1348, merchet was paid on about two-thirds of peasant marriages, the richer peasants paying more and several fines being pardoned because of poverty. There was an exceptionally large number of marriages in 1349 in the wake of the Black Death, but merchet payments declined rapidly afterwards and had almost disappeared by 1400.[79] This situation can be compared with Winslow in Buckinghamshire, another manor of the abbey St Albans, where there was considerable evasion of merchet in the two decades before the Black Death, and even more in the 1350s, when forty-two villeins left the manor.[80] The weakening of seigneurial controls had a beneficial effect on villein status. Where the lord was able to maintain control over his tenants, however, merchet continued to be levied in the fifteenth century. The *Liber Gersumarum* of Ramsey Abbey recorded 426 merchet payments from twenty-nine manors between 1398 and 1458.[81] This did not include all the marriages which took place, but the abbey was clearly still able to exert its authority.

Payments were made by both men and women. Of the 204 marriage licences recorded in the fourteenth-century court book of Winslow, eighty-eight were purchased by men and eighty-one by women, with only a minority paid for by parents or others. Most licences cost between one and two shillings but could be considerably more, possibly for richer families; there is no evidence of women paying less than men. On the Ramsey manors, 33 per cent of the licences were paid for by women, 33 per cent by the father and 26 per cent by the bridegroom. In addition, 21 per cent of the licences gave the woman the right to marry whom she liked. There was also wide variation in the amount of the fines. The amount was much less for marrying a villein within the village, and those paid for by brides were cheaper than those bought by fathers and bridegrooms.[82] The size of the fine was probably related to the financial standing of the purchaser.

The evidence of the merchet fines indicates that, although many peasant marriages took place within the village, some men and women married elsewhere. There is a widely held assumption that people rarely moved from their birthplaces before modern times, but a variety of evidence shows this to be a fallacy. On the lands of the abbey Ramsey, marriages were taking place within a radius of fifteen miles. [83] Social and economic changes between the twelfth and fifteenth centuries encouraged the movement of people. The growth of towns presupposed immigration from the villages around them or, in the case of the largest centres, from much further afield. Peasants moved to new settlements, and came into the towns to sell and buy at the markets and fairs. There were increasing opportunities for making social contacts, although it is very difficult to document actual cases of migration, and women's migration before the Black Death has been described as 'largely invisible'. After the Black Death, there may well have been extensive migration by teenage boys and girls entering apprenticeship or servanthood, as has been found for York and Yorkshire, and such migration must have had an effect on marriage. [84]

There are signs in the eleventh and twelfth centuries that lords exercised a measure of control over marriages in towns. The customs of Newcastle-upon-Tyne at the time of Henry I specified that merchet did not exist in the town. The fine of childwite, paid by a father whose daughter gave birth to a bastard, was levied in London before Henry II's charter of 1155. John's charter to Bristol of c. 1189 allowed the burgesses to marry and to give their sons, daughters and widows in marriage without their lord's licence; moreover, the lord was to have no rights of wardship and marriage over the burgesses. [85] Although some seigneurial controls remained in the smaller towns, the growth of self-government in the larger centres led to the disappearance of such restrictions. Parental and family controls might well remain, but young people away from home would have had more freedom to choose their marriage partners, as was the case with those working in craftsmen's households in York after the Black Death. Possibly, this situation goes back to the thirteenth century. In a case concerning the marriage of Alice, niece of Ralph the baker, to John the blacksmith in London about 1200 no reference was made to her parents. It is probable that Alice made her own choice. [86]

At the end of all the negotiations, the wedding itself had the colour and ritual of the ceremony at the church door, followed by feasting and conviviality. This applied at all social levels, although relatively little is known about peasant weddings. It was a time of gift-giving and celebration. The wedding celebrations of Richard earl of Arundel's daughter Elizabeth and Thomas Mowbray, earl of Nottingham, at Arundel Castle in 1384 lasted for a week. The wedding was attended by Richard II and Anne of Bohemia, and Earl Richard gave a present to each member of their household. When Mary de Bohun married Henry Bolingbroke, the future Henry IV, his two sisters each gave her a silver-gilt goblet and ewer, and she received jewels from her new father-in-law, John of Gaunt. The guests were entertained by ten royal minstrels, together with four in the service of Gaunt's brother, Edmund, earl of Cambridge.[87] Once the celebrations were over, the couple embarked on married life.

3

Wives and Mothers

On 14 September 1323 Thomas de Hale agreed to maintain his daughter and son-in-law, Richard de Bruche, in accordance with their gentle status, using the property which had been granted to the couple by Richard's father, Henry. Richard was to train as a lawyer, spending one year at Oxford, and four years as an apprentice at the Court of Common Pleas, and receiving £1 13s. 4d. each year for his food and clothing.[1] Presumably, his wife continued to live with her father, and the couple were unable to set up their own household for at least five years. Such arrangements, where the young couple lived with parents at the start of their marriage, are found relatively frequently in the middle ages, but for the most part marriage marked the beginning of an independent life in a nuclear household, using the property, goods and money conferred by the parents at marriage.

The pattern of nuclear households dates from at least Anglo-Saxon times, although many couples had parents and relatives living close at hand. Research on the Halesowen court rolls for the period between 1270 and the Black Death shows that most people lived in nuclear households, although there were also households with extended families. The number of extended families fell after 1349.[2] The rise in population between about 1000 and 1300 meant that by the late thirteenth century, with land in short supply, the son found that his best hope lay in a grant from the family holding. Some, however, chose to move to new settlements or growing towns, and in East Anglia the growth of the land market lessened the dependence on the family for land. The high level of mortality after the Black Death, together with the much greater availability of land and urban work, increased the amount of migration, and many families in towns in particular lacked close kindred nearby.

Whether the newly married couple settled near their relations or not, they lived their lives very much under the eyes of their neighbours.

There was little privacy until the late middle ages, and then only for the better off who could afford larger houses and more rooms. Quarrels were overheard by servants and neighbours, and, in an age when most activities were community-based, gossip was rife. Women were usually blamed for gossip, and, as they went around getting water, grinding flour or baking bread, news of what was happening was bound to circulate. Both borough and manorial courts attempted to punish gossiping, with apparently little effect, as when the tithing jury at Nottingham in 1407–8 presented Alice Brown, Isolda Osborn, Agnes Ostler, Cecily Mold, Denise Baxter and especially Helen Mylner as common scolds.[3]

The wife was expected to take charge of the household and in due course of the children. Her upbringing normally fitted her for her duties, just as her husband made use of his training in farm work or a craft. The man was the head of the household and his wife was expected to obey him. It was the husband who was responsible for property and who exercised public duties such as taking office in the courts or parish church and paying taxes. His wife was expected to conform to the communal code of behaviour. She might appear in the local court for such offences as gossip, theft, or breaches of the assize of bread and ale, but did not owe suit of court, since she held no property in her own right. She could, however, do much to enhance her husband's reputation by her behaviour and hospitality, and was expected to be able to take her husband's place in his absence and to help with the farm or business.

Relationships between husbands and wives ranged from the happy to the humdrum and the incompatible. Most couples managed to stay together and evolve a working partnership; it was easier for a couple to survive by combining their different skills than for someone on their own. The church advocated a loving relationship, but a hard-headed and practical viewpoint was often needed in the medieval world. Looking at individual couples, much of the evidence of affection is. During the late fourteenth and early fifteenth centuries, tomb depictions show husband and wife holding hands, as with Richard II and Anne of Bohemia at Westminster Abbey, John de la Pole and Joan Cobham at Chrishall, Essex, and Ralph Grene and his wife at Lowick, Northamptonshire. This may well have been more than a conventional gesture; there was certainly a close relationship between Richard and

Anne, and the contract for the Lowick tomb laid down the details of the sculpture.[4]

Actions by husband or wife throw more reliable light on their feelings, and miracle stories sometimes illuminate a marriage. Letitia Lamede's husband took her by wheelbarrow in 1279 from London to Evesham, to the shrine of Simon de Montfort. She suffered from dropsy and was half paralysed. The journey took ten weeks, but on arrival she was immediately cured.[5]

Few women wrote their own letters and modes of expression were formal; many have not survived, and most letters from wives date from the fifteenth century when they were written in English. Yet some letters show a close, affectionate relationship between husband and wife. Margery Brewes remained in love with John Paston III after their marriage, in one letter addressing him as 'my own sweetheart', and in another wanting to join him in London, as she felt that it was a long while since she had lain in his arms. Elizabeth Stonor was not as open with her feelings in her letters to her husband, but she too felt that it was a long while since she had seen him; she was very worried when she heard that he was ill, wanting him to come to her or to send her horses so that she could join him. Both women were primarily concerned in their letters with business, Margery promising to watch her tongue if she spoke to the duchess of Norfolk on John's behalf. Men similarly combined affection and business, John Bourchier greeting his wife most lovingly before announcing in the same sentence that he was a prisoner in France and asking her to raise his ransom.[6]

Affectionate descriptions in wills cannot be taken at face value, since they may well have been inserted by the scribe. The terms of the will, however, can throw light on the couple's trust in each other and sense of partnership. The frequent practice of husbands appointing their wives as executrices of their wills points to their faith in their good judgement and efficiency. The bequest of businesses and of guardianship of children testified to the same qualities. Husband and wife can often be seen as a team working in the interests of their family. Thomas Austyn, citizen and mercer of London, left the guardianship of his son and two daughters and of his apprentices to his wife, Alice, on his death in 1391; £100 was bequeathed to each child, the daughters' money constituting their dowries. Alice died less than four years later and provided for the payment of the debts of her husband and herself, and for a servant to run the shop until her son had completed his apprenticeship and could take over. The widow and executrix of Adam in Ye Lane, a London citizen and cooper, who died in 1392, remarried, but ensured in her own will of 1398 that the provisions of Adam's will should be carried out.[7]

Concern for the family and realisation of wives' abilities are also apparent in landholding. It was generally taken for granted that the husband held his own and his wife's land, and the only time that a woman would hold land as an independent woman, or *femme sole*, would be when she was widowed. Yet this was not invariably the case. Very occasionally, a married woman is found holding land independently of her husband. According to the Yorkshire Domesday, Asa held her land free of the control of her husband Beornwulf even when they were living together; he could neither grant, sell nor forfeit it. After their separation, she held all her land as its lady.[8] Alienation of land by husbands posed a danger to their wives in that they could lose their dower. Charters of the twelfth century sometimes associated the wife with the grant or recorded her consent, and from the late thirteenth century the practice of examining the wife separately when her husband was alienating land may have given her some safeguard. In some cases, however, it is probable that coercion or fear of her husband lay behind her consent.

In the later middle ages, the wife gained more responsibility for the family land as joint tenure of property became increasingly common. Such tenure ensured that the family would continue to hold the property in the event of the death of husband or wife, thus bypassing the interests of king or lord. Joint tenures are found among military and free landholders from the later thirteenth century, and among unfree tenants in the fourteenth century. The legal basis was established by the first chapter of the statute of Westminster II of 1285, known as *De Donis Conditionalibus*. Thus, in 1309, Walter son of Humphrey paid 50s. to the honour court of Clare, so that he and his wife might be enfeoffed jointly of his manor of Borley, Essex. From the late fourteenth century, deathbed transfers were recorded in manor court rolls which could well benefit a wife. A manorial official heard the dying man's wishes, reporting them to the court where the transfer was recorded on the roll. In 1400 John Martyn, saddler of Saffron Walden, Essex, surrendered his holding to the use of his wife Margery for her lifetime. John died soon afterwards.[9]

Common interests in land and business, and the need for both husband and wife to contribute to the viability of the household, provided a basis for marital partnership. The couple, however, might well face difficulties in their relationship. The wife was expected to be subordinate but still had her own views and feelings. In writing to Eleanor de Montfort, countess of Leicester, about 1250, the friar Adam Marsh criticised her for her quick temper as well as for her extravagance of dress. Adam did not believe in husbands having everything their own way (he spoke to Sir Warin de Montchensy about treating his wife properly and with respect), but he expected wives to be submissive.[10] The same message comes across in advice literature, and both the Knight of La Tour-Landry and Christine de Pizan expected wives to be obedient and quiet in public, voicing any criticism when they were alone with their husbands.

It was taken for granted that the husband had the right to chastise his wife for disobedience, although the punishment should not be excessive. There must, however, have been many women who lived in fear of domestic violence, and some husbands are recorded as killing their wives, as when, in March 1271, Walter le Bedel asked his wife to come with him to Renhold barn to get a bushel of wheat. Once there, he struck her on the head and threw her body into a stream. In 1500 Simon Warner of Norwich alleged that Thomas Banburgh beat his wife, threw her down the stairs, set his foot on her breast (as one would break a goose breast) and pulled her by the arms till she had no breath in her body.[11]

Most women probably retaliated to violence verbally, but occasionally a wife killed her husband. Amicia, wife of Simon de Atherfield on the Isle of Wight, was burned at the stake for his murder in 1211; Simon has been described as 'a martyr to his wife' and a cult grew up at his tomb. Juliana Murdak was condemned for the murder of her husband, Thomas, in 1316; she was apparently helped by members of her household, and possibly persuaded by Sir John de Vaux, who married her three days after the murder. A few years later, in 1328, Elizabeth Pugeys received a pardon for helping in the deaths of her husband and brother-in-law, murders connected with an inheritance dispute.[12]

Problems arose within a marriage which could not have been fore-seen. Trouble might arise with mothers-in-law. Walter le Archer of Halesowen assaulted his mother-in-law when she excluded him from a family party. A Lincoln court case alleged that a mother was interfering in her son's marriage. Wives might be neglected and cut off from social life. Writing to her brother, George Plumpton, in the mid fifteenth century, Katherine Chadderton described the lonely life of her sister, Dame Isabel, whose husband was 'always in trouble'. She asked her brother to find a young woman, preferably a relative who was strong and able to work, to act as her companion. Sickness might strike unexpectedly; Elizabeth Scrope found shortly after her marriage in 1486 that her husband, William, Viscount Beaumont, was mentally ill. He never recovered. Debt might also prove a serious problem, and this was probably the reason why Joan de Mohun sold Dunster, Somerset, to Elizabeth Luttrell shortly after her husband's death. Incompatibility is difficult to gauge from the evidence, but many husbands and wives had to come to terms with unfaithfulness, and there was little the wife could do if her husband took another partner. The court of the deanery of Wisbech, Cambridgeshire, recorded in 1468–69 that Robert Sawer did not want his wife to sleep with him but had driven her out of the house and instead he kept Agnes Pullam from her husband. [13]

Serious problems of incompatibility might arise in arranged marriages. John de Warenne, earl of Surrey, married Edward I's granddaughter, Joan de Bar, in 1306; he was nineteen and she was ten. A few years later, John was in a relationship with Matilda de Nerford, and seeking a divorce on grounds of consanguinity, claiming that he had been forced into his marriage. It was alleged that he and Matilda had entered a con-tract to marry before 1306. He did not obtain his divorce, but it appears that he and Joan lived largely separate lives. They had no children. John died in 1347, his will referring to Isabel Holland as his wife. Obviously, there was a serious age gap between John and Joan, but other couples managed to bridge this. Possibly, trouble between them started when they began to live together as husband and wife. [14]

A somewhat different marital breakdown came to light in mid-fifteenth-century Colchester, when John Neuport and his wife, Alice, claimed property left to her by her former husband, William Prentys. William had died suddenly and did not have time to draw up a will.

It was alleged that John and Alice had connived at his death, and John was in the house on the night he died. William was reported to have said before he died that Alice should have none of his goods if she married John. Some time after William's death, John brought a paper will to the scrivener, John Spaldinge, who objected that it had an old date but was written in a new hand. The will was in fact a forgery.[15] There is no indication in this chancery case as to why William and Alice's marriage had foundered, but clearly things had gone badly wrong.

Marital offences were usually dealt with by the church courts, and the preponderance of legal material means that more is heard of the breakdown of relationships than about successful marriages. Recent research on the courts at Canterbury, Rochester, Ely and York has brought out the range of marital problems in medieval England, much of the business being concerned with adultery and fornication, concubinage, and clandestine and irregular marriages. In the consistory court of Rochester in 1363–4, forty-eight of the seventy-five cases concerned fornication and seventeen adultery, and the court was intent on enforcing its view of regular marriage. At the Ely consistory court between 1374 and 1382, the 122 marriage cases comprised about one-quarter of the total business, eighty-nine of these cases dealing with problems arising from clandestine marriage. Many of the cases concerned alleged or actual bigamy. At York, a high proportion of the precontract cases were brought by female plaintiffs.[16]

Some of the cases concerning clandestine marriage constituted an attempt to prove the marriage invalid and open the way to marriage with someone else; poor women, those without any sort of dowry, were the most vulnerable. Separation and divorce were more acceptable in the Anglo-Saxon period than after about 1150, but certain aspects of the earlier serial monogamy continued to be found. Separation, described as divorce from board and bed (*a mensa et thoro*), and maintaining the bond of marriage, was allowed by the church in cases of adultery, apostasy, heresy, violence or when both partners wished to enter the religious life. Annulment, or divorce from the marriage bond (*a vinculo*), was allowed in cases of invalid, forced or under-age marriage, consanguinity (without a dispensation), precontract, bigamy, crime on the part of the husband, and impotence. Impotence involved the inspection of the man by a group of mature women who tried to excite him sexually.[17]

Comparatively few cases of separation and divorce appear in the rolls of the church courts. They comprised ten out of ninety-eight cases at Canterbury between 1372 and 1375, and at York 19 per cent of the cases in the fourteenth century and 13 per cent in the fifteenth concerned separation or annulment.[18] The low figures are probably misleading, as the examples of Robert Sawer and Earl John de Warenne show how men deserted their wives for another woman. John even hoped that Isabel Holland would have a child to inherit his estates. Whether the case went through the courts or not, there is no doubt that marital breakdown and *de facto* divorce did occur.

In 1191, towards the end of his life, Earl William de Roumare secretly confessed to the bishop of Lincoln that his first wife, Alice, claimed after they were married that they were related. She asked for an annulment, and William agreed, although he did not think that they were kin. Both remarried, but William had the matter on his conscience. Pope Celestine III decided that William should do penance and remain with his second wife. Another late-twelfth-century Lincoln case concerned John who was married to Alice but committed adultery with Maxilla. He later married Maxilla while Alice was still alive, and continued to live with her after Alice's death; they had ten sons. In this case, Celestine III decreed separation, penance, and continence for the rest of their lives. They were both old but were to make provision for their children's support to the best of their ability.[19] In the later case of Margaret Camoys, her elopement with William Paynel was followed by John, her husband, quitclaiming her to William by charter. This only came to light when William and Margaret claimed dower from John's estate in 1300. By then they had regularised their relationship.[20]

Annulment took time to secure, and some women undoubtedly had a hard time. Lucy Thweng, of Yorkshire, married William Latimer, who became one of Edward I's household knights. The marriage ran into difficulties and she was willingly abducted from home nine years later. It took another nine years to secure a divorce, and in the meantime she had become the mistress of Nicholas Meinill, with whom she had a son. Eventually, they agreed to separate, and her second and third marriages were apparently less eventful.[21] With the nobility, political considerations became entangled with divorce. In the mid twelfth century, Aubrey de Vere, earl of Oxford, attempted to divorce his wife after his father-in-law, Henry of Essex, was judged guilty of treason. Aubrey did not want a wife from a disgraced family and kept his wife in custody. Pope Alexander III refused an annulment and apparently the earl took his wife back.[22] Nothing is known of their later relationship.

Couples undoubtedly encountered problems in their married lives, yet most marriages lasted for life. This was not simply due to the difficulty of securing a separation or divorce. Rather, the successful running of the household, and therefore the survival of the family, depended on both husband and wife whose roles were complementary. For most people, life was precarious, and it was not until about 1300 that the spectre of starvation was lifted. Although life improved for many in the later middle ages, there were still bad times. The partnership of husband and wife was vital.

The strong sense of family in the middle ages meant that couples looked forward to the birth of children, with sons being especially welcome to secure continuity. Only children born during the marriage counted as potential heirs.[23] Moreover, even young children could give some help in the household, and they provided support during old age. The wife took responsibility for the children, especially when they were young, and the combination of childcare with running the household and helping her husband meant a constant round of work; although the husband was the main breadwinner, his wife also often worked to earn money. The sheer amount of work was not always appreciated by husbands, who sometimes accused their wives of wasting time gossiping to the neighbours. According to the *Ballad of the Tyrannical Husband*, the husband felt aggrieved on his return from a day's ploughing to find that his dinner was not ready. His wife treated him to a tirade with her account of broken nights getting up to see to the children, cooking, housework and childcare during the day, milking the cows and making butter and cheese, looking after the poultry, brewing ale and making cloth and linen.[24] She felt that she looked after the family well and got no thanks.

Many women, at all social levels, found that they were pregnant frequently from their late teens or early twenties until the menopause. Numbers of children per family varied, but rich families had on average more children than the poor. At Halesowen between 1270 and 1349, the mean number of children over the age of twelve in families reconstituted from the court rolls has been estimated as 5.1 in rich, 2.9 in middling and 1.8 in poor families; 4 per cent of rich families had seven or eight children, but the highest figure for middling and poor families was six. The figures dropped markedly after the Black Death, and between 1350 and 1400 the mean number of children over twelve has been calculated as three in rich families, two in middling and 1.4 in poor; 10 per cent of rich families had four or five children, but for poor and middling families the maximum number was four.[25] Court roll material does not exist before the thirteenth century, and for the Anglo-Saxon period the size of families can only be guessed at. It is likely, however, that family size reached its peak during the three hundred years of population growth before c. 1300.

The number of children over twelve represent the survivors, as women usually had more pregnancies than surviving children. Some women found, however, that they were unable to have children, while others ceased to conceive because of illness, malnutrition or damage during childbirth, malnutrition being especially serious in the early period of the middle ages.[26] Although there is some information on the number of infant deaths in particular families, there are no overall figures. It has been suggested that between 200 and 300 out of every 1,000 babies died in their first year; only 500 survived at the age of five, and mortality continued to be high until the age of ten.[27]

Some families may have tried to limit the number of children by birth control, although the church set its face against this. *Coitus interruptus* is referred to in a wide range of church writings, especially in the early fourteenth century when there was widespread poverty and famine as a result of overpopulation. The presence of the topic in confessors' manuals suggests that birth control was in fact widely practised. Women's knowledge of herbs and plants, and their responsibility for medical care, also points to the use of contraception, and in England plants such as pennyroyal and Queen Anne's lace could be used as contraceptives or to induce early abortions.[28] Infanticide may also have been more widespread than appears in the records, although it was difficult to distinguish it from accident in the event of drowning or overlaying in bed by the parent, inducing suffocation, as in the case of Stephen and Joan Tiler who smothered their daughter as she was lying between them in bed. Babies might also be exposed, burnt or secretly buried, possibly

1. Infant mortality: Thomas, son of Giles Grevile of London, merchant (d. 1492); the baby is completely swaddled. Brass at Stanford Rivers church, Essex. By permission of Martin Stuchfield.

in cases where the child was illegitimate and the mother extremely poor. More women than men were accused of infanticide, but the number of prosecutions was small, thirteen cases being recorded at Rochester between 1447 and 1455.[29]

Although compilations by university scholars such as Bartholomew the Englishman, Vincent de Beauvais and Giles of Rome contained sections on children and their upbringing, it is unlikely that they were of much practical use to the women of the medieval world. Women probably learned most of what they knew about pregnancy, childbirth and childcare, all of them regarded as women's concerns, from talking to female friends and neighbours. In addition, from the thirteenth century, information and advice were given by confessors and in vernacular treatises. Doctors might be consulted by the wealthy, but the midwife was usually responsible for the birth, although a doctor might be called. When Joan Basset's son was born at Huntingfield, Suffolk, in 1301, the doctor was summoned from Norwich and arrived on the day of the birth.[30]

Medical knowledge was limited, although the use of herbal treatments could be effective, as the Anglo-Saxon Leechbooks show.[31] Charms and amulets were important, as in the Anglo-Saxon grave at Barton Court Farm, Oxfordshire, where a woman was buried with her new-born baby an amulet purse.[32] Medical knowledge increased in the West from the twelfth century, but childbirth remained a dangerous time for women, and recourse to the supernatural continued. St Margaret of Antioch was especially invoked at childbirth, as was the Virgin Mary. Cecily Neville, duchess of York, made a pilgrimage to Walsingham before one of her confinements, and the girdle of the Virgin Mary was often lent by Westminster Abbey to elite women in childbirth; two monks journeyed to Knaresborough, Yorkshire, for the birth of the eldest son of Elizabeth, countess of Hereford. Lady Juliana Grimbaud feared that she was in great danger during childbirth and invoked Simon de Montfort; she was delivered of a fine boy.[33]

From 1215, annual confession before Easter communion was the occasion for social, as well as religious, instruction. William de Pagula, author of the early fourteenth-century *Oculus sacerdotis* (*The Eye of the Priest*), was probably connected with the diocese of Salisbury.[34] His approach to pregnancy and childcare was sensible, if not always practicable. Pregnant women should avoid heavy work, and were recommended to breastfeed their babies. Parents were to keep a constant eye on their babies, not tie them in their cradles, and ensure that their mouths were not covered. Warning was given of the danger of suffocating the baby if it was in the same bed as the parent.

The fourteenth and fifteenth centuries saw a number of gynaecological treatises in the vernacular which were read by women as well as men. The male translator of *The Knowing of Woman's Kind in Childing* explained that literate women were more likely to read English and could then pass on their knowledge to the illiterate. The treatises were derived from the late-twelfth-century works attributed to Trotula of Salerno, the most famous of a number of women practitioners working there in the eleventh and twelfth centuries. Trotula was probably not the author of the treatises, but there is no doubt of their popularity, with over one hundred manuscripts surviving.[35] They combined classical, Arab and empirical medicine, and became the basis for later medieval views on female physiology and pathology, the vernacular works sometimes adding extra information.[36]

Little could be done to alleviate the sufferings of the mother in childbirth; the mother of John Musard, for one, never forgot the pains she suffered. Adam Sare remembered the birth of Alice de Newentone, because at the time he was in a garden where he heard the cries and groans of the baby's mother. Puerperal fever and post-natal depression, as suffered by Margery Kempe, were further dangers.[37] Because of the risks of childbirth, women came to confession and took communion beforehand. Deaths of mother and child were frequent, and the midwife had to be ready to baptise a baby unlikely to live.[38] Elizabeth, countess of Hereford and daughter of Edward I, lost her first child, as did Mary de Bohun, wife of Henry Bolingbroke. Mary herself died in childbirth in 1394. Margaret Beaufort was never able to have another child after the birth of Henry VII.

Care during childbirth was provided by women. Women of the nobility and gentry and wealthy townswomen would have a midwife in attendance; other women relied on relatives, neighbours and friends. Midwives were well rewarded; the woman at the birth of Mary de Bohun's son, Thomas, received forty shillings. Early in her first pregnancy, Margery Brewes wrote to her husband, John Paston III, that the

midwife, Elizabeth Peverel, was suffering from sciatica, but had promised to arrive at the due time, even if she had to be brought in a
barrow.[39] Once the baby was born, the news was brought to the father.
Fulk son of Warin was especially congratulated on the birth of a son as
all his other children were girls. News soon spread among neighbours,
kinsmen and friends, and messengers were rewarded. Edmund de
Colevile's grandparents gave the messenger jewels worth £5 for bringing
news of the birth.[40]

Baptism took place at Easter and Whitsun until about 1200, but after
that, provided that the baby was strong enough, the baptism usually took
place at the parish church within a day or so of the birth.[41] The baby was
carried by the midwife or nurse, accompanied by the godparents. It was
usual to have two godfathers and a godmother for a boy, and two god-
mothers and a godfather for a girl, and the baby was often named after
a godparent. When Philip Paynel was born in 1269, his great-uncle,
Philip Basset, was invited to be his godfather and sent two friends to
the baptism to give him the name Philip. John de Forstebury, also of
Wiltshire, approached Sir William de Lyllebon in 1286 to be his son's
godfather, but William had to refuse, as his mother was remarrying on
the same day. Godparents sometimes gave presents, John le Hauekere
receiving 6s. 8d. and a gold ring from his godfather. A close relationship
often developed between godparent and godchild, and godchildren were
often remembered in wills. Joan de Treviur, for instance, was said to
have especially loved her godson, Otto de Bodrugan.[42]

The mother did not attend the baptism, as she was recovering from
the birth. The time for celebration came when she attended the ceremony known as churching to give thanks for the birth of her child. She
was met at the church door by the priest, who recited the thanksgiving
prayers and sprinkled her with holy water; then followed her attendance
at mass.[43] On the day of the churching, the father usually held a feast
for his friends and neighbours. John de Forstebury asked his guests to
remember the day and year of his son's birth, a sensible precaution, as
he died before his son came of age. The feast after the birth of John de
Grey in about 1300 was also well remembered twenty-one years later,
since the abbot, priors and almost all the other good men of the region
had been present.[44]

The feast points to pride in both baby and family, but the question arises as to how medieval parents regarded their children and whether there were effective family relationships. This has aroused considerable argument between historians over the past forty years.[45] Obviously, some parents loved their children more than others, and love was not necessarily shown in the same way as at the present day. Love was rarely expressed in writing, but medieval parents saw childhood as a distinct phase of life, and high infant mortality did not preclude loving relationships. Parental care in the face of disability points to love and the desire to do one's best for the child. A feeding bottle, probably for an Anglo-Saxon child with a cleft palate, has been found at Barton upon Humber.[46] Some mothers were desolate at the loss of a child and parents took their children to shrines in search of a cure. Matilda de St Hilary, wife of Roger, earl of Hertford, became hysterical on her return from mass to find her infant son, James, apparently dead. She implored St Thomas of Canterbury to revive him, although those around her urged her to accept that the child was dead. Her chaplain spoke sternly, accusing her of being stupid. Yet after two hours the child revived, and Matilda in thanksgiving went on pilgrimage to Canterbury. Such expression of emotion was, however, rare. The unruly and warlike Gilbert de Clare, earl of Gloucester, explained that he would be arriving late at Edward I's court because one of his young children was ill, but urged his correspondent not to divulge this. Scenes of parents and children together are also rare. Osbern Bokenham wrote of how he talked to Lady Bourchier on Twelfth Night, 1445, while her four sons were engaged in the revels and dancing.[47]

Love of children can be seen in the care taken over burials. About half of the Anglo-Saxon children who died after infancy had at least one possession in their graves. A child of eight was buried with a tiny brooch and beads, and another, younger child with a small pot and brooch. Similar care was taken later, as when the baby Humphrey de Bohun was brought down from Knaresborough for burial in Westminster Abbey in 1304 and an elaborate funeral was followed by the ringing of bells and prayers for his soul. Some parents chose to be buried near their children, as did Thomas Austyn, citizen and mercer of London, in 1391.[48]

In both their vocabulary and law-codes, the Anglo-Saxons saw children as different from adults. It was not until the age of ten or twelve that they considered the child able to take responsibility for his or her actions.[49] The distinction was made more explicit in the didactic works of thirteenth-century schoolmen and were reflected in the ways in which children were brought up.[50] Vincent de Beauvais wrote *De eruditione filiorum nobilium* (*Of the Education of Noble Sons*) in 1247–49 at the request of Queen Margaret of France, and was concerned with the education of girls as well as boys. He, like other schoolmen, distinguished between infancy, to the age of six or seven, and later childhood up to puberty. It was in this later period that boys and girls were educated in religion and social and occupational skills. Children were to be disciplined, but not too severely, and the children of better-off parents were to be taught useful occupations and how to manage their inheritances.[51]

Parents took these stages of childhood into account. The mother was primarily responsible for the baby and the young child, whether boy or girl. In most families, she carried out the care herself, breastfeeding the child for up to two years and thus delaying a further pregnancy. Elite families from Anglo-Saxon times onwards employed a wet-nurse, and normally appointed a mistress to take charge of the children, although the mother remained in overall control. Details are known of many mistresses of royal children, and a letter of 1306 from Edward I to Margery de Haustede throws light on her responsibilities. Margery was looking after his second family, the children of Queen Margaret. The king was surprised that Margery had sent no news of the children; he wanted to know how they played and behaved, and wished to have her opinion of baby Eleanor.[52]

Wet-nurses were widely employed by noble and gentlewomen, and either lived in the household or had the baby in their own homes. Mary de Bohun's accounts record purchases of clothes, shoes and beds for both children and nurses. Elizabeth de Brompton was seen lying in her cradle in her nurse's chamber. According to the accounts of the de la Pole household at Wingfield Castle, Suffolk, in 1416–17, Isabella, daughter of Earl Michael the younger, boarded with her nurse, Joan Baker, in the neighbouring village of Fressingfield at the cost of 6*d.* a week. Mothers played with their children; one witness at John Musard's proof of age remembered seeing the young boy running with his mother.[53]

Children had their balls and toys, although it can be difficult to recognise toys in archaeological excavations. Anglo-Saxon girls who were buried with keys, weaving battens and spindlewhorls may have used them as part of their play of imitating adults. Lead and tin toys have been found in London, together with a miniature jug and a finger puppet.[54] Dolls are referred to by the early fifteenth century. Other toys were presumably made out of perishable materials, and many children would have created their own toys out of sticks and stones and made up imaginary games. Some mothers taught their sons from books, the most famous example being the future King Alfred being introduced to a book of poetry by his mother. Eleanor of Castile purchased a psalter and seven primers in 1290, and her daughters, Elizabeth and Mary, probably received some of them. John Tiptoft, earl of Worcester, was taught morals and literature by his mother at home.[55]

From the age of seven, the training of boys and girls diverged, the mother remaining primarily responsible for her daughters. According to Vincent de Beauvais, girls should receive an education in religion, morals (especially chastity), humility and manners. He permitted reading, music, sewing and weaving. In his opinion, girls should be kept at home and not allowed to gad about. This training he saw as the prelude for marriage.[56] Similarly, the Knight of La Tour-Landry saw the education of his daughters in religious, moral, and social terms. He wrote his book in 1371–72, because he was concerned that he often had to be away from home while his daughters were growing up and he wanted to provide them with plenty of good advice. He was somewhat puritanical on the subjects of dress and make-up, but there is no doubt of his love for his daughters. Although he hankered after romance, his wife believed firmly in arranged marriage. The work became widely known, Caxton publishing it in an English translation in 1484. Caxton may well have translated the work for Queen Elizabeth Woodville, who at the time had five young daughters. Christine de Pizan wrote on similar lines in her *Treasure of the City of Ladies.*[57] All these authors were writing for families of the elite but the qualities they wished to foster applied widely.

An interesting comparison can be drawn with the poem, *How the Goodwife Taught Her Daughter*, which circulated after the Black Death and set out ideals of life for girls. In addition to its use by mothers, it may have been used by mistresses of apprentices and servants who were responsible for the girls during their teenage years.[58] The girl should not wander round the town and frequent alehouses, but work hard, carry out her religious duties, and help the poor and sick. Much of the advice was geared towards her future married life; she should love and respect her husband, avoid extravagance, manage her house and servants wisely, and be hospitable to her neighbours. Her own children should respect her and should be punished for disobedience. She should raise a dowry for her daughters. With their marriage, the cycle began again.

Much of the teaching was given by example, especially the practical skills of housekeeping and childcare. Daughters of peasants and towns-people were expected to help in the house from an early age, going for water and looking after babies and toddlers. Skills for earning money were learned at the same time, such as spinning and weaving, brewing ale, shopkeeping and marketing, or running an inn. A servant girl was expected to spin, clean and cook. Social skills were absorbed from mother, mistress and neighbours or on visits to friends. The mother's example was crucial in learning religious practice, and it was her and the godparents' responsibility to see that the girl was confirmed when the bishop visited the neighbourhood. Godparents were expected to teach the Lord's Prayer and the creed.

Daughters of wealthier families learned embroidery, music and danc-ing. They also had to learn how to supervise and manage servants, as the Ménagier of Paris expected his wife to do. He considered that his wife should know how to do all the jobs around the house and garden, and also how to direct and care for her servants.[59] Anglo-Saxon girls were buried with household goods, pointing to their adult responsibilities.[60] Judging by the efficiency with which many widows ran estates and busi-nesses, it is likely that they had begun to learn their skills by listening to parents and servants. Girls mingled with the life of the household and had the opportunity to meet officials and servants as well as their social equals, as the story of Richard Calle and Margery Paston makes clear. For most families, privacy was limited, even at the end of the middle ages.

It is likely that mothers of the elite were more careful than the par-ents of the poor over guarding the chastity of their daughters. Leyrwite fines were levied in manor courts in certain parts of the country and appear to have especially affected the poor. They point to widespread sexual activity, and poems of the later middle ages show considerable enjoyment of sex.[61] A girl who left home for service may have had greater freedom to meet boys and girls of her own age unsupervised by her parents, but it is also possible that poorer parents were not as concerned with their children's chastity as their better-off neighbours or the gentry or nobility, whose ideas on family presupposed that their daughters would be virgins when they married. Chastity and a good reputation went together. The close connection between bride and property in the arranged marriage is paralleled by developments in the law of rape, where in the later middle ages the woman's rape was seen in terms of theft of property belonging to her father or husband.[62] On a practical point, mothers were also aware of the dangers of early childbearing, so, in some cases of early marriage, consummation was delayed. Both Eleanor of Castile and Eleanor of Provence, the mother and grandmother, pressed for the delay of the marriage of Edward I's daughter, Eleanor, to Alfonso of Aragon.[63]

Not all authorities approved of girls learning to read, but many saw it as a way of increasing religious understanding, and the image of St Anne teaching her daughter, the Virgin Mary, to read was popular. Literacy among the elite increased in the later middle ages, although learning to write does not seem to have been a major concern, as there was usually a clerk at hand to write letters to a woman's dictation. Using the Old Testament example of Deborah and the story of St Katherine of Alexandria, the Knight of La Tour-Landry argued that reading was profitable to all women, since it provided a better understanding of their religion. His daughters learned from these and other examples how to behave at mass and conduct their private prayers.[64] Such material, however, inculcated more than religious teaching. Lives of the virgin-martyrs were included in the household manuscripts of the fourteenth and fifteenth centuries owned by noble, gentry and wealthy mercantile families. These works provided both entertainment and education. A number of Osbern Bokenham's female saints' lives were written at the request of women, such as the Life of St Mary Magdalen for Lady Bourchier, and the Life of Elizabeth of Hungary for Elizabeth de Vere, countess of Oxford.[65] St Elizabeth combined activity in the world with the religious life and could be regarded as an exemplar of the 'mixed life', advocated by Walter Hilton and popular among fifteenth-century women. St Katherine of Alexandria was a model girl, beautiful, quiet in manner and dress, intelligent and courageous, a good household manager, and with a deep religious faith. St Margaret of Antioch was also a model, since she was an attractive girl of great faith and courage. Such teaching was not limited to the elite. The stories of the saints were popularised in sermons, wall paintings and on rood screens, such as those still to be seen in Norfolk parish churches.

Reading and book ownership did not only teach religion and morals; but also the recital of Anglo-Saxon poetry introduced children to the great deeds of the past and stories of heroes and monsters. From the twelfth century, romances were popular and read aloud. They opened up an imaginary world very different from the girl's own experience. She might dream of the Knights of the Round Table but had to be realistic as far as her own prospects were concerned. In the long run, literacy had its practical uses when she was running her own household (and possibly estates or business as well) and needed to check supplies and expenditure. During Eleanor Townshend's widowhood at the end of the fifteenth century, estate documents were written in English so that she could understand them, and she kept a record of her agricultural sales and of the leases she agreed to.[66]

The mother was not solely responsible for her daughters' upbringing. For particular skills, she needed help and advice. Walter de Bibbesworth produced his treatise to enable Denise de Montchensy to teach her children French in the thirteenth century. Some girls may have gone to school; a statute of 1406 referred to the right of men and women of any status to send a son or daughter to school. Some children were taught in nunneries; Elizabeth de la Pole was taught by a friar when she was at the nunnery of Bruisyard.[67]

On occasion, girls and boys were sent away from home, and another woman became responsible for them. Foster mothers are found in the Anglo-Saxon period, and the early-eleventh-century will of the atheling Æthelstan referred to his grandmother who brought him up and to his foster mother who was bequeathed an estate 'because of her great deserts'.[68] Children of the elite were sent to other households to gain more experience of social life, and to make connections which would stand them in good stead in later life; in 1380 John of Gaunt sent his daughter, Katherine, to live with Joan de Mohun, and Jane Howard entered the household of Countess Elizabeth de Vere in 1466.[69] Below that level, many girls went into service, but fewer girls than boys were apprenticed. Training as a craftswoman gave a girl a marketable skill for adult life.

Mothers were responsible for their daughters until they married. Children's lives did not always turn out as planned, as the Paston family found. Margaret Paston regarded Margery's marriage as unforgivable, although she remembered her Calle grandchildren in her will.[70] Margaret expressed her love for her family very much in material terms and this love continued into their adult lives. Many women, like Margaret Paston, lost their husbands and had to cope with their families on their own. Widowhood constituted a distinct stage in a woman's life, presenting her with new problems as well as opportunities, and opening up new fields of relationships.

2 The widow: Christina, widow of John Bray esquire (d. 1420).
Brass at Felsted church, Essex. By permission of Martin Stuchfield.

4

Widows

Death struck families suddenly and at any age. The hayward, Reynold Stad of Eaton Socon, Bedfordshire, went out to look after his lord's meadow in 1267, fell with the 'falling sickness' (probably a heart attack or a stroke) and died immediately. His wife had the shock of discovering his body.[1] Until about 1300, men, women and children might well be weakened by malnutrition and die of starvation.[2] The Black Death of 1348–49 carried off between one-third and one-half of the population. Infectious diseases took their toll and the late fifteenth century saw the arrival of the sweating sickness, often a killer. Many women died in childbirth, and accidents and violence accounted for a large number of deaths. Wives of men fighting in the king's armies might not learn for months if their husbands had died in battle, while merchants' and sailors' wives might well wonder during long absences if they had been deserted or if their husbands were dead.

Many women outlived their husbands, as much less is heard of widowers than widows. Some 79 per cent of later medieval Yorkshire merchants left a widow, and, out of 442 merchants with named wives, only ninety-one survived their wives; of these, fifty-three married more than once, although it was unusual for them to have more than two wives.[3] A man's loss of his wife did not affect his own landholding and livelihood and, by the custom of curtesy of England, he continued to hold his wife's land for life if the couple had had children.[4] It was taken for granted that a widower would continue to bring the children up if they were still young, and that he would probably remarry.

By contrast, the widow had to face considerable change. Widowhood presented women of all social levels with problems but also opportunities. The widow, unlike the great majority of wives, was regarded as a *femme sole*, a woman entitled to her own legal identity, able to plead in the courts, run a business or lands and make her own decisions.

Yet many widows faced difficulties on bereavement. Their entitlement to dower often gave rise to disputes within the family, as well as on occasion with the lord or king, while the question of remarriage might have profound effects on their children and on their natal and marital families.

Some widows suffered extreme grief on the deaths of their husbands. During Edward I's reign, it was reported that Margery de Anlatheby had been an idiot since her husband's death and her son had been taken away from her soon after.[5] Many women must have grieved but realised at the same time that they had to take action to secure their future and that of their children. Moreover, a show of grief was not approved of in the middle ages. On his visit to Queen Berengaria, widow of Richard I, St Hugh of Lincoln found her almost heartbroken. He calmed her by speaking of the need for courage in the face of bereavement. A similar line was taken by Bishop Despenser of Norwich when writing to his niece, Constance, after the execution of her husband, Thomas, Lord Despenser, in 1400 and the forfeiture of his estates to the crown for treason. The bishop emphasised that it was a great sin to be utterly consumed by grief. Lady Despenser should be guided by reason and recover what she could of the family's lands and reputation. The bishop would help her where he could.[6]

Bishop Despenser was right to stress the practical tasks facing the widow. Widows of all social levels throughout the middle ages had to secure their dower and see to the guardianship of their children. Furthermore, from the thirteenth century onwards, when the church exercised jurisdiction over wills, widows often acted as their husbands' executrices and this entailed immediate as well as long-term action, sometimes lasting for the rest of their lives. Husbands often trusted their wives' judgment, practical ability and knowledge of their affairs; Ealdorman Ælfheah in c. 970 expected his wife to maintain the lands he left her according to the confidence he had in her. An analysis of fifteenth-century Norfolk gentry wills shows that out of 271 wills, the wife acted as executrix in 140, usually with other family members and friends. Nobles, craftsmen, artisans and peasants all appointed wives as their executrices and in wealthy families in particular the carrying out of a will entailed a considerable amount of work. Although many of the surviving wills were drawn up by the better-off, humbler people were leaving wills by the fifteenth century at least and peasant wills are referred to in manorial court rolls. Occasionally, a wife refused to act as executrix. The reason is usually unclear, but may sometimes have been rooted in the fear of being liable for the testator's debts; one executrix in Cambridgeshire was dismissed before the final account because of her poverty. [7]

The executors' first concern was to organise the funeral, for which the deceased had often laid down detailed provisions; the celebration of requiem masses followed the funeral and executors were sometimes expected to provide a tomb. John Hastings, earl of Pembroke, for instance, bequeathed £140 for a tomb like that of Elizabeth de Burgh. Guests had to be invited, and the service, almsgiving and subsequent feast organised. Henry, duke of Lancaster (d. 1361), wanted no extravagance at his funeral, but the guests were to include the royal family, his wife, sisters and brothers, and other great lords. [8] Arrangements for requiem masses were often complicated. Sir John Gildesburgh (d. 1389) wanted to be buried in his parish church of Wennington, Essex. After payment of his debts, his goods were to be divided between his wife and the executors, of whom she was one. Masses were to be celebrated for the benefit of his own soul and the souls of his parents, friends, benefactors and all the faithful departed. Twenty-five chaplains, in groups of five, were responsible for these for a year at Wennington, the Greyfriars' and Blackfriars' churches in London, the Blackfriars' church in Chelmsford and at Walden Abbey. Five more chaplains were to celebrate masses at five parish churches in Essex and Suffolk for a year, and money for commemorative masses was left to other parish churches, Walsingham Priory, the Franciscan church at Ware, Hertfordshire, and the Burghersh chantry in Lincoln Cathedral. All this must have taken much organisation. Commemoration was of necessity much simpler below the level of the gentry. William Seman of Little Cornard, Suffolk, in 1446 wanted to be buried in the churchyard of St Gregory's church in Sudbury and for a friar to celebrate masses for his soul, and for his parents and benefactors, for a year as soon as possible after his death, if his goods were sufficient to cover the cost. [9]

To obtain probate, the executors took an oath that they would prepare an inventory of the deceased's goods and submit a final account. Once the inventory was drawn up, the executors might administer the estate. [10]

Where a group of executors had been appointed, a smaller number might act; Amice, widow of Sir Eustace de Hacche, in 1307 appointed her co-executor as her proctor to make the inventory. Anastasia, widow of Sir Thomas FitzHenry, in 1400 took the oath as executrix and administration of goods was granted to her. In 1433, the earl of Salisbury and John Quixley, on behalf of the other executors, including the widow, Countess Joan Beaufort, presented their final account for executing the will of Ralph Neville, first earl of Westmorland, were questioned on it, swore to its truth and were given their quittance.[11] The earl had died in 1425.

Relatively little is known as to how executors carried out their work. Their first duty after the funeral was to pay the debts of the deceased, but his or her goods were not always sufficient to cover them. The testator's unbequeathed goods were sold to raise money; the 1366 will of Matilda de Vere, countess of Oxford, referred, for instance, to two wine bowls purchased from the executors of Elizabeth de Burgh.[12] In rural communities, payment of debts was sought at the manor court. The debt of 20s. paid by Agnes, widow of William del Lane, to Peter de Lewes at Wakefield, Yorkshire, in 1331 may well have been linked to her role as William's executrix. The following year, Eva, widow and executrix of William de Colley, was sued by William de Birkes for the *maritagium* of William de Colley's daughter, Juliana; Eva denied the charge.[13] Widows whose husbands had held office are found accounting for their late husbands, whether they had been wives of a manorial reeve or of an office-holder under the crown. Some widows were owed money by the crown for military service overseas, which might or might not be paid. Eleanor, countess of Ormond, accounted for the receipts and expenses of her husband, Sir Thomas de Dagworth, while he was in charge of Brittany between 1345 and 1347, and Joan, widow of John de Copland, constable of Roxburgh and keeper of Berwick, for his office for the years 1360–64.[14]

In addition to the execution of her husband's will, the widow had to secure her dower and see to the guardianship of her children. In most cases, the mother acted as guardian of minor children, often with some male supervision and the oversight of the manor or borough court. This is likely to have been the case in the Anglo-Saxon period, and, although there were local variations in custom, the mother was usually named guardian in manorial court rolls, as at Brigstock in Northamptonshire, and Walsham le Willows in Suffolk. Here, in 1328, Matilda, widow of William Coppelowe, sought custody of William's son and heir, aged two, from the manor court at the same time as her dower. She was granted custody. A similar situation applied to free tenants and to gavelkind tenants in Kent. A case of 1332 at Great Waltham and High Easter in Essex, however, shows that the mother was not always appointed guardian.[15] Among London citizens in the later middle ages, the mother was generally accepted as guardian, subject to the supervision of the city authorities. Guardianship was arranged by the mayor and chamberlain, sureties were taken and by the early fifteenth century the city required a bond for the children's wealth to be provided. Mothers were encouraged to remarry. The mayor's court had the final say in the ward's apprenticeship and marriage.[16]

With children of the nobility and gentry, the situation varied over time. From at least the tenth century until Tudor times, mothers were not solely responsible for their children, as the latter were placed in other households as part of their education. Henry I laid down in his coronation charter that either the widow or a relation should act as guardian of children and land in the event of a minority, but as rights of wardship developed in the twelfth century, it became more usual after about 1150 for guardianship to be in the hands of lord or king.[17] During the later middle ages, royal and seigneurial rights of wardship and marriage became useful sources of money and patronage, but because of joint tenures and enfeoffments to uses, the estates increasingly remained under the family's control and mothers often resumed responsibility for guardianship. Thus, in the late 1290s, the young Gilbert de Clare, earl of Gloucester and Hertford, lived with his mother and stepfather, Joan of Acre and Ralph de Monthermer, who administered his estates. He moved to the household of Queen Margaret at the age of ten in 1301.[18]

However guardianship was organised, there were dangers. In Normandy, the mother was not allowed to act as guardian, and literature has plenty of stories of the potential danger to the heir from mother and stepfather, dangers which also existed in fact.[19] The later middle ages saw occasions when a mother's incompetence damaged an estate, as happened on the lands of the Courtenay earls of Devon in the 1430s.[20] Earlier, waste committed by king or lord caused considerable grievance, as did control over the heir's marriage. The Magna Carta attempted to prevent waste of the ward's land, and laid down that heirs should not be disparaged in marriage and relations should be informed before the marriage was contracted, but waste by the guardian always remained a problem.[21]

The securing of her dower was the other immediate concern to the widow after her husband's death. The great majority of widows were entitled to dower, but from about 1250 the common law considered that they were only entitled to it if they had been old enough to have sexual relations with their husbands; they forfeited dower in the event of divorce and sometimes adultery.[22] Down to the thirteenth century, dower was settled by the bridegroom's family on the bride as part of the marriage settlement, the arrangement being confirmed at the church door during the wedding. The amount of dower varied in Anglo-Saxon times, wills showing that it ranged from a few estates to a major share of the husband's land. The Domesday Survey for Nottinghamshire and Derbyshire, for instance, referred to a half share, but the share was usually less than one-third in the Norman period, and the widow kept her *maritagium*.[23] Such arrangements are recorded in charters, like the death-bed gift in the mid twelfth century by Baldwin fitz Gilbert to his wife, Adeline de Rollos, of three estates in Northamptonshire and Lincolnshire for her support. In the 1140s, Adam son of Warin provided for his second wife and her children by creating one-fifth of a knight's fee on the Essex–Suffolk border, to be held of his eldest son and heir.[24]

From the late twelfth century, attempts were made to introduce greater definition into rights to dower. The Magna Carta in 1215 reiterated the principle laid down by Henry I in his coronation charter that the widow should receive her dower and marriage portion, but specified that her marriage portion and inheritance were to be handed over immediately after her husband's death, and her dower assigned within the forty days she was allowed to remain in her husband's house. She should make no payment for her lands. The reissues of the Magna Carta in 1217 and 1225 laid down that dower was to comprise one-third of all the land which was her husband's during his lifetime, unless she had been dowered with less at the church door.[25] In the course of the thirteenth century, dower came to be interpreted as one-third of the lands held by the husband on his wedding day, and also the lands he acquired after his marriage.

Women often found that their rights to land came under threat. Thurketel Heyng thought it necessary to lay down in his will that his wife's portion was never to be contested; she was to hold it and grant it as she pleased.[26] The number of dower cases brought by military and free tenants in the royal courts in the late twelfth and thirteenth centuries testifies to the problems women encountered in obtaining their dower; 20 per cent of the cases on the royal court roll for Michaelmas term 1225 concerned dower.[27] Church courts were only involved if questions arose over the validity of the marriage, or divorce or adultery. It is understandable why families were reluctant to allocate dower, and argued that the widow had quitclaimed her rights, or that her husband was not seised of the land. Their land might be too small to support two households and it might already be supporting a dowered widow. The new widow might be the heir's stepmother and not particularly liked. She might even be of about the same age as the heir and likely to survive for many years. Poverty among the thirteenth-century gentry led to widows selling their land, as when Matilda, widow of Robert Abetot, granted James de Beauchamp her land in Acton Beauchamp, Worcestershire, in return for a food and clothing allowance.[28]

Dower cases were often long and complex, and involved women of all ranks from noblewoman to freewoman.[29] Individual cases point to the difficulties which women faced. In the early 1220s, Gunnora de Bendenges had to prove that she had been legitimately married to John fitz Hugh, because John had made a bigamous second marriage and died on crusade. A similar situation is apparent in a letter of 1220 from the bishop of Norwich, declaring that Ascelina's marriage to Robert Chevre had been valid; this enabled her to claim dower successfully in thirty acres in Wixoe, Suffolk.[30] The final concord at the end of a dower case in the royal courts provided the widow with a sure title to land, as in 1204 when Azilia, widow of Robert Basset, and William Basset reached an agreement over her dower in Drayton Beauchamp, Buckinghamshire, and Long Marston, Hertfordshire.[31]

The number of dower cases in the royal courts dropped from the later thirteenth century, probably because women had other ways of accessing land through joint enfeoffments which precluded the loss of estates by the family in the event of a minority. Further change came with enfeoffments to uses, found in the second half of the fourteenth century with the nobility and later with the gentry. This ensured continuity during a minority and greater flexibility in the transfer of land. Feoffees also provided for the widow's jointure and she ceased to be entitled to common law dower. It may well have been felt that widows had benefited too much from their lands in the later middle ages; certainly some sons had found themselves straitened in their activities. [32]

Boroughs had their own customs over dower. In the 1220s, dower at Lincoln was assigned from the tenements held by the husband at the time of his death. In thirteenth-century Wilton, the widow could choose to have her 'free bench' (a share in the husband's dwelling) for life, or to receive £5 as dower. In Bakewell, Derbyshire, she received one-third of her husband's holding. In later medieval London, the widow was allowed her 'free bench' until her own death or remarriage. She received one-third of the property held by her husband at the time of their marriage, or one-half if there were no children; she was also assigned one-third or one-half of her husband's chattels under the custom known as *legitim*, and this wealth she could dispose of as she chose. Urban property could also be left by will, and many wives benefited from this; William Smyth of Colchester divided his lands and goods equally between his wife and son in 1486, and the following year John Dalton of Hull made a threefold division between his wife, his children, and the good of his soul. The borough courts took action where necessary in dower cases; the City of London had its own writ of dower and heard cases in the court of Husting. [33]

Village widows claimed their dower at the manor court at the same time as they sought custody of an under-age heir. Local customs varied, but in the later middle ages the widow was mostly allocated one-third or one-half of her husband's land, which she might or might not continue to hold if she remarried. Under gavelkind tenure in Kent, the widow held half of her husband's land. [34] Some widows, as at Brigstock and Walsham le Willows, were free to dispose of parts of their property. At the manor court at Walsham le Willows, dower comprised one-half of the husband's land. In 1328 Matilda, widow of William Coppelowe, was allocated a messuage and seven acres of land, and swore fealty as a villein. She was expected to maintain her property. Dower might be agreed outside the court: Christina, widow of Walter Kembald, had the court's permission in 1317 to come to an agreement over dower with Simon Kembald. Widows who had been jointly enfeoffed had to prove this to the court; in 1332, Alice Heton showed the Wakefield court the charter testifying that she had been jointly enfeoffed with her husband and was therefore entitled to continue as tenant. Disputes over dower came before the courts. At Wakefield in 1333, the relations in one case asserted that they had met the claim for dower, and in another it was claimed that the husband had never held the land concerned. The dower holding had to be properly maintained. At Little Leighs, Essex, in 1313, Amice, widow of John de Rachham, risked losing a large part of her dower, which consisted of all her husband's holdings, because she had let the buildings fall into a bad state of repair.[35]

Serious problems arose among the nobility and gentry when the husband had forfeited his estates for rebellion and treason. During the Anglo-Saxon period, the wife's dower was regarded as excluded from her husband's crimes, although the tenth-century kings did not always accept this. It was therefore particularly important for wills to be guaranteed by the king, and Wulfgeat of Donington, for one, asked his lord the king to be a friend to his wife and daughter. Royal favour was important. Eadgifu, third wife of Edward the Elder, enjoyed power during the reigns of her sons, Edmund and Eadred, but lost favour under Eadwig. Although her lands were restored under Edgar, she lived in obscurity.[36]

Political crises and rebellion continued to affect widows and their landholdings in the Norman period and later, and some kings manipulated the situation in their own interests. According to the treatise attributed to 'Bracton', dating from the 1220s, treason should be punished by the perpetual forfeiture of the traitor's lands; no heir should hold anything from his father's or mother's inheritance. Yet this approach was regarded as too drastic, and in the aftermath of the Barons' Wars the Dictum of Kenilworth of 1266 made provision for rebels to redeem their lands. Special provision was made for individual widows, as when Sibyl de Dive was granted one of her husband's manors for the maintenance of herself and her children.[37]

Further developments took place later as a result of tenurial changes. According to the statute, *De Donis Conditionalibus*, the statute of treasons of 1352 and the position taken by the Appellants in 1388, entailed lands were exempt from forfeiture, although the Appellants considered that the exemption did not apply to enfeoffments to uses. Richard II took a more extreme line in 1398, making entailed lands, those held to use and those in fee simple subject to forfeiture. This policy was followed by the acts of attainder of the fifteenth century. From the widow's point of view, according to the Appellants and the acts of attainder, she had the right to her inheritance and jointure because these predated her husband's treason, but she could only claim them after her husband's death when she was a *femme sole*. Her right to dower was not protected unless the sentence of treason was reversed.[38]

In practice, the woman's access to land depended on the attitude of the king, her political connections, and whether royal favourites or kinsmen had their eye on the forfeited estates. After the Merciless Parliament, Richard II issued letters on behalf of a number of women to whom inheritances and jointures were returned. The lands of Michael de la Pole, earl of Suffolk, were forfeited, but manors in Lincolnshire and Nottinghamshire were returned to his son and his wife, Katherine Stafford, because they had been jointly settled on the couple. Katherine's 'cousins and allies', the earl of Warwick and others, requested the estates' return. Women who had been left landless also received some of their husbands' land, as in the case of Anne, widow of Sir James Berners, until she remarried or received other help.[39]

Certain periods were especially vindictive. Many cross-border families, holding land in England and Scotland, suffered during Edward I's Scottish wars. Eleanor Ferrers, for instance, lost her English lands after her second husband, Sir William Douglas, was imprisoned in England in 1297. She was dependent on Edward I for maintenance, and only regained her lands two years later after William's death.[40] Many widows were in difficulties after the battle of Boroughbridge of 1322, partly as a result of their husbands' rebellion, and partly because of the greed of the royal favourite, Hugh le Despenser the younger, who aimed to build up a great principality in south Wales. Even the widow (Marie de St-Pol) and co-heirs of Aymer de Valence, earl of Pembroke (d. 1324), who had never been a rebel, found themselves under heavy pressure because of the earldom's Welsh estates; Marie had difficulty in securing her dower. Marie's great friend, Elizabeth de Burgh, lady of Clare, who had been implicated in the rebellion along with her husband, found herself forced to relinquish her inherited lordship of Usk. She left an account of the harassment to which she most unwillingly succumbed.[41]

Similar pressure was put on wives and widows of attainted husbands during the Wars of the Roses. Elizabeth, countess of Oxford, was forced to hand over land to Richard, duke of Gloucester, in 1473–74 when according to her son she was threatened and imprisoned and feared for her life. Her husband and eldest son had been attainted early in Edward IV's reign; her second son fought for the Lancastrians at the battle of Barnet, later seized St Michael's Mount in Cornwall and only escaped from Yorkist imprisonment shortly before the battle of Bosworth. He secured the reversal of the acts of attainder after Henry VII's accession when he enjoyed high favour with the king.[42]

The majority of widows, fortunately, did not have to suffer similar traumas. Most, having buried their husbands and secured dower, came to terms with their new lives and had to decide whether or not they wished to remarry. As a *femme sole*, the widow had the right to choose her new husband – but a wise widow sought advice from family and friends. At times, pressure was undoubtedly applied by kings and lords, as well as by families, fortune-hunters and potential abductors. As with first marriage, economic factors played a part. A young, rich widow might well remarry. If a poor widow wanted to remarry, however, she stood less chance, especially if she had a large number of children. Some widows wanted to remarry for companionship or to secure a stepfather and extra resources to help in bringing up their family; others might marry for love, sexual attraction or for a useful family alliance. A number of women apparently decided that there were good reasons for not marrying again. Some later medieval husbands set their faces against remarriage, possibly for property reasons.[43]

English law accepted widows' remarriage, although late Anglo-Saxon law required the widow to wait for twelve months, otherwise she forfeited her morning-gift and dower.[44] The church was more ambivalent. Although Gratian and later commentators thought that the widow had the right to remarry, they saw only the first marriage as fully sacramental; Pope Alexander III forbade a nuptial blessing for the second marriage, although it is probable that many parish priests contravened this.[45]

Remarriage in the villages depended partly on the economic situation and partly on local custom. A fine often had to be paid to the lord. Manors where the widow held her dower for life might well see more remarriages than those where dower was lost on remarriage and also when the heir came of age. During the years of expanding agriculture, manorial lords took an interest in the marriage of widows as well as of girls, although attempts to enforce widows' marriage in Norfolk met with only limited success. Unmarried men were also alive to the prospect of marrying a widow. At Cottenham, Cambridgeshire, in the early fourteenth century the main type of property transfer among villeins was through the marriage of landed widows, but there is no sign of the widows being forced to marry against their will. The number of marriages fell after the famines of 1315–22 and more markedly after the Black Death.[46]

Numbers of remarriages varied from place to place. At Halesowen, six out of ten widows are known from the court rolls to have remarried in the early fourteenth century, with fewer remarriages after 1349. Eight out of 106 widows remarried at Brigstock and five out of thirty-four at Iver in Buckinghamshire. Possibly, the low figures were due to the nature of local farming and the lower pressure on arable land; Iver had a pastoral economy, while at Brigstock land could be acquired via the land market and the forest provided a variety of occupations. At Thornbury, Gloucestershire, the widow's decision to remarry was closely linked to her form of tenure, and more women with customary holdings remarried than those with gavel land. Customary holdings owed heavy labour services while the main obligation on gavel land was the money rent.[47]

If a woman chose not to remarry, she ran her holding herself. No question was raised as to her ability to do this and women were capable of doing all but the heaviest farmwork, for which they hired labour. It was rare for a woman to lose her holding, but a court at Chatteris, Cambridgeshire, heard in 1287 that Agatha de Chedesham had been ejected from her eight acres of land because of her extreme poverty.[48] Possibly, Agatha was too old to manage her holding; in any case, arrangements were made for her to be given food. Women entered into varied arrangements if they needed help. At Cottenham in 1326, Maria Buk bound her son to take all responsibility for the holding; he was to receive

3 Family: William Turnor (d. 1473) with his two wives, Margaret and Margery; Margaret had four sons and six daughters, and Margery one son and two daughters. Brass at Berden church, Essex. By permission of Martin Stuchfield.

half the crops and the land was to revert to him after her death. Over thirty years earlier, after Cecilia Saleman's amercement for leyrwite in 1290, her mother made an agreement with her and Henry Cosyn, presumably her partner, under which they were to marry and serve her for the rest of her life. They were to receive food and clothing and one acre of land to cultivate at their own expense. It is not clear if they were to receive the mother's land after her death.[49] It looks as if the mother got the best of the bargain.

In old age, women on their own, as well as single men and married couples, entered into maintenance agreements, handing over their land to their children or to others in return for living space, some livestock and a small area of land or, alternatively, an allowance of food and clothing. In the mid fourteenth century, Matilda Hamond of Ingatestone, Essex, handed over her messuage and eight acres of land to her son in return for two rooms, a curtilage and fifteen shillings a year for life. About one hundred years later, Margaret Chapeleyn conveyed her holding in Horsham St Faith, Norfolk, to John Chapeleyn and his heirs in return for a share of the house and outbuildings, and a cow, pig and poultry.[50]

In the towns, a practical and realistic attitude prevailed and a widow with property or a thriving business was likely to have suitors. In London, poor, older widows stood less chance of remarriage than widows of merchants and wealthy craftsmen, who often remarried within the same trade as their first husbands. The tendency to remarry increased in the fourteenth and fifteenth centuries. Thomasine Percyvale, said to have come to London as a servant from Week St Mary in Cornwall, had three husbands, all members of the Tailors' Company.[51] Thomasine had wealth and connections to offer, the latter being particularly valuable in view of the importance of close-knit networks among town elites.

Similar patterns emerge in provincial towns. Lucy, widow of John Sayer, shearman and bailiff of Colchester, took the advice of her husband's executors over remarriage, choosing as her second husband Thomas Halke, a man of wealth and reputation and one of the Colchester aldermen. Two years after his death she married Thomas Profete of Nayland, Suffolk, a rich and thrifty man. There were extensive marriage networks, involving both girls and widows, in the northern towns of Beverley, York and Hull.[52] By the fifteenth century, wealthy urban women were marrying into the gentry and nobility. Elizabeth Stonor was the widow of a London mercer, Thomas Ryche, when she married William Stonor in 1475.

Patterns of remarriage among noblewomen varied over the middle ages. It is found occasionally among Anglo-Saxon noblewomen, although not often among queens, who found that they had greater influence over their children and at court if they remained widows. It is likely that our knowledge of remarriage is minimal as wills reveal little about marital history. Æthelflaed, daughter of Ælfgar, ealdorman of Essex, and second wife of King Edmund (d. 946), probably remarried Ealdorman Æthelstan as her second husband, but there is no reference to him in her will.[53]

Evidence is more plentiful in the Norman period, when rich widows, like heiresses, were often treated as objects of patronage. According to his coronation charter of 1100, Henry I promised a baron's widow her dower and marriage portion, and he stated that he would not give her in marriage without her consent. Yet, although there were some lengthy widowhoods, pressure was probably brought to persuade widows to remarry since Henry was anxious to reward his *curiales* and secure loyalty among his barons. Lucy, daughter and heiress of Turold, sheriff of Lincoln, married in turn Ivo de Taillebois, Roger fitz Gerold and Ranulf Meschin, earl of Chester (d. 1129), the last marriage being conferred by William II. On Ranulf's death, Lucy paid a fine to have her inheritance and dower, and, according to the Pipe Roll of 1130, offered one hundred marks to hold her court, and 500 marks to remain unmarried for five years.[54] It appears that the widow's age and status enabled her on occasion to dictate terms, provided that she had the money for the fine. As she grew older, she would become less attractive to a *curialis* anxious to found a dynasty.

It has been calculated for the period 1069–1230 that out of fifty-eight dowager countesses twenty-five married once, twenty-six twice, seven three times and one four times.[55] In other words, a considerable number of widows did not remarry. Under the Angevins, the relationship between crown and widow was often as much financial as personal. When Hawise of Aumale was widowed in 1189 after a ten-year marriage, Richard I brought pressure to bear to persuade her to marry a Poitevin, William de Forz. On his death, Richard arranged for her marriage to

Baldwin de Béthune in 1195 and paid at least part of the wedding expenses. Widowed again in 1212, Hawise made an agreement with King John that in return for a fine of 5000 marks she could have her inheritance and dower freely, hold her honour court and not be forced to remarry.[56]

According to the Magna Carta, a widow was not to be compelled to marry, on condition that she gave security that she would not remarry without royal or seigneurial assent.[57] There were, however, times down to the early fourteenth century when kings married widows off to their favourites. From the reign of Edward III, however, royal consent became largely a formality. Even if the widow remarried without consent, as did Margaret de Brotherton, royal favour was usually soon recovered. It was when they were widowed that a number of noblewomen chose men of lower rank than themselves, although still within knightly society. Joan of Acre, daughter of Edward I and widow of Gilbert de Clare, earl of Gloucester and Hertford (d. 1295), was attracted to a squire in the earl's retinue, Ralph de Monthermer, and married him, to her father's fury. After shortlived marriages to two successive earls of Stafford, Anne, daughter of Thomas, duke of Gloucester, and Eleanor de Bohun, chose Sir William Bourchier, a younger son of an Essex family.[58]

Remarriage at any level in society brought readjustments in family relationships and problems could certainly arise. Stories of the wicked stepmother have a factual basis and stepfathers could equally abuse their position, although it should not be assumed that this invariably occurred. Family tensions could likewise arise between mother or father and their children, as the Paston family were well aware. In the Anglo-Saxon period, the details of family quarrels were often not recorded. The reasons lying behind the late tenth-century attacks by Wulfbold on his stepmother's lands are unknown, although they may have been related to a dower settlement.[59] Fuller information is available for the later middle ages. The second marriage of Ralph Neville, earl of Westmorland, to Joan Beaufort resulted in her children being favoured at the expense of the earl's heir, born to him and his first wife.

Step-parents often took steps to preclude future tension. Matilda Mogge of Barking, Essex, made her will with her husband's consent in 1466. She wanted her feoffees to let her husband, William Mogge, hold her land for eight years after her death and for it then to pass to her son,

John Hacche (clearly a son by a previous marriage), on condition that he was 'of good rule, conversation and governance' during the eight years; if not, or if he died, the land was to be sold and the money given to her two children, John Saunders and Joan, wife of Thomas Ledes.[60] Matilda must have married three times and was anticipating possible trouble between son and stepfather. In his will of 1494, John Lord Scrope bequeathed all his goods at Bolton Castle and all his cattle in Yorkshire to his heir, provided that the latter gave comfort and help to his widow. His stepmother's will of 1498, with its bequests to the Scrope family, reveals no signs of tension.[61]

The concentration on dower and remarriage may make it appear that the widow was only concerned with her personal interests, but in fact her involvement with children and family continued throughout her life. Letters provide the best indication of the ups and downs in her relationship with sons and daughters and further information can be gleaned from bequests in wills. Margaret Paston continued to work for the well-being of her marital family all her life, but her letters betray exasperation at times, as when she upraided her eldest son, John II, for not seeing to his father's tomb, or made it clear that she wanted her sons, John III and Edmund, out of the house so that she could save money for her daughter Anne's dowry.[62]

A more poignant situation faced Hawise de Neville in the mid thirteenth century. Her son, Hugh, had been an adherent of Simon de Montfort and lost his lands in 1265, although he was subsequently pardoned and the estates partly restored. He took the cross and went to the Holy Land as a crusader, leaving his mother and his brother, John, in charge of his affairs in England. He was promised 500 marks from the money collected for the crusade, but it never materialised; as his mother said in a letter to him, such funds went to the great lords. Hawise was in the unenviable position of being unable to send Hugh the money which he wanted, and also of having to salvage the Neville family fortunes after the Barons' Wars. She urged him to apply direct to the pope for his crusading money, and to hasten his return to England to see to his affairs. As she put it in her letter, 'We know well that it would be very great dishonour and it would be as we think a great sin to suffer that you and yours be disinherited by your negligence'. Hawise died in 1269, probably the same year as Hugh died in the East.[63]

It was not only as mothers that widows were of use to their families. The medieval family was always aware of its wider kinship, both male and female. Although it was more usual to turn to male kinsmen for advice and help, sisters and grandmothers might well be called on as well. William de Ferrers of Groby appointed his sister, Philippa Beauchamp, one of the supervisors of his will of 1368, as did Henry, duke of Lancaster, whose sister, Lady Wake, was appointed an executrix.[64] Occasionally, a group of sisters remained in close touch with each other throughout their lives, providing mutual support. Of the nine daughters of Richard Scrope, one became a nun at Barking, and the others married into the nobility and gentry of Essex and East Anglia. The will of Elizabeth Beaumont, countess of Oxford (née Scrope), of 1537 left bequests to all her sisters and their husbands and children who were still alive; Mary and Jane were both present when the will was drawn up and both served as executrices. Elizabeth's marriage to the thirteenth earl of Oxford (d. 1513) may have helped to draw the family together and to foster their connections at court.[65]

The sparse references to grandmothers are partly the result of low life expectancy, since grandparents had often died before their families needed their help. The atheling Æthelstan made a bequest for the soul of his grandmother, who had brought him up.[66] The wills of the later middle ages show that when grandmothers were still alive they remembered their grandchildren in their wills, giving them personal and household items, or contributing to a girl's dowry.

Grandmothers might play a more active role. Agnes Paston (d. 1479) was anxious to block her granddaughter Margery's marriage to Richard Calle. She played her part in the family's property disputes and gave presents to her grandsons.[67] The circumstances for a grandmother's intervention had, however, to be propitious. Elizabeth de Burgh had one son and two daughters, all of whom had children, but, although close to them all, she was only involved in the affairs of her Ferrers grandchildren. Their father, Henry de Ferrers of Groby, died in 1343 and their mother Isabella six years later, so Elizabeth kept a watchful eye on the three children, having them to stay in her household and being involved in the negotiations for their marriages. A similar line was taken by Katherine Stafford, countess of Suffolk, after the battle of Agincourt. In 1480, Elizabeth Lady Latimer made landed provision for her daughter,

Katherine Dudley, who had been widowed and lacked a livelihood, and she arranged for feoffees to make an estate worth £100 a year for her younger grandson, Thomas. Elizabeth's husband had been declared a lunatic in 1451 and had died in 1469, and her eldest son was killed in the same year, leaving two very young sons.[68]

Occasionally, grandmothers indulged in blatant favouritism. Joan Beauchamp, lady of Abergavenny, made no reference in her will to her granddaughter and heiress, Elizabeth, who married Edward Neville. She wanted instead to safeguard the lands given to three members of her family who would not otherwise inherit, her grandsons, James, John and Thomas Butler, and she left each of them money to defend these livelihoods.[69]

Widows also transmitted the memories and traditions of their marital and natal families. In her will of 1399, Eleanor Bohun, duchess of Gloucester, remembered the priory of Lanthony by Gloucester and the abbey Walden in Essex. Lanthony was a Bohun foundation and Walden became a family house when the Bohuns became earls of Essex in 1236. Eleanor's father, Earl Humphrey, was buried in the abbey. Her bequests to her son Humphrey included the poem, *The History of the Knight of the Swan*, in French, and a psalter with her father's arms on the clasps; the swan was the Bohun badge, and Eleanor wanted the psalter to remain in the family, passing from one heir to the next. Humphrey was also bequeathed his father's armour, with a cross placed over the heart, and a gold cross of his mother's which was her best loved possession.[70]

Some widows of the elite combined their concern for their families with a religious life. Many Anglo-Saxon noble widows entered a nunnery or were in some way affiliated to one. Edith, queen of Edward the Confessor, retired after 1066 to Wilton, although she remained in touch with the outside world. Wynflaed, in her will of *c*. 950, was closely connected with a religious community, possibly Shaftesbury, while maintaining control of her estates.[71] Entry into a monastery offered security and protection; the widow was away from the politics of the court but not completely cut off from secular affairs. Widows continued to enter religious houses after 1066, but in smaller numbers by the later middle ages. Alternatively, they might spend their last years as a monastic boarder, as did Eleanor Wyndham (d. 1505), mother of Elizabeth Beaumont, who boarded at Carrow nunnery in Norwich with her daughter, Jane.[72]

With the religious vocation, there was always the danger of a change of mind and it was unwise to make a precipitate decision. Elizabeth Juliers, countess of Kent, lost her husband in 1352 and was veiled as a nun at the Cistercian abbey of Waverley in Surrey. Eight years later, however, she married Sir Eustace Dabricescourt. The archbishop of Canterbury allowed the marriage but sentenced the couple to penance, including, for Elizabeth, the recitation of certain psalms every day, a yearly pilgrimage to the shrine of St Thomas of Canterbury, and a diet of bread and pottage once a week.[73]

Many well-off widows in the later middle ages chose to become vowesses, taking an oath of chastity before the bishop but continuing to live in their own household and to administer their property. In the last years of her life, Cecily Neville, duchess of York, divided her day between religious service, prayer and reading, and the work connected with running a large household and estate. She got up at seven o'clock, and said matins of the day and matins of the Virgin Mary with her chaplain before hearing low mass in her chamber and having breakfast. She spent the morning in the chapel. At dinner, she listened to a religious reading from the lives of Jesus or the saints or from one of the medieval mystics. She then spent an hour with all who had business with her. After a short rest, she spent the rest of the afternoon in prayer. When the bell rang for evensong, she enjoyed a drink of wine or ale, and said the evensongs of the day and of the Virgin Mary with her chaplain before hearing evensong sung in the chapel. At supper, she went over the reading which she had heard at dinner with those who were present. She enjoyed some time after supper with her gentlewomen in recreation. At seven o'clock, she had a drink of wine and spent time in private prayer. She was in bed by eight o'clock.[74]

A few women took the vow in their husbands' lifetime, notably Margaret Beaufort, the mother of Henry VII. During the fourteenth century, 28 per cent of vowesses were wives or widows of knights, 14 per cent were townswomen and 8 per cent noblewomen, the figure for townswomen rising to 32 per cent in the early sixteenth century. Not all women kept their vow and a subsequent marriage was not regarded as invalid.[75] Some husbands specified in their wills that property bequeathed to their wives was only to remain in their hands while they were widows, as in the case of Alice, widow of the London grocer,

William Lynne, who took the vow within three months of her husband's death. William Herbert, earl of Pembroke, stated in his will that his wife had promised to take the vow so as to be better able to execute his will and help their ten children.[76]

For a few women, widowhood might last for forty or fifty years. After the grief of loss and bereavement, and the anxieties arising from her husband's will and the securing of dower, the widow continued to have family and community responsibilities, whether she remarried or not. She might have responsibility for a farm, shop, business or estate. Even when her children were grown up, had married and sometimes moved away, she might be called on for help and support. Most women remembered their children in their wills.[77]

5

Work

Childcare and running the household took up most of a woman's time. In addition, she helped her husband with farming his land, marketing and craft work, and from time to time engaged in work outside the household or as a *femme sole*. Although the husband was expected to support his family, any extra money earned by his wife came in useful, to pay the rent, save for a daughter's dowry or purchase items needed by the household. Widows were occupied in a similar round of work, with the added responsibility of supporting their households. Other women on their own had to support themselves, including teenagers working away from home, deserted wives and women who never married; these groups were to be found particularly in the towns where there were growing numbers of women on their own after the Black Death.[1] Such women were predominantly poor.

With the husband holding his wife's property during marriage, and with many poor widows, it was rare for a woman to have money to invest in training or business. Moreover, for both wife and widow, work had to be fitted in with housework and childcare, both of which had higher priority. A woman therefore might work before marriage and the arrival of children, then work as she could when she had free time, and work full-time again if she needed to or if it was in the family's interests for her to do so as a widow. There was a marked life-cycle and sporadic pattern in women's work, and she might well not confine herself to a single way of earning money. The wife of John Aldewyn, butcher of Romford, Essex, in the late fourteenth century, brewed ale while her husband was getting his business established and again when he retired. In between, John became a prosperous businessman, selling meat and other foodstuffs, trading with Londoners and building up his landholdings.[2]

Lack of capital meant that a woman had to make the most of her skills as a housewife and possibly craft skills as well. Hence, she was mainly engaged in low-grade occupations similar to her household work, in domestic service, brewing, spinning and marketing. She must often have found that her various tasks left her exhausted. The professions were largely closed to her; she might receive an elementary education but the universities were open only to men. Her practice of medicine was of low status compared to that of university-trained physicians.

Not only was the work often menial but it was not necessarily always available. In the Anglo-Saxon period, women would have been engaged in agricultural and domestic work, food preparation and brewing, and spinning and weaving for their own households – probably very rarely for money. The economic expansion between the tenth and early fourteenth centuries, with the doubling of population, growth of towns, industry and trade, and an increasing use of money, opened up work opportunities for women. Even then, the development was by no means uniform over the country. Market towns developed later in the north of England than in the south. Textile manufacture was found in many of the larger towns in the twelfth century but then declined, only expanding again in the later fourteenth century. The drastic fall in population after the Black Death encouraged women's employment, and the level of wages in relation to prices meant that standards of living were higher than before. The mid-fifteenth-century slump and the decline of much urban industry by 1500, however, had a serious impact on the work of both men and women.[3] Women tended to take on a variety of jobs, being dependent on what was available.

Women were found in domestic service throughout the middle ages. Women in service came under the authority of the householder, who took over the role of the woman's father or husband, but there is no doubt that young girls could be at risk when away from their families. References to women servants in Anglo-Saxon times are sparse and it is likely that many were slaves. Their work centred on household tasks. According to Ine's laws, a lord moving to a new estate might take with him his reeve, his smith and his children's nurse. Women's wills occasionally refer to servants, sometimes in connection with their manumission. About 950, Wynflaed bequeathed a female weaver and a seamstress to her granddaughter. Probably about fifty years later, Wulfwaru referred to all her household women to whom she left a finely decorated chest.[4]

Slavery declined after the Norman Conquest, but female servants continued to perform similar household work. However, it is only after the Black Death that it is possible to estimate the number of women employed. According to the poll taxes of 1377–81, male and female servants, including apprentices, comprised a sizable proportion of the urban population, but were less numerous in rural areas. Those in service amounted to 10 per cent of the taxable population in Rutland in 1377, as compared with 15.5 per cent in Colchester and 22.8 per cent in Hull; the figures for 1381 were 27.5 per cent in Chichester and 14.7 per cent in Northampton.[5]

Women were usually servants rather than apprentices and less likely than men to be in elite households, although here the number of women increased in the fifteenth century. Little documentary evidence is available as to their ages, but many appear to have been young and mobile, not staying long with any one employer, although according to the Statute of Labourers of 1351 a year's contract was regarded as the minimum.[6] There may well have been a sizeable number of older women servants and examples are found of wives living apart from their husbands while in service.[7] Both men and women left bequests to female servants, occasionally specifically for their marriage. In 1404 Thomas Wodecoke, janitor of St Mary's Abbey at York, left a sum of money to his servant, Joan de Middleton, and in 1490 Marion Mathew was bequeathed an amount of Spanish iron by her employer, Thomas Wood, draper of Hull.[8] For a poor widow on her own, taking service with a woman who was better-off might well be a safeguard against destitution in old age. Whatever the age of the servant, work was rarely specialised and might involve working in the house and on the farm and possibly also at a craft. In the poem, 'The Servant Girl's Holiday', the girl rushes through her chores in order to go out with her boyfriend. Normally, she would be spinning, sweeping, cutting rushes for the floor, laying the fire, bringing the herbs into the kitchen, seeing to the milk and kneading dough.[9]

It is not certain whether the high proportion of servants listed in the poll tax returns reflects growing work opportunities after the Black Death, as there is no statistical information before 1348. The poll tax figures may reflect a situation going back to the early fourteenth century at least. Service continued to be a common occupation for men and women into early modern times. In Coventry in 1523, a town then in decline, female servants were to be found in 441 households, of which 55.8 per cent kept one servant and 8.2 percent four or more; in comparison, male servants were employed in 242 households. Living-in servants comprised almost one-quarter of Coventry's population.[10]

Young servants worked hard and received a general training for their future lives. Some met their marriage partners while employed in a household. Some were sexually exploited by their employers. In the mid fifteenth century, John Nubold of Lichfield committed adultery with his servant, Margaret Wakefield, and was suspected of carrying on the relationship after she moved to Newcastle-under-Lyme.[11] Servants received their board and lodging but wages were low, if they were paid at all. Pay for women was certainly lower than for men, although it might rise as the servant became more experienced. The wages of a woman in service at Writtle, Essex, in the early fifteenth century rose from one shilling to 6s. 8d. a year during four years of employment. The maids at Mote in Sussex did much better, receiving between 13s. 4d. and 16s. a year, together with board, lodging and clothes. According to the statute of Cambridge of 1388, the yearly pay for a female labourer and a dairymaid was set at six shillings each.[12]

Whether they were servants, single or housewives, women in the countryside and small towns helped their husbands or employers with farmwork, carrying out labour services or working for pay. The amount of money earned from such work was small, since employment opportunities for women were limited and much of the work was part-time. While he was directly exploiting his estates in the thirteenth and fourteenth centuries, the lord of the manor employed a maid, to look after the farmyard and make pottage for the workers, and in some cases dairymaids. Women were capable of doing most agricultural work in the fields and are recorded hoeing and weeding, haymaking, reaping, carrying corn, winnowing and threshing, and breaking stones for road-mending.[13] Women were most in evidence at haymaking and harvest-time, the busiest periods of the whole year. In 1283, at Seven-hampton in Wiltshire, Margery Willam was fined 6d. at the manor court because her daughter slandered the bailiff while they were reaping the lord's grain. At Houghton on the Ramsey Abbey estates five years later, Beatrice Cuttepoce failed to come to do harvest boon works. It was customary for the lord to have first call on the labour of both men and women at haymaking and harvest, and for a woman who was able to reap not to glean; gleaning was left to the old and the children. It was generally considered that the poor had the right to glean.[14]

The anonymous thirteenth-century treatise *Husbandry* set the wages of male reapers at 2*d.* a day and female at 1*d.*, while according to the Statute of Labourers of 1351, reapers were to receive 2*d.* a day during the first week of August and 3*d.* in the second. This was the time of labour shortage after the Black Death, when harvest workers moved to other places in search of higher pay than that laid down by the statute. Seventeen men and women were fined for doing this at Ramsey in 1379 and in 1362–63 Margaret, wife of John le Bere of Wantisden, travelled twenty miles to Ilketshall in Suffolk for reaping.[15] Women were being prosecuted at the same time in Essex, such as Isabella, daughter of Gilbert Rouge of Sturmer, who was said to have taken 4*d.* a day and food at harvest-time, and Isabella, daughter of William Spendelove, accused of moving from place to place. Women were on the move in other counties as well. In some areas, such as parts of eastern England and the West Country, women received the same pay as men, but this was rare. The female reapers and binders at Minchinhampton, Gloucestershire, in 1380, were paid 4*d.* a day, the same rate as men. However, female harvesters in Sussex in the fifteenth century always received lower wages than men, and on the whole in agricultural work women tended to do low-grade jobs for lower pay.[16] Even when they were paid an equal wage at harvest, it has to be remembered that the harvest period was short, and, although women's wages made a welcome addition to family finances, a woman on her own needed additional employment or other means of support.

Women engaged in a number of money-making occupations. It is significant that a statute of 1363, while restricting men to a single trade, allowed women brewers, bakers, carders, spinners and workers in wool, linen and silk to continue to work in several trades.[17] Brewing ale was widespread among women in both town and country and information about it becomes plentiful with the enforcement of the thirteenth-century assize of bread and ale. Ale was widely drunk and had to be brewed frequently, since it went sour after a short time. Before 1350, brewing gave women more profit and status than most other types of work. It was a household occupation in which women engaged along with their family and servants. A coroner's roll of 1270 reported an accident in Lady Juliana de Beauchamp's brewhouse in Staploe, Bedfordshire, where two female servants were carrying a tub of grout, intending to tip it into a boiling vat. One of them slipped and fell into the vat. Although she was quickly pulled out, she was scalded so badly that she died next day. [18]

The importance of women as ale-brewers in the thirteenth and early fourteenth centuries has been illustrated at Brigstock in Northamptonshire. Women dominated the business and fall into two distinct groups, the 273 minor brewers and the thirty-eight ale-wives. The first group brewed mainly for their own households but sold any surplus. The ale-wives were major producers. They were married women, some of whose husbands were important in the community and who were long resident on the manor. Often interrelated, they were frequently involved in large-scale brewing over a period of about twenty years. They did not brew throughout the whole period, but brewed intermittently, presumably when they had no more urgent concerns to attend to. [19]

Brigstock was an arable farming community where new land was being taken into cultivation and where Rockingham Forest provided pasture, hunting and poaching. The men had plenty to do while their wives were brewing. Men may have played a more prominent role in the trade on more pastoral manors, such as Iver in Buckinghamshire – 73 per cent of the brewing fines at Iver were levied on men. In some places where court rolls record men's names, however, they may well have been paying the fine on behalf of their wives, exercising their authority as head of the household. At Alrewas, Staffordshire, it appears that men took responsibility for their wives' fines and debts, and that many of the women listed were widows or single. [20] This may well have occurred widely.

Brewing was also important to townswomen. Brewing, and to some extent ale retailing and keeping taverns, was in women's hands in Shrewsbury, and forty-eight women were fined for brewing and retailing in March 1400. There was a substantial number of brewers at Norwich, with fines often levied on husband and wife together, probably as a licence to brew. Fifty-seven people were listed in Conesford leet in 1288–89, eighty-four in Mancroft leet, eighty-one in Wymer, and sixty-four in the leet of *Ultra Aquam*. At Colchester, ale-brewing was largely in the hands of women, who paid a small fine, again as a licence to brew. Their number was considerable. The 112 ale-wives of 1311 constituted the highest figure before the Black Death. The growth of the town in the later fourteenth century led to an expansion of brewing and there were 235 brewers in 1405. The brewers included the wives of the leading men of the town who served as bailiffs and members of parliament.[21]

There are signs that brewing was becoming more commercialised after the Black Death, with women on their own finding that they could no longer compete, in spite of the growth of the market due to the improvement in diet. This process continued in the fifteenth century with the rise of the alehouse, as in Sussex where the industry became concentrated in fewer hands. Some women, however, were still able to earn a useful supplementary income. Elizabeth Baker of Battle, Sussex, worked as a brewer for twenty-two years after the death of her husband in 1460, helped for part of the time by her married daughter, Margaret. She was also a landholder, possibly engaged in dairying or cattle-rearing, and she sold linen cloth. In Havering, Essex, seventy-eight women who started brewing between 1420 and 1449 continued to brew for an average of 11.3 years. By the early sixteenth century, however, women were ceasing to brew ale in England.[22]

The other reason for the fall in the number of women brewing ale was the growing popularity of beer. Beer made use of hops and kept much better than ale. Its manufacture was mainly in the hands of professional beer-brewers. Colchester was importing beer from north Germany in the late fourteenth century, and hops were imported in large quantities from the mid fifteenth century. Some of the beer-brewers were immigrants from the Low Countries, such as Peter Herryson and Edmund Hermanson, both from Brabant. By the mid 1470s, a foreigner was brewing beer in Rye, Sussex, and foreigners were brewing beer a little earlier at Minehead in Somerset.[23]

Women's involvement in victualling was less significant than in brewing. Working as a butcher or fishmonger necessitated a larger outlay of capital than most women had. On the whole, there were fewer female than male bakers, although at Brigstock in the first half of the fourteenth century the number of women outstripped the men. It was more usual for wives to help their husbands and for widows to take over the businesses when their husbands died. In Shrewsbury, the butchers' wives were regularly fined for leaving dung and entrails in the street; they often carried on the business as widows until their sons were old enough to take over.[24]

Judging by the court rolls, many women in town and country, ranging from the poor to the better off, worked as hucksters, petty traders and stallholders retailing food and drink. They were almost certainly involved in retailing from early in the middle ages, but their offences against market regulations were only recorded once court rolls began to be kept in the thirteenth century. The most prevalent offences were forestalling and regrating, buying up goods on the way to market to force the price up, or purchasing in the market itself to sell later in the day, again at a higher price. Twenty-two out of the thirty-five regraters at Shrewsbury in March 1400 were women, and women traders were numerous in the borough of Halesowen.[25] Women retailers sold a wide range of foodstuffs. In the late fourteenth century at Exeter, they sold flour, salt, oats, ale, poultry, eggs, butter and cheese, and, at Coventry between 1377 and 1380, fish, poultry, ale, dairy products, eggs, fruit and charcoal; sixty-three out of 139 regraters and forestallers prosecuted at Coventry in these years were women. At Norwich in 1312–13, nine women in one ward were amerced for regrating oats and thirteen for regrating cheese. In 1390–91, the wife of Henry Lant was fined for buying poultry in the market on Saturday and selling them at the gates of the cathedral on Sunday; this had caused a great outcry.[26] In some boroughs, such as York, hucksters might enjoy the freedom of the city, and in late-fourteenth-century Norwich, hucksters were fined for not being citizens.[27] In Bristol, tapsters, hucksters and food retailers enjoyed the status of portmen or portwomen, although it was decided in 1470–71 to put an end to this.[28]

Running an alehouse or an inn might be combined with petty trading. At Chester, women with husbands who were craftsmen kept taverns. Some hucksters also ran alehouses in the city's cellars. Many of these women were *femmes soles*, responsible for their own business and debts. Women ran inns in other towns, including Durham and Nottingham.[29] At Chelmsford, Essex, Mabel Wymond took over an inn in the High Street after her husband's death, and Nicola Osteler ran her husband's inn and stalls by the bridge, continuing his quarrel with the bishop of London over damage to their property when the bridge was rebuilt.[30] Wives also ran village inns while their husbands followed another occupation. Inns attracted the attention of the courts for being disorderly and the haunt of criminals. In 1370, at Thornbury, Gloucestershire, Juliana Fox was expelled for using her inn as a brothel and for the reception of thieves. From the late fifteenth century the growing concern of the courts with public order and social control made it increasingly difficult for women to run alehouses.[31]

Women engaged in cloth-making from early times, the development of the textile industry in England making use of many of their basic skills. The twelfth-century urban industry produced cloth for the home market and for export, but decline set in about 1200 and thirteenth-century cloth-making is found mainly in the country and small towns, for instance in north Essex and Norfolk. In Norfolk, because of dense settlement, landholdings were often very small and intensively farmed and the growth of the linen and worsted industries must have brought welcome money into peasant households. This was an area of weak manorial control, enabling the peasantry to take up by-employments.[32] In the country as a whole, the industry grew rapidly after the Black Death, both in the large towns and countryside, and was particularly concentrated in east and south-east England, the West Country and parts of Yorkshire. Despite the recession of the 1430s and 1440s, and urban decline in the late fifteenth century, the industry flourished into the sixteenth century. Development in other counties, such as Derbyshire, could be short-lived; here, the industry emerged in several villages about 1355 and employed up to a quarter of the population in the 1370s, but it collapsed after 1380.[33]

Textiles provided employment for women in the places where the industry was established, but mainly they did low-grade work in their own homes. The largest group of female workers in late-fourteenth-century Exeter were in the textile industry, washing, combing, spinning and weaving wool. Women rarely had the capital to become dyers, fullers or shearwomen themselves. At York, only four out of about fifty-nine dyers were women in the 1380s, though a widow was able to take over her husband's dyeing business.[34] Women worked in the early and laborious stages of preparing flax and hemp, and in washing and spinning wool. The wool had to be washed to get rid of grease, and then carded or combed, preparatory to spinning. Spinning was often done on the distaff and so could be combined with watching the children or visiting neighbours. Some references to the spinning-wheel are found in the late middle ages; when Joan Powdych of Emneth, Norfolk, listed her household goods in 1467, she included a spinning-wheel.[35]

The spinner might be self-employed or work for an entrepreneur. In fifteenth-century Norfolk, she bought her wool, combed and spun it and sold the yarn to yarn hucksters who sold it on to the weavers. The piece-rate in the mid fifteenth century was generally 2d. for a pound of spun woollen yarn. Spinning brought work into the household but a woman relying on spinning for her support would be poor. Alternatively, she might receive wool from a clothier who made a money payment for the yarn; truck payments were forbidden by statute. Spinners were quite capable of defrauding the clothier by selling some of his wool and making up the weight with oil or water. Some clothiers, however, had a good relationship with their workers; Thomas Spring II of Lavenham, Suffolk, left one hundred marks to his spinners, fullers and tenters.[36]

Women had woven cloth from early times, using the warp-weighted vertical loom, and this was still being used for linen and worsted in Norfolk into the fourteenth century. The horizontal treadle loom was introduced into north-west Europe in the eleventh century; it was essential for long bolts of cloth and appears to have been taken over by the male worker. Women continued to weave, as in York where they probably had small businesses, or like the woman reported to the court of the deanery of Wisbech in the late 1460s for weaving on Sunday at the time of divine service.[37] By then, however, several towns were restricting weaving to men. In Bristol in 1461, the weaver was allowed to employ his present wife but no other women were to work as weavers, since skilled men were out of work and living as vagrants. The weavers' guild at Shrewsbury decreed in 1448 that a woman who lost her husband was only to continue to weave for three months so as to complete outstanding work. The worsted weavers of Norwich in 1511 allowed men and women to possess looms at home but no woman was to weave worsted because, it was said, she was not strong enough.[38] Women were increasingly restricted to the preparatory processes.

Silkwomen enjoyed much higher status. They were found predominantly in London in the fourteenth and fifteenth centuries and were

usually from mercers' families or married to mercers. They manufac-
tured sewing silk, ribbons and laces, silk corses and fringe. In 1483 Alice
Claver supplied the great laces of purple silk and Venetian gold thread
for the purple velvet mantles worn by Richard III and his queen at their
coronation, together with other luxury materials. The silkwomen did
not have their own guild but had the right to train their own apprentices. Four indentures of female apprentices survive, including two to
silk throwsters and one to a silkwoman. The prestige of the craft is
reflected in the fact that apprentices are known to have come from
Yorkshire, Lincolnshire, Buckinghamshire, Warwickshire and Norfolk.[39]

Silkwomen brought their own petitions for the remedy of grievances,
presumably with the backing of the mercers. The petition of 1368 has to
be considered in the context of bad relations between the London mercers and the merchants of Lucca. When the silkwomen alleged that a
merchant, Nicholas Sardouche, was buying up all the silk in London and
forcing the price up, a compromise was reached over the price. Mid-
and late-fifteenth-century petitions were directed against foreign
imports. In 1455 it was asserted that Lombards and others were importing poor-quality ribbons, laces and corses, and thrown silk. These
imports were consequently forbidden for the next five years. In 1483 the
target was thrown silk from Cologne, on which an embargo was
imposed by acts of parliament until 1505.[40]

It is possible to reconstruct the lives of some of the silkwomen. Isabel
Fleet came to London from Dursbury, Cheshire, and trained as a dyer,
throwster and corse weaver. She married a mercer, William Fleet, from
Fleet in Lincolnshire. They lived near Cheapside, where Isabel had her
shop in the Mercers' Crown Seld from at least 1425–26 until 1448–49.
Husband and wife trained their own apprentices and Isabel left money
to five female apprentices in her will of 1455. Silkwomen and their families had close marital, business and friendship connections. Beatrice
Fyler was another silkwoman married to a mercer and appears to have
run a profitable business. She was a friend of Alice Claver, who acted as
her executrix in 1479 along with Beatrice's daughter, Joanna, in all probability a silkwoman and married to a mercer, John Marshall, who had
had her brother, Edward, as his apprentice.[41]

The growth of crafts, especially in London and the larger provincial
towns, presented women with opportunities for employment in the

clothing, leather, metalwork and building trades. Some women were apprenticed to a particular craft, such as Agnes, daughter of Thomas le Chaloner of Coventry, who was apprenticed to Robert Raulot, a maker of leather purses, in 1336; he was to instruct her in the craft and provide board and lodging, while her father supplied her clothes. Many other women were presumably trained by their husbands. A woman might work with her husband, or as a wage-earner in another household, or as a *femme sole*. She might be engaged in several occupations, be an artisan or run a business. Adam Hecche, armourer of York, left his daughter all his tools for making chainmail in 1404. In her will of 1458, the widow Emmot Pannall of York referred to her saddler's workshop. The year before, John Rodes, fishmonger, left his wife a ship and his share in the house on the quay by the salt hole under Ouse Bridge. [42]

Levels of wealth varied widely. Some women must have found it hard to make a living, especially if they were on their own. Some won a reputation for their luxury craft work, such as Leofgyth, who held land in Wiltshire in 1086 and did gold embroidery for the royal family, and another embroiderer, Mabel of Bury St Edmunds, who worked for Henry III between 1239 and 1244. [43] After the Black Death there were employment opportunities for women, partly because of the labour shortage and partly as a result of the rise in living standards. Women are found working as tanners, skinners, curriers, glovers, saddlers and shoemakers; as founders, armourers, blacksmiths, ironmongers, pinners, needlers and occasionally as goldsmiths; as building labourers or supplying building materials; as seamstresses, embroiderers, tailors, cappers, hosiers and dressmakers; and as candle-makers.

Craft guilds existed from the twelfth century and proliferated in the late middle ages as a means of controlling craftsmen and artisans. A woman generally belonged to a guild because her husband was a member and as a widow was allowed to carry on his craft. In certain towns, such as Coventry, wives and unmarried women were allowed to belong to a guild as *femmes soles*. There were no guilds specifically for women, as at Paris and Cologne. Few references to women are found in craft guild regulations and it was rare for a woman to hold office. Women participated in the guild's religious, charitable and social activities, attended assemblies, and, if running a business, were expected to follow the rules on employment, apprenticeship and search. [44]

A number of widows ran successful businesses, as sometimes did daughters. Isabella de Copgrave of York was still in charge of her husband's tilehouses when she died in 1400. Agnes Ramsey, daughter of a master mason, William Ramsey of London, acted as his executrix and carried on his workshop for many years; in 1358–59, she made the tomb of Queen Isabella in the Greyfriars church in London, according to the agreement reached with the queen during her lifetime. Matilda Penne of London (d. 1392–93) is one of the apparently few women working as a skinner, taking over the business after her husband's death in 1379–80. She must have had some training, as she had the ability to buy skins and make them up into fur-linings. She trained her own apprentices and appears to have carried on the business until her death. Also unusual were women like Johanna Hill and Johanna Sturdy, working as bell-founders and running workshops in Aldgate in the mid fifteenth century. Johanna Hill was left the business by her husband and in 1440–41 was making bells for the church of Faversham in Kent. Her stamp also survives on bells in Devon, Buckinghamshire, Essex, Hertfordshire, Suffolk and Sussex. Johanna Sturdy ran the same foundry in the late 1450s, when she replaced Johanna Hill's tenor bell at Faversham.[45]

The women who had a trading and not just a manufacturing role had the best chance of prospering, in spite of the risks involved. Like silk-women, they usually had wealthy and influential marital and family connections, and as widows continued their husbands' businesses, sometimes until their sons were old enough to take over. During the thirteenth century, several Jewish women are known to have been active in their husbands' businesses, both as wives and widows. Unlike Christian wives, they were able to hold property in their own right and manage moneylending businesses in their own name. Henna, wife of Aaron of York, acted as his business partner in the 1250s. The position of the Jews, however, became increasingly vulnerable well before their expulsion in 1290. Licoricia of Winchester, the richest Jewess of the thirteenth century, lost much of her fortune through the very heavy royal tallages of the 1250s, and Henna was forced by Edward I's ordinances to sell all her property in York by 1280. Women, like men, were subject to imprisonment and mistreatment.[46]

A number of Englishwomen operated as traders. Women cloth traders are found at York, where several were freemen. At Exeter in the late thirteenth century, the most successful female merchants sold cloth and may also have supervised some of the cloth-finishing processes; they were widows, carrying on their husbands' trade.[47] In London, women imported and exported cloth and were members of the Staple. Margaret Croke continued to run her husband's business for a short time after his death in 1477, exporting wool and woolfells.[48] Women in provincial towns, such as Margaret Rowley and Agnes Kyte of Bristol, both of whom were widows, also engaged in overseas trade. Margaret Rowley imported wine and woad from Bordeaux in 1479, immediately after her husband's death. Agnes Kyte traded with her son, and, in her will of 1488, left him all the merchandise beyond the sea which he was already in charge of. Denise Holme of Beverley exported wool and wool-fells between 1465 and 1470, from the time of her husband's death until shortly before her own. Marion Kent of York exported cloth and lead and imported a wide range of merchandise in the early years of her widowhood while her children were growing up. She was exceptional among *femmes soles* in being a council member of the York mercers' guild in 1474–75.[49]

These women were unusual in later medieval England. The growth of towns and, more particularly, conditions after the Black Death meant that urban women with wealthy and influential connections were able to work and prosper. They had legal and social advantages. In the fourteenth and fifteenth centuries, the wives of London citizens were able and expected to trade as *femmes soles* and run their husbands' businesses as widows, while enjoying their dower. They obtained their freedom of the City through their marriage and so were able to trade.[50] Their position was comparable to women engaged in trade or running businesses elsewhere. These women could be said to be enjoying a 'Golden Age', but they were a tiny minority among working women.

Most working women were poor, and, although there were more openings for them after the Black Death, some of their earlier occupations, such as brewing, were declining. Much of their work in textiles and crafts was low-grade, and their role in weaving was also in decline. They were hit hard by the mid-fifteenth-century recession, and in Sussex and elsewhere this led to unemployment in the cloth industry as well as to a reduced demand for agricultural labour, the cloth industry not recovering until the 1490s.[51] By the late fifteenth century, pressure was brought by powerful guilds on male and female artisans. Small mercers in London in the thirteenth century ran their own shops and travelled with their goods, those of silk and linen being made by their wives; by the fifteenth century, the Mercers' company was marginalising them. The Mercers' company brought pressure to bear on lesser mercers and shepsters by forbidding credit to the poorer shepsters and making it difficult for them to buy linen. The Mercers also sought to enforce quality controls over silk embroideries and church vestments, which affected both men and women.[52]

At about the same time, some guilds were forcing retirement on widows if they remarried. In 1487, the York textwriters and illuminators allowed an apprentice to continue to be trained by his master's widow as long as she was a *femme sole*. The York butchers in 1498 insisted that a man of another craft who married a butcher's widow was to have nothing to do with butchering until he had reached an agreement with the city chamber and the guild.[53] With the rise in population after about 1500, there were fewer openings for women at a time when falling wages and rising prices made their earnings more essential to the household.

Because of their sex and lack of access to university education, women were excluded from the professions and could not enter the priesthood, law or medicine. Some women were employed in the book trade, and worked as bookbinders, scriveners and painters. Matilda Myms of London, widow of John the painter, bequeathed all her materials to her apprentice; she also ran an alehouse.[54] Women also had medical knowledge, learned presumably at home, and looked after their own families and neighbours. John Paston III asked his wife Margery to send a plaster for the knee of James Hobart and a note saying how long it should be left on the knee and that it should be covered with cloths to keep the knee warm.[55] Women worked as midwives, and a few names of female doctors, who were regarded with suspicion by male practitioners, are known. During the thirteenth and fourteenth centuries, women apprentices and surgeons worked in London, most of them with fathers or husbands who were barber surgeons. The situation was similar in Lincoln, Norwich and York. During the fifteenth century, women surgeons disappeared in London, although not in York. Women also worked as nurses, providing care for hospital patients.[56]

Prostitution was widespread, especially in the towns, and records from the thirteenth century onwards point to sporadic regulation by the authorities. From at least 1266–67, prostitutes were forbidden to live in the City of London, an order which had to be repeated. In 1382, Cock Lane in Smithfield and Southwark were designated for prostitutes, the lordship of the bishop of Winchester in Southwark becoming the main centre for the stews. Prostitutes were expelled from York in 1301 when the royal court was based in the city, but they returned within a few decades. Other places, such as Exeter and Westminster, levied fines on prostitutes which virtually gave them a licence to operate. Distinctive dress was adopted in some towns, such as the striped hood in London, Great Yarmouth and Bristol.[57] On the whole, towns tolerated prostitution as a social necessity, while at the same time keeping a watchful eye to prevent disorder and to make money for the town through the levy of fines.

Although prostitution was widespread, many prostitutes worked on a casual basis, soliciting as prostitutes when they could not find other work. Many of the women were poor and turned to prostitution when they could not find employment in spinning, dressmaking or retailing. Aliens such as Flemings in Southwark or Scotswomen in York (where the Scots were much disliked) were sometimes forced into prostitution. In York, certain women acted as procuresses but the brothels were small and prostitutes solicited in alehouses and elsewhere in the city. In 1504 Katherine Rasen and others were accused of keeping a chain of brothels in Westminster and other places round London. At Lichfield, Joan Wright was accused in 1465–66 of keeping a brothel and procuring girls as prostitutes, but it was more usual for women to open their houses to all comers. There seem to have been plenty of clients, often clergy in a cathedral city. Between 1441 and 1451, in the cathedral chapter act book of York, eighty-six presentments concerned forty-five clergy, while seventy-nine concerned fifty-nine laymen.[58]

Organised or municipal brothels, of the type found in southern Europe, were rare in England and only found in Sandwich, Southampton from the late fifteenth century, and Southwark from the mid fourteenth.[59] The distinction between the more casual organisation usually found in England and the municipal brothels of southern Europe has been attributed to the contrasting marriage patterns of the two areas and the 'honour and shame culture' of the south.[60] Great importance was attached to the virginity of the bride, and marriage in Italy tended to be at a young age for girls, soon after puberty, but at the age of about thirty for men. In contrast, in England, marriage partners tended to be in their late teens or early twenties, making for a companionate marriage.

London, like Sandwich and Southampton, had an Italian community and a large number of foreigners living in the city or passing through. Ordinances were drawn up in the fifteenth century to regulate the Southwark stews and to protect the prostitute from the stewholder, who was to be a married man and to use his house solely as a brothel and not as a shop or inn. He was not to sell food, drink, fuel or candles; this provision was designed to prevent him from gaining a hold over the prostitutes through their becoming indebted to him; he was not to lend a prostitute more than 6s. 8d. He was only to keep two servants, an ostler and a laundress, so he would not be able to use his servants as prostitutes. He was not to keep boats to bring clients from the city, and no client was to be kept in the house against his will. The house was to be closed on holy days, except in the middle of the day.

No married or pregnant woman was to stay in the house as a prostitute. Every prostitute was to have free access to her chamber and her rent was fixed at no more than 14d. a week. No woman was to be kept in the house against her will. The prostitutes were not to keep any male friends in their rooms. Regulations were laid down as to their dress and manner of soliciting. They had to leave Southwark for most of the day on holy days and at night when there was a parliament or council in session at Westminster. Punishments were laid down for infringements of the ordinances.[61]

By the late fifteenth century, English towns were tightening up on their regulations for prostitutes. Prostitutes were expelled from Leicester in 1467, and in 1482 York decreed that they were to live in the suburbs. Ten years later, the Coventry authorities showed deep suspicion of women on their own. Strong and healthy single women under the age of fifty were forbidden to rent houses or rooms, but to go into service; women with a bad reputation were to be evicted by their landlords.[62] Such regulations were a further pointer to women's worsening employment prospects in the early modern period.

6

Noblewomen

Throughout the middle ages, the nobility were at the top of the lay social hierarchy, under the king, and enjoyed a position of wealth, power and influence derived largely from their estates. Along with the kings, many noblemen were well-known figures, leading armies, playing a prominent role in council and government, and, on occasion, mounting rebellion. Chroniclers do not give their womenfolk such prominence, yet, in addition to their importance as heiresses and mothers, women had a significant role to play in the locality through their landholding and patronage; this role sometimes had national political ramifications. As both wives and widows, women could be found running estates, exercising jurisdiction and building up the reputation and prestige of the family.

There was considerable variety of wealth and landholding within the nobility and this is apparent from the earliest laws of the Anglo-Saxon kings. The laws of Æthelberht of Kent distinguished between eorl and ceorl, noble and peasant, and provided compensation according to her class for the breach of guardianship of a widow of noble birth. In the eleventh century, there was a great economic and social gulf between a man such as Godwine, earl of Wessex, and a thegn with five hides of land.[1] Similarly, in the Norman period, there are distinctions between the great barons, lesser lords and knights. During the later middle ages, greater definition was given to the nobility by the concept of parliamentary peerage, but there were still great differences between the higher nobility and the rest, and between the knights, esquires and gentry. There was, moreover, considerable upward and downward mobility. Yet, despite these divergences, there were always common factors uniting the nobility: their military ethos, land tenure and service, local and national social and political networks, and a common political and religious culture. From the late twelfth century, the values and ties of chivalry existed throughout the nobility.

Noblewomen owed their position partly to their birth but mainly to their marriage. Marriage took them into a new family, one that was sometimes distant from where they had grown up. As well as taking on the roles of wife and mother, they had to adapt to their husbands' interests and get to know new people and an unfamiliar environment. They saw themselves as part of their marital family, but many also retained connections with the family of their birth through their religious patronage and sometimes their place of burial.

Anglo-Saxon marital interests were served in some instances by husband and wife drawing up their will together, as did Ulf and Madselin in the mid eleventh century, when they were about to go on pilgrimage to Jerusalem. In the late tenth century, Brihtric and Ælfswith declared their will in the presence of their kindred. Husbands granted lands to their wives in the expectation that their wishes for the future disposal of the estate would be carried out. Ealdorman Ælfheah of Hampshire (d. 971) referred to his confidence that his wife would maintain the property, and he reminded her to be generous in her almsgiving for the benefit of their souls. Other testators were more concerned with their obligations to their natal families. Both Æthelflaed, second wife of King Edmund, and her sister, Ælfflaed, wife of Ealdorman Byrhtnoth of Essex, were concerned to carry out the wishes of their father, Ælfgar, ealdorman of Essex, notably his bequests to the religious community at Stoke-by-Nayland in Suffolk. Ælfflaed also showed her loyalty to her husband in confirming three promised estates to the church of Ely and giving a ring which matched the one given as Byrhtnoth's burial fee.[2]

This identification with both marital and natal families continued until the end of the middle ages, although the situation was sometimes complicated by remarriage. Many husbands and wives of the fourteenth and fifteenth centuries stated in their wills that they wanted to be buried together. Cecily, duchess of York, for instance, wanted to be buried next to her 'most entirely best beloved lord and husband', Richard, duke of York, at Fotheringhay in Northamptonshire. Certain wives, however, chose burial with their natal family. Philippa, countess of March, stated that she was to be buried at the abbey of Bisham, founded in 1338 by her father, William, earl of Salisbury, rather than in the Mortimer abbey Wigmore. Mary, Lady Roos (d. 1394), chose to be buried next to her husband in the choir of Rievaulx Abbey, but wanted her tombstone to be like that of her Orreby grandmother in the church of Boston, Lincolnshire.[3] Sometimes, the choice was influenced by the woman being the last survivor and heiress of her family. Isabel, countess of Warwick, wished to be buried with her Despenser ancestors in Tewkesbury Abbey in 1439 and Margaret Paston chose the aisle of her natal family church at Mautby, where her ancestors were buried. Occasionally, choices were dictated by age and piety as well as family considerations. Marie de St-Pol, countess of Pembroke, buried her husband, Aymer de Valence, in Westminster Abbey and the mourners depicted on the tomb included members of her family as well as his, probably at her instigation; she herself was depicted twice. On her death in 1377, over fifty years later, she preferred burial in the Franciscan habit in the Minoresses' abbey Denny, Cambridgeshire.[4]

The noblewoman's sense of her identity was also reflected in her seal. This emphasised her social standing and authority. Seals go back to the Anglo-Saxon period, but the earliest surviving laywoman's seal is that of Queen Matilda, wife of Henry I. Noblewomen were using seals from the late 1130s, and by about 1250 the practice had spread throughout society. Women's seals of the twelfth and thirteenth centuries were usually oval in shape and contained the standing figure of a woman, with the emblems of a lily or a hawk.[5] From the mid twelfth century it became increasingly usual to incorporate heraldry, and the arms chosen reinforced their sense of identity. These armorial bearings point to pride in both marital and natal families. The earliest example is the seal of Rohaise de Clare, countess of Lincoln, dated after 1156, which made use of her natal Clare family chevrons. The same device was used by her daughter, Alice, wife of Simon de St Liz III, earl of Huntingdon and Northampton.[6] Both women probably considered the Clare arms more prestigious than those of their husbands.

Armorial seals became more popular during the thirteenth and fourteenth centuries, replacing the seal with the standing lady by about 1400. A few ladies adopted double-sided seals, but these disappeared during the fourteenth century. The use of the husband's arms was common and Margaret de Neville (d. 1338) included the shields of both her husbands. Many women included their father's as well as their husband's arms, as did Marie de St-Pol, countess of Pembroke.[7] A considerable amount of information could be conveyed on the seal. Elizabeth de Burgh, lady of Clare (d. 1360), included the arms of her three husbands, the Clare chevrons representing her father's family, the leopards of the king of England and the emblems of the crown of Castile and Leon; her mother was Joan of Acre, daughter of Edward I and Eleanor of Castile.[8] Noblewomen like Elizabeth had complex identities of which they were proud.

Noblewomen saw themselves as integrated into their families and were conscious of their status in society. The question arises, however, as to how much authority they could really exercise, in view of their subservience to their husbands and their property being under their husbands' control during marriage. Widows enjoyed greater independence but their actions usually continued to be within the context of their family. The noble wife's primary obligation was providing an heir, as the birth of at least one boy was regarded as crucial for securing the continuity of the family. Yet her duties went further and she was expected to contribute to the family's well-being and prestige. Just as peasant and townswomen led active lives within marriage and exercised authority, especially as widows, so noblewomen often succeeded in forging a partnership with their husbands and were able to take their husband's place on the estates and sometimes in war. Their activities as wives depended on circumstances, on the extent of their husbands' absence and on their role in national and local politics. Once widowed, they were expected as *femmes soles* to administer their lands and provide for their children.

Like other women, noblewomen's responsibility for the household gave them an important and prominent role. Anglo-Saxon riddles refer to the feasts which the woman had to cater for and the clothing to be provided. She was expected to hold the keys of the household. Comments made about queens apply equally to noblewomen. Husband and wife were expected to be generous, the wife to be a good counsellor, loved by her people, cheerful and trustworthy, and keeping her husband's secrets. All these qualities were highly regarded throughout the middle ages. At a feast, she greeted her husband first and hastened to give him the first cup.[9] Little is known of the structure of the Anglo-Saxon noble household; most attention is focused on the lord's band of followers rather than on the servants or slaves who ensured that everything ran smoothly.

The masculine ethos of the household continued into the early modern period, although more women servants are found in great houses in the fifteenth century.[10] Most household officers and servants were male, as were the estate officials. There was always a small group of women who waited on the lady; the women who were bequeathed clothes and furnishings by Æthelgifu in the late tenth century possibly came into this category. Children's nurses and mistresses were female, as were washerwomen. In the mid twelfth century, Amicia, countess of Leicester, gave a sum of four shillings a year to one of her waiting women on her marriage to one of the earl's men, and a little later Matilda de Percy, countess of Warwick, referred to Juliana, her chamberlain. Agnes de Condet (d. 1222–23) left her lady-in-waiting ten marks, a robe of scarlet and a mantle, and sheets and a coverlet.[11]

During the later middle ages, noblewomen regularly remembered both male and female servants in their wills. Margaret Paston wanted her servants to continue to be employed in the household for six months after her death, and singled out Agnes Swan to receive a gown, girdle and twenty shillings. In 1401, Isabella, widow of Sir Walter Fauconberg, provided in her will for her confessor and Beatrice Lady Roos to reward her servants. Elizabeth Mohun, countess of Salisbury (d. 1414), listed her servants in hierarchical order, starting with her chaplains and ladies and ending with the grooms of the household departments, who received between one mark and forty shillings each. The more prestigious servants received valuable goods as well as money; her chaplain, Sir Hugh, was bequeathed a gold vestment, a missal and a breviary to pray for her, and her chief lady-in-waiting, Agnes Grene, was left one hundred marks because of her long service, together with two of her best robes lined with trimmed miniver.[12]

Noble households were usually itinerant until at least 1300. Bishop Robert Grosseteste advised Margaret de Lacy, countess of Lincoln, to make plans at Michaelmas, after the harvest, as to how many weeks she was going to spend on each manor over the coming year. He advised her not to burden any place by too long a stay, since the manors had to contribute to her income as well as her food supply. Although the estates produced most of the household's food, she had to purchase wine, wax, spices and cloth for liveries, and he advised her to do this twice a year at the great fairs. He clearly expected the lady to be in control of her household, although her marshal had to enforce her orders. Servants should be honest, loyal and hardworking, or be dismissed. There was to be no strife or faction. Guests were to be treated courteously. In Grosseteste's view, the lady should always be present in the hall at mealtimes, seated at the centre of the high table so that she could see everything that was going on. Meals had to be served in an orderly fashion, each servant knowing what he or she had to do. The lady's presence in the hall brought her honour and tangible benefits. [13]

It was only with the more settled lifestyle of the later middle ages that there came to be more privacy in great houses and, although lords and ladies were encouraged to eat in hall, there was a growing tendency for them to have their meals separately. [14] Grosseteste's remarks about the lady's overall control, however, still applied. Cecily Neville, duchess of York, daily set aside an hour after dinner to give audience to all who had business with her, and four times a year proclamation was made in the market towns round her residence in the castle of Berkhamsted to find out if the lady's officers and servants had paid her debts. Elizabeth, Lady Zouche, was personally concerned with provisioning and purchases, while Elizabeth Stonor signed her accounts. [15] Such women were not ciphers within their households.

Household accounts show that households varied considerably in size, according to the wealth and status of the lord or lady; they were organised hierarchically in terms of rank, and departmentally according to function. In 1418–19, Alice de Bryene of Acton, Suffolk, paid £44 in wages to her maid and chamberlain, squires, chaplains, clerks of the chapel, grooms and pages; in addition, they received her livery, and both wages and livery depended on their rank in the household. Two years later, the household of Elizabeth Berkeley, countess of Warwick, comprised about fifty people. The division of the household into departments goes back to early times, but it became much more specialised in the households of the higher nobility in the fourteenth and fifteenth centuries, although strict departmental divisions did not always apply in practice. In addition to the hall, chamber and chapel, the service area comprised the pantry for the supply of bread, the buttery for wine and ale, the kitchen for meat and fish, the poultry for birds, eggs and dairy produce, and sometimes other departments as well. [16]

For the higher nobility, the later medieval household was not necessarily a single unit. The distinction between the great household and a
smaller itinerant household probably goes back to early times. Elizabeth
Berkeley was in charge of the inner household in 1420–21 while her husband, Richard Beauchamp, had his foreign household with him in
France. A few women's households were distinct from their husbands'.
Elizabeth de Burgh, countess of Ulster, married to Edward III's second
son, Lionel, duke of Clarence, had her own household in 1357.[17]

The household, whatever its size, constituted a community in its own
right. Here the lady lived her life and carried out her duties, here her
children were born and spent their early years. At least part of a noblewoman's day was spent in her chamber with her ladies, but she would
also be seen in the hall and chapel. Over time, the lady lived among
familiar faces. Servants might spend many years in the same household,
some joining as pages and receiving subsequent promotion. In the 1350s
Elizabeth de Burgh, lady of Clare, was employing many of the same men
and women who had been with her over ten years ealier. The servants
received board and lodging, livery, wages, and sometimes gifts and
bequests. The chapel served the spiritual needs of the household; Elizabeth de Burgh's chamber account of 1351–52 records the offerings made
at mass on behalf of the lady and her household.[18]

The household was, however, much more than a self-sufficient community. It had its part to play in building up the lord's or lady's reputation in the locality and further afield through its splendour and display,
and through the exercise of hospitality. Officials were sent out from the
household to administer the estates, to hold manorial and honour
courts, and to defend the family's rights in the royal courts and in parliament. Land and lordship were the foundation of noble power and had
to be maintained and defended throughout the middle ages. Without the
household to carry out her business, the lady's policies could not have
been executed. Robert Grosseteste expected his wife to be as aware of the
state of affairs on her lands as in her household, but urged her to have a
trustworthy steward, bailiffs and clerks to carry out the everyday work.[19]

Both wives and widows had responsibilities for land, some wives
working in partnership with their husbands and taking over from
them when they were away from home. Very occasionally, a wife
was responsible for her own inheritance. Elizabeth Berkeley succeeded

to the Lisle estates through her mother, and during her marriage to Richard Beauchamp the receiver paid the money over to the keeper of Elizabeth's household; the earl, however, kept the Despenser inheritance which he gained from his second marriage under his own control. Anne Neville, duchess of Buckingham, had at least some part in running her estates after her second marriage to Lord Mountjoy, and her officials regarded her as head of the household. [20] Widows did not necessarily have a completely free hand on their estates; dower or jointure belonged to the marital family and reverted to them on the widow's death and the widow's own landed inheritance passed to the heir. Widows might come under threat from their male relations, as when Godgifu, widow of Earl Leofric of Mercia, lost estates to her grandsons, Edwin and Morcar. [21]

Twelfth-century charters make it clear that noblewomen were involved in the family's affairs. The extent of involvement varied but the number of charters in which wives advised their husbands and witnessed grants points to their having a political role which continued during their widowhood. The title of countess in the twelfth century probably denotes some political responsibility. Occasionally, charters referred to lands belonging to the wife's inheritance but many charters dealt with estates and tenants belonging to the husband's lordship. Mabel, wife of Robert, earl of Gloucester, illegitimate son of Henry I, witnessed four of her husband's charters. She gave her consent to his foundation of the abbey of Margam as its endowment came from her lands. The importance of her political role is apparent in the treaty between her husband and Miles of Gloucester, earl of Hereford, since she was made responsible for ensuring that her husband kept his side of the agreement; if not, she was to see that he did. Mabel, as countess, had a key role in the Gloucester lordship, and may have been left in charge of the estates when her husband was overseas with Geoffrey, count of Anjou. As a widow, she controlled the honour of Gloucester's Norman lands on behalf of her son, Earl William. [22] Her daughter-in-law also played a key role in the lordship, witnessing three-quarters of her husband's charters and issuing her own charters as a widow. [23]

Margaret de Bohun exemplifies the roles which a woman could play in her estates. She was the daughter of Miles of Gloucester and married Humphrey de Bohun, steward of Henry I, who died about 1165. Between the death of her father in 1143 and the death of her husband, Margaret lost her four brothers, all of whom died without heirs. Miles's lands were divided between his three daughters, Margaret receiving his lordship in Herefordshire and the office of constable of England. She exercised lordship as a widow for over thirty years, dying in 1197. The office of constable passed to her son, Humphrey (d. 1181), by the 1170s, and subsequently to her grandson and his descendants.[24]

As lady, Margaret met her obligations to the king as her overlord. She returned the *carta* listing her knights to Henry II in 1166, recording seventeen knights' fees of the old enfeoffment and 3¾ of the new.[25] She accounted to the Exchequer for the aid for the marriage of the king's daughter in 1167–68, and, at the end of Henry II's reign and under Richard I, for scutage due from her lands.[26] In her lordship, Margaret followed the pattern set by her father. She confirmed earlier grants of land to tenants, and made her own landed rewards to those who served her. She also confirmed her tenants' grants, as with the land given by William de la Mare to the abbey of Gloucester. There are only occasional references to her officials, who are described by their Christian name and office, such as Alexander the butler and Wimund the chamberlain. Margaret's actions have to be seen in her family context and her son and grandson are occasionally found witnessing her charters.[27] Both widows and grantees saw it as advantageous to have the heir's consent.

The family context is particularly apparent in Margaret's grants to the priory of Lanthony Secunda and her confirmations of earlier endowments. This Augustinian priory had been founded by Miles of Gloucester in 1136 to receive the monks who fled from Llanthony Priory in Monmouthshire. Both Miles and Margaret were buried there and Miles's widow, Sibyl de Neufmarché, entered the religious life at the priory. Margaret was generous in her benefactions and also concerned to fulfil her brothers' grants. She gave all her land in Quedgeley, Gloucestershire, held by her father and grandfather, to free her brothers' souls from the danger of damnation, since they had promised on their succession to give five librates of land for the benefit of their mother's soul. Walter had also promised ten librates for the salvation of Henry II. Her own grant was made for the salvation of Henry II, her son Humphrey, daughter Matilda and all her sons and daughters, and for the souls of her parents and husband, their deceased sons and daughters, her brothers, sisters, relations, predecessors and heirs.[28] The patronage of Lanthony Secunda priory by the Bohun family and their descendants continued into the fifteenth century, when Anne, countess of Stafford and granddaughter of the last Bohun earl of Hereford, made gifts to the priory and was buried there. [29]

The growth of professional administrators in the thirteenth century led to more bureaucratic strictures on estates; in addition to their stewards, receivers and bailiffs, members of the nobility had their councils and auditors by 1300 and attorneys to conduct their litigation. Direct demesne farming in the thirteenth and fourteenth centuries necessitated close supervision by the officials. There was, however, still an important role for the lord or lady to exercise ultimate control. Robert Grosseteste expected the lady to know where her property was situated and how it was stocked, and how the size of the harvest could be calculated and checked. [30] Moreover, the lady still had her feudal obligations to the crown, exercised rights of wardship, marriage and aids over her vassals, and exerted influence and patronage over the people and churches of the locality.

Joan de Bohun (d. 1419) was the widow of the last Bohun earl of Hereford, and like her twelfth-century predecessor, Margaret, an important landholder and patron, exercising lordship, particularly in Essex. [31] She was the daughter of Richard FitzAlan, earl of Arundel (d. 1376). Her husband died in 1373, leaving two daughters who came into Edward III's wardship and who inherited the Bohun estates. Joan's dower made her a major Essex landowner. The late fourteenth and early fifteenth centuries were a time of transition in estate exploitation, and to start with Joan pursued a mixed policy of direct farming and leasing, farming decisions being made in consultation with her council. Arable and livestock farming was carried on, grain being produced for the market as well as for consumption, and labour provided by the services of her peasants. Some of her manors were attacked during the Great Revolt of 1381. After the Revolt, Joan continued to be an energetic landowner; expansion being especially apparent at Saffron Walden, where the dyeing and fulling of woollen cloth was encouraged. [32] It became clear, however, that direct farming of the manors was no longer profitable and the estates were leased out.

By Joan's time, feudal relationships between lord and vassals still existed but were of little practical importance, except for the lord's rights of wardship and marriage. Instead, Joan was at the centre of a strong network of county gentry who served as her officials and counsellors; in return, she acted as arbitrator, feoffee in property transactions and intercessor with the royal government. The upward mobility of men such as Robert Darcy owed much to thier service to Joan and the contacts gained through her with the nobility and the crown.

Countess Joan and her circle acted together in their religious patronage, especially in the founding of chantries. Joan also joined with the Essex elite as a member of St Helen's religious guild at Colchester. Monastic patronage was less significant than in the twelfth century, but Joan, like her Bohun predecessors since becoming earls of Essex, was a patron of Walden Abbey, financing new building and giving vestments, altar vessels and relics. Her piety was extolled by the abbey.[33]

Joan gained wider responsibilities as a result of the deposition of Richard II and the accession of her son-in-law, Henry IV, in 1399. Like other noblewomen, she was given custody of forfeited estates, a remarkable number being in her hands in the early fifteenth century. Her service on government commissions was exceptional for a woman and underlined the trust that the king had in her. Both he and his son, Henry V, saw that she was rewarded. Both Margaret and Joan de Bohun exercised their responsibilities as widows vigorously and in the interests of their marital family.

In the mid fifteenth century, Margaret Paston was largely responsible for her family and lands in Norfolk during her husband's absences in London as well as after his death. The survival of letter-collections makes it possible to obtain much more personal details of a woman's role. John Paston I sent instructions as to what his wife was to do; she responded with accounts of her activities. She was not only responsible for running the estates but also defended the landed interests of the family and represented their concerns to influential patrons; on occasion, she had to defend the manors themselves.[34] All this was important for an ambitious, upwardly mobile family of lowly origins, keen to secure the Fastolf inheritance. Margaret's concern for her children to make good marriages was at least partly due to her desire for the Pastons to gain a secure position among Norfolk gentry families.

Responsibility for land, lordship and patronage was an important part of many noblewomen's lives, particularly when they were widows. This responsibility was not limited to England; several, like Mabel, countess of Gloucester, journeyed across the Channel to take charge of lands in Normandy, although the number of course diminished after the loss of Normandy in 1204. A few noblewomen still had lands in France after 1204, however, and Marie de St-Pol, countess of Pembroke, travelled periodically to her French lands during the Hundred Years War.[35]

Women took on political roles, occasionally as crown office-holders, and more often at court, in war or during rebellion. The use of the title *vicecomitissa* by Bertha de Glanville may well indicate that the wife of a sheriff was thought to have public duties.[36] Ela, countess of Salisbury, served as Sheriff of Wiltshire in 1227–28 and 1231–36, accounting in person at Michaelmas 1236. The office had been held by her husband, father and grandfather, although a later case in the royal court laid down that she had no hereditary right to the office. The ceremonial leadership taken by earl and countess in the county was seen when Ela and her husband, William Longespee, earl of Salisbury, laid foundation stones for the new Salisbury Cathedral in 1220.[37]

Mistresses of royal children or ladies-in-waiting for the queen were recruited from noble and gentry women. Matthew Paris provides a eulogy of Cecilia de Sanford, the mistress of Henry III's sister, Eleanor. Eleanor married William Marshal the younger and, as a widow, she and Cecilia took the vow of chastity in the presence of St Edmund of Abingdon, archbishop of Canterbury. Eleanor broke her vow and married Simon de Montfort, but Cecilia remained a vowess until her death. Her funeral at St Albans was attended by knights and nobles as well as by the abbot and monks.[38]

The roles of maid of honour and lady-in-waiting at court became more important with the growth of court culture and centralisation from the later fifteenth century. Ladies-in-waiting were often related to the queen, both Elizabeth Woodville and Elizabeth of York employing members of their own families. The women received board and lodging and a money fee; Elizabeth Woodville paid her ladies-in-waiting £40 a year if they were of noble birth, or £20 if not.[39] Their influential position at court enabled them to become useful intermediaries for their families and localities.

Involvement in court politics occurred through the need to defend inheritances. Much of the Berkeley estate was entailed to the male line in 1349, with the result that Elizabeth, only child of Thomas Berkeley (d. 1417), was excluded from that part of the inheritance, the manors passing to her cousin, James. Elizabeth and her husband, Richard Beauchamp, earl of Warwick, were unwilling to accept this, and, with the earl away in France, Elizabeth appeared before the king's council in 1421 to argue her case. Nothing was achieved before her death the following year. Although a settlement was reached in 1425 which lasted until the earl's death in 1439, the quarrel was then renewed and concluded only in 1609.[40]

Castles on occasion were placed in the charge of women. Nicola de la Haye, who inherited the office of constable of Lincoln Castle from her father and passed it to her husbands, herself defended the castle twice. In 1191 she and her husband sided with Count John against the Chancellor, William Longchamp, bishop of Ely, who headed the regency council during Richard I's absence on crusade. Richard of Devizes asserted that she acted like a man in her defence of the castle. In 1217 she defended the castle for King John against the rebels during the civil war following the Magna Carta. Women continued to be appointed as castellans during the later middle ages, Isabella de Vescy being in charge of Bamburgh Castle between 1304 and 1311 and after 1312.[41] She enjoyed high favour under Edward I and Edward II and this is probably why the Ordainers insisted on her removal in 1311.

Noblewomen were sometimes involved in warfare during times of rebellion, when they acted alongside their husbands. It is rare to find a woman's statement of political belief, but Isabella, countess of Arundel, complained to Henry III personally in 1252 that he had turned his back on justice. She pointed out that the king had several times sworn to observe the Magna Carta in return for grants of taxation, but that he had shamelessly broken his oath. She failed to get a favourable decision in the custody case she had brought before the king. Elizabeth de Burgh made her views known in 1326 in her protest against her treatment by the Despensers. She drew attention to the disagreements in 1321–22 between Edward II and the great men of the land over certain oppressions which were contrary to the law of the land. She also protested over the wrongful use of royal power by the younger Despenser.[42] Grievances over favourites and over the undermining of the law were frequently expressed in political confrontations.

Concern for their families often drove women to take action and they were not deterred by the thought that it might result in the forfeiture of their estates. They might use stratagem, open conflict or siege in their attempts to achieve their ends. Gytha, widow of Earl Godwine and mother of King Harold, remained a landowner in the south west after the Battle of Hastings. She was involved in the Exeter rising against the Conqueror but fled with other noblewomen after Exeter surrendered. She took refuge on the island of Flat Holme in the Bristol Channel for a time and then went into exile at St Omer with a great store of treasure.[43] The seizure of Lincoln Castle in 1141 by Ranulf, earl of Chester, during the civil war under Stephen, was aided by a trick in which his wife and Hawise, countess of Lincoln, played a key part. By chatting to the wife of the knight who should have been defending the castle, they distracted attention from Earl Ranulf who overpowered the castle's royal guards and took possession. Petronilla, countess of Leicester, supported her husband during the rebellion of 1173–74 and was captured with him at the battle of Fornham; William of Newburgh commented on her manly spirit, but Jordan Fantosme was disparaging; although she advised the earl to fight, she fled after the battle, nearly drowned in a ditch and lost her rings in the mud.[44]

Eleanor de Montfort actively supported her husband in 1265. During the summer, she and her household moved from Hampshire to Kent, where she was concerned to secure the support of the Cinque Ports and entertained the burgesses of Winchelsea and Sandwich. After the battle of Evesham and her husband's death, she continued to hold Dover Castle until it fell to Lord Edward in the autumn. Elizabeth de Burgh joined her husband, Roger Damory, in the rebellion against Edward II and was captured at her castle of Usk in 1322; Damory died soon afterwards. At the end of the middle ages, Margaret Beaufort worked behind the scenes to secure the accession of her son, Henry VII.[45]

Political and estate activity overlapped with the noblewoman's social life, and at least part of her success in supporting her family depended on social networking. It was essential that she should be seen to be involved with her fellow nobles and gentry. Throughout the middle ages, the nobility and gentry were a closely interrelated group and it was taken for granted that members of the extended family would be called on when needed. In addition to kin, extensive networking took place with neighbours and friends. Contacts were maintained by messengers and letters and during the later middle ages the letters became more informative, giving political news, information about lands and dependants, and family details. Although written formally, many letters point to affectionate relationships, as in Robert Lovell's letter to his mother-in-law, Alice de Bryene, and in the correspondence between Philippa of Lancaster, wife of John I of Portugal and Bishop Despenser of Norwich. Many noblewomen enjoyed entertaining friends and neighbours; Elizabeth de Burgh's visitors arrived thick and fast during the summer of 1350 after the Black Death.[46] Quite apart from the pleasures of social contacts, visiting, feasting and hunting and hawking, success in litigation or petition depended on knowing the right people with influence and power.

In this the household came into its own, providing the setting for social, political and religious contacts, and advertising the lady's splendid lifestyle, wealth and influence wherever she happened to be living. Hospitality gave the opportunity for conspicuous consumption and the means of displaying her possessions, in strong contrast to the majority of the medieval population. Social gatherings are most fully documented in the household accounts of the later middle ages but can also be traced in some of the earlier charter witness lists. The charter issued by Henry I recording Richard Basset's arranged marriage to the daughter of Geoffrey Ridel was witnessed by the bride's mother (Geva, daughter of Hugh, earl of Chester), her kindred, members of the earl of Chester's household, members of the Basset family, and others of Henry I's 'new men'.[47]

Elizabeth de Burgh's Christmas feast at Usk in 1326 displayed hospitality with strong, political overtones. Elizabeth's main concern when Queen Isabella invaded England in the autumn of 1326 was to recover Usk from the younger Despenser. She moved west and was back at Usk at least by mid-November. Her celebration of Christmas at the castle publicised her return and gave her the opportunity to preside over a gathering of her officials, supporters and friends. For Christmas dinner, two hundred goblets and one hundred decorated dishes were purchased. For drink, the buttery supplied 8½ sesters of wine and 230 gallons of ale. Two boars' heads were served and the kitchen cooked beef, bacon, pork, mutton and venison. This meat would have been for all those present, but for the lady, her higher officials and important guests a wide variety of birds was provided, including chickens and pullets, three swans, two herons, two bitterns, twelve geese and thirteen partridges, together with twelve piglets. The kitchen used eight hundred eggs on Christmas Day.[48]

The rich and colourful furnishings of the hall and the display of plate were seen by a wide spectrum of people, and their descriptions doubtless helped to reinforce the lady's reputation in the neighbourhood. According to the lists of those having meals in the house of Alice de Bryene at Acton, Suffolk, in 1412–13, not only the gentry were entertained. On 10 August, 1413, for instance, the list included Sir Andrew Boteler and his wife, maid, chaplain, squire and two grooms; eight boon workers, involved in the harvest; and two men and two women from Sudbury who were nameless. Hospitality was extended to all social groups and to strangers and travellers. Churchmen were also entertained, like the two friars from Norwich on 29 September 1412, and two friars from Sudbury exactly four months later. On 1 January 1413 three hundred tenants were given hospitality, in addition to the named guests, an anonymous harper providing music for the occasion.[49]

The noblewoman was, almost invariably, a patron of the arts, employing numerous craftsmen to ensure that her setting did credit to her and her family. Many noblewomen updated and refurbished their residences. Sometimes a new house was constructed, as by Elizabeth de Burgh in the outer court of the Minoresses' convent outside Aldgate in the 1350s, when she decided to spend part of the year in London. Joan Beauchamp, lady of Abergavenny (d. 1435), undertook substantial refurbishing of her residence at Rochford, Essex, in 1430–33. The principal buildings were in the inner ward. Here the chimney of the great chamber was rebuilt, and a boarded ceiling provided in the parlour, while the posts in the hall were painted by a London craftsman to look like marble; presumably, this was an aisled hall. A new chapel was built of brick, with a cellar underneath. New building near the gatehouse possibly comprised lodgings, as these were added to many great houses in the fifteenth century.[50]

Some women of the higher nobility, like Elizabeth de Burgh, employed goldsmiths and illuminators in their households, but it was more usual for possessions to be purchased. The accounts of Henry

Bolingbroke and his wife, Mary de Bohun, record the merchants and craftsmen who supplied the rich materials and furs which were made up into clothes for the family and household, or were sometimes used as gifts. In 1387–88, for instance, Peter Swan was paid £2 for embroidering with harebells a short, black cloak for the lady; the cloak was lined with Baltic squirrel. Katherine Swynford and her daughter, Joan, received their Christmas livery, a robe of blue and white brocade, lined with trimmed miniver. Presents of expensive clothing were made to the lady's sister, Eleanor, duchess of Gloucester.[51] Plate and furnishings are mostly known from descriptions in wills, since relatively few objects have survived. The items recorded in the will of Joan Beauchamp were luxurious and colourful. Her grandson, James, was bequeathed a pair of gilt basins decorated with her arms, a bed of cloth of gold embroidered with swans, and a green tapestry embroidered with branches and flowers in different colours.[52]

Noblewomen, like queens, were patrons of authors, copyists, illuminators and printers, and the growth of literacy encouraged ownership of books: romances for recreation and psalters and books of hours for religious devotion. Books were commissioned or purchased from professional writers and illuminators. From at least the twelfth century, noblewomen were patronising authors. Alice, wife of Robert de Condet, commissioned a translation of part of the Book of Proverbs into French, while Constance, wife of Ralph fitz Gilbert, was the patron in 1136–37 of Gaimar's *Estoire des Engleis*. Matthew Paris dedicated his Life of Archbishop Edmund of Abingdon to Isabella, countess of Arundel, and his French saints' lives circulated among noblewomen. Osbern Bokenham's saints' lives were sponsored by a number of women from East Anglia. Mary de Bohun patronised manuscript illumination in the 1380s, following the example of her natal family who were the most important patrons of this form of art in the fourteenth century; one work portrays Mary at prayer, adoring the Virgin Mary.[53]

At the end of the middle ages, Margaret Beaufort and other women connected with the court were patrons of William Caxton and Wynkyn de Worde. Margaret Beaufort was one of the few laywomen known to have made their own translations; her translation of part of *The Imitation of Christ* by Thomas à Kempis was issued in 1504 and *Mirror of Gold for the Sinful Soul* two years later. Eleanor Hull was another learned noblewoman who translated French devotional texts, probably in the 1420s, including a commentary on the Seven Penitential Psalms.[54]

It is not possible to calculate the number of noblewomen owning books or the size of their collections. The majority of books have not survived and relatively few women made wills, which in any case did not necessarily list all their books. Nevertheless, an analysis of noble-women bequeathing religious literature shows that their number grew after about 1350, and some merchant and gentry women were following their example in the fifteenth century. In addition to their books of hours, psalters and service books, the most popular form of religious lit-erature was saints' lives, although references are also found to didactic and mystical works and books of meditation.[55] All these allowed the noblewoman to engage in personal piety.

The value set on books is occasionally reflected in comments in wills; Anne Harling left her god-daughter, Anne Fitzwater, a primer with silver and gilt clasps as a remembrance to pray for her. Where informa-tion on book ownership is plentiful, it appears that noblewomen had broad tastes. In 1466, Alice Chaucer, duchess of Suffolk, transferred a number of works from Wingfield Castle, Suffolk, to Ewelme in Oxford-shire, including service books and didactic works, Christine de Pizan's *Book of the City of Ladies*, and a romance.[56]

Book ownership brought women into contact with a wide range of people. Margery de Nerford (d. 1417) probably had a collection of between fifteen and twenty volumes, some of them copied for her by her chaplain. She lived mainly in London, and, as well as her contacts among the nobility and at court, she and William de Bergh, parish priest of the church of St Christopher-le-Stocks, had a common interest in books and joined forces in founding a chantry in the church. William bequeathed most of his books to Margery, and both of them had con-tacts with the nunnery of Denny. Margery also had friends among the London elite, and John Whatley, mercer, acted as her executor. Accord-ing to her will, both he and the abbey of Denny received copies of her books.[57]

Noblewomen's cultural patronage was largely directed to enhancing their position in the eyes of their peers and neighbours, but their choice of books enabled them to develop their individual tastes. Their personal piety and devotion to the saints were enhanced by their books of hours.

Their religious practice also had its public dimension and their patronage of religious houses and hospitals had a direct bearing on their
influence in the locality, as in the case of the Bohun family and the
monastery of Lanthony Secunda.[58]

Their foundation of colleges in the universities of Oxford and Cambridge has given a few medieval noblewomen a memorial down to the
present day. The colleges were designed as religious communities where
prayers would be offered for the founders' souls, but also where training would be provided for young men who would often become their
chaplains and administrators. The prestige of the founder and her family would be always remembered. The earliest benefaction was Balliol
College at Oxford, a foundation imposed as a penance on John de Balliol about 1257. Its permanent endowment was provided by his widow,
Devorguilla of Galloway, using money John had left for the purpose. She
purchased property in Oxford in 1284–85 for the scholars to live in and
endowed them with land purchased in Northumberland. She also issued
the original statutes, providing for the communal life and studies of the
scholars.[59]

The two friends, Elizabeth de Burgh and Marie de St-Pol, probably
made their foundations at Cambridge in consultation with each other.
Elizabeth was approached in the mid 1330s to help the poorly endowed
University Hall, but she insisted on becoming sole patron before taking
generous action. She made her main grants to Clare Hall, as it was
renamed, in 1346, provided an income for the college of £60 a year, and
she issued statutes in 1359, the year before her death. Marie de St-Pol was
making plans for the foundation of the Hall of Valence Marie from 1341,
but the actual foundation took place in 1347. Like Elizabeth, she published statutes for the college, stressing the educational provision, and
she left it one hundred marks and relics and ornaments in her will. The
college soon became known as Pembroke Hall.[60]

The outstanding later Cambridge benefactor was Lady Margaret
Beaufort. Margaret endowed divinity professorships at Oxford and
Cambridge and a preachership at Cambridge in 1503–4; daily lectures
were to be given and were to last for an hour, except in Lent. Her concentration on Cambridge for her principal endowments was largely due
to the influence of John Fisher, a Cambridge theologian who became
bishop of Rochester in 1504. In addition to benefactions to Jesus College

and her interest in Queens', she founded Christ's College and St John's, although the latter was unfinished at her death.

The foundation of Christ's College involved the takeover and expansion of God's House, founded in 1439 with the aim of training grammar masters to teach in schools. Margaret envisaged a considerable expansion, as during the negotiations of 1504 a college with property worth £100 was anticipated. The following year, Margaret incorporated God's House into the larger foundation, to be named Christ's College, which was to support a maximum of sixty scholars. The college was established for the increase of the Christian faith and, according to papal letters, was to be devoted to the study of theology and the arts, while the grammar teaching of God's House was retained. Margaret was empowered to draw up the college statutes. She had her own rooms in the college and probably resided there from time to time. When finished, the college had twelve fellows and forty-seven scholars, with Margaret having the right to appoint masters and fellows.[61]

All four female founders took a businesslike approach to their colleges. As with the administration of their estates, they showed themselves capable of exercising power and authority, and carrying their plans through to a successful conclusion. They were influential figures in their own regions and in the country as a whole, establishing reputations which would outlast them. In many respects, their activities were like those of queens; they had many similar duties to perform and at the same time enjoyed social occasions and the recreations which went with them. It remains to be seen whether queens were equally able to exercise authority and influence.

7

Queens

Queens occupied a unique place among medieval women. The queen was not only the wife and mother of kings, but her coronation also gave her an official status within the realm. Many of her activities were comparable to those of noblewomen, but her responsibilities and powers of intercession extended to the kingdom as a whole. The degree of power exercised by the queen fluctuated over the middle ages, depending on the circumstances and political climate of the time, the attitude of her husband, and the queen's own ambitions. Basically, however, her authority and influence stemmed from her roles as wife and mother.

The church played a prominent part in sanctioning the position of the queen and in the rituals which surrounded her, and it is significant that several queens played a significant role in Bede's account of the Conversion. In the late sixth century, Æthelberht of Kent married the Frankish princess, Bertha, who, as a practising Christian, may have secured a favourable hearing for St Augustine's mission and influenced her husband's conversion to Christianity. King Edwin of Northumbria's marriage to Æthelberht's daughter, Æthelburh, was conditional on her being allowed to practise her religion and Edwin was subsequently converted by Paulinus, the priest who had accompanied her to the north. Edwin's survival to become king of Northumbria was, according to Bede, due to a queen's intercession. Edwin had sought refuge at the court of Raedwald of East Anglia, who was faced with deciding whether to kill him or hand him over to his Northumbrian rival, Æthelfrith, a decision that was reversed by his queen's persuasion. Rather later, when most of England was converted, the synod of Whitby was summoned by King Oswiu of Northumbria, who found that his celebration of Easter did not coincide with his wife's; he followed the Irish custom while Eanflaed, who came from Kent, adhered to the Roman practice.[1]

Queens were therefore already active in the sixth and seventh centuries, often using their powers of persuasion, regarded throughout the
middle ages as the acceptable way for women of all social groups to take
action. The Anglo-Saxon Chronicle records only one woman as ruler:
Cenwealh of Wessex died in 672, after which his widow, Queen
Seaxburh, reigned for one year.[2] Yet, although the activities of some
queens are known, many others are obscure figures, and, in view of the
prevalence of divorce and serial monogamy down to the late Anglo-
Saxon period, they could not even assume that one of their sons would
become king. In fact, it was not until the thirteenth century that primogeniture became the normal custom for royal succession. The status of
early queens varied, Mercian queens enjoying more importance than
those of Wessex. Legends of evil queens grew up in Wessex and elsewhere, such as the story of Eadburh, daughter of Offa of Mercia and wife
of Beorhtric of Wessex, who was said to have poisoned her husband. It
was only from about the middle of the tenth century, as the kings of
Wessex extended their rule over much of England, that their queens
came to be significant figures in their own right.[3]

It was from this time that the queen's coronation became established
practice. The first woman known to have been crowned was Judith,
daughter of Charles the Bald, on her marriage to Æthelwulf of Wessex
in 856. The consecration and coronation of Carolingian kings and
queens had taken place since 751, and Judith's father probably thought
that coronation would safeguard her position in England; Æthelwulf
was a man with grown-up sons, marrying a teenage bride. Certainly
his conferring of the title of queen on Judith was unusual for the West
Saxons. At her coronation, Judith was anointed with chrism, the holy oil
normally reserved for the consecration of bishops and the anointing
of kings. The comparison in the accompanying prayer with the Old
Testament women, Judith and Esther, implied that the queen was a
woman of power, inclined to mercy, chaste and virtuous. No reference
was made to the queen's fertility, but this later became a feature of the
queen's coronation.[4]

No further queen's coronation appears to have taken place for over
one hundred years, until Ælfthryth was crowned with her husband,
King Edgar, at Bath in 973.[5] From that time, queens were usually
crowned with their husbands if they were already married at the time

of the king's succession, or on their own if the marriage took place after it. Through coronation, they gained official status. Over the centuries, certain changes took place in the coronation *ordines*, but the essence of the ceremony – anointing and crowning followed by mass – remained constant. A feast took place after the coronation and pageantry gradually became more elaborate.

A late medieval queen's coronation was described in the *Liber Regalis* of *c.* 1375, probably drawn up by Abbot Lytlington of Westminster, and is supplemented by the *Liber Regie Capelle*, written in 1449.[6] When the king and queen were crowned together, both went in procession to Westminster Abbey, the queen's procession following the king's. The queen wore a purple robe, and her hair was loose, confined only by a gold circlet ornamented with jewels. In front of her walked three lords carrying her regalia: the rod with a golden dove on the top; the gilt sceptre, also topped by a dove; and the crown. The queen walked under a canopy carried by the barons of the Cinque Ports and was supported by two bishops; noble ladies followed. After prayers at the entrance of the church, she proceeded to her throne, which was placed to the left of the king's and was lower than his, emphasising her subordination.

After the king was crowned, the queen moved to the high altar and was anointed on the head and breast. To the accompaniment of prayers, she was then given the ring, the crown was blessed and placed on her head, and the sceptre was put in her right hand and the rod in her left. She was then led back to her throne and mass began. After mass, the processions returned for the coronation feast. At the feast for Katherine of Valois in Westminster Hall, the queen sat in state with the archbishop of Canterbury and the bishop of Winchester on her right, and the king of Scots, the duchess of York and the countess of Huntingdon on her left, with the countess of Kent sitting under the table by her right foot and the Countess Marshal by her left. The Earl Marshal knelt on her right holding a sceptre and another sceptre was held on her left.[7]

The coronation regalia and prayers emphasised the queen's special status in the realm, and her position as king's wife and mother; the archbishop's prayer on her arrival at the abbey stressed her fertility. As at Judith's coronation, women of the Old Testament were invoked, but of greater importance was the invocation of the Virgin Mary. Like Mary, the queen was regarded as virgin and mother; she arrived at her coronation as a virgin, symbolised by her loose hair, and she was expected to bear the king's children. This dichotomy is found even when the queen was already a mother, as the coronation of Elizabeth Woodville shows. [8] The special relationship between the queen and the Virgin Mary went back to Anglo-Saxon times. The frontispiece of the *Liber vitae* of the abbey of New Minster, Winchester, depicted Emma and her second husband, Cnut, either side of an altar, with angels above, and, above them, the figures of the Virgin Mary and St Peter flanking Christ. Emma was given the title of Queen and placed beneath the image of the Virgin Mary. The earthly queen was linked to the queen of heaven, both women fulfilling the role of mother and providing a guarantee for the future through their sons. [9]

Most Anglo-Saxon kings made marriage alliances with native noble families, as exemplified by Edward the Confessor's marriage to Edith, the daughter of the powerful Earl Godwine. A few kings made a foreign marriage, such as Æthelberht of Kent, and Æthelred II and Cnut who in turn married Emma, sister of Duke Richard II of Normandy. Such marriages were made with the intention of strengthening foreign alliances and were the outcome of political considerations. The selection of a foreign queen became normal practice after 1066. Not only were the kings French but they also had extensive lands and interests on the Continent. Moreover, there were usually sound political reasons for their alliance. This was particularly apparent with Henry I's first marriage to Edith-Matilda, daughter of Malcolm Canmore and St Margaret of Scotland, and descended from the West Saxon ruler, Æthelred II. Her father had planned earlier to marry her to Alan the Red, count of Brittany and Richmond, but this had been prevented and Matilda probably continued to live with her aunt in the nunneries at Romsey and Wilton. Questions arose in 1100 as to whether she had made her profession as a nun, but her marriage went ahead, the alliance reinforcing the Normans' hold on the English throne. [10] The most spectacular gain of land and lordship was made by Henry II. Two years before his accession, he married Eleanor of Aquitaine, heiress to the duchy of Aquitaine, soon after her divorce from Louis VII of France.

Royal marriages provide an interesting commentary on political events. In the wake of the loss of Normandy in 1204, it was important to secure the English lands in south-west France, and marriages were concluded with neighbouring ruling families: Richard I married Berengaria of Navarre; John, Isabella of Angoulême; Henry III, Eleanor of Provence; and Edward I, Eleanor of Castile. There was a change of direction from the late thirteenth century in the light of the escalating disputes with the kings of France over Gascony and the outbreak of the Hundred Years War. Edward I's second marriage to Magaret, the sister of Philip IV, and Edward II's to Philip's daughter, Isabella, were planned to secure peace with France. With the Hundred Years War going badly for England, it was hoped that Richard II's marriage to Anne of Bohemia would secure support from the Holy Roman Empire. The recognition of Henry V as heir to the French throne in the treaty of Troyes of 1420 was sealed by his marriage to Katherine of Valois, while Henry VI's marriage to Margaret of Anjou has to be seen in the context of defeat at the end of the Hundred Years War and the hope that the marriage would bring peace. As was to be expected in the middle ages, few love matches took place. The Black Prince fell in love with and married Joan of Kent, the widow of Thomas Holland, but died before his father. Edward IV, the first king for over three hundred years to marry an English noblewoman, secretly married a widow, Elizabeth Woodville, to the dismay of his council.[11]

The queen's wedding was usually the subject of lengthy negotiations. Quite apart from the diplomatic aspects of the match, the bride's beauty and virtue were taken into account and she was expected to be pious and charitable. It was essential for the marriage to be valid and the necessary dispensations to be obtained from the papacy. Her likely ability to bear children was important and with this in mind many brides were married in their teens. As with other ranks in society, however, there was some feeling against girls being married too young. Margaret Beaufort urged the postponement of her granddaughter's marriage to James IV of Scotland, because she was afraid that the marriage would be consummated at too early an age.[12] Since Margaret had given birth to Henry VII at the age of thirteen, and had never been able to have any more children, she knew what she was talking about. Elizabeth of York agreed with her mother-in-law.

In fact, much more was involved than just the consummation of the marriage. The bride was often going to a foreign country where she would not only meet an unknown husband but also face an unknown royal family and court. She might well have to learn a new language and she often had few attendants from her own country. A measure of maturity was essential for her to come to terms with her situation. As with the nobility, the relationship between husband and wife developed after the wedding, and there were a number of happy marriages, as with William the Conqueror and Matilda of Flanders, Edward I and Eleanor of Castile (who were rarely parted), and Richard II and Anne of Bohemia. By contrast, the marriage of Henry II and Eleanor of Aquitaine can best be described as stormy.

In addition to the personal factors and diplomatic advantage, financial and landed concerns were matters of negotiation. As was customary from the eleventh century, the dowry was the concern of the bride's family and dower of the bridegroom's. The dowry, however, did not always materialise. It was agreed at the negotiations that Anne of Bohemia's dowry would be settled later; it was never paid, as her brother, the Emperor Wenzel, could not afford it. Chroniclers commented on Margaret of Anjou's lack of a dowry.[13] The queen's dower developed over the middle ages. Late Saxon and Norman queens had their own landed resources, providing them with wealth and a measure of political power. Most of the lands were part of the royal estates, and from the tenth century it became customary for certain places to be regarded as the queen's land. The queen's holdings were extensive; in 1066, Edith's landholding inside and outside Wessex was valued at between £1,570 and about £2,000 a year. With some of the lands situated in the north midlands and on the Welsh border, the queen had political and military responsibilities.[14] A similar system operated after the Conquest, with the Conqueror and Henry I granting their queens their own estates, some of which had been held by Anglo-Saxon queens.[15]

The practice of giving queens estates for their support during their husband's lifetime lapsed after 1154 and Eleanor of Aquitaine instead received money payments when she was in England. The dower assigned to queens in the second half of the twelfth and early thirteenth centuries only came into their hands after their husband's death, as was the case with women in other social groups. By the end of Henry III's reign, the importance of land as giving financial support to the queen during the king's lifetime was again realised. Eleanor of Provence became more powerful and financially skilful as she grew older. When she married, she was dependent on royal grants paid into her wardrobe, but she gained control over her resources, including the queen's gold, sums from the Jews, revenues from wardships and grants of land.[16] The importance of being a skilful manager is apparent throughout the later middle ages. Eleanor of Castile became unpopular through her acquisition of new lands and harsh exploitation of her rights, leading to complaints from Archbishop Pecham and an inquiry after her death. Elizabeth Woodville appears to have been a careful manager, in contrast to the extravagance of Margaret of Anjou, although some of Margaret's problems were the result of difficulties in securing her dower revenues. Philippa of Hainault fell so hopelessly into debt that her affairs were taken into her husband's hands in 1363.[17]

Dower in the late thirteenth and fourteenth century was normally set at £4,500, and this was also the figure for Elizabeth Woodville's dower; for the wives of Henry IV, Henry V and Henry VI, dower amounted to approximately £6,500. Problems arose when more than one queen was in receipt of dower, and dower lands usually passed from one queen to the next. On her death in 1318, the lands of Margaret of France passed to her niece, Queen Isabella. Political changes also affected dower. On Edward II's deposition in 1327, Isabella took royal lands into her own hands, increasing her dower to 20,000 marks, while Elizabeth Woodville lost her dower when Richard III seized the crown and her marriage was declared invalid.[18]

All queens had their own households. These merged with the king's when they were together and became more elaborate with the passage of time.[19] Anglo-Saxon queens in the eleventh century had their own households, servants and officials and this remained the case after 1066. The household was sufficiently flexible to meet new needs, as when the queen's wardrobe was created for Eleanor of Provence in 1236. The size of the household changed according to need. During the lifetime of her father-in-law, Henry III, Eleanor of Castile had a small household, but this grew substantially when she became queen. Queen Isabella's household in 1311–12 numbered about 180 people, including her principal officials, ladies and damsels, clerks and household servants. Although her nurse, Theophania de St-Pierre, was French, the great majority of the household were English. Administration became more elaborate in the fourteenth and fifteenth centuries, when the queen's council developed to advise her, make appointments and carry out judicial and executive functions. Councillors and officials tended to move between the king's and the queen's service. [20]

Ritual and ceremonial were essential to the court, as a means of advertising the wealth and power of the king and communicating the virtues of his rule. From the time of her arrival in England, the queen had a ceremonial role to play, and her entry into London reflected her subjects' expectations. These were echoed on her later visits around the realm. Her reception was a splendid occasion. Matthew Paris commented on the arrival of Eleanor of Castile in 1255, the Londoners putting on their best clothes to receive her, and her reception including processions and music. The house where she lodged was furnished in the Spanish style with silk hangings and decorated tiles. Matthew was suspicious of the number of Spaniards she brought with her and of the king's generosity towards them. [21]

For the state entry of Margaret of Anjou into London in 1445, the queen was met on Blackheath by the mayor, aldermen and sheriffs, clad in scarlet, and the craft guilds, wearing blue gowns with embroidered sleeves and red hoods, who escorted her through Southwark to the City. There she was welcomed by sumptuous pageants. Some underlined the importance of peace. There was a pageant of peace and plenty on the Southwark side of London Bridge, and Noah's Ark on the bridge itself, symbolising the cessation of God's anger. The way to the Kingdom of Heaven was set out in the City. Grace, God's chancellor, greeted Margaret at Leadenhall, and St Margaret in Cornhill. At the Great Conduit in Cheapside, there was a pageant of the five wise and five foolish virgins; the heavenly Jerusalem was displayed at the cross in Cheapside, and the Resurrection and Last Judgement at the gate to St Paul's Cathedral. Verses by John Lydgate were recited at each pageant. Two days later, Margaret was escorted to her coronation at Westminster by the London crafts. [22]

Of all the queen's duties, the birth of children was crucial, and, in view of infant mortality, the birth of several sons was to be welcomed. From the eleventh century, however, childlessness was not a reason for divorce, and Edith, wife of Edward the Confessor, Berengaria of Navarre and Anne of Bohemia remained queens, despite having no children. [23]

Several queens had large families. Eleanor of Castile probably had four-teen children, many of whom died in childhood. Of her four sons, only the youngest, Edward II, grew to adulthood; five of her nine daughters grew up, but one of them, Eleanor, died when she was nineteen.[24] As with noblewomen, the physical care of the children was provided by mistresses and nurses, and children might be established in their own households from an early age. Queens often took a close interest in their children's upbringing and subsequent marriage, and occasionally sided with them against the king. Matilda of Flanders incurred the Con-queror's wrath for supporting her eldest son, Robert, against his father, and Eleanor of Aquitaine backed the young Henry in his revolt against Henry II.[25]

By the fifteenth century, the birth of a royal baby was surrounded by elaborate pomp and ceremonial which displayed the baby's legitimacy and the hopes for the future of the dynasty. As with other social groups, the birth itself was the concern of women. About a month beforehand, the queen withdrew from court to her chamber, which had been spe-cially furnished, in the company of her ladies. Once the baby was born, church bells were rung and messengers sent out to spread the news. Nei-ther the king nor the queen was present at the baptism; the godparents were expected to be at court ready for the ceremony. The queen emerged from her chamber for the ceremony of churching about forty days after the birth. Preceded by a duke carrying a candelabra and fol-lowed by a duchess carrying the chrism cloth used at the baptism, the queen was escorted to the chapel by two dukes, with lords walking in the front of the procession and ladies behind. Prayers were said at the entrance to the chapel, the queen was sprinkled with holy water and an antiphon of the Virgin Mary sung. Mass was then celebrated and at the offertory the queen moved to the altar, still escorted by two dukes, and offered gold, the candelabra and the chrism cloth. Afterwards, she returned to her chamber where a feast was held.[26]

The queen played her part in the ceremonial life of the court. Her life was punctuated by religious observance which had its own forms of rit-ual. On formal occasions, she sat in state alongside the king and wore her crown. Such occasions enabled the royal family to display itself to the leading men of the realm and foreign visitors and reinforce its power, while at the same time cementing the unity of the kingdom.

The queen took part in royal progresses, being greeted in the towns she visited by pageants which had their own political message. During times of civil war, she had a particular responsibility to strengthen the royal dynasty. Margaret of Anjou in the late 1450s aimed at establishing the Lancastrian power-base in the midlands. Her visit to Coventry in 1457 was part of this policy. Here she saw the Corpus Christi plays, except for the Last Judgement which could not be seen 'for lack of day'. The plays were particularly appropriate as they brought out the parallel between the celebration of the body of Christ (*corpus Christi*) and the need for social unity and wholeness, personified by the mayor in the context of the town and the king and queen in the context of the realm. Elizabeth Woodville's stay in East Anglia in the summer of 1469, when the York-ist dynasty was under threat, had a political purpose and she was treated to a programme of pageants at Norwich. York proclaimed its message of dynastic peace when Henry VII and Elizabeth of York visited the city in 1486, in one pageant making use of the union of the red and white rose as bringing prosperity to York. [27]

Much of the court ceremonial was celebratory and recreational. As in the stories of courtly love, ladies played their part in inspiring their knights, issuing challenges, supporting them in tournaments and dis-tributing prizes, as well as joining in the feasting and dancing afterwards. From the early thirteenth century, tournaments were regarded as a major social occasion and ladies attended regularly, sitting in special stands; many were injured when the stands collapsed in Cheapside in 1331. Both men and women made extravagant vows, as when Queen Philippa vowed not to be delivered of the baby she was expecting until she and Edward departed to campaign in France; the child was Lionel of Antwerp. Edward III held fifty-five tournaments with great splendour and pageantry in the thirty years after his acces-sion in 1327. [28] In 1375 his mistress Alice Perrers, dressed as 'lady of the Sun', led the procession from the Tower of London through the City to Smithfield, where the jousting lasted for three days.

Much less is heard of tournaments in the first half of the fifteenth cen-tury but they were revived under Edward IV, who saw chivalry as a means of exalting his kingship. In 1466, Elizabeth Woodville and her ladies issued a challenge to her brother, Anthony Lord Scales. Anthony, Bastard of Burgundy was invited as his opponent and the tournament took place at Smithfield the following year. After two days of fighting, a great feast was held at the Grocers' Hall in the City. The plan to continue the tournament for another week came to nothing because of the death of Philip the Good, duke of Burgundy. This tournament had diplomatic overtones, as the Yorkists were anxious for an alliance with Burgundy. In a chivalrous culture, tournaments and meetings of knightly orders such as the Garter had a serious as well as a recreational side, and in the fourteenth century especially they fostered knightly training and bonded lords and knights. Queens and noblewomen were admitted to the fraternity of St George and received Garter robes, although they were not necessarily given them every year. There were often family or political reasons why they were included at a particular time.[29]

Because of her position as the king's wife, the queen exercised a measure of political influence through intercession and patronage. In her *The Treasure of the City of Ladies*, Christine de Pizan strongly advised the wise princess to use intercession to influence her husband, and queens are found interceding with kings and with subjects throughout the middle ages. The most graphic example is Queen Philippa kneeling in tears before Edward III and interceding for the lives of the leading burghers of Calais. Froissart's imaginary addition that the queen was heavily pregnant added to the drama of the scene.[30]

The nature and extent of the queen's patronage are apparent in the letters of Margaret of Anjou from soon after her marriage until the late 1450s and the outbreak of the Wars of the Roses. The letters cover a wide variety of subjects, including dower, estate matters and her love of hunting. Many of the letters, however, concerned her attempts to get jobs and marriages for members of her household, not all of which were successful. A widow, Lady Jane Carew, was praised for her beauty and virtue and urged to marry Thomas Burneby, one of the queen's stewards; Jane in fact married the brother of the earl of Oxford. Margaret wrote to Katherine de la Pole, abbess of Barking, asking her to exercise good ladyship to the royal squire, Robert Osberne. She suggested Matilda Everyngham as the prioress of Nuneaton priory. She recommended her gentlewoman Margaret Stanlowe to Edmund Beaufort, duke of Somerset, and wrote to the chancellor of Oxford University asking for a benefice for one of her clerks. She intervened to expedite the business of members of her household.[31] Patronage was also exercised by gift-giving, especially at New Year. Generosity was highly regarded and jewels and plate made welcome presents. In 1452–53, Margaret of Anjou made such gifts to ninety-eight named recipients and also gave presents to the lowlier members of her household. Financial difficulties meant that the gifts were less lavish than five years before.[32]

Queens were in a position to benefit their families and some did so substantially. The position of Eleanor of Provence as queen of England brought rewards and advancement to her Savoyard relatives and their dependants. Her uncle, Peter of Savoy, received considerable rewards in England, and Eleanor was involved in the plan to marry her sister, Sanchia, to Henry III's brother, Richard of Cornwall, and to promote Boniface of Savoy to the archbishopric of Canterbury. Girls related to the ruling house of Savoy married into the English nobility. Such a policy caused resentment and Eleanor became unpopular for her promotion of the Savoyards.[33]

Elizabeth Woodville's marriage to Edward IV opened up preferment for her father and siblings. She employed relatives in her household, including her sister Anne, her sister-in-law Elizabeth Lady Scales, and her brother John, her master of the horse. Her father was appointed treasurer and constable by Edward IV and raised to the rank of earl. Family marriages into the higher nobility secured even greater advancement, the Woodvilles virtually cornering the marriage market. Five of the queen's sisters were married by 1466, and her brother John married the dowager duchess of Norfolk, Katherine Neville, a most unequal marriage with the bridegroom aged about twenty and the bride about sixty-five. As with Eleanor of Provence, the rapid advancement of the queen's family caused resentment, and the earl of Warwick singled out several of them as 'seditious persons' in his manifesto of 1469, alleging that they had damaged both king and realm.[34]

Every medieval queen exercised influence through intercession and patronage. Occasionally, and especially between the tenth and twelfth centuries, the queen played a more active role. The degree of her activity depended on circumstances, contemporary opinion, the position and attitude of her husband and her own ambitions. The West Saxons of the ninth and tenth centuries, in contrast to the Mercians, were suspicious of queens, although their suspicions apparently diminished by the later tenth century. Some queens, however, played a political role behind the scenes. Eadgifu, the third wife of Edward the Elder, has been described as a key figure during the reigns of her sons, Edmund and Eadred, and unsuccessfully supported Edgar as Eadred's successor rather than his brother, Eadwig. Ælfthryth, Edgar's third wife and anointed queen, backed the claim to the throne of her son, Æthelred II, arguing for the strength of his claim as the son of an anointed queen.[35]

One woman of the early tenth century, however, stands out as an effective ruler. Alfred the Great married his daughter, Æthelflaed, to Ealdorman Æthelred of Mercia who died in 911, possibly after a long illness. From 910 until her own death in 918, Æthelflaed worked in close alliance with her brother, Edward the Elder, king of Wessex, to defeat the Danes and drive them north of the River Humber. She was already building a burh (fortress) in 910, when the West Saxon and Mercian armies were victorious over the Danes at Tettenhall in Staffordshire. Up to 915, she was building burhs in the north-west and Cheshire; the year 916 saw her sending an army into Wales. In 917, her army was fighting in the east midlands and captured Derby, followed by Leicester in 918 when the Danes of York promised to accept her overlordship. Unfortunately, she died soon afterwards. Edward deprived her daughter, Ælfwyn, of all authority in Mercia and took her to Wessex.[36] He did not want a potential rival in Mercia.

The last two Anglo-Saxon queens, Emma and Edith, were both described as queens and as sharers in rule.[37] Little is heard of Emma during the reign of her first husband, Æthelred II, which was marked by warfare and English defeat; her marriage to Cnut, probably in 1017, according to her own account, brought peace, and she provided Cnut with a link to the Anglo-Saxon past. Her importance is seen in the extent to which she witnessed documents, and this is also true of Edith during the reign of Edward the Confessor. Edith intervened in the affairs of the realm, although her attitude to the succession after the Confessor's death is unclear. Both women exerted their power as wives. Emma, however, also used her position as mother after Cnut's death in 1035 in an attempt to put her son, Harthacnut, on the throne, but she failed and was driven into exile. Once Harthacnut became king in 1040, on the death of his half-brother, Emma proved to be a powerful queen mother. She made a deliberate decision to back her son by Cnut rather than her sons by Æthelred, and she was deprived of lands and treasure by Edward the Confessor in 1043.[38]

After the Norman Conquest, the scope for queenly action was increased by the need for regents. The queen, in her role as the king's wife, was an obvious choice, provided that the king considered her able and trustworthy. William the Conqueror left his wife Matilda and Roger of Montgomery in Normandy as regents when he crossed to England for the Hastings campaign, and Matilda was also regent in the duchy in 1067, 1069 and 1080. The survival of a writ issued in her name and the record of her presiding over a land plea point to her also acting in William's place in England. She presided over pleas alongside her husband and they gave judgement jointly. Matilda was a prominent figure at court, attesting sixty-one diplomas, and she was normally described as queen. Occasionally, she was described in more detail: a grant to the abbey of Holy Trinity, Caen, described her as wife and queen, daughter of Baldwin, 'duke' of Flanders, and niece of Henry, most illustrious king of the Franks.[39] Her daughter-in-law, Matilda of Scotland, first wife of Henry I, played a similar role as regent and in attesting charters.[40] Adeliza of Louvain played a much smaller part in government, although she was present at councils and wore her crown alongside the king.[41]

The outbreak of the civil war between Stephen and the Empress Matilda meant that Matilda of Boulogne, wife of King Stephen, played a prominent role, although like her predecessors she derived her power from her position as king's wife. Through her determination, she succeeded in securing Stephen's return to power after he was taken prisoner at the battle of Lincoln in 1141 and the Empress Matilda looked set to take over the realm. *The Deeds of Stephen* described her as using her feminine wiles along with manly resolution and courage. Failing to gain her husband's release and her son Eustace's inheritance by negotiation, she was ready to fight. The Empress fled in face of the Londoners and Matilda's army which grew as she gained allies by pleading and bribery. She and her brother-in-law, Bishop Henry of Blois, besieged the Empress's forces at Winchester, the capture of the Empress's half-brother, Robert, earl of Gloucester, facilitating the negotiations for Stephen's release.[42]

All three Matildas acted as subordinates to their husbands. Although an heiress could succeed to her father's lands, the idea of a daughter succeeding her father as ruler was one which medieval people were reluctant to accept. After the White Ship disaster of 1120 and the loss of his only legitimate son, Henry I tried to ensure the succession of his daughter, Matilda, married to the Emperor Henry V and subsequently to Geoffrey, count of Anjou. The barons swore to recognise her as heir in 1127 and again in 1131. Yet her second marriage was unpopular and Stephen's speed in seizing the crown on Henry I's death in 1135 put her at a serious disadvantage. The nearest that she came to the throne was in the summer of 1141 after the battle of Lincoln. She was unable, however, to gain possession of London and alienated the Londoners by her demand for tallage. Her arrogance was off-putting and she showed a lack of judgement and understanding of people. She never became queen, but her role as mother was significant, since she transmitted her claim to the throne to Henry II.[43]

The year of Henry II's accession, 1154, marks a watershed for queens, who gradually ceased to play as significant a political role as in the previous two centuries. Government became more formal and bureaucratic than in the late Anglo-Saxon and Norman periods. Eleanor of Aquitaine was regent on Henry II's continental lands for brief periods in the first half of his reign and was active in England during the king's absence, with writs being issued in her name. From the time that she and her sons rebelled against Henry in 1173, however, she was held prisoner; and, although she appeared in public occasionally in the last years of the reign, she was not fully released until after Henry's death.[44] During these years, she had no opportunity to exercise authority. Although Eleanor of Provence occasionally acted as regent, and mobilised troops in France for her husband against Simon de Montfort, later queens were rarely active in politics.[45] Their ceremonial role became increasingly important.

Few queens acted as guardians to sons who were under-age. The number of minorities after the Conquest was relatively small, but in England, unlike France, the practice of using the queen mother as regent never developed. Instead, male members of the royal family and magnates governed by means of a minority council. On the death of John in 1216, in the middle of civil war, William Marshal was appointed regent of the nine-year-old Henry III. There was no role in England for his mother, Isabella of Angoulême, who soon returned to France and married

Hugh X of Lusignan. Joan of Kent and Katherine of Valois had no formal, political position during the minorities of their sons, Richard II and Henry VI.

In contrast, three mothers took vigorous action on behalf of their sons, aiming to secure their position as rulers. On the death of her husband in 1189, Eleanor of Aquitaine was in her late sixties, but showed her strength and abilities in securing England for Richard I. She was in charge of the kingdom until Richard arrived. Subsequently she accompanied Richard's bride, Berengaria of Navarre, to Messina for her wedding. She played a part in suppressing John's revolt against Richard. After the king's release from captivity, she retired to the abbey of Fontevrault, but emerged after his death to ensure Aquitaine's loyalty to John.

Isabella of France aimed at gaining power by means of her son. Her invasion in the autumn of 1326 culminated in the capture of her husband, Edward II, the elimination of his favourites, the Despensers, and the king's abdication and murder. Although his son, Edward III, was crowned king, the next three years saw control exercised by Isabella and her lover, Roger Mortimer, earl of March, in the face of increasing discontent. It was only when Edward seized power in 1330 and executed Mortimer that he was able to take over as effective king.[46]

Only one queen, Margaret of Anjou, made a formal claim to the regency. She did this as wife rather than mother since Henry VI was struck with madness in 1453–54 while Margaret was pregnant for the first time. The birth of her son, Edward, in October 1453, strengthened her hand, as she could claim that she was acting on behalf of her son, in the same way that Queen Isabeau had acted for the mad Charles VI of France. Margaret claimed the regency early in 1454 for as long as her husband was ill and the prince too young to rule, but Richard, duke of York, was created Protector and Defender of the realm on 27 March 1454. The king recovered early in 1455. In the following years, Margaret exercised power without a formal title and was the dominant influence at court in the later 1450s. She was responsible for making the alliance with Scotland, involving the cession of Berwick, and bringing a northern and Scottish army south to win the second battle of St Albans. After Edward IV's victory at Towton in 1461, she continued to work to secure Henry VI's return to the throne; although successful in 1470–71, the Yorkist victories at Barnet and Tewkesbury and the deaths of Henry and Edward led to her living in France, where she died in 1482.[47]

The queen's active political role in the middle ages was usually limited and only rarely was she in the forefront of events. Yet her use of religious and cultural patronage gave her a different type of power. The queen was expected to be pious and charitable and her religious observance was based on attendance at daily and seasonal services and processions, devotion to the saints, especially the Virgin Mary, and personal meditation with her books of hours. Elizabeth of York's charity ranged from offerings in chapel to payments to men going on pilgrimage on her behalf and casual almsgiving.[48]

Queens got to know church leaders and on occasion exerted influence through them. Eadgifu had the support of Archbishop Dunstan in backing Edgar's succession rather than Eadwig's in 955, and Bishop Æthelwold of Winchester probably supported Ælfthryth in the succession dispute of 975–78.[49] A strong friendship is apparent in the correspondence of Matilda of Scotland with Archbishop Anselm in the early twelfth century, although there were limits as to what the queen could do. Matilda was concerned for his health and urged him to reduce his fasting. Anselm appreciated her letters and gifts, and urged her to protect English churches, especially monasteries. He also wanted her to persuade Henry I to reject his council's advice over lay investitures, an admonition seconded by Pope Paschal II. Matilda knew well that she could not influence the king on a matter of policy which in his view affected his throne and the security of the kingdom.[50]

As indicated in Anselm's letters, the queen was regarded as the protector of churches and this was true throughout the middle ages. It is most strongly expressed in the *Regularis Concordia* of c. 970, in which the king is seen as the protector of monasteries and the queen of nunneries. Matilda of Scotland exercised protection over Malmesbury Abbey and in 1105–6 asked Anselm to confirm Eadwulf as the new abbot. Anselm at first refused because he interpreted her messengers' present of a goblet as a bribe. He later relented and Eadwulf's appointment was confirmed. Later queens were regarded as protectors, as seen in the relations between Eleanor of Provence and the Cistercian nunnery of Tarrant in Dorset.[51]

During the great period of growth in the religious orders between the tenth and thirteenth centuries, queens in cooperation with churchmen were in the vanguard of new movements, providing a lead which could be followed by others. Often they wanted to provide a memorial and prayers for members of their family. Royal mausolea, such as the abbeys of Reading, Faversham and Westminster, were normally under the king's patronage, but queens supported their efforts. There was a personal incentive for the foundation of nunneries, particularly in the late Anglo-Saxon and Norman periods, although queens retired to nunneries throughout the middle ages. Ælfthryth founded nunneries at Wherwell and Amesbury in Wessex, and Edith largely rebuilt the abbey of Wilton.[52]

The relationship of patron and nunnery brought mutual benefits. Pope Nicholas II gave his approval to the marriage of William the Conqueror and Matilda of Flanders on the condition that husband and wife each made a religious foundation; William founded the abbey of St Stephen, Caen, for monks, and Matilda Holy Trinity, Caen, for nuns. Although the grants of lands in Normandy and England to Holy Trinity were made in the names of William and Matilda, the queen is recorded as making purchases to give to the abbey. Probably in 1083, shortly before her death, with the king's agreement, she made a number of personal bequests to the abbey, including her crown and sceptre, a chasuble made at Winchester by the wife of Ealdred, a cloak embroidered with gold to be used for a cope, altar furnishings, all the accoutrements of a horse and all her vases except those given away in her lifetime. She was buried in the abbey, where her tombstone survives. Crowds of poor people came to her funeral. Her epitaph cited her family, her foundation of the abbey and her generosity to those in need.[53]

All these houses were Benedictine. With the growth of new orders after about 1100, there was a change of direction in queens' patronage. The Augustinian canons, introduced into England about 1100, were patronised by Matilda of Scotland and Henry I's court. The queen was renowned for her piety and charity, although William of Malmesbury criticised her for excessive generosity, which led to harsh exploitation of her tenants. In 1108, with Henry I's agreement and on Anselm's advice, she founded the Augustinian priory of Holy Trinity, Aldgate, endowing it with property in London and Exeter. Her example was followed by

Stephen's queen, Matilda of Boulogne, who granted the priory the hospital of St Katherine by the Tower of London, with the stipulation that it should maintain thirteen poor people there.[54] Matilda of Boulogne also patronised the new orders of the Savignacs and the Knights Templar. For her foundations of the late 1130s and 1140s, she made use of the lands of her natal inheritance, commemorating her father, Eustace, count of Boulogne, as well as her husband and children. Savigny had been founded between 1112 and 1115 in the county of Mortain, the Norman county granted to Stephen by Henry I, and Matilda affiliated her abbey at Coggeshall, Essex, to Savigny. Her principal grants to the Templars comprised Cressing Temple and the manor and half hundred of Witham, again in Essex.[55] Through their patronage, these two queens encouraged interest in the new orders, while at the same time keeping up their links with the older, Benedictine houses.

The same is true of the queens of the thirteenth and early fourteenth centuries, although their patronage was primarily directed towards the friars, especially the Franciscans and Dominicans. Eleanor of Provence had a particular concern for the Franciscans, as had Margaret of France, the second wife of Edward I, and her niece, Isabella, wife of Edward II. Eleanor provided for the burial of her heart in the Greyfriars' church in London at her death in 1291. It was Margaret and Isabella, however, who facilitated the building of the church. In 1301–2, Margaret secured land and houses in St Nicholas's parish, valued at sixty marks, for the site of the choir, and she spent 2,000 marks on the church, which was still unfinished at her death in 1318. Isabella spent at least a further £700, and Queen Philippa and others also contributed. Margaret was described in the Greyfriars register as the 'first founder of our new church' and was buried in the choir before the high altar. Isabella and the heart of Eleanor of Provence were also interred in the choir.[56]

Eleanor of Castile was both pious and generous, and patronised the Dominicans, who had originated as a Spanish order. She was regarded as a foundress of the priories in London and Chichester, and prepared the chapel in the London church where her heart was to be buried. She and her children were admitted to confraternity in the order in 1280. She made gifts to the priory at Oxford and gave money to provide food and drink for the provincial chapters in 1289 and 1290. Her preference for the Dominicans probably explains why her mother-in-law,

Eleanor of Provence, founded a Dominican house at Guildford to com-
memorate her grandson, Henry, who died in 1274.[57]

Like noblewomen, several queens turned to patronising university
colleges in the later middle ages, encouraging learning, training future
churchmen and administrators, and providing for the commemoration
of their souls. Eleanor of Castile left money in her will to the University of Oxford. Of greater significance was Philippa of Hainault. The
Queen's College, Oxford, was established in the early 1340s by Robert
de Eglesfield, a clerk in the queen's household, with Philippa as co-
founder. Grants of money and property were made by Philippa and
Edward III, and Philippa's example may well have encouraged further
donations. In 1350 the college's income from property amounted to
£66 6s. 5d. and Philippa herself petitioned the pope for confirmation
of her foundation.[58]

Cambridge had to wait about another hundred years for its Queens'
College and again an appeal was made to the queen for help. The college dates from 1448 after Andrew Doket had approached Margaret of
Anjou; the first court was built and the college was dedicated to St Margaret and St Bernard. Margaret was following the example of her
husband with his more lavish foundation of King's College, and, when
she asked him for permission to make her foundation, said that she was
acting to the praise and honour of the female sex. The college was, however, still unfinished when Edward IV became king, and Doket prevailed
on Elizabeth Woodville to re-establish the College as Queens'. Anne
Neville and Richard III also gave property to the college. Elizabeth's
statutes laid down that the college was to have a president, twelve fellows, studying arts or theology, and three young Bible clerks studying
the arts. Margaret of Anjou had provided for a lecture in theology twice
daily for the increase of faith, but it is not clear if this was ever carried
out. A free public lecture in divinity was, however, in place by 1484–85.[59]

Religious patronage contributed to the queen's influence in both
church and kingdom and to her personal reputation for piety. Many
medieval queens were literate and educated. Edith is described as beautiful, religious and good, very intelligent, and very well educated at
Wilton, knowing Latin, French, Danish and Irish; she was a great reader
and skilled in painting and needlework.[60] Queens like her had an interest in art and literature and were ready to patronise it. Patronage

redounded not only to their own enjoyment but also to their prestige and that of the court. In some cases it may have helped to spread continental ideas. Eleanor of Castile kept up with her family all her life and employed Spaniards in England. In addition to her interest in books and illumination, she helped to spread Spanish ideas about furnishings and gardens and possibly also about painting. Anne of Bohemia encouraged the widespread continental cult of St Anne in England.[61]

Queens Emma and Edith probably both commissioned the literary works associated with them, which put forward their version of the events with which they had been involved. The *Encomium Emmae Reginae* (*Praise of Queen Emma*), written by a Flemish monk in 1041–42, portrayed Emma as sharing rule with Cnut and bringing peace to England. The events of 1035–41, with the succession struggle after Cnut's death and the eventual accession of Harthacnut, are described from Emma's point of view. This was the time when she was visited by Alfred, her younger son by Æthelred, who was slain during his visit; it is an obscure episode and the *Encomium* blames Earl Godwine for his death. *The Life of King Edward* was written in the aftermath of the Norman Conquest. Attributed to a monk of St-Bertin, it extolled Edward's saintliness and Edith's role in promoting this through her presence at court, the establishment of peace during the reign and their religious benefactions at Westminster and Wilton. Edith was the daughter of Earl Godwine and the work argued for Godwine's loyalty during the crisis of 1051–52 and in support of Edith's actions at the time of the Northumbrian rising against her brother, Tostig, in 1065. She was powerless to prevent the events of 1066.[62]

No other queen provided a literary justification of her actions. Matilda of Scotland is more typical of medieval rulers in acting as a literary patron and is outstanding in the amount of patronage she offered. As the daughter of St Margaret of Scotland, she had the *Life of St Margaret* written to provide a model for her own life. Both mother and daughter were well educated, pious and charitable, both were bound up with family and children, both wished to increase religion and establish peace and justice. Matilda also commissioned the *Gesta Regum Anglorum* (*Deeds of the English Kings*) from William of Malmesbury, asking for a full account of her predecessors. William himself said that she always supported good literature and promoted those who loved it; he saw the Empress Matilda as following in her mother's footsteps and offered the completed work to her. Queen Matilda also patronised poets and commissioned the *Voyage of St Brendan* in Anglo-Norman.[63] Her patronage was continued by Adeliza of Louvain, who commissioned a French bestiary from Philip de Thaon and a Life of Henry I, now lost, from David the Scot. Her name took the place of Matilda's in three of the four copies of the *Voyage of St Brendan*.[64]

Much has been written about Eleanor of Aquitaine, troubadour culture and courts of love at Poitiers at the centre of her duchy of Aquitaine. A lot of this has to be jettisoned in the light of recent research, but it is clear that both Henry and Eleanor patronised art and literature, including the poet Bernard of Ventadour.[65] Romance, with its tales of war, love and chivalry, became a favourite form of literature for queens in the later middle ages, together with religious works. Eleanor of Provence purchased and read romances and enjoyed classical and Arthurian stories; she probably owned a psalter and an illuminated apocalypse, and possibly a book of hours. Two works were written for her, *La estoire de Seint Aedward le Rei* by Matthew Paris, and *Rossignos* by John of Howden. John included classical and Arthurian heroes and also crusaders, taking his stories down to Eleanor's lifetime. Eleanor of Castile likewise enjoyed romances and her scribes and illuminator produced manuscripts for her. She exchanged books with her half-brother, Alfonso X of Castile, and commissioned a translation of the *Art of War* by Vegetius as a present for her husband. At the time of her death in 1358, Queen Isabella possessed romances from the Charlemagne cycle, some about the Trojan war and three Arthurian romances; she also owned service books and a book of homilies.[66] Queens continued to enjoy romances and religious texts to the end of the middle ages. By then, they were patronising printing.

Several queens predeceased their husbands. For those who survived them, there were a number of options. Some widows went into retirement, such as Edmund's second wife, Æthelflaed of Damerham; she was childless and, although she came from a powerful natal family, little is heard of her for the rest of her life.[67] Many of the foreign queens, such as Margaret and Isabella of France, remained in England after their husbands' deaths, living on their dower lands. Not all queens lived in retirement. Eleanor of Aquitaine was exceptional in her activity as queen mother. In contrast to Eleanor's activities, Joan of Navarre, widow of Henry IV, was arrested in 1419 and deprived of her dower on the accusation that she was planning Henry V's death by witchcraft. She spent the next three years as a prisoner, although she was treated leniently and enjoyed a comfortable life. She was able to entertain nobles and churchmen. She was freed shortly before Henry V's death. It is likely that Henry had his eye on her dower, at a time when he needed money for the French war; she was never put on trial, although the charges were never dropped. She gradually recovered her possessions after her release and lived the rest of her life in peace.[68]

Some queens, both before and after the Conquest, retired to nunneries, although they were not necessarily professed as nuns. Eleanor of Provence retired to the nunnery of Amesbury in 1286, along with two of her granddaughters, and died there five years later. Elizabeth Woodville ended her life in the abbey of Bermondsey.[69] A queen's remarriage might well have political repercussions. Adeliza of Louvain married William d'Aubigny, and welcomed the Empress Matilda and Robert of Gloucester at Arundel Castle when they landed in England in 1139. Isabella of Angoulême's marriage to Hugh X de Lusignan caused difficulties for Henry III in his attempts to secure his lands in south-west France, in spite of Isabella's protestations that she was acting in Henry's interests. Katherine of Valois made a clandestine second marriage with Owen Tudor which had political implications for the future.[70]

Even in death, the queen still drew the attention of the realm and served as a focus for unity. Eleanor of Castile died at Harby, near Lincoln, in 1290, and, as her body was brought south to Westminster, it could be seen dressed in the royal robes, with crown and sceptre. Her royal regalia were buried with her. The twelve Eleanor Crosses were built at the places where the funeral cortège rested for the night on its journey. Eleanor's tomb effigy seems to represent her at the time of her coronation, while the heraldry on the tomb chest recalled her ancestry, inheritance and marital arms. Both the individuality and the official role of the queen were recognised, and through her the importance of the king and their heirs.[71] Eleanor, like her predecessors and successors, was both wife and mother, but at the same time had the unique rank, status and power of queen.

8

Religious Women

In contrast to the majority of medieval women, who were wives and mothers with all the family responsibilities that these roles entailed, nuns and anchoresses lived enclosed lives focused on prayer; both were vowed to chastity, but nuns lived in communities and anchoresses on their own or in small groups. Yet, despite the expectations of church reformers, they were not cut off from the world, and the concerns of family and community always impinged on their lives to a greater or lesser degree. Their lives and work, which can only be understood in the religious, social and political context of their time, changed considerably over the middle ages in line with contemporary attitudes and expectations. Religious houses of the seventh and eighth centuries, with their responsibilities for conversion to Christianity and pastoral care, were very different from the royal nunneries of pre-Conquest Wessex and still more from the houses which proliferated in the wake of the monastic reforms of the late eleventh and twelfth centuries. Few nunneries were established after 1200 but these included houses with a high reputation, such as the Bridgettine house at Syon and the Dominican nunnery at Dartford.

Double monastic houses for men and women, under the rule of an abbess, were founded from the early years of the Conversion. They opened up for women a way of life other than marriage, and gave them the opportunity to take up new responsibilities and exercise power. According to Bede, the main driving-force came from the royal families and many were established at royal villas, with kings offering their daughters to the new foundations. The first child of Edwin of Northumbria was a daughter, born just at the time that Edwin survived an assassination attempt, and he vowed that he would become a Christian if he was victorious over the West Saxon ruler who had sent the assassin. As a pledge, his baby daughter was given to Bishop Paulinus to be dedicated to Christ as a nun. Widows also sought refuge in monastic houses. When Edwin was killed in battle in 632, Paulinus fled with Queen Æthelburh and two of her children to Kent, where she became a nun at Lyminge.[1] Other royal women were ready to become nuns, some entering houses in Francia, because, as Bede pointed out, there were few nunneries in England early on; Eorcengota, daughter of King Eorcenberht of Kent, entered Faremoûtier-en-Brie.[2]

Although the rules of life differed from one monastery to another, all nuns were expected to be chaste and devout. Their life centred on the daily round of services in church and learning was highly prized. Aldhelm of Malmesbury (d. 709) wrote his treatise on virginity for Abbess Hildelith and the nuns of Barking; presumably, learning and knowledge of Latin flourished at Barking, for Aldhelm's style was extremely elaborate and florid. Guthlac, who became a hermit at Crowland, began his religious life under Abbess Ælfryth at Repton, where he was taught to read and sing psalms, and learned about the Scriptures and the monastic way of life.[3] The double houses served as minsters for their region and were important as a means of bringing Christianity to new areas.[4] The abbess had a powerful and influential role in public life and considerable responsibilities inside and outside the monastery. Abbess Tette of Wimborne, sister of King Ine of Wessex, is described as able and skilled in ruling, setting a pious example and ensuring strict discipline without alienating her nuns.[5]

The house at Whitby under Abbess Hilda (614–80) exemplifies the religious, cultural and political importance of the double monasteries. Hilda was a kinswoman of King Edwin and baptised at the same time. In her thirties, she planned to enter the Frankish house at Chelles, but was recalled by Aidan to Northumbria, where she became a nun and later abbess at Hartlepool; here she received King Oswiu's daughter, Ælfflaed. She established the double house at Whitby in 657, a house which was influenced by Roman, Frankish and Irish practices. Whitby became renowned for its learning, and it was here that Caedmon discovered his gift for composing and performing religious songs and was persuaded by Hilda to become a monk. *The Life of St Gregory the Great* was written at Whitby in the early eighth century. Hilda stressed the importance of studying the Scriptures for both monks and nuns, and five men from Whitby were promoted to bishoprics. Bede stressed

the importance of her example of religious fervour and good life in the
monastery and locality, and she had a political role in advising kings,
ealdormen and ordinary people. In 664 she hosted the synod at Whitby
which determined that Northumbria should follow the practice of the
Roman rather than the Irish church, the argument focusing particularly
on calculating the date of Easter. Bede described Hilda as a woman
devoted to the service of God; although she sided with the Irish church,
she accepted the decision in favour of Rome.[6]

Many of the royal abbesses became saints. Hilda's name was included
in the *Calendar of St Willibrord* of the early eighth century. Other saints
included Æthelthryth, daughter of King Anna of East Anglia, who
refused to consummate her marriage with Ecgfrith of Northumbria and
at length became a nun at Coldingham, subsequently founding the
abbey of Ely in the Fens. The abbey was established on the land of
her first husband, Tonberht. She was succeeded as abbess in 679 by her
sister, Seaxburh, widow of Eorcenberht of Kent, and foundress of
the house of Minster-in-Sheppey where she had retired as abbess after
her husband's death. Milburh (d. 715), daughter of a Mercian king and
his Kentish queen, became the second abbess of her father's foundation
at Much Wenlock and was renowned for her saintly life and death. Her
sister, St Mildred, returned from Chelles to become a nun and later
abbess at Minster-in-Thanet.[7]

The double monasteries brought considerable advantages to royal
families. They offered prayers for the dead and for the living. The reputation of a royal family was enhanced when several of its members
became nuns and saints. Double houses also provided a haven for
widows, where they could have an active role in the locality without
causing a threat to the throne. Monastic learning contributed to the
growth of a written culture, opening up the way towards development
in government, while minster churches established centres of royal
influence. They could also foster a kingdom's unity. In Northumbria,
the provinces of Deira and Bernicia each had their ruling dynasties.
Oswiu of Bernicia sought to unite them through his marriage to Eanflaed, daughter of Edwin of Deira. Oswiu's support of Whitby helped to
create a common Northumbrian culture. Hilda was related to Edwin,
but her close links with Aidan and Oswiu, her responsibility for his
daughter, Ælfflaed, and her influence over the Northumbrian church

proved her loyalty to the Bernician ruling house. It was at Whitby that Oswiu, his queen and members of his family were buried, and, according to the Whitby *Life of St Gregory*, the bones of King Edwin were reburied there also.[8]

During the eighth century, nuns played a significant part in the Anglo-Saxon missions to the Continent. St Boniface, who received papal permission to preach in Frisia and Germany in 719, relied extensively on Anglo-Saxon helpers, both men and women, as well as on the gifts and prayers of the English church. In his letters to women, he dispensed spiritual advice while at the same time asking for support. In answer to Abbess Bucge, who consulted him over making a pilgrimage to Rome, he advised her to go in order to gain peace of mind but to wait until the Saracen attacks round Rome were over. He asked Abbess Eadburh, of Minster-in-Thanet, to copy the Epistles of St Peter in gold so as to impress the heathen and to provide him with the Scriptures; it appears that the abbess had received many requests from him.[9]

Leofgyth stands out among Boniface's helpers. In addition to Boniface's correspondence, she was described in the *Life* written by Rudolf of Fulda in 836, based on an earlier account derived from the information of four of her nuns. She wrote to Boniface, who was her kinsman, soon after 732, recalling his friendship with her father, sending him a gift and asking for his prayers. She also asked for his help with her writing, an art which she had begun to learn from Abbess Eadburh at Minster-in-Thanet. According to the *Life*, she was educated at the double monastery of Wimborne under Abbess Tette. Boniface asked Tette to send Leofgyth to support his mission and made her abbess of the double monastery of Tauberbischofsheim, where she built up a reputation for learning, teaching her nuns the importance of prayer and study, but not allowing excessive austerity; she thought that understanding, especially in reading, was lost through lack of sleep. The story was told that, as the young nuns read the Scriptures to her while she rested, any omission or mistake was immediately corrected by the abbess. Shortly before his martyrdom in Frisia in 754, Boniface urged her to remain in Germany and wanted her to be buried with him in the same grave; in 780 she was interred near him in the monastery of Fulda.[10] Several other Anglo-Saxon nuns worked in Germany, such as Tecla (d. *c.* 790), sent from Wimborne by Tette to become a nun under Leofgyth and then abbess of Ochsenfurt and later of Kitzingen, and Walburga (d. 779) who after her time at Wimborne and Tauberbischofsheim, where she became skilled in medicine, became abbess of Heidenheim.[11]

During the period of Conversion in both England and Germany, nuns and abbesses enjoyed greater influence over lay society than for the rest of the middle ages and abbesses, in particular, were prominent in religious and political affairs. Yet, even in the early period, not all houses reached a high standard. Bede commented on slack discipline at Coldingham, and, in his letter to Bishop Egbert of York in 734, he complained of so-called monasteries for monks and nuns which did not follow the monastic way of life and needed thorough reform. Reform was attempted by the church councils of the eighth century, but, from the point of view of later church reformers, the double houses did not conform to the standards they expected for nuns. The concept of the double monastery was suspect; nunneries always needed the ministration of priests, but the idea of a community of monks and nuns went contrary to the emphasis on chastity and enclosure, as the Gilbertines and Bridgettines were to find later. Archbishop Theodore only grudgingly accepted double houses and they disappeared by the end of the ninth century.[12]

The Viking raids of the ninth century have often been said to have caused the collapse of monastic life. Some nunneries were probably damaged at that time. In Kent, the Vikings ravaged Sheppey in 835; in 851, they wintered for the first time on Thanet and spent the winter on Sheppey four years later. However, other factors were more significant in explaining the decline.[13] As the age of Conversion gave way to consolidation, the establishment of more dioceses put church organisation much more into male hands. The Carolingian religious reforms laid more stress on the regulation of convents and on the adoption of the Rule of St Benedict; this became widespread in England with the monastic reforms of King Edgar in the tenth century. Political and family developments also had a bearing on the fate of monastic houses. Minster-in-Thanet became embroiled in the struggle between Cenwulf of Mercia and the church of Canterbury in the early ninth century. Wimborne ceased to be a nunnery after the rebellion of Æthelwold against his cousin, Edward the Elder, in 900; he seized Wimborne, where his father, King Æthelred of Wessex, had been buried, together with one of the nuns.[14] Edward did not tolerate any community which was a focus of loyalty for a rival. Family continued to have a considerable influence on houses and the strong rights which family members had over its land might well result in a house being ephemeral, although the practice from the late tenth century of making grants to institutions rather than individuals gave some guarantee of continuity.[15]

The reign of Edgar saw the revival of monasticism associated with Saints Dunstan, Æthelwold and Oswald. Abbesses were present when the *Regularis Concordia* was drawn up and the nunneries were placed under the protection of the queen.[16] Little is known, however, about the process of reform within the houses, although it is clear that the authority of the abbess was less than it had once been. Apart from Barking, the best known Benedictine enclosed houses were situated in central Wessex and closely linked to the West Saxon royal family, receiving royal patronage and offering, in return, prayers, safe havens and burial. They were subject to royal interference and the nuns can hardly be said to have made a complete retreat from the world.

Shaftesbury was founded by King Alfred, who placed his daughter there as first abbess. The abbey also received grants from the tenth-century kings. It provided the burial place for Ælfgifu, the first wife of King Edmund, and, of much greater significance, for Edward the Martyr, murdered during the succession dispute after Edgar's death. Wilton was likewise closely associated with the royal dynasty. Ælfflaed, second wife of Edward the Elder, and her two daughters were buried there; and Wulfthryth, Edgar's divorced wife, lived there as abbess with her daughter, St Edith. Both women may have been involved in the succession dispute after Edgar's death. According to Goscelin of St Bertin, Edith was offered the throne after the murder of Edward the Martyr. Whatever the truth of the story, she was recognised as a saint by 1000.[17] Girls who were brought up at Wilton did not necessarily become nuns; Edith left to marry Edward the Confessor, although she always maintained her connection with the abbey, while Matilda of Scotland became the wife of Henry I.

These nunneries were exclusive institutions, situated in Wessex and only catering for a proportion of the women who wanted to follow a religious life. Other women might live as vowesses, either in their own household, or in informal groups, or attached to a monastic house, something which continued into the twelfth century. The late Anglo-Saxon period was a time of new liturgies, enabling a widow to devote herself to the religious life. From the mid tenth century, more such women were living outside nunneries.[18] Some of these vowesses can be identified from their wills. Wynflaed, in her will of c. 950, gives details of her clothing, including her best holy veil and her nun's outfit. She left one of her estates to Shaftesbury Abbey. She was probably closely connected with a religious community, possibly Shaftesbury, but she was not an enclosed nun because she was in control of her lands and possessions.[19] Æthelgifu may well have been a vowess with her own community; her will refers to unfree women chanting the psalter and she was closely connected with the monks of St Albans.[20] The Domesday Book refers to informal groupings, such as the twenty-eight nuns living alongside the abbey of Bury St Edmunds, and Leofgyth, a nun on her own, holding two messuages in Warwick. About 1102 Anselm wrote to a small, informal community of Anglo-Saxon nuns and their chaplain, urging them to persevere in the religious life and to pay attention to the smallest details, advising them on how to avoid evil thoughts and explaining the root causes of good and evil deeds.[21]

The lives of religious women continued to be diverse after 1066, but there is little sign of nuns in the north until after c. 1150. In the confusion of the Conquest, many women fled to nunneries, posing a problem later for Lanfranc as to whether they should be counted as nuns.[22] The established nunneries retained most of their lands, although occasional losses are recorded in The Domesday Book, and remained the wealthiest down to the Dissolution. Norman girls were entering these houses within twenty years of the Conquest. Shaftesbury had a Norman abbess from 1074 and sometimes a member of the higher nobility was appointed, as when Cecily, daughter of Robert fitz Hamon, was abbess about 1107. The Normans who entered as nuns came from the vicinity of Shaftesbury and were not from the wealthiest families. Most made entry gifts of land worth about £2, probably less than their fathers would have given for a dowry on marriage. Their families anticipated spiritual benefits in return for their gifts.[23]

Some of the nunneries made a deliberate attempt to foster their reputation in the eyes of the Normans through hagiography. A Fleming, Goscelin of St-Bertin made his career in England and wrote lives of a number of female saints, including Edith of Wilton and Wulfilda of Barking. He also composed his *Liber confortarius* for Eve, whom he had known as a girl at Wilton and who had left to become a recluse at Angers. Goscelin worked for Herman, bishop of Sherborne, but was dismissed by his successor, Osmund, about 1079. After this, he sought hagiographical commissions and probably ended his life at St Augustine's, Canterbury.[24] His saints' lives may have encouraged Norman recruitment.

Anselm's letters to English nunneries show a fatherly interest in their spiritual progress and he regarded the relationship as reciprocal. About 1094 he wrote to both Abbess Eulalia and the nuns of Shaftesbury, and Abbess Matilda and the nuns of Wilton, encouraging them in the conscientious observance of the Rule of St Benedict so as to climb to heaven, step by step. In both letters, he asked for their prayers, and Abbess Matilda was urged to obey and love Bishop Osmund of Salisbury. Anselm was strict when he thought it necessary. The abbess and nuns of Romsey were threatened with an interdict in 1102 if they continued to venerate Earl Waltheof as a saint. Two years later, during his exile, Anselm told Abbess Eulalia and her nuns that he knew that they hoped for a letter from him; he urged them to live as if always in the presence of their guardian angels. He thanked them in 1106 for their prayers during his exile, and ordered them to obey the abbess, keep the peace and think of no sin as trivial.[25]

The twelfth century saw a great expansion in the number of monastic houses, largely as a result of the rise of new religious orders, such as the Augustinians and Cistercians, and their appeal to people of all social groups. Nunneries grew in number but not to the same extent as male houses, and they were often poor. Many patrons, both men and women, preferred to endow monks rather than nuns, as had also been the case in the late Anglo-Saxon period. In the fourteenth century, Michael de la Pole opted for a Carthusian foundation in place of his father's plan for a house of Franciscan nuns, believing that God's will would be served with greater vigilance and devotion by monks than by nuns.[26] Because they could never be ordained as priests, the nuns could not celebrate the requiem masses which became increasingly popular from the thirteenth century.

Anselm's letters claim, however, that nunneries had spiritual benefits to offer, although it is probable that their appeal was distinct from that

1. The significance of lineage: Dorothy Clopton, wife of Thomas Curson esquire, in heraldic costume. Stained glass window at Long Melford church, Suffolk, second half of the fifteenth century.

2. Marriage: Bride and groom in the foreground, with the priest behind and the clerk holding the service-book. Panel on the Seven Sacrament font, Great Glemham church, Suffolk.

3. Baptism: The priest stands behind the font, with the godparents on the left, the godmother holding the baby; the clerk holds the service-book. Panel on the Seven Sacrament font, Great Glemham church, Suffolk.

4. Penance: A graphic depiction, with the priest absolving the penitent (in the pew) while the devil holds onto a man awaiting confession. Panel on the Seven Sacrament font, Great Glemham church, Suffolk.

5. Death: the administration of the sacrament of extreme unction by the priest to the dying man; the wife weeps at the foot of the bed. Panel on the Seven Sacrament font, Badingham church, Suffolk.

6. Old age: An old woman with her distaff and her cat. Misericord from Minster-in-Thanet church, Kent.

7. The temptation of fashion: the devil sits between the horns of the woman's head-dress. Misericord from Minster-in-Thanet church, Kent.

8. The birth of Jesus: the Virgin Mary is lying down with her maid behind her; Joseph is excluded from the birth, sitting on the right; contrary to custom, Mary is visited by the three Wise Men. Alabaster panel at Long Melford church, Suffolk.

9. Work and religious practice: the wife of John Chapman with her rosary at her shop door. Carving at Swaffham church, Norfolk.

10. Lacock Abbey, Wiltshire, the nunnery founded by Ela countess of Salisbury in 1229: the north and east ranges of the cloister, rebuilt in the Perpendicular style; the windows above date from after the Dissolution. By permission of the Conway Library, Courtauld Institute of Art, London.

11. Lacock Abbey, Wiltshire: the warming house, dating from about 1247; the bronze cauldron by Peter Waghevens of Malines dates from 1500. By permission of the Conway Library, Courtauld Institute of Art, London.

12. John and Katherine Goodale, portrayed on the pulpit that they gave to the parish church; the figures are the same size as the Fathers of the Church, portrayed on the other four sides. Burnham Norton church, Norfolk.

of the male houses. Many nunneries differed in layout from the typical monastic plan and sited their cloisters and the surrounding conventual buildings on the north rather than the south side of the church. Sometimes the cloister had to be placed to the north because of the nature of the site and the source of the water supply, but there was also a conceptual reason why northern cloisters were built, especially in south-east, east and northern England. The association of the north with cold and the south with heat symbolised the different natures of men and women. It was believed that the body was made up of the four humours corresponding to the elements of fire, air, earth and water, and in women the cold and wet elements of earth and water were predominant. Moreover, on the rood, the Virgin Mary stood on the right of the figure of Jesus on the cross (the north side), and certain elements in the liturgy were associated with the north side of the church, notably the women's arrival at Christ's tomb on Easter morning and finding it empty. All this symbolism had an enduring impact on the life of the nuns and was reflected in the plan of the nunnery.[27]

There is no doubt that many twelfth- and thirteenth-century women wished to become nuns. Christina of Markyate was determined to reject marriage in favour of life as a recluse, in spite of the opposition of her parents and suitor. Not all women had so powerful a motivation and some may have become nuns as a result of family pressure or because of a dislike of the prospect of marriage. Virginity was extolled by the medieval church.[28] The twelfth century, however, saw a virtual end to the practice of child oblation, so women were entering nunneries in their teens or later, at an age when they knew what becoming a nun involved.

The main problem that the nuns faced lay in churchmen's attitudes to the religious life for women; the church's emphasis lay on enclosure and chastity, and it was worried about the number of priests needed to minister to the nuns. Informal groups of women attached to male houses were regarded as unsuitable, so women were expected to live in enclosed communities. Of the new orders, the Augustinians accepted nuns, but the Cistercians set their faces against women until 1213. In 1220 and 1228 they again attempted to put a stop to the incorporation of nunneries, although without complete success. Several English Cistercian nunneries started off as informal groups.[29] The Premonstratensian canons originally accepted women but soon changed their minds.[30]

Two reformers, however, accepted a form of double house. Robert of Arbrissel founded Fontevrault as an abbey for men and women under the rule of an abbess. The house was patronised by the Plantagenet royal family and three daughter-houses were established in England at Amesbury, Nuneaton and Westwood in Worcestershire. Of greater importance for England was St Gilbert of Sempringham, whose foundation of a double house at Sempringham in Lincolnshire became the mother-house of the Gilbertine order. The problems which he faced reflect the difficulties which women encountered in seeking a religious life. His original foundation about 1130 was for a group of anchoresses at his parish church of Sempringham. He subsequently added lay sisters to work in the convent and then lay brothers to work on the land. Finally, probably in the 1150s, he added a group of priests to minister to the convent's spiritual needs.[31]

The arrangements were essentially informal. The Cistercians refused to take over his two houses in 1147 and events soon showed that a more structured organisation was essential. The case of the nun of Watton, about 1163, highlighted the danger of men and women living in the same community. The nun, who had entered Watton as a child, was found to be pregnant; her lover was one of the canons, so she was imprisoned and forced to castrate her lover. The scandal was hushed up but the fact that no baby was born did not alter the fact that serious trouble had occurred.[32]

Trouble of a different kind erupted with the lay brothers' revolt of 1165–67, protesting against the strictness of Gilbert's rule.[33] Although Gilbert was exonerated by the papacy and the lay brothers' conditions eventually improved, again a more structured organisation was essential. The priests and nuns each had their own cloister, and the church was partitioned so that men and women could not see each other. All the inmates owed obedience to the master and the men were responsible for both property and supplies. Gilbert's was the only English order for women but it only numbered twenty-six houses, many of which were in Lincolnshire and Yorkshire, and only eleven of the houses were double, reflecting the problems of mixed communities and the growing emphasis on enclosure for women. Gilbert, however, catered for a real need in making provision for unmarried women and widows. His provision of lay sisters also encouraged peasant women to live a religious life.

The patrons of nunneries came from a variety of social groups, including the royal family, churchmen, nobles and knights. Many foundations were made by a husband and wife, sometimes as an establishment for a daughter, or by a widow, sometimes for herself. The use of the woman's marriage portion for foundations was widespread. Some priories grew out of a group of anchoresses or out of a hospital. Although some foundations, like Bishop Gundulf's nunnery at Malling in Kent, were made soon after the Conquest, many date from the second half of the twelfth century.

To take a few examples, King Stephen and Matilda of Boulogne established the nunnery at Lillechurch, Kent, for their daughter Mary, who moved there from the nunnery of Stratford atte Bow. Mary had a chequered career, since she became abbess of Romsey in the 1150s but married Matthew, younger son of the count of Flanders in 1166, probably against her will, when her brother's death left her sole heir to the Boulogne lands. She ended her life as a nun in northern France. Such events are reminiscent of the late Anglo-Saxon period. Godstow, Oxfordshire, was a noble foundation but was later patronised by Henry II, whose mistress, Fair Rosamund, was buried before the high altar. Henry refounded Amesbury as a daughter-house of Fontevrault, while Nuneaton was established by Robert, earl of Leicester, and his wife, Amice. Stixwould, Lincolnshire, was founded by Lucy, widowed countess of Chester, about 1139–42, and she may have become a nun there. On a lower level, Redlingfield in Suffolk was endowed in 1120 by Emma de Redlingfield with her manor and the parish church. Marrick in north Yorkshire was founded in 1154–58 by a knight, Roger de Aske, whose daughters became nuns there. Nun Appleton was established a few years earlier by Alice de St Quintin whose mother had founded Nunkeeling and whose uncle founded Nun Monkton.[34]

Some nunneries had a chequered early history. Crabhouse priory in Norfolk originated as a women's hermitage, but faced ecclesiastical harassment and was forced to move after a serious flood about 1200. By the early thirteenth century, it was established as an Augustinian nunnery. Thetford priory began with a group of female hermits after it ceased to be a cell of the abbey of Bury St Edmunds about 1160, and developed into a Benedictine nunnery. Aconbury priory in

Herefordshire began as a community of the Knights Hospitallers and subsequently became Augustinian.[35]

Most nunneries were established by 1200. Some noblewomen, however, made their own foundations in the thirteenth century. The Augustinian abbey of Lacock, Wiltshire, was founded in 1229–30 by Ela, countess of Salisbury, and widow of Henry II's illegitimate son, William Longespee. It is likely that she always intended to enter her own foundation; she became a nun in 1237 and abbess two years later, holding the office for about twenty years. She founded the abbey for the souls of all her family, past, present and future, and, in close cooperation with her eldest son and the crown, endowed it with land in Wiltshire and Gloucestershire. The *Register of St Osmund* describes her as 'a woman indeed worthy of praise because she was filled with the fear of the Lord'.[36] Isabella, countess of Arundel, founded the Cistercian abbey of Marham in Norfolk in 1249, giving the nunnery the land in Marham which her father, Earl William de Warenne, had given her at her marriage.[37] Somewhat later, in the 1280s, Matilda de Lacy, countess of Gloucester, refounded the house of Augustinian canons at Canonsleigh in Devon as a nunnery for canonesses. She died before completing the foundation and it was only in her grandson's time that the endowment was complete.[38]

In contrast to the number of women's houses belonging to the mendicant orders in continental Europe, there were few such houses in England. Possibly this was because there was less urban development in England than in northern Italy and parts of Germany; possibly it was because by the thirteenth century fewer English foundations were being made. The patrons of the English mendicant nunneries tended to belong to the elite, and the four houses for Franciscan nuns were established by a small interrelated group among the higher nobility. The nuns were known as Minoresses. They followed the Isabella Rule, laid down by Isabella, sister of Louis IX of France, for the nunnery at Longchamp which she founded in 1255. The nuns pursued an enclosed, contemplative life; although they took the vow of poverty, they were allowed to hold property in common.[39]

In 1294, Denise de Montchensy founded a house for Minoresses at Waterbeach, Cambridgeshire, having had the project in mind for over ten years. About the same time, the London house outside Aldgate was

established by Blanche, queen of Navarre, a niece of Louis IX of France
and second wife of Edmund, earl of Lancaster. Her great-niece, Marie
de St-Pol, countess of Pembroke, acquired the site for the house at
Denny in 1327, and twelve years later received a royal licence to move
the Waterbeach nuns to Denny. Although Waterbeach opposed the
move, the merger had been effected by 1351. The fourth house, Bruisyard
in Suffolk, was founded in 1364–67 by Lionel, duke of Clarence, for his
mother-in-law, Matilda of Lancaster.[40]

All these founders had a personal and religious interest in their foundations. Lionel's first wife, Elizabeth, countess of Ulster, was buried at
Bruisyard and Marie de St-Pol at Denny. Matilda of Lancaster is said to
have long wanted to become a nun. After two marriages, she became an
Augustinian canoness in 1347 at Campsey Ash in Suffolk. She moved to
Bruisyard for a more peaceful life, free from the crowd of nobles who
came to Campsey. Contact with the Minoresses was widely appreciated
in lay society. Elizabeth de Burgh built her London house in the 1350s in
the outer precinct of the Aldgate convent, a house later occupied by
Lucy, countess of Kent, and Margaret Howard, duchess of Norfolk.[41]
Dartford was the only house of Dominican nuns founded in England. It
was founded by Edward III in 1346 but, because of the Black Death, the
first nuns, four of whom came from France, only entered it ten years
later. It enjoyed a high reputation in the late middle ages.[42]

The few houses established in the late middle ages belonged to
orders which had a high religious reputation among the laity, such as
the Carthusians. Henry V chose this order for his foundation at Sheen.
The house at Syon belonged to a more recent order founded in the late
fourteenth century by St Bridget of Sweden. She envisaged a double
house where the life was based on religious devotion, poverty and study.
The nuns and monks lived in separate parts of the monastery but shared
the church. The order was patronised by the Danish royal family,
including Henry V's sister, Queen Philippa. Syon was founded at Isle-
worth, Middlesex, in 1415 by Henry V, who envisaged a community of
sixty nuns and twenty-five monks, each with their own head. The house
attracted nuns from the nobility, gentry and merchant families and
enjoyed a high reputation in noble society.[43]

The trend towards enclosure culminated in Pope Boniface VIII's
decretal, *Periculoso*, in 1298 which laid down that all nuns should be

enclosed. They were not to leave the nunnery; visitors were to be vetted; and abbesses and prioresses were to carry out business by proxy. Such provisions were hardly feasible. John Pecham, archbishop of Canterbury, in his visitation of Barking Abbey in 1279, wished to safeguard the chastity of the nuns, but was aware that priests, servants and workmen were inevitably present in the monastery, and there were occasions when nuns should leave the abbey, such as to see a parent who was dying. All he could do was to lay down rules to minimise contact and safeguard the nuns.[44] It was not possible to be completely cut off from the world. Nuns were bound to be influenced by their families and their early lives. Moreover, a reciprocal relationship existed in the later middle ages between the nunnery and the world outside; although lacking the religious and political significance of the Conversion period, the nunneries offered a variety of services in return for family and neighbourhood support.

Girls usually entered the nunnery in their mid teens, at the age when their sisters might well be getting married. They could be professed as nuns at the age of sixteen. They were drawn from families of nobles, knights, gentry, and wealthy yeomen and townsmen. The payment of a dowry precluded women from lower in the social scale. The system of the dowry came under attack in the twelfth century since canon lawyers saw it as simony, the purchase of a position in the church. Yet many nunneries would have found it difficult to accept women without some form of endowment, and gifts of land, money or goods continued to be made.[45] Moreover, the entrant was usually expected to provide her clothing and bedding. When Joan Samborne entered Lacock in 1395, she brought a veil, a worsted cloak, cloth and furs for cloaks, tunic and underclothes, a bed and bedclothes, and a bowl and spoon, at an estimated cost of £12. The requirements for Blackborough, Norfolk, were more specific and cost between £5 and £7; in addition to her clothing, the entrant was expected to bring two mattresses, two pairs of sheets, two pairs of blankets and two coverlets, and other goods included a napkin and towel, ewer and cup, and a basin.[46]

Nunneries were often crowded in the thirteenth and early fourteenth centuries when the population of England reached its medieval peak. Some episcopal visitations forbade further admissions because of the poverty of the houses; in 1315, Archbishop Greenfield of York forbade further admissions of nuns and sisters at Sinningthwaite without his licence.[47] The twenty-four nuns at Amesbury at its refoundation by Henry II increased to seventy-seven in 1256 and 117 about 1300; in 1256 there were eighty-seven nuns at Nuneaton. Romsey had ninety-one nuns in 1333. There was a considerable fall in the number of monks and nuns after the Black Death, although some nunneries, like Syon and Shaftesbury, remained fairly populous. At Marham, there were seventeen inmates in 1377 but seven in 1536, while Bruisyard had fifteen inmates at both dates. Romsey had only eighteen nuns in 1478. In the 1430s, there were said to be hardly enough nuns at Elstow, Bedfordshire, to chant divine service, and new entrants were to be encouraged.[48]

Some nuns were not suited to the monastic life. A number became pregnant and it is hard to imagine how they settled if they were readmitted to the nunnery. Some ran away, such as Isabella Gervays of Winchester, who connived in her own abduction and returned to the nunnery pregnant. Conditions were especially difficult in the north during the Scottish wars around 1300; a nun ran away from Coldstream when war was pending and two nunneries were dispersed.[49] A somewhat different problem was posed by noble nuns who, though professed, adopted a largely lay lifestyle. Isabella of Lancaster, who became a nun at Amesbury in 1327 and later prioress, administered her own property, maintained a virtually lay household, visited her family for long periods, and received noble visitors.[50]

A detailed analysis of the nuns' social origins has been made for East Anglia, based on all the nuns who can be identified between 1350 and 1540. We know that 6 per cent of the nuns came from the parish gentry, 32 per cent from the county gentry, 14 per cent from the towns, and only 4 per cent each from the nobility and yeomanry. Nuns and their families often opted for a nunnery near their home, if this was available, although the presence of a nun who was a kinswoman might well affect their choice of house. At Dartford, most nuns and prioresses appear to have come from the gentry, London merchants' families, and the families of men in royal service; very occasionally, a nun belonged to a noble or the royal family. Most nuns came from the home counties and East Anglia, but the high reputation of the house brought entrants from Yorkshire and Glamorgan. Yorkshire nunneries, such as Marrick, also attracted women from the local gentry, and the prioresses of

Nun Appleton often had local connections. Some nunneries, including the houses of the Minoresses, drew wealthier inmates, and the house outside Aldgate attracted noble, gentry and merchant women. The reputation of some houses transcended regional loyalties. Barking Abbey drew nuns from East Anglia as well as from Essex and the London area, including Katherine de la Pole, daughter of the earl of Suffolk, who was elected abbess in 1433.[51]

The nun's day, as was the case earlier in the middle ages, was punctuated by the *Opus Dei*, the services in church. Between the services, she devoted herself to prayer and reading; manual labour was performed occasionally but was not a normal part of the day. It was a life of silence, apart from the period of recreation. She ate her main meal at midday, listening to a religious reading. At Elstow in the early fifteenth century, each nun was to have a dish of meat or fish three times a week, together with bread and ale.[52] Pittances, or extra dishes, were served on special occasions. The convent met in the chapter house for a weekly meeting.

It can be assumed that entrants would have had religious teaching at home. They received further training in reading, the chant and the Rule of the house during their novitiate. The thirteenth-century Nuneaton Book, with its sacred and recreational reading, was probably designed for novices or children educated in the convent. How much the nuns understood of the Latin of the services is unknown. Episcopal visitations were primarily concerned with the performance of the services and at Barking in 1279 Archbishop Pecham stressed that the services were to be celebrated 'devoutly and wholly'. They were not to be shortened, especially the night offices of matins and lauds, and compline was to be said at the proper time. Every nun should attend the services unless she was ill or engaged in convent business. Special provisions were made for the mass of the Virgin Mary and the celebration of Holy Innocents' Day. Nuns were allowed to take communion at mass on all the major feasts and on the anniversaries of their professions.[53]

Whatever their knowledge of Latin, many nuns were able to read French or English and used these languages for their prayers. There is, however, little evidence of nuns composing literary works after the Conquest, although they contributed verses to the memorial rolls which circulated among monastic houses. In 1113, the nunneries of St Mary's, Winchester, Amesbury and Shaftesbury wrote Latin verses in the mortuary roll of the abbess of Caen, and Wherwell added the names of some of their nuns who had died. Three saints' lives in the Anglo-Norman period were written by women, two of whom were certainly nuns. *Vie Seinte Audrée*, the Life of St Audrey, alias Æthelthryth of Ely, was written in the thirteenth century by Marie, who may have been a nun of Chatteris and who dedicated her work to the saint. The story stresses the saint's virginity, her two unconsummated marriages and her subsequent foundation of the abbey at Ely. The other two lives were written at Barking, which retained its Latin culture into the twelfth century. Clemence of Barking in the late twelfth century produced a French verse life of the virgin martyr St Katherine of Alexandria, and, at about the same time, an anonymous nun wrote a *Vie d'Edouard le Confesseur*. This can be linked with the growth of the cult of Edward the Confessor as a virgin saint. Beatrice of Kent, abbess of Lacock, is said to have written an account of Ela, countess of Salisbury.[54] Other works may well have been written by nuns who remain unknown because of the authors' anonymity.

More is known of the nunnery's books, although again our knowledge is partial because libraries were broken up at the Dissolution and the books dispersed or destroyed. For many nunneries only one or two books have been traced, such as the Sarum Breviary from Polsloe, Devon, or the two psalters and a compilation of lives of the saints from Campsey Ash. Denny had a fifteenth-century copy of the Northern Homily Cycle, in English. The compilation from Campsey Ash is the largest known collection to have been in a nunnery's possession. The saints' lives were written in Anglo-Norman in the late thirteenth century and the manuscript was used for reading in the Campsey refectory in the early fourteenth century. The lives chosen for inclusion focus on East Anglia and it has been suggested that the manuscript was probably commissioned by Isabella, countess of Arundel.[55]

Further information is found in testamentary bequests, and, although the bequests were made to the individual nun, it was often intended that the book would eventually go into the convent library. These books included saints' lives, spiritual guides, and mystical and moral works. Agnes Stapleton in 1448 left books in French and English to the nunneries at Arthington, Denny, Esholt, Nun Monkton and Sinningthwaite. Elizabeth Fincham divided her books between her son and daughter; the daughter was a nun at Shouldham in Norfolk and the books were to be shared with the other nuns.[56] It is possible that the nunneries continued to follow the Benedictine practice of issuing a book to each nun at the beginning of Lent; this is known to have happened at Barking.[57] The use of French and English mirrored contemporary social practice and ensured that in a changing world nuns were able to lead a life of religious devotion.

Knowledge of continental mystical writings in the late middle ages is found among the Carthusians, at a few nunneries such as Syon, Dartford, Barking and the houses of the Minoresses, and also among some of the higher nobility. The work of a thirteenth-century German mystic, Mechtild of Hackeborn, is not referred to in England until after the foundation of Syon, and the earliest mention comes in the will of Eleanor Roos in 1438; Eleanor was buried at the Carthusian monastery of Mount Grace in Yorkshire. *The Myroure of Our Ladye*, written in the first half of the fifteenth century, was in the nuns' library at Syon. It assumed that the nuns would have the Scriptures in English. It recommended the nuns to read, among other authors, Richard Rolle, Mechtild of Hackeborn and St Bridget as a way of enabling them to engage in affective contemplation of Christ's Life and Passion, and of the Virgin Mary and the saints. The will of Cecily Neville, duchess of York, of 1495 shows her interest in mystical works and her links with Dartford and Syon. She left her granddaughter, Bridget, who was a nun at Dartford, a copy of the Golden Legend, the *Book of Special Grace* by Mechtild of Hackeborn and a Life of St Katherine of Siena. Another granddaughter, Anne, prioress of Syon, received the *Revelations* of St Bridget, a work on the life of Christ attributed to Bonaventure, and Walter Hilton's book on the contemplative and active life. The Bonaventure, a popular introduction to mystical religion, was translated into English by Nicholas Love, prior of Mount Grace.[58]

The growth of privacy at the expense of communal life reflected contemporary society and caused concern in the visitations. The trend was setting in by 1300 and bishops attempted to regulate it; they realised that they could not set the clock back. Many sought to ensure that the nuns slept in their dormitories, and Bishop Gray's injunctions for Burnham in the 1430s laid down that no boys, men or laywomen over the age of fourteen were to sleep there. At St Mary of the Meadows, Northampton, the bishop found that the nuns ate in the refectory three days a week and wanted them to increase this to four. Several visitations mentioned households of nuns within the convent and the Elstow injunctions provided for their supply of fuel. At Godstow in 1432 there were to be only three households of nuns in addition to the abbess's household, with between six and eight nuns in each.[59]

The fear of contact with the world underlay many of the episcopal injunctions. Privacy could lead to lack of supervision and transgressions of the Rule. Therefore at Elstow, probably in 1422, the prioress and sub-prioress were to spend more time in the cloister so as to oversee the nuns and preserve silence. At Godstow, no layperson was to be entertained in the nuns' chambers, as the Oxford scholars alleged.[60] Nuns were only to go out of the nunnery with the permission of the prioress and were to be accompanied. Dissensions were to be settled and rebellious nuns corrected. The nuns of Wilberfoss in 1308 were not to wear red or indecent clothes, or long supertunics like laywomen. The nuns of Yedingham were not to wear girdles or other ornaments on their habits. There was particular concern for the maintenance of chastity, a serious problem in the Yorkshire nunneries in the early fourteenth century, when the situation was certainly exacerbated by the Scottish wars and famine. In Yorkshire in the first half of the fourteenth century, sixteen nuns broke their vow of chastity and twenty-three left their convents without licence. In contrast, there were only about fifteen cases in the two hundred years between the Black Death and the Dissolution.[61]

Bishops realised that, in spite of *Periculoso*, nunneries could not be cut off from the world. They had their property to manage, and lay society expected them to cater for boarders and children, and to give alms. The link with family remained strong, especially for nunneries with a small endowment glad of further gifts. The property held by the nuns comprised lands and churches, and, where the nunnery church was shared by the parish, a close relationship emerged. All these responsibilities required women of ability and determination, and gave them the opportunity for a more powerful role than they would have exercised as wives.[62]

Each house was headed by an abbess or prioress. Although the nunnery had to obtain a licence to elect a new head from the crown or bishop, and report the result to the patron, the election was made by the nuns themselves. The feast after her election introduced her to the locality. The feast at Wilton on 13 September 1299, to celebrate the election of Emma la Blounde and the feast-day of St Edith, lasted several days and was attended by laypeople as well as by the nuns. The menu was comparable to a noblewoman's feast, with sixteen swans, thirteen peacocks and three boars being served, as well as more ordinary food.[63]

Under the abbess or prioress were the obedientiaries, such as the sacrist in charge of the church and the cellarer in charge of the estates. Their work was reviewed once a year in full chapter when the women were either reappointed or replaced. Research on East Anglia points to an element of meritocracy among the office-holders. Only a minority came from wealthy families, with none coming from the nobility and only 16 per cent from the county gentry; 65 per cent, in contrast, came from the parish gentry. Several of these women held more than one office and were presumably chosen for their administrative abilities. Margery Palmer became prioress at Carrow in 1485, having been cellarer for forty-four years, while Anne Martin, who entered Carrow in 1492, became cellarer by 1514 and was later placed in charge of the infirmary.[64]

The abilities of an abbess are epitomised by Euphemia at Wherwell in the mid-thirteenth century. She doubled the number of nuns from forty to eighty and was a prudent and honest administrator as well as being pious and charitable. She provided a new infirmary and rebuilt the farm buildings on several manors. She rebuilt the bell tower when the old one fell down through decay (none of the nuns being injured, however). The presbytery was also rebuilt when it was in danger of collapse. The church was ornamented with crosses and reliquaries and provided with books and vestments. Her work testified to the glory of God, the well-being of the abbey and the welfare of the nuns.[65]

Effective financial management was very much on the bishop's mind at times of visitation. Some religious houses ran into serious debt and maladministration, as at Ankerwyke in 1441. At Elstow, probably in 1422, two of the senior, highly regarded nuns were to be chosen as treasurers, and they and the abbess were to hold the keys of the common chest. Expenditure was to be decided by the abbess and the 'sounder part' of the convent. Receivers and servants were to collect revenues faithfully and pay them all over to the convent. Every nun who was an office-holder was to present her accounts to the convent once a year. No leases were to be made by the abbess without the consent of the majority of the convent.[66] Similar regulations are often found for other houses in the later middle ages.

Accounts were drawn up by male officials or by the nuns themselves. At Marrick, accounts survive for 1415–16, compiled by the bursar, sacrist and the granger, who was a man and presented his grange account. The sacrist received about £9 in offerings and tithes; the church was used by the parish, while the nuns had the choir, and £5 6s. 8d. was paid to the chaplain. The bursar was the principal financial official, handling receipts of over £64, mainly from rents and sales of grain and stock; as was often the case at this time, arrears were high, and it was difficult to collect rents. The resources had to be carefully managed and little was spent on luxuries.[67]

Nuns were expected to exercise hospitality and almsgiving, both of which placed a heavy burden on their finances. They also educated children. When Margaret, duchess of Clarence, was with her husband in France between 1418 and 1421, her two daughters and their servants stayed at Dartford. The prioress was paid 6s. 8d. a week for the girls' board and further payments were made for their household. Such functions were subject to careful regulation in the visitations, although pressure could be brought to bear on nunneries to take in particular people. At Burnham in the 1430s, no women over the age of fourteen or boys over eight were to lodge in the house without the bishop's permission; existing lay lodgers were to be removed, and no corrodies or pensions were to be granted without permission.[68] A corrody enabled its purchaser to receive maintenance from a religious house; the money was welcome at the time of purchase but the support might well cost the house more in the long run. Some lodgers proved unsuitable, such as Lady Audley at Langley priory in 1440, since her twelve dogs caused uproar in the church; although she paid 40s. a year rent for her house and kept it in repair, the bishop insisted on the removal of the dogs. Most lodgers were women who paid for their board and lodging. Some houses attracted considerable numbers, such as the 250 at Carrow priory between the late fourteenth century and c. 1450.[69]

Contacts with lodgers and family brought a worldly element into the nunnery. On the whole, however, the relationship between nunnery and locality was beneficial to both sides. Laypeople received confraternity, prayers and burial. Anne Harling enjoyed confraternity at Syon and several East Anglian houses, including Blackborough, Bruisyard, Campsey Ash, Carrow, Marham and Shouldham. Alice Ewer, the widow of John Ewer, an esquire attached to Barking Abbey, chose to be buried in the nuns' cemetery next to her husband. Margaret, widow of Sir John Stapilton, wanted to be buried in the priory church of St Clement's, York; she left money to the convent for food on the day of her burial, and a silver and part-gilt salt-cellar to the prioress, which was to pass from one prioress to the next. She also provided for a fit and honest chaplain to celebrate mass for her and her husband's souls in the nunnery church for a year after her death. The nuns were to sing the requiem mass on the eighth day after her death, each receiving 3s. 4d.[70]

When they were buried elsewhere, men and women might still leave bequests in return for prayers. Thomas, earl of Warwick, in 1369 left his daughter, Margaret, a nun at Shouldham, a ring, a cup with a cover, and forty marks, and his granddaughter, Katherine, also at Shouldham, a gold ring and £20. Margaret Teye, a member of the Essex gentry, was buried in St John's Abbey, Colchester, but left embroidered cloths to the abbess of Barking to pray for her soul and those of her friends, and money to the chaplains and convent to hold a solemn dirge and mass for her and her husband's and all her friends' souls. An indenture of 1352 gave details of the celebration of John Goudlyne's obit at Lacock on 3 August every year. The full funeral service and requiem mass were to be sung, and each nun was to say the seven penitential psalms with the litany. John's soul was to be especially commended on other days among Lacock's benefactors, as recorded in their book of obits.[71]

In return for their religious and social services, the nuns relied on the support of neighbours, kindred and friends. This is shown dramatically at Crabhouse in the time of Prioress Joan Wygenale (1420–45), who rebuilt much of the priory with the help of her cousin, Edmund Perys, parson of Watlington, and, after his death in 1427, of another cousin, Master John Wygenale, parson of Oxburgh. By 1427 she had rebuilt the barn, built her own chamber, and enclosed the priory with a wall. She then decided to demolish the church, which was rebuilt and refurnished. After 1427 she rebuilt the hall and constructed a new malt-house. This burnt down in 1432 but was rebuilt on a bigger scale with a dovecote. The bakehouse was repaired and enlarged. The church tower was heightened. The dormitory, which was probably the original one, was in a bad state of repair in 1435 and the prioress feared that the sisters would be injured, so it was taken down and rebuilt over a period of seven years. Farm buildings were reconstructed. The work was complete in 1444. Crabhouse's benefactors received the nuns' prayers and religious services. Edmund Perys was buried there, as were the parents of Master John Wygenale. Another benefactor, William Harald, who paid for the lead to roof the church, was buried in the Lady Chapel. Money was bequeathed to pray for the souls of Edmund Eyton, John Watson and Stephen Yorke. The Trinity guild which met in the church also gave money.[72]

Over a period of nearly one thousand years, the role played by nunneries changed in conformity with contemporary ideas and expectations. Family and locality were important to the nuns over the whole period, although in different ways. Abuses occurred from time to time in individual houses and were handled to a large extent by the visitations. It would be unrealistic to expect that high standards would always be maintained or an ideal religious life achieved. Throughout the period, women were living a devotional life but were not divorced from the world. Yet, in the later middle ages, many nunneries were following a humdrum existence compared to the Continent. There is no parallel to the women saints who numbered about one-quarter of all the canonisations in the thirteenth, fourteenth and fifteenth centuries. Many emanated from Italian houses, some of them nuns, others, like St Catherine of Siena, attached to convents as members of a third order. Mysticism flourished among Dominican nuns in Germany and at the convent of Helfta in Saxony.[73] In contrast, the two English women mystics, Julian of Norwich and Margery Kempe of King's Lynn, followed the life of anchorite and laywoman.

The life of the nun did not suit all religious women and some preferred solitary, although not necessarily isolated, lives as hermits and anchoresses.[74] The service by which the anchoress was enclosed in her cell included part of the funeral service. She was regarded as dead to the world and ready to devote the rest of her life to prayer and contemplation. Such a step entailed careful preparation and became more regulated in the later middle ages. In 1435 Beatrice Franke, a nun of

Stainfield in Lincolnshire who wished to become an anchoress at the parish church of Winterton, was examined before her enclosure, and the people of Winterton were asked for their agreement.[75] It was important to safeguard the anchoress's maintenance. Her cell was usually attached to a church, with a window overlooking the altar so that she could participate in mass and a window looking out into the world. Although she was exhorted not to gossip, she had the opportunity to counsel laypeople.

Anchoresses were dead to the world but still valued by society, and they were patronised by kings, nobles, gentry and merchants, as well as by churchmen. They are found throughout the middle ages and many presumably went unrecorded. Seventy-three anchoresses have been identified in the diocese of Norwich and this is in all probability not the full number.[76] Documentary references are usually sparse and short but go back to the early period; the sister of Guthlac of Crowland being an anchoress at Peakirk came to his burial in 714. Margery Kempe consulted Julian of Norwich in 1413 as to her visions and tears, and many others probably sought more mundane advice. Bequests in wills testify to the reputation of anchoresses. Elizabeth Lady Darcy in 1412 left 6s. 8d. to the anchoress at Mansfield and 13s. 4d. to the anchoress at Kneesall, both in Nottinghamshire. Beatrice Lady Roos left 40s. each to the anchoress of Leake and the anchoress of Nun Appleton.[77]

The advice given to anchoresses varied over time. Goscelin of St-Bertin wrote his *Liber Confortarius* for Eve, who had been brought up from childhood at Wilton but left *c.* 1080 to become a recluse at Angers. He envisaged a religious life based on prayer and wide reading, a tribute to Wilton's cultural achievement in the eleventh century. The works recommended included the Desert Fathers, late classical histories, and *On the Consolation of Philosophy* by Boethius. No other writer recommended this amount or standard of reading. Aelred of Rievaulx, writing in the early 1160s at the request of his sister, produced a work which enjoyed wide influence. He based the life of the anchoress on the Rule of St Benedict, and gave his sister advice on her food, clothing and daily routine. He saw reading as a way into meditation and into Cistercian spirituality.

The *Ancrene Wisse*, a treatise written in the west midlands in the early thirteenth century for a group of three women living as anchoresses, also became influential in monasteries and the lay world. Although influenced by Aelred, it was very much a product of its time and its emphasis on penance reflected the work of the Fourth Lateran Council. The author was concerned to plan the structure of the anchoress's external life so as to enable her to concentrate on the inner life of the heart. He therefore laid down details of largely vegetarian meals, warning the women to eat enough to sustain life and not to fast on bread and water without the permission of their confessor. Visitors, even visits from family, were discouraged. The anchoress was allowed to have a maid, and a pet cat, but was expected to live frugally on alms. She was allowed to sell what she made, presumably from sewing, but was not to set up a business. Her clothes, shoes and bed-coverings were to be plain, warm and well made but she was not to wear jewellery. She was not to teach children and was warned not to gossip. These practical details provided the outer framework of her life, but most of the treatise concentrates on her inner life and control of the senses, eschewing temptation, and going to confession and performing penance. Devotions were to be performed throughout the day.[78] In contrast to Goscelin, there is no expectation that reading and study would be part of daily life, nor is there any idea of a spiritual union with Christ as found with the thirteenth-century German mystics.

Mysticism was much more in evidence in the fourteenth and fifteenth centuries.[79] The Yorkshire mystic Richard Rolle lived as a hermit at Hampole in the first half of the fourteenth century and acted as spiritual guide to the Cistercian nunnery there. Two of his works, *The Commandment* and *The Form of Living*, were written for the nun, Margaret Kirkby, the latter when she was preparing to become an anchoress in 1348. Rolle focused on the love of Jesus and the love of the soul for God. Margaret was urged to concentrate on the vision of Christ with her whole heart, and to meditate on Christ's suffering and death so as to purify herself: the fire of love would burn away sin, rescuing her from temptation.[80]

The best-known anchoresses in medieval England were Christina of Markyate (d. *c.* 1160) and Julian of Norwich (d. after 1416). They were very different. Christina is known through her *Life*, written by a monk of St Albans, which describes the difficulties she had to overcome before living her life as a recluse.[81] Christina, or Theodora as she was originally called, was born into a leading family in Huntingdon. She was attractive and her parents planned her marriage to Burhred. The betrothal took place but she refused to consummate the marriage, saying that she had taken a vow of chastity on a visit to the abbey of St Albans. The result was stalemate, since Burhred refused to release her. After a time, she escaped from home and lived as a recluse with an anchoress at Flamstead, and then moved to the hermitage of Roger of St Albans at Caddington. Roger died in 1122 and about the same time Burhred released her from her betrothal. Her difficulties were not completely over, but she was consecrated as a recluse and remained connected with St Albans, where she exerted influence over Abbot Geoffrey. Others joined her, and in 1145 she became head of a Benedictine priory at Markyate. Christina's experiences bring out the depth of women's vocations in the twelfth century, together with the amount of family pressure which could be brought on a girl to marry and the importance attached to the family's local reputation. She may not have been able to read and her religious life probably comprised recitation of and meditation on the psalter. The St Albans Psalter, produced for her at St Albans about 1120, would have enabled her to meditate on the life of Christ, the life of St Alexius and on the other stories illustrated, helping to deepen her religious devotion.

In many respects, Julian of Norwich stands in strong contrast to Christina. Little is known about her, apart from what she touches on in her *Revelations of Divine Love*. At about the age of thirty, in 1373, she suffered from a serious illness and it was thought that she was about to die. While she was ill, she had a series of visions centred on Christ and his crucifixion and these she put together in the shorter version of the *Revelations*; the longer version was considerably later, probably the result of her meditations as an anchoress. Her concern with the sufferings of Christ is typical of the late middle ages and her description is vivid. Through visualising the suffering, she was given a vision of the all-embracing love of God and the conviction that because of God's love everything would be well. She saw men and women as finding peace through union with God; because of God's nature, he is both Father and Mother, and nourishes and feeds mankind. Although this idea was expressed in the early church, it is not found in medieval England before Julian. Her reputation was probably limited to Norwich and Norfolk;

only one fifteenth-century manuscript survives of the short version, and three post-Reformation manuscripts of the longer version of the *Revelations*.[82]

In view of the importance attached to private religious practice among late medieval nobles, gentry and townspeople, it is significant that the other famous woman mystic of the fifteenth century was Margery Kempe, born about 1373 into the urban elite of King's Lynn and married to John Kempe. She lived the life of a working wife and mother. After about twenty years of marriage, and the birth of fourteen children, she wanted to live a life of chastity but her husband was unwilling to consent. In the end he agreed, in return for Margery's promise to pay his debts. Margery still regarded herself as responsible for him and nursed him when he was old and senile. Margery had a vision of Christ when she was suffering from post-natal depression after the birth of her first child, but her life as a visionary really began once she embarked on her life of chastity. Her visions centred on the life of Christ, of the Virgin Mary swaddling Jesus and of his presentation in the Temple at Jerusalem, and she experienced a mystic marriage to Christ when in Rome in 1414. She journeyed widely on pilgrimage in England, the Continent and the Holy Land. Although she had the support of some religious figures, she provoked resentment and unpopularity. Early on, she was accused of Lollardy at Canterbury, an understandable charge in view of the tensions at the time. In King's Lynn, one friar refused to allow her to attend his sermons and her outbursts of weeping disturbed fellow-worshippers. Her companions on foreign pilgrimages found her difficult and she was often left in the lurch. It was only towards the end of her life that her religious insights were appreciated, as seen in her admission to Lynn's Trinity Guild in 1438. She was illiterate but knew of later medieval mystical works. Her contemporary influence was small, however; she dictated her experiences but the work was lost and only rediscovered in 1934.[83]

The experiences of religious women in the middle ages were diverse. In spite of the views of the church on women and chastity, they played an important part in the conversions of England and Germany, and were often in the forefront of religious, political and cultural affairs in the Anglo-Saxon period especially. Throughout the middle ages, whether as nuns or anchoresses, women had an important role in their neighbourhood and with their families. Their religious practice over-lapped with the lay world as their contacts with nobles, gentry and townspeople show. It remains to see how the majority of laywomen viewed their responsibilities towards their neighbours and their involvement with their parish church.

9

Charity and Lay Religion

From the time of the Conversion, religious practice centred on the Christian church, owing allegiance to the pope at Rome. Pagan sites and festivals were adapted to the new religion. Pagan practices, however, persisted; it was not until 640 that Eorcenberht ordered the destruction of pagan idols in Kent, and the Sutton Hoo ship burial displays both pagan and Christian elements. Pagan practices continued to be regularly condemned by churchmen and presumably went underground as the church gained a stronger grip on the country.[1] Heathen Vikings who settled in the east and north in the ninth and early tenth centuries were quickly converted. Links with Rome existed from early on and were strengthened with the development of canon law and the growth of ecclesiastical jurisdiction in the twelfth and thirteenth centuries. Unlike certain parts of Europe, England was unaffected by heresy well into the later middle ages; it was only from the late fourteenth century that the authorities faced the Lollard heresy in certain parts of the country. The majority of the population, however, remained orthodox and fifteenth- and early-sixteenth-century evidence indicates that religion in the parish churches was flourishing.

For laywomen of all social groups, there were two overlapping elements in Christian practice: worship of God and love of one's neighbour, as laid down in the Golden Rule of the Gospels.[2] All men and women were expected to engage in charity in accordance with their own ability and local need. Medieval charity did not only comprise the relief of the poor but gifts to religious men and women and to pilgrims; benefactions to nuns, already discussed, were also regarded as a form of charity. The manumission of slaves in the period down to the twelfth century was regarded as a charitable act as was the repair of roads and bridges, and the relief of prisoners.

Charity implied a mutual relationship. Help was given in return for

prayers, and the prayers of the poor were considered particularly effica-
cious. Charity was essentially in private hands, most being given by
individuals, although by the end of the middle ages some help was given
by parish churches and guilds. This meant that charity was selective and
much depended on those in authority in the community. In the late
thirteenth and early fourteenth centuries, leyrwite was often levied on
poor women among the unfree peasantry and unmarried mothers were
sometimes excluded from receiving alms. Before 1500, local courts leet
were taking a strong line against those whom they regarded as undeserving, including single women and prostitutes, gamblers and
drunkards.[3] This attitude became more marked in the Tudor period. In
a large city, such as London, the poor might sink without trace. Poverty
was widespread in the middle ages but it is essential to distinguish
between different degrees of poverty. Many families were struck by temporary poverty because of the death of father or mother, a bad harvest
or a slump. Others lived permanently near to destitution and picked up
work if and when it was available. Children and old and disabled people were especially vulnerable, as were widows with young children;
these groups were often singled out for charitable bequests in later
medieval wills.

Some medieval people attempted to tackle these problems through
the foundation of hospitals and almshouses, many of the hospitals being
for the old and the long-term sick or for lepers who were segregated
from society. The evidence for hospitals goes back to the years after the
Norman Conquest. They were established as religious houses, often following the Augustinian rule, and the inmates were expected to pray for
their benefactors. Women worked as sisters in the hospitals. Queens
were responsible for some of the foundations; Matilda of Boulogne
founded the hospital of St Katherine by the Tower of London in 1147,
with a master and brothers and sisters, to care for thirteen poor people,
and Eleanor of Castile converted the foundation in 1273 into an
almshouse for a master, priests, brothers and sisters, and eighteen poor
bedeswomen and six scholars. Another London hospital, St Mary without Bishopsgate, was established in 1197 by Walter and Rosia Brune. It
was refounded in 1235 and in 1303 had a prior, twelve canons, five brothers and seven sisters; there were 180 beds in 1535.[4] Such a structure was
typical, although many foundations were smaller. The largest hospital in

England, the Augustinian St Leonard's at York, was staffed by a master, thirteen canons and eight sisters, while St Giles's hospital in Norwich had, according to its statutes of *c.* 1257, a master, four priests, two clerks, four lay brothers and three or four women to care for thirty or more infirm poor.[5] Although these hospitals continued to the Dissolution, many collapsed because of insufficient endowments and in some cases were refounded.

The spiritual care of the patient was regarded as paramount. The sisters provided physical care and their work was certainly tough. No hospital had a paid medical staff until Henry VII founded the Savoy hospital in 1505, with a paid physician, surgeon and apothecary.[6] Probably at least some of the sisters had or gained medical skills; a Sister Anne, 'medica', is referred to at St Leonard's, York, in 1276, and at St Giles's hospital in Norwich the sisters had their own garden where they could grow herbs. According to the St Giles's hospital statutes, the women were to be aged about fifty and to be 'of good life and honest conversation'. They were to care for the sick and change the sheets and bedclothes as needed, to attend divine service and follow the rule of St Augustine. They wore white tunics, grey cloaks and black veils and lived within the hospital, eating and sleeping in their own house, which no one else was to enter without the master's permission. The women owed obedience to the master and they and the brothers were to take a vow of chastity and own no property.[7] The desire to safeguard the women's chastity is apparent in the hospitals, as in the nunneries.

According to visitations, some sisters were badly treated and given inadequate food and clothing, as at St Bartholomew's hospital in London in the early fourteenth century and at St Mary's without Bishopsgate in 1431. The brothers and sisters at St Leonard's, York, complained in 1287 that they were receiving less food than earlier on; the meat which was served three times a week no longer included mutton, and the beef and pork were of poorer quality than before. By 1287 they were given money for their clothes but the poor complained that they no longer received the old ones.[8] During the fourteenth and fifteenth centuries, the sisters in some hospitals were no longer responsible for physical care and this was entrusted to servants and corrodians. The change took place at St Leonard's, York, by 1364 and in several London hospitals by the early fifteenth century, while maids took the place of lay brothers at St Leonard's by 1450. Laywomen replaced sisters at St John's hospital in Oxford by 1390.[9] The sisters might still have had supervisory duties but often no longer carried out the gruelling physical work.

What of the female inmates? In addition to the poor, aged and chronically sick, who presumably benefited from regular meals and cleanliness, some hospitals catered for pregnant women. St Bartholomew's hospital in London cared for unmarried mothers for some time after the birth of the baby. In the event of the mother's death, the hospital brought up and educated the child. The hospitals of St Mary without Bishopsgate and St Thomas in Southwark also looked after women in childbirth and the former provided for orphans. Provision for pregnant women was also found in provincial towns, as in St John's hospital in Oxford and St Paul's in Norwich. Women lepers were also catered for, the hospital of St Nicholas in York being founded for lepers in the early twelfth century. By 1300 all the inmates were women.[10]

Many of the older hospitals faced economic problems after the Black Death, largely because of the fall in rents, and there were also difficulties due to fraud and maladministration. They turned to corrodies as a means of improving their finances. This met a social demand for a place in the hospital where those who could afford it could end their days in security, a demand which is also reflected in the foundation of almshouses in the late middle ages. In return for a sum of money, the corrodian was guaranteed food and sometimes lodging in old age. Corrodies were purchased by men or women or a married couple. Although the money paid for the corrody was welcome, the long-term maintenance of corrodians created financial problems, even though they might work in the hospital or kitchen or at spinning and carding wool. Between 1392 and 1409 at St Leonard's hospital, York, the average minimum life expectancy for a female corrodian was 10.7 years, as against 8.1 years for men. The minor corrodians, or livery-holders, at St Leonard's were fed by the hospital kitchen and lived either in their own homes or in housing provided by the hospital. A corrody at St Leonard's cost at least £20 and most were more than £40; they usually supported a married couple with one or two servants. Women paid about the same amount to become sisters. Some women were admitted as corrodians by royal demand, such as Matilda de Weston, rendered destitute after her husband was killed by the Scots.

The most expensive corrody cost £81 and was secured by John de Cundall and his wife in 1394. They were to receive food every week: fourteen of the better white loaves and six other loaves, eight gallons of the better ale and six of the ordinary ale, and 12*d*. in money to purchase food from the kitchen; each year they were to be allocated a bushel of salt, a bushel of oaten flour, a stone of candles, and 10,000 turves and three cartloads of wood for fuel. John was to receive a suit of livery as a yeoman of the hospital once a year. If his wife survived him, she was to receive half the amount of food and fuel, but not the livery. [11]

Women continued to bequeath money to hospitals in the fourteenth and fifteenth centuries, as when Katherine Peverel in 1375 left 6*s*. 8*d*. each to the hospitals of St James, Chichester; St Katherine, Shoreham; St Nicholas, Lewes; and St James near Seaford. [12] The emphasis, however, was very much on benefactions to almshouses, which were established by rich merchant families and the landed elite. Cecily Plater founded a maison dieu in St Andrewgate at York, and York women gave a high priority to bequests to maisons dieu and almshouses, such as Margaret Kirkham who left 20*d*. to each maison dieu in the city. [13] On a grander scale, William de la Pole and Alice Chaucer, duke and duchess of Suffolk, founded God's House at Ewelme in 1437 for two priests and thirteen poor men. These were to pray for Henry VI and the founders during their lifetimes and their souls after death; they were also to pray for the souls of the king's ancestors, and for the parents, friends and benefactors of the duke and duchess, and for all the faithful departed. Margaret Lady Hungerford completed but modified her father-in-law's foundation of Heytesbury hospital in Wiltshire. The 1472 foundation was for a warden (the chaplain), twelve poor men and one woman. Mass was to be celebrated every day in Heytesbury parish church for the king and queen, the Hungerford family and others, as well as for all the faithful departed. [14] The emphasis on male inmates reflects the contemporary trend.

In addition to gifts to hospitals and almshouses, women engaged in individual acts of charity and collaborated in the fundraising for their parish church. They were aware of the prospect of hell for those who committed the deadly sins and failed to do good works; hell was graphically depicted in paintings of the Last Judgement in parish churches. Contemporary needs evoked a practical response and for many women charity comprised an extension of their work as housewives. Many carried out good works in their daily lives, exemplified by the church's teaching on the seven works of mercy. These were derived from Christ's parable of his Second Coming, when those who had performed good works would be separated from those who had not and be welcomed into the kingdom of heaven, while those who had done nothing would be condemned to eternal punishment.[15] The works were listed as feeding the hungry, giving drink to the thirsty and hospitality to the stranger, clothing the naked, and visiting the sick and prisoners. To these was added the burial of the dead. Housewives were able to offer hospitality, help their neighbours with childcare and in cases of illness, and keep an eye on the aged. As they moved round the village or town to chat to their neighbours or to make purchases, women were in a good position to find out how other families were faring.

Church ales and help ales called on women's skills as brewers and probably existed from the Anglo-Saxon period onwards. Historians have focused most attention on the church ale as raising money for the parish church, but they were also held to tide neighbours over a crisis, or to provide money for a couple when they married or when a child was born. Conviviality and enjoyment were combined with fundraising. In an age when poverty could strike suddenly, the help provided by an ale could prove invaluable. It is probable, however, that neighbours were selective in those whom they chose to help.[16]

It was not only the elite who made charitable bequests to the church and the poor. It was usual to leave money to the parish church, often for tithes forgotten. Bequests were made to the friars much more often than to monks or nuns, and also to the poor, although this latter trend became more marked in the sixteenth century. Taking examples from less well-off testators in fifteenth-century Suffolk, Agnes Ide of Glemsford in 1421 left 6s. 8d. for tithes forgotten, 10s. to the friars of Clare, and 3s. 4d. each to the friars of Babwell, Cambridge and Sudbury. Margaret Boole left money to the nuns of Thetford and Redlingfield (her daughter was a nun there) and to the friars at Thetford and Babwell. Isabel Fysch of Worlington provided that money from the sale of her lands was to be used for her funeral, payment of her debts and legacies, with the residue divided equally between the fabric of the parish church, road-mending, relief of the poor and the celebration of masses.

Margery Muryell of Hawstead left 10s. to be spent on local roads, and the residue of her goods was to be used 'wisely' in deeds of charity. Mariola Wedyrdene of Bildeston left 6d. each to the poor of the town. [17]

The wills and household accounts of the elite show a similar pattern of carrying out works of mercy in the course of their daily lives and a concern for the needs of the locality. Just as minster or parish priests encouraged charity among their congregations, so women of the elite were advised by their chaplains and confessors. Some of the charitable work of Margaret de Brotherton, duchess of Norfolk, originated as penances laid down by her confessor, such as the repair of roads and bridges near her castle at Framlingham. [18] Some charitable concerns changed over time, although the relief of the poor is found throughout the middle ages. Æthelgifu in her will of 980–90 left gifts to the church in return for prayers and masses and freed a number of her slaves, including her goldsmith and his family, and the priest at Langford, Bedfordshire, who was to hold his church for life provided that he kept it in repair and celebrated three masses a week for her husband and herself. [19]

Bequests to religious houses are found before and after the Conquest, but references to manumission ceased with the disappearance of slavery. Concern for the poor continued, however, as in the Bristol will of Alice Hayle of 1261, who wanted her household goods and clothes, and one sow and three piglets, sold to raise money for religious services and the poor for the benefit of her soul and those of all the faithful departed. [20] Later wills continue to mention almsgiving, sometimes to be arranged by the executors after all legacies had been distributed. Katherine Peverel made such an arrangement for the benefit of her soul and those of her two husbands. Many women of the elite wanted the poor as mourners at their funerals so as to gain the benefit of their prayers.

Testators tended to become more selective in their almsgiving in the fourteenth and fifteenth centuries, either by specifying particular places or categories of poor people. Beatrice, Lady Roos, in 1414 left ten marks to be distributed among her tenants, especially the needy in Roos and 'Munkwyk', and £10 to poor tenants in Melbourne, Seaton Ross and Storthwaite. Joan Beauchamp, Lady Abergavenny, was much more lavish in 1435: 100 marks to the poor at her funeral; 200 marks to her poor tenants in England; £100 to the poor in her lordships in the form of clothing, bedding and livestock; £100 towards the marriages of poor girls in her lordships; £100 for roads and bridges; and £40 for the relief of prisoners. She coupled concern for her own estates with groups of people in need. In the distribution of the remainder of her goods in her will of 1355, Elizabeth de Burgh singled out an even greater variety of good causes: poor religious; women who had fallen on hard times; poor gentlewomen burdened with children; poor parish churches which needed better furnishings; poor scholars; the repair of roads and bridges; poor householders and merchants; poor prisoners; and other works of charity for the salvation of her soul. [21]

All noble and gentry households, religious houses and hospitals dispensed alms and food at their gates, and the numbers who were fed could be substantial, such as the 800 fed by Eleanor de Montfort on 14 April 1265. Some noblewomen maintained poor people in their households and some bequests represented a continuation of a lifetime's charity. Katherine de Norwich fed thirteen poor people on bread and herrings in 1336, and Beatrice, Lady Roos, left 6s. 8d. each to seven poor old men of her household. Elizabeth de Burgh's chamber account of 1351–52 shows that, in addition to her almsgiving at the gate, she gave alms to religious and laypeople on her travels, to pilgrims and to children who were baptised in her presence in Clare parish church. A special distribution of bread and herrings to the poor was always made on St Gregory's day, 12 March, the anniversary of the death of her third husband, Roger d'Amory. Like most noblewomen, money was given to the poor on Maundy Thursday and in 1352 fifty poor people were given 9d. each, roughly approximating to her own age, and a further sum was given to the almoner for the poor. Towards the end of her life, disbursements of money were made at her residences. [22]

There is no means of telling the degree to which almsgiving contributed to the relief of the poor. Far more was spent on a lavish lifestyle and conspicuous display than on charity. It was taken for granted that there would always be poor people in society but there was also firm acceptance of the idea that the poor should be helped. Possibly, the help was most effective in villages and small towns where the inhabitants knew each other and where the parish church, guilds and local people provided relief, even if there was a tendency to help those thought to be deserving.

Religious worship focused on the seven sacraments of the church.

These included the principal rites of passage of a woman's life, namely, baptism soon after birth, confirmation, marriage and the anointing of extreme unction just before death. They also comprised the two sacraments of regular religious observance, mass and penance.[23] Although religious observance became more elaborate as the number of churches and priests increased, and people learned more about Christianity, there are threads of continuity linking the Conversion period with the later middle ages. Baptism was emphasised from the start as the initiation into Christianity: by the early eighth century the importance of infant baptism was stressed in royal law codes and by church councils. The discipline of penance was also emphasised, although it is improbable that it could have been enforced among the laity. In its concern for pastoral matters, the council of 'Clofesho' of 747 urged the appointment of priests fit to preach, baptise, celebrate mass on Sundays and holy days, and to teach the Creed and Lord's Prayer in English. These concerns were reiterated in Wulfstan's Canons of Edgar about 1000, when almsgiving, payment of tithes and the abandonment of pagan practices were also prescribed. The need to teach men and women about their faith was widely recognised.[24]

Because of the size of dioceses, only a limited amount of teaching could be given by the bishop at his cathedral. Minster churches grew up, serving a smaller area, sometimes served by monks and nuns, and sometimes by communities of priests. Some of the minsters fostered the cult of a local saint and attracted pilgrims as well as local people, as at Ely and Wimborne. By about 800, the English lowlands were covered with a network of minsters and most places were within about six miles of a church – within walking distance for most people. Attendance at the minster was expected on the great festivals. Parish churches evolved from the second half of the tenth century, when landowners established proprietary churches on their estates and in the towns. They gradually superseded the minsters, although some of the latter survived. The parish system, as it was to last down to the nineteenth century, was virtually complete by about 1200.[25] During the late Anglo-Saxon period, several women are known to have established estate churches. In her two wills of the late tenth or eleventh century, Siflaed endowed her village church at Marlingford, Norfolk, with five acres of land, a meadow, a homestead and two wagon-loads of fuel. She provided for her priest,

Wulfmaer, and his descendants to serve it as long as they were in clerical orders.[26] This was clearly a proprietary church, Siflaed describing it as 'my church' and Wulfmaer as 'my' priest.

Once parish churches were in place, and had become the main focus for the laity's religious worship and teaching, men and women were brought into greater contact with the church and the sacraments. Although the elite and their households generally worshipped in private chapels, licences for chapels usually safeguarded the rights of the parish church and the beneficiary was expected to attend from time to time. In about 1230 Sir William Mauduit was allowed to attend mass in his own chapel because of the difficulty of reaching his parish church of Tillingham, Essex, especially in winter, but he, his wife and household were to attend mass in Tillingham church at Christmas, Easter, Pentecost, and the festivals of the Nativity of St John the Baptist, the Assumption and Nativity of the Virgin Mary, All Saints and St Nicholas.[27] Nobles and gentry also had the money to buy papal privileges, such as the right to choose their own confessor and to have a portable altar. But even women of the higher nobility, such as Elizabeth de Burgh, sometimes worshipped at the parish church, provided for preachers and contributed to the building fund.[28]

Building on the work of earlier councils, the Fourth Lateran Council of 1215 spelled out in detail the practices and way of life expected of the laity. Its work was taken up and furthered by diocesan synods and their statutes, and by confessional and preaching manuals. Bishop Richard Poore, for instance, issued statutes for his diocese of Salisbury in 1217–19, basing them on the Third and Fourth Lateran Councils, and on statutes issued in Paris in the early thirteenth century and by Archbishop Stephen Langton in 1213–14. His statutes discussed the sacraments in detail, explaining how they should be taught and put into practice. He also included statutes on the ornaments of the church and on tithes, which often caused friction between priest and parishioner.[29]

In particular, men and women were expected to take communion at Easter, having gone previously to confession, and four sermons a year were to be preached in every church. Friars provided additional sermons in the towns. The teaching applied to both men and women. Husbands were expected to direct their wives, and parents their children, while wives, in spite of their subordination and supposed irrationality, were expected to use their arts of persuasion to correct the behaviour of their husbands. [30] Parishioners were to be instructed in the faith, in the ten commandments of Moses and the two of the Gospels, and in the seven sacraments, seven works of mercy and the seven deadly sins. The teaching was ethical and moral as well as theological.

The growth of parish churches meant that people encountered more teaching in visual form than formerly . Although much disappeared after the Reformation, enough survives to show what was regarded as important in the later middle ages. The emphasis in depictions of Christ's life was put on His birth and on His suffering, death and resurrection. The saints, and especially the Virgin Mary, were depicted in fresco, stained glass, and on rood screens and pews. Many churches were dominated by a painting of the Last Judgement over the chancel arch, reinforcing the importance of a good life and vividly depicting the peace of the kingdom of heaven contrasting with the tortures of hell. The fifteenth-century seven sacrament fonts of Norfolk and Suffolk may have been designed to reinforce orthodoxy and showed the sacraments in the context of everyday scenes. [31] For the majority of parishioners, the church, even of a poor parish, was the richest and most colourful building they were likely to enter, and the colour of the images was supplemented by the richness of the altar vessels, crosses, vestments and books which every church was expected to have for the celebration of the sacraments.

There is no means of gauging the depth of religious belief and practice, but the evidence points to women making full use of their parish church. The principal service on Sundays and holy days was mass, which men and women were expected to attend, although they were often segregated in different parts of the church. Children also attended but could be noisy. The service was in Latin and in the late middle ages the view of the celebrant was restricted by the rood screen, which shut off the chancel and high altar. The congregation, however, was expected to participate. In her deposition of 1429 against the Lollard heretic Margery Baxter, Joan Clyfland described what she had said to Margery as to what she did every day in church, presumably while attending mass. On entering the church, she genuflected before the cross, said the Lord's Prayer five times in honour of the cross, and the Hail Mary five times in honour of the Virgin Mary. [32]

The *Lay Folks' Mass Book*, originally dating from about 1200, explained the structure of the mass through the priest's movements and actions. Laypeople were expected to be reverent during the service and not cause a disturbance; one man was fined in the deanery of Wisbech for chattering during mass. The congregation was to listen to the priest when he was speaking or chanting, and pray their own prayers when he prayed silently. Prayers were included for the laity, who were expected to know the Creed and the Lord's Prayer. The climax of the service came at the consecration, with the elevation of the host, believed to have been transformed from bread into the body of Christ; this doctrine of transubstantiation had been laid down at the Fourth Lateran Council. Mass brought the whole community together. The congregation was sprinkled with holy water. In the prayers, the priest called on the congregation to pray for all in authority, and for the parish, those in need, the household providing the holy loaf, those who had died recently and the parish benefactors. Before he took communion, the priest kissed the pax which was then kissed by the congregation, symbolising the peace of the community. The holy loaf was blessed at the end of the service, distributed, and taken home with the holy water. At certain times of year a procession of parishioners made offerings of money and food, such as the eggs at Easter. Once a year, the dead were remembered at a requiem mass, when all the names on the parish bede-roll were read. Mass emphasised not only the individual but, the unity and wellbeing of the parish, recalling the wholeness of Christ's sacrifice for mankind.[33]

Men and women took a pride in their parish churches. As it became more usual in the fifteenth century for those lower in the social scale to make wills, so it can be seen that both the wealthy and the less well-off made gifts. Alice Warde of Fornham All Saints, Suffolk, left 6s. 8d. to the fabric of the church, while Margaret Coket in 1462 bequeathed £2 for the repair of Ampton church and its ornaments and four marks towards the repair of Sporle church in Norfolk. The gifts recorded in the 1368 visitations by the archdeacon of Norwich were made by married couples as well as by individuals. At Cawston, Robert and Agnes Starlyng presented a chalice and two red satin copes embroidered with gold leaves. Idonea, widow of Robert de Sparham, gave a 'new and good' missal bound in red leather, while Margaret Hopperlerye gave a 'great and good' psalter. Idonea also gave two new hearse cloths of black worsted, embroidered with the letters *R* and *I* in gold. At the top of the social scale, Alice, duchess of Suffolk, remodelled the chancel of Wingfield church, which contained the tombs of her husband's ancestors.[34]

The records of All Saints church in Bristol are particularly interesting in that they record gifts made during the benefactors' lifetime, showing their degree of commitment during their lives. Gifts consisted of property, money or church furnishings. In the thirteenth century, Alice Hayle gave the tenement called the Green Lattice in the High Street and also made bequests to the church in her will. During the late fifteenth century, when furnishings were becoming more elaborate, wealthy merchants and their wives made generous gifts. Alice, widow of the merchant Henry Chestre (d. 1471), gave a new carved front to the rood altar in the south aisle, with the images of St Anne, St Mary Magdalen, St Giles, St Erasmus and St Anthony, and a new rood loft, carved with numerous images. It is likely that there was considerable consultation before major donations were made. Alice took the advice of the worshipful men of the parish and of the carvers before embarking on her project for the rood loft.[35] It was important to ensure that the plans would be carried through; a case came before the court of the dean and chapter of Lincoln in 1346 where a mother had handed over land to her son, who was to provide a candle to burn before the altar of the Virgin Mary, a condition which was not being met.[36]

Mass centred on Christ's sacrifice for the redemption of mankind and was therefore a service for both the living and the dead. Death and the afterlife were ever-present concerns in the middle ages but the greater prominence given to purgatory from about 1200 led to a great increase in requiem masses for the souls of the dead; it was believed that the time spent in purgatory could be shortened by the prayers of the living. Over time, new devotions were incorporated into the masses. Men and women were concerned for their own salvation as well as for their families, and sometimes for their friends and benefactors, and for all Christians.

Commemoration depended on one's means as well as one's preferences. The best-known form of commemoration was the chantry, providing for daily or weekly masses, first found in the twelfth century but increasingly popular from the thirteenth, and supported by an endowment in land or money. Some were established in perpetuity, others for a term of years.[37] Alternatively, money might be bequeathed for a specific number of masses after the funeral, for trentals or sets of thirty masses, or masses on the anniversary of death. An obit on the anniversary of the funeral involved its re-enactment.

Women took advantage of all these forms of commemoration. Although noblewomen continued to make use of religious houses and many wanted masses celebrated by the friars, the parish church came increasingly to be used. Philippa Mortimer, countess of March (d. 1381), left £200 to her father's abbey of Bisham, where she was buried, on condition that her anniversary was celebrated by the monks for ever. William de la Pole and Alice Chaucer, duke and duchess of Suffolk, founded their chantry chapel in Ewelme parish church, where Alice was buried, next to their almshouse and near their palace. Elizabeth, widow of Sir Thomas Carrewe, founded her chantry in 1451 in the chapel of St Nicholas on the south side of Luppitt parish church in Devon for the souls of herself and her husband, their parents, sons and daughters, and her fellow grantors, whose names were to be displayed above the chantry altar. The chantry was endowed with property in Devon which was put into the hands of feoffees. Elizabeth stipulated that the chaplain was to assist the vicar at the parish mass on Sundays and holy days.[38]

Other arrangements were less lavish. Mary, Lady Roos, who was buried near her husband in the choir of Rievaulx Abbey in 1394, bequeathed £24 for priests to celebrate masses for one year for the benefit of her soul and those of her husband and parents. Jane Prynce of Theydon Garnon in Essex in 1473 arranged for an honest priest to pray for three years for her and her husbands, their parents, friends and all Christian souls. Alice Snapes of Maldon wanted two trentals of masses organised by her executors in 1410. It is unusual to find a daughter's will, but Margaret Wareyn of Long Melford, Suffolk, provided for a chaplain to celebrate masses for her and her father's soul for a year.[39]

Devotion to the saints, and especially to the Virgin Mary, found throughout the middle ages, intensified from the twelfth century. Many noblewomen possessed relics, often of the true cross, and had devotions to particular saints. Rosaries were being used for prayer in the late middle ages and were bequeathed in wills. For women who were literate, psalters and books of hours enabled them to deepen their religious lives and engage in individual devotion. In the fifteenth century, some women owned mystical works, especially in northern England where the contemplative life was strongest. Elizabeth Sewerby possessed works by Richard Rolle, the *Revelations* of St Bridget of Sweden, and works on the life and passion of Christ.[40]

Poorer women expressed their devotion to the saints and hopes of their intercession by leaving money to the lights which burned before the images. At West Ham, Beatrice Fissh (d. 1379) left 12*d.* each to the high altar and St Mary's altar, and 6*d.* each to the altars of Holy Cross and St Nicholas. She bequeathed a kerchief and a silver-gilt clasp to the image of the Virgin Mary. Twenty years later, Alice Billyng left 20*d.* each to the lights of the Virgin Mary, St Nicholas and Holy Cross. In the mid fifteenth century, Joan Barsawers left 12*d.* to the light of the Virgin Mary, as did Alice Grenstede, who also left 2*d.* to the light of St Anne, a cult which was then growing in popularity. Margaret Harlyston bequeathed 12*d.* to the light of the Virgin Mary, 8*d.* to St Nicholas, and 6*d.* to St Christopher, while Christiana Throssher left 4*d.* each for the lights of the Virgin Mary and St Christopher, 2*d.* for the light of St Anne, and 3*d.* for the light of All Saints.[41]

Religious guilds and confraternities provided for intercession and commemoration for men and women who could not afford individual masses.[42] A few guilds are found in the Anglo-Saxon period, but they proliferated in the fourteenth and fifteenth centuries, providing for funerals, anniversary masses, charity, and social and recreational activities. They catered for both the living and the dead. Most guilds were open to men and women, the women often joining with their husbands; in East Anglia at the end of the middle ages, women may well have constituted at least one-third of total membership. Some guilds required entry fines and all expected regular fees to maintain lights, chaplains and charitable payments. In addition, offerings might be expected at masses.[43] The poor were thus precluded from membership but all other social groups were included.

The fraternity of Holy Trinity in the church of St Botolph without Aldersgate in the City of London was founded in 1374 when each brother was to offer one penny to maintain thirteen tapers round the Easter Sepulchre. Within a few years, because of the growth of the fraternity, each brother was to pay 12*d.* a year to maintain the lights and support the guild chaplain. Lists of members in the guild register show that some paid considerably more.[44] Married couples and women on their own, probably widows, were among the members.

Although women were accepted as members and sometimes founded guilds, they seldom held office, just as it was very rare for a woman to serve as churchwarden of the parish church, a reflection on women's subordination in the medieval world. When Holy Trinity guild at St Botolph's was refounded in 1446, two men and one woman were named as founders, the woman being Dame Joan Asteley, formerly nurse of Henry VI.[45] Women were involved in the foundation of some of the Cambridgeshire guilds. Occasionally women are mentioned as holding guild stock. Alice Spenser, who with her husband had helped to found St Christopher's guild at March in 1472, was holding stock in the early 1480s. Women might also serve as guardians of a particular light. At St Thomas's church in Launceston, women served as officers of All Hallows guild only in 1491 and 1497.[46]

Parish guilds reflected the local social hierarchy and included men and women of different status, as with the Holy Trinity guild at St Botolph's without Aldersgate. Most of the members lived locally and probably few were wealthy. Brewers comprised the largest group of tradesmen who can be identified. Of the 667 members between 1377 and 1463, seventy were clergy. The prioress of Clerkenwell nunnery entered the guild in 1402–3. Some members of the nobility also joined, such as William and Joan, Lord and Lady Willoughby, and William and Margaret, Lord and Lady Roos, in 1408–9.[47] A few urban confraternities gained a nationwide reputation and attracted noble and gentry members as well as their own townspeople. The guild of Holy Trinity at Coventry attracted some of the leading nobles of the realm and it was usual for the wife to join as well as the husband. The same was true of the Corpus Christi guild at York, the late medieval festival of Corpus Christi becoming popular after about 1350. A widow, Alice Neville, Lady FitzHugh, joined in 1473, soon after the death of her husband, and her children, Richard, Roger, Edward, Thomas and Elizabeth, joined at the same time. Other well-known northern families, such as the Scropes, Constables and Parrs, were members of the guild.[48]

Many parishes had several guilds dedicated to a variety of saints and some had guilds for particular age and gender groups. In Cornwall,

Bodmin had its guilds for maidens and young men, St Neot, North Petherwin and Poughill guilds for young men, Stratton and West Looe for maidens, and St Neot and Poughill for wives. Women's guilds grew up in the late fifteenth century and enabled women to combine in fundraising, worship and social activities, in addition to their individual jobs in church of washing and cleaning. These guilds were concentrated in the south and west, especially in Devon and Cornwall. Many had a special devotion to the Virgin Mary, the maidens of St Ewen's church in Bristol, for instance, raising money for her light. Other female saints were venerated, and the maidens of St Margaret's church, Westminster, had a special role in the parish procession on the feast of St Margaret.[49]

It was the responsibility of each guild to devise its statutes, specifying its religious observance and charity. The main focus was on the mass, but the inquiry into guilds of 1389 points to considerable variety. At Maldon in Essex, members paid ¼d. a week to support the chaplain and pay for five candles to burn before the image of the Virgin Mary at high mass and the mass of the Virgin on Sundays and feast days. One requiem mass was held each week, and a calendar of obits was to be kept. Each brother was to be remembered at his year's mind, and all brothers and sisters were to say the psalter of the Virgin Mary three times a year, praying for the living and the dead. The guild of Corpus Christi at Grantham, Lincolnshire, was established about 1339 by the devotion of the townsmen. Brothers and sisters joined in the Corpus Christi procession and each made a voluntary offering at the mass. Afterwards, they ate together and each married couple gave food to a poor man; the guild also gave food to the friars. The guild chaplain celebrated a daily mass at the altar of Corpus Christi. It was noted that the members had recently collected two marks for church ornaments. Here the guild combined religion, charity and enjoyment.[50]

Both guilds and parish churches catered for social as well as religious life. Although the prospect of purgatory and depictions of the Last Judgement and Hell cast an element of fear over medieval religion, there was also time for recreation and fun. The numerous guildhalls built in the fifteenth century provided a place for meetings and also for refreshments or feasts after funerals, obits or guild assemblies. The church's year combined fasting and celebration, the solemnity of the mass and entertainment. Guilds held processions as well as their feasts, such as the

Bodmin Riding which was held in early July on the Sunday and Monday after the feast of St Thomas of Canterbury. Ale was sold on the Sunday to raise money, and on the Monday the prior of Bodmin presented a garland. The procession then moved from the priory to the end of the town, where there were games and sports.

The guild of St Helen at Beverley held its procession on the saint's feast day. It was led by a fair young man dressed as the saint, accompanied by two old men, one carrying a spade and the other a cross; this symbolised St Helen's discovery of the true cross in Jerusalem. The sisters of the guild followed the saint, walking two by two, then the brothers and finally the aldermen of the guild. When the procession reached the Franciscan church, where the guild was based, mass was celebrated at St Helen's altar. The guild then had a meal of bread, cheese and beer.[51]

Although all churches celebrated the major feasts, their calendars of celebrations varied. In the early sixteenth century, Great Dunmow, a small market town in Essex, celebrated Plough Monday at the start of the farming year in January, May Day and the feast of St Andrew on 30 November; the celebrations were as much secular as religious. The Lord of Misrule presided over dancing at Christmas, and the Corpus Christi play was put on for the town and the surrounding villages. At Long Melford in Suffolk there were processions on Palm Sunday and at Corpus Christi, and on three days at Rogationtide to beat the bounds of the parish; food and drink was supplied each day. There were bonfires and tubs of ale, and sometimes food, on Midsummer Eve (23 June), the Eve of Saints Peter and Paul (28 June), St James's Eve (24 July), and St Thomas's Eve (20 December).[52] Many of the outdoor festivities took place in the spring and summer. Presumably all parishioners could take part, although women are unlikely to have been involved in the organisation. The inversion of the social order, with the Lord of Misrule or the Boy Bishop at Christmas, provided an opportunity to let off steam. Many parishes celebrated the late medieval festival of Hocktide on the second Monday and Tuesday after Easter, when the women held men to ransom, reversing their usual subordination.

Pilgrimage combined devotion to a particular saint as intercessor and miracle worker with the carrying out of a penance, the desire to secure salvation, possibly the search for a cure, and the opportunity to travel and get away from everyday routine. Many women went on pilgrimage on their own behalf or for others throughout the middle ages. There was some prejudice against female pilgrims, and in later medieval Rome they were not allowed to visit certain chapels in the basilicas of St John Lateran and St Peter. It is likely that many more people went on pilgrimage than are recorded and that the majority visited local shrines, close to their homes; the shrine of Henry VI at Yarmouth, first mentioned in 1485–86, received offerings of 22s. 8d. in that year.[53] The popularity of shrines waxed and waned over the middle ages. New ones grew up round the tomb of a particular holy person or image, but the centralisation of the church and the development of a formal procedure for canonisation of saints meant that unofficial shrines were often regarded as suspect in the later middle ages. Simon de Montfort, Thomas of Lancaster and Henry VI were never officially canonised, although in their time they attracted large numbers of pilgrims.

Women were attracted to recognised and unofficial shrines. In the late fourteenth century, women were admitted to see the miracle-working crucifix at Meaux Abbey in Yorkshire in the hope that this would increase devotion, but were stopped when it was found that they strayed into the cloister and conventual buildings.[54] Early in the century, the bishop of London ordered an inquiry into the miracles which were reported at Ashingdon parish church in Essex and were attracting huge crowds. He wanted the image approved if veneration was to continue. In fact, nothing further is heard of it and the shrine was probably closed down. A local cult at Whitstone in Cornwall was investigated about the same time.[55]

Some early shrines, such as that of St Cuthbert at Lindisfarne and then at Durham, were always attractive to pilgrims. The same is true of the shrine of St Æthelthryth at Ely. In the later middle ages, her cult was especially popular in the Fens and women bequeathed gold rings to the shrine in the fifteenth century. St Cuthberga was the patron of the eighth-century nunnery at Wimborne, and in the fifteenth century she was venerated in the parish church on 31 August, when the church was cleaned, the Lady chapel lit and a fair was held in the churchyard. Many gold and silver rings were offered to the saint's image.[56] These saints were seen as having a special relationship with their church and as being protectors of their communities.

The most popular shrines in England in the later middle ages were those of St Thomas Becket at Canterbury and of the Virgin Mary at Walsingham. These drew large numbers of pilgrims from the late twelfth and mid thirteenth centuries respectively. Pilgrims, however, made their own choice of shrines. There were many small shrines dedicated to the Virgin Mary, as seen in the pilgrimages carried out by proxy for Queen Elizabeth of York, at Windsor and Eton, Caversham, Worcester, Northampton, Dover, Barking and elsewhere. In her will of 1440, Isabel Turnour of Sudbury, Suffolk, wanted her daughter, Christine, to go on pilgrimage to Walsingham in her place, so as to fulfil her promise; in return, she was to receive clothing, religious objects and jewellery. Men often expected their proxies to be male, but Nicholas Culpeper in 1434 wanted his wife to complete his promised pilgrimages to Canterbury and Walsingham. Anne Harling, Lady Scrope, divided up the great gold beads of her rosary, laced with crimson and gold silk, leaving ten to the shrine at Walsingham, ten to Our Lady of Pew at St Stephen's chapel, Westminster, ten to the shrine of St Edmund at Bury, and ten to the shrine at Canterbury.[57]

Some women went on pilgrimage abroad with their husbands or on their own, often to Rome or Santiago de Compostella. King Alfred's sister, the wife of Burgred of Mercia, was buried at Pavia, possibly having been on her way to Rome. William of Warenne and his wife, Gundrada, set out for Rome but were unable to get there because of the war between Pope Gregory VII and Henry IV. Santiago was popular among English pilgrims in the later middle ages and in 1434 about fifty ships carried 2,310 pilgrims. Jerusalem was a more unusual goal. Ulf and his wife, Madselin, drew up their will soon after the Norman Conquest before starting for Jerusalem.[58] In 1310 Robert Fitzwalter and his wife were said to be about to start for Jerusalem. Elizabeth de Burgh was dispensed from her vow to go to the Holy Land and Santiago but visited many shrines in England, including Canterbury, Walsingham and Bromholm.[59] The mystic Margery Kempe was an enthusiastic pilgrim, as both a wife and a widow. Among the English shrines that she visited were York, Bridlington and Beverley, Walsingham and Norwich, and the shrine of the Holy Blood at Hailes. She went to Syon, possibly for the Lammas Day indulgence on 1 August. At Norwich she visited the tomb of Richard Caister, vicar of St Stephen's church, who had supported her and her visions. Abroad, she went to the Holy Land in 1413 and visited the shrines in Rome and Assisi on the return journey; she travelled to Santiago in 1417 and to Wilsnack and Aachen in 1433. Her *Book* gives a vivid account of her experiences.[60]

For the Lollards of the late middle ages, the veneration of saints, images, lights, requiem masses and pilgrimages of the late medieval church were anathema, as was the doctrine of transubstantiation at mass. The Lollard heresy derived from the work of John Wycliffe and also from the attitudes of the late fourteenth century, when among both orthodox and heretics there was an emphasis on personal unworthiness and contempt for the body, and a desire for simplicity. Unlike many of her contemporaries, Margaret Courtenay, countess of Devon, specified in 1391 that she wanted a simple funeral.[61] Contempt for the body was most vividly portrayed in the tombs depicting the dead person richly dressed, while underneath the naked body was shown decomposing, as with the tomb of Alice Chaucer at Ewelme.

The Lollard knights of Richard II's reign display a mixture of orthodoxy and heresy, and both literacy and vernacular devotion encouraged personal religious views. Less is known about their wives, but at least one woman agreed with her husband's move from orthodoxy to heresy. About 1400 Sir Thomas Latimer and his wife, Anne, presented a Lollard, Robert Hook, to the living of Braybrooke in Northamptonshire where they resided; two years later, Hook was one of the witnesses and executors of Anne's will. In her will, Anne commended her soul into God's hands, stressing her unworthiness and making no reference to the Virgin Mary or the saints. She provided for her burial at Braybrooke but there is no reference to the funeral or to commemoration. She made several charitable bequests: £2 towards the repair of the chancel and parsonage at Braybrooke; £2 towards the bridge which had been begun by her husband; and £20 to the poor. Small bequests were made to her brother and servants and the residue of her goods was bequeathed to the poor.[62]

With other wives of the Lollard knights, the situation is less clear-cut. Both Alice Sturry and Perrin Clanvow made their wills as widows. Perrin's husband, Sir Thomas, was heir to the prominent Lollard, Sir John Clanvow. In her will of 1422, Perrin Clanvow wanted a simple burial and may have had some heretical material among her religious books. Yet she provided for requiem masses and overall appears to have been orthodox. Possibly her views changed as she grew older. Alice, who was the widow of Sir Richard Sturry and died in 1414, may not have agreed with her husband's religious views. Her will points to orthodoxy in its references to the Virgin Mary and the saints, requiem masses and bequests to monks and friars.[63]

After the Oldcastle rebellion of 1414, relatively little is heard of heresy among the knights and gentry, although it continued to be found occasionally among urban elites. The church focused its attention mainly on craftsmen, artisans and servants in the towns and villages of east and south-east England, London, Yorkshire, the west and parts of the midlands. Investigations were carried out particularly after 1414 and around 1500, but little is heard of heresy in the mid fifteenth century. Beliefs and practices varied. It has been argued that Lollardy gave women greater prominence than they normally enjoyed, but this is apparent in only a few cases.[64] The majority of women found late medieval orthodox religion attractive and related to its practices. Moreover, the tradition of female subordination was deep-rooted. Although some Lollards saw women as having priestly powers and accepted that they could preach, it is improbable that there were Lollard women priests. Yet the Lollard desire to have no intermediary between themselves and God explains why one Norfolk couple considered that any pious man or woman was a priest.[65]

Examinations of heretics, in the diocese of Norwich between 1428 and 1431, in Kent in 1511–12 and in Coventry at the same time, show that Lollardy was based in the household, and that heresy was transmitted within the family and from family to servants. Although not all the members of the household accepted Lollardy, the mistress was the key to the dissemination of ideas in view of her role in the upbringing of her children and supervision of servants. At Coventry in 1511–12, Robert Hachet said in his examination that his wife knew of his secrets and beliefs but did not agree with them. Joan Gest became a heretic during her time in service and introduced her husband to heresy. According to the testimony of the Grebill family of Tenterden in Kent, the father taught his two sons about Lollardy when they were aged about seven. The mother, Agnes, was present and had long held Lollard beliefs. The whole family were Lollards, except possibly for a daughter. Agnes Grebill was the only member of the family who refused to recant. It was usual to examine both husband and wife, not just the head of the household, as in the case of John Godsell, parchment-maker of Ditchingham, Norfolk, and his wife, Sibyl.[66]

Much of the information about grassroots Lollardy comes from these examinations. This has its disadvantages, since the investigation was structured, with set questions to be asked. The answers of the Lollards themselves may easily have been changed to a certain extent. The beliefs expressed focused on certain of the sacraments, especially mass and transubstantiation, on late medieval practices, and on the priesthood and church hierarchy. Sibyl Godsell's answers were on the same lines as her husband's, and typical of other Norfolk heretics. She had little time for the sacraments of baptism, confirmation and penance, and the consent of the parties was sufficient for marriage without solemnisation in church. Only God, not a priest, could forgive sins, and the consecration of the host at mass did not transform the bread into the body of Christ. This denial of transubstantiation undermined the whole importance of the mass which, as already seen, was at the heart of medieval doctrine. Sibyl described the pope as Antichrist and any pious man or woman as a good priest. She did not hold with fasting, images and pilgrimages, and the pious had no need to pay tithes and offerings to churches. These beliefs could be expressed in much more vivid and earthy terms, as in the deposition of Joan Clyfland against Margery, wife of William Baxter, a wright, of Martham. Margery asserted, among other things, that no greater honour should be given to images and crucifix than to the gallows; they were made by lewd wrights and coloured by lewd painters. Regarding pilgrimages, she thought of Thomas of Canterbury as a traitor and heretic, and declared that she would never go as a pilgrim to Mary of Falsyngham, nor to any saint or other place.[67]

Lollards met in their houses to read the Bible and Lollard tracts in English, and women exercised their customary duty of hospitality. Margery Baxter invited Joan Clyfland and her maid to come to her chamber at night and hear her husband read the Scriptures; her husband, she said, was the best teacher of Christianity. Similar meetings were held by other Norfolk Lollards. Women helped Lollard priests and were less suspect as they moved round the county. Margery Baxter knew the condemned heretic, William White, whom she regarded as a saint.

She took him into her home and concealed him for five days, and carried his books from Yarmouth to Martham. She was present when he was burnt at the stake.[68] Women like Margery had their own social networks which they could draw on. Margery Locock of Coventry, wife of Hugh Stubbe and then of Henry Locock, a girdler, talked with heretics during both her marriages and heard Roger Landesdale reading heretical books in his house.[69]

Women therefore played a role for which they were well fitted because of their work and status as housewives. It is rare, however, to find women leading house groups. Alice Rowley, however, was an exception. She married William Rowley, a mercer (d. 1505), who rose to be mayor of Coventry and master of the Trinity guild. Alice continued her husband's business after his death. Her son, Thomas, served on Coventry's common council and as sheriff. Both men were orthodox in their religious beliefs but Alice was a Lollard by about 1491, when she converted Joan Warde to heresy; in 1506, Alice was suspected of heresy but sixteen women swore to her good reputation. Probably she became more active as a heretic after her husband's death. She was literate and had her own books. Juliana Yong recorded her teachings, such as her denial of images and pilgrimages, and of transubstantiation. Alice herself admitted that she had read publicly at Lollard meetings. She was examined in 1511–12 and sentenced to a harsh penance; she also had to watch the burning of Joan Warde.[70]

For most medieval people, religion under the aegis of the church encompassed divine worship and practical charity in the community, the celebration of mass for the living and the dead, the enjoyment of feasts and plays, and the fear of the Last Judgement mitigated by the intercession of the Virgin Mary and the saints. All these are found throughout the social hierarchy. Members of the elite could contribute more by way of patronage, but much of the work on medieval churches and their furnishings was carried out by the accumulation of small sums from men and women. The care of the poor, the sick and orphan children was widespread, even though it was usually carried out informally. Degrees of piety cannot be measured but many medieval people were involved in their church and showed considerable pride in what was achieved. Religious faith and practice combined with local feeling and the importance attached to family in the medieval world.

10

Death

Even if they were well provided for, many women must have been lonely in old age. Many were widows and had lost their children through marriage, migration or death. Joan de Bohun (d. 1419), countess of Hereford, Essex and Northampton, was described at the end of her long life as conducting herself like Anna in the temple at Jerusalem, devoting herself to prayer and meditation.[1] She had been a widow for nearly fifty years and had lost her husband while her two daughters were still children. Both predeceased her, Mary dying in childbirth in 1394 and Eleanor ending her life in 1399; of her two sons-in-law, Eleanor's husband, Thomas, duke of Gloucester, was murdered in 1397, while Henry IV, Mary's husband, died in 1413. She got on well with Henry V, although it is not known how much contact she had with him and his siblings. Eleanor's daughter, Isabella, became a Minoress, her son, Humphrey, and daughter, Joan, died soon after their mother. Only Anne, who married into the Stafford and Bourchier families, survived her grandmother. Joan might well have felt isolated and have had sad memories at the end of her life.

Margaret Cappes spent most of her life in Hornchurch, Essex, and wanted to be buried in the parish churchyard.[2] She died in London towards the end of 1477. Her three daughters had moved away from home, probably when they married. Agnes married John Gardiner, a London citizen and tallowchandler; Joan married William Reynold, a tanner of Stondon Massey; and Alice Grose lived in Maldon. Presumably, Margaret moved to London as a widow to be near one of her daughters. Sons were also likely to move, especially if they were ambitious and upwardly mobile. The son of Agnes Fylour of Bristol became a London mercer and was not best pleased when Alice bequeathed a house to the church of All Saints.[3]

It is likely that Agnes and women like her found the parish church with its varied activities a refuge in old age. They may also have relied on their servants for company or on a circle of women friends. The bequests to other women in many widows' wills testify to such networks. Joan Boleman of Rattlesden, Suffolk, who died in 1440, divided her clothes among four women, left a peck of malt to seven others, while an eighth woman received half a bushel of maslin; one man was bequeathed one bushel of peas and one bushel of malt. Joan had a daughter, Alice, and she and her husband, Robert Legat, were appointed executors and received the residue of her goods.[4] Such female networks might exist during marriage but probably became of greater importance in old age.

The evidence of wills provides the best clue as to women's attitudes and priorities at the end of their lives. Wills cannot give the whole picture as they do not record lifetime giving, and it has to be borne in mind that the testator was often on her death-bed and may have been prompted or forcefully persuaded to make particular bequests. Nevertheless, wills provide a guide and indicate that most women had a similar outlook. Two wills can be taken as throwing light on common interests, both of them orthodox in belief and coming from different parts of the country. Joan Turbeville was the widow of a London citizen and vintner who died in 1433, appointing Joan as his executrix. Joan herself died in 1438.[5] She committed her soul to Almighty God, her creator and saviour, and to the Virgin Mary and all the saints, and wanted to be buried next to her first husband, John Warde, in the church of St Nicholas Cole Abbey in the City. Her funeral was to be carried out immediately after her death, with the whole service of the dead, as was fitting. She left money for prayers, for the fabric of St Nicholas's church and that of St Margaret Pattens, and 3s. 4d. each to the churches of East and West Tilbury in Essex. Ten marks were bequeathed to Simon Berston, described as the little boy living with her, with the money being kept at the Guildhall until he came of age; if he died before that, the money was to be spent on an honest chaplain to celebrate masses for a year in the church of St Margaret Pattens for her soul, the souls of her three husbands (John Warde, Robert Grey and David Turbeville), and the souls of all the faithful departed. Clothes, jewellery and plate were bequeathed to three women, presumably her friends, and 20s. to her servant, Agnes Eley. The rest of her goods were to be disposed of for the

good of her soul. In particular she wanted an honest chaplain to cele-
brate masses for a year after her death in the church of St Nicholas Cole
Abbey, the beneficiaries including herself and her husbands, Matilda
Turbeville, David's daughter, and all the faithful departed.

Joan, the widow of Sir Robert Hilton of Swine in Yorkshire, made her
will in 1432.[6] She described herself as belonging to the Catholic faith
and commended her soul to Almighty God, the Virgin Mary and all
the saints. She planned to be buried in the parish church of Swine, on
the north side of the entrance to the choir, and left a draught animal or
40s. for her mortuary and £6 13s. 4d. to pay for her funeral. 66s. 8d. was
to be distributed to the poor, 20s. was to be spent on the fabric of the
church, and 40s. was bequeathed to the vicar to pray for her soul. 6s. 8d.
was left to each order of friars in Beverley and Hull, 6s. 8d. to the prioress of the nunnery of Swine and 3s. 4d. to each nun, and 40s. to the
nunnery of Nunkeeling. Her beds, clothes and household goods were
divided between her two daughters, Isabella and Elizabeth, a book of
romance was bequeathed to her sister, and a bed and a gold cross to
John Constable of Halsham and his wife; John was appointed supervi-
sor of the will. Her niece, Margaret, the daughter of her brother, Robert
Constable, was bequeathed £13 6s. 8d., clothing, a bed and a book of
romance; Robert was her principal executor and goods and money were
left to him and the other two executors. Other bequests were listed,
some of which may have been to servants. The remainder of her goods
was to be disposed of by her executors for the benefit of her soul and
that of her husband.

Women's wills varied in detail, but these two sum up their priorities
at the end of their lives. Their primary concern was for the fate of their
souls and they wanted a fitting funeral and prayers. With noblewomen,
the funeral was often spectacular and constituted their final piece of lavish display, ensuring that they would be remembered. For her funeral in
Westminster Abbey, where her tomb can still be seen, Eleanor de
Bohun, duchess of Gloucester, wanted her body to be covered by a black
sheet which had a white cross on it and her arms in the middle of the
cross. Her funeral hearse was surrounded by lights at the corners and by
fifteen godfearing, old, poor men, wearing gowns and large hats and carrying torches, who were to stand five at the head and five on each side,
and pray for her soul, her husband's soul, her benefactors, all the living

and the dead and all Christians. In return, they were to be given a pair of shoes, a pair of linen sheets and 20d.[7] Eleanor, like other women, whatever their status, was concerned for her salvation.

The fate of the soul, however, was not women's only concern. They looked beyond themselves to their husbands and family. Many women in the later middle ages chose to be buried next to their husbands, Joan Turbeville choosing burial by her first husband; Jane, the widow of John Prynce, lord of Theydon Garnon in Essex, wanted to be buried by her first husband in the church of St Katherine Cree if she died in London or alternatively by her last husband at Theydon Garnon.[8] The provision of prayers for the husband's soul was also widespread. Children usually received the bulk of the personal bequests and women's wills often went into household furnishings, clothes and plate in great detail. Not every child was necessarily mentioned and girls who had already received their dowries might well be omitted. Yet the universality and number of these bequests point to the strength of the family tie and the mother's desire to be remembered by her children. It is rarer to find references to grandchildren but they point to the same conclusion.

Testators looked beyond their nuclear family to their marital and natal families and to their friends. Joan Turbeville remembered a step-daughter and Joan Hilton her brother and niece. It was usual to leave money or goods to the servants of the household and Joan Turbeville singled out her maid for a special bequest. Legacies to institutions and places with which they were connected, even if they were small, indicate the desire for commemoration. Throughout their lives, women were aware of what was going on in their communities and this is reflected in their bequests to the poor and to religious houses. Certainly such bequests were made in return for prayers but at the same time they benefited the locality; religious and social concerns were intermeshed. Joan Hilton remembered her local nunnery and parish church, while Beverley and Hull were the two nearest towns to Swine.

These concerns for family and local society are found throughout the middle ages. Whatever their position in the social hierarchy, most women's lives were taken up with family and household. The changes which took place in the economy, government and the law did not alter this. Society, church and government grew more complex and sophisticated by the late middle ages and many women lived more comfortable lives and had more possessions than they had had in earlier centuries; serfdom virtually came to an end and housing and living conditions improved. Opportunities to work increased with the growth of towns and trade, even if most of the work was of low status. There was no longer the danger of starving to death. Yet there was no guarantee that the improvements would last. Even in the later fifteenth century, women found that certain areas of employment were closed to them and this presaged the fewer openings and lower wages of the Tudor period. As the population grew in the sixteenth century, housewives found it more difficult to contribute to the family budget, while inflation made it harder to maintain standards of living.

Over the medieval period, nuns experienced greater changes than housewives in the role they played in society. Their lives continued to centre on the worship of God but the influence they exerted in the Conversion period changed to a much more limited impact in the later middle ages. Worship, however, became increasingly elaborate for both nuns and laywomen at the end of the middle ages, as did the opportunities to contribute to the church's images, lights, altars and screens. No one living then could have imagined that all this would be swept away in the next fifty years, along with the beliefs in the commemoration of the dead and the need for prayers to help them through purgatory. The religious houses, supported by generations of laypeople were dissolved. With the Tudor Reformation, a new era began for women in England.

Notes

Notes to Chapter 1: Women's Worlds

1. C. Rawcliffe, *Medicine and Society in Later Medieval England* (Stroud, 1995), pp. 29–34, 171–75.
2. Genesis, chapter 3.
3. A. Blamires, with K. Pratt and C. W. Marx, eds, *Woman Defamed and Woman Defended* (Oxford, 1992), pp. 144–47.
4. K. Gravdal, *Ravishing Maidens: Writing Rape in Medieval French Literature and Law* (Philadelphia, Pennsylvania, 1991), pp. 6–9; K. M. Phillips, 'Written on the Body: Reading Rape from the Twelfth to Fifteenth Centuries', in N. J. Menuge, ed., *Medieval Women and the Law* (Woodbridge, 2000), pp. 125–44; J. B. Post, 'Sir Thomas West and the Statute of Rapes, 1382', *Bulletin of the Institute of Historical Research*, 53 (1980), pp. 24–30.
5. P. S. Gold, *The Lady and the Virgin: Image, Attitude and Experience in Twelfth-Century France* (Chicago, Illinois, 1985), pp. 43–73.
6. L. R. Poos, 'Sex, Lies and the Church Courts of Pre-Reformation England', *Journal of Interdisciplinary History*, 25 (1994–95), pp. 585–607; W. H. Longstaffe and J. Booth, eds, *Halmota Prioratus Dunelmensis*, Surtees Society, 82 (1886), pp. 38, 144, 160.
7. P. Franklin, 'Peasant Widows' "Liberation" and Remarriage before the Black Death', *Economic History Review*, 39 (1986), p. 197; P. Franklin, 'Politics in Manorial Court Rolls: The Tactics, Social Composition and Aims of a Pre-1381 Peasant Movement', in Z. Razi and R. Smith, eds, *Medieval Society and the Manor Court* (Oxford, 1996), pp. 162–98; R. H. Hilton, *The English Peasantry in the Later Middle Ages* (Oxford, 1975), pp. 109–10.
8. M. M. Sheehan, *The Will in Medieval England: From the Conversion of the Anglo-Saxons to the End of the Thirteenth Century*, Pontifical Institute of Medieval Studies, Studies and Texts, 6 (Toronto, 1963), pp. 303–6. Technically, the will deals with land and the testament with personal possessions, but the term 'will' is widely used to cover both.

Notes to Chapter 2: Marriage

1. M. A. Meyer, 'Early Anglo-Saxon Penitentials and the Position of Women', *Haskins Society Journal*, 2 (1990), pp. 47–61.

2. J. G. C. Anderson, ed., *Cornelii Taciti De origine et situ Germanorum* (Oxford, 1938), chapters 7, 18–20.

3. B. Colgrave and R. A. B. Mynors, eds, *Bede's Ecclesiastical History of the English People* (Oxford, 1969), pp. 78–103.

4. Ibid., pp. 150–57; W. H. Stevenson, ed., *Asser's Life of King Alfred* (Oxford, 1904), p. 16.

5. J. T. McNeill and H. M. Gamer, eds, *Medieval Handbooks of Penance* (New York, 1938), pp. 209–10.

6. Ibid., pp. 184–86, 192, 196, 209; D. Whitelock, ed., *English Historical Documents, c. 500–1042* (London, 2nd edn, 1979), pp. 392–94, 410–15, 462–63; F. L. Attenborough, ed., *The Laws of the Earliest English Kings* (Cambridge, 1922), pp. 4–9, 14–15, 68–77; A. J. Robertson, ed., *The Laws of the Kings of England from Edmund to Henry I* (Cambridge, 1925), pp. 200–3.

7. Whitelock, ed., *English Historical Documents*, pp. 396–97; Attenborough, ed., *Laws of the Earliest English Kings*, pp. 24–27.

8. Whitelock, ed., *English Historical Documents*, pp. 465–66, 475–76; Robertson, ed., *Laws from Edmund to Henry I*, pp. 210–13. The reckoning of degrees of consanguinity is discussed by J. Goody, *The Development of the Family and Marriage in Europe* (Cambridge, 1983), pp. 134–46.

9. Whitelock, ed., *English Historical Documents*, p. 901; W. Stubbs, ed., *Memorials of St Dunstan*, Rolls Series (London, 1874), p. 32.

10. Whitelock, ed., *English Historical Documents*, p. 393; Attenborough, ed., *Laws of the Earliest English Kings*, pp. 14–15; McNeill and Gamer, eds, *Medieval Handbooks of Penance*, pp. 195–96, 210.

11. P. Stafford, *Queens, Concubines and Dowagers: The King's Wife in the Early Middle Ages* (London, 1998), pp. 71–81; P. Stafford, *Queen Emma and Queen Edith: Queenship and Women's Power in Eleventh-Century England* (Oxford, 1997), pp. 236–46.

12. M. C. Ross, 'Concubinage in Anglo-Saxon England', *Past and Present*, 108 (1985), pp. 3–6, 13–15; Stafford, *Queen Emma and Queen Edith*, pp. 73–74; Stafford, *Queens, Concubines and Dowagers*, pp. 64–65.

13. Whitelock, ed., *English Historical Documents*, pp. 463, 816–22; Robertson, ed., *Laws from Edmund to Henry I*, pp. 202–203; M. Tangl, ed., *Die Briefe des Heiligen Bonifatius und Lullus* (Monumenta Germaniae Historica, Epistolae Selectae, i, Berlin, 1955), pp. 146–55; A. W. Haddon and

W. Stubbs, eds, *Councils and Ecclesiastical Documents Relating to Great Britain and Ireland* (3 vols, Oxford, 1869–78), iii, pp. 350–56.

14. W. J. Millor and H. E. Butler, eds, *The Letters of John of Salisbury*, i (London, 1955), pp. 153–56.

15. McNeill and Gamer, eds, *Medieval Handbooks of Penance*, p. 195; R. R. Darlington and P. McGurk, eds, *The Chronicle of John of Worcester* (3 vols, Oxford, 1995–98), ii, pp. 532–35.

16. Whitelock, ed., *English Historical Documents*, pp. 467–68.

17. The morning-gift ceased to be made in the twelfth century.

18. Whitelock, ed., *English Historical Documents*, pp. 593, 596–97; A. J. Robertson, ed., *Anglo-Saxon Charters* (Cambridge, 1956), pp. 148–51. The mancus was equivalent to thirty pennies. Used as a unit of account, it was sometimes issued as a coin.

19. F. Pollock and F. W. Maitland, *The History of English Law before the Time of Edward I* (2 vols, Cambridge, 1898), ii, pp. 15–16, 292. From the late thirteenth century, the dowry usually comprised a sum of money.

20. D. Whitelock, ed., *Anglo-Saxon Wills* (Cambridge, 1930), pp. 68–69.

21. A. Farley and H. Ellis, eds, *Liber Censualis vocatus Domesday Book* (4 vols, London, 1783–1816), i, fos 48v, 170r; ii, fol. 431v. Grants of *maritagia* continued to be made in the twelfth and thirteenth centuries, as when Philip de Kyme, with the consent of his wife and heirs, granted a tenement in Hallington, Lincolnshire, to Robert, son of Richard, when Robert married his daughter, Hawise; F. M. Stenton, ed., *Documents Illustrative of the Social and Economic History of the Danelaw*, British Academy Records of the Social and Economic History of England and Wales, 5 (Oxford, 1920), p. 351.

22. Ibid., i, fol. 218; J. Ward, ed. and trans., *Women of the English Nobility and Gentry, 1066–1500* (Manchester, 1995), pp. 91–92.

23. Whitelock, ed., *English Historical Documents*, pp. 602–3; Robertson, ed., *Anglo-Saxon Charters*, pp. 150–53; P. Stafford, 'Women and the Norman Conquest', *Transactions of the Royal Historical Society*, 6th series, 4 (1994), pp. 241–42; A. Williams, *The English and the Norman Conquest* (Woodbridge, 1995), pp. 12, 199–202.

24. Farley and Ellis, eds, *Domesday Book*, ii, fol. 232r; Williams, *The English and the Norman Conquest*, pp. 101–2; J. A. Green, 'Aristocratic Women in Early Twelfth-Century England', in C. W. Hollister, ed., *Anglo-Norman Political Culture and the Twelfth-Century Renaissance* (Woodbridge, 1997), p. 69; E. Searle, 'Women and the Legitimization of Succession at the Norman Conquest', *Proceedings of the Battle Conference on Anglo-Norman Studies*, 3 (1981), p. 164; H. Clover and M. Gibson, eds, *The Letters of Lanfranc Archbishop of Canterbury* (Oxford, 1979), pp. 166–67.

25. D. M. Stenton, *The English Woman in History* (London, 1957), pp. 28–30; Stafford, 'Women and the Norman Conquest', pp. 221–49.

26. F. E. Harmer, ed., *Select English Historical Documents of the Ninth and Tenth Centuries* (Cambridge, 1914), pp. 3–5.

27. Whitelock, ed., *English Historical Documents*, p. 465; Robertson, ed., *Laws from Edmund to Henry I*, pp. 208–9; Williams, *The English and the Norman Conquest*, pp. 207–9; H. R. Loyn, 'Kinship in Anglo-Saxon England', *Anglo-Saxon England*, 3 (1974), pp. 201–2; J. Crick, 'Women, Posthumous Benefaction and Family Strategy in Pre-Conquest England', *Journal of British Studies*, 38 (1999), pp. 399–422.

28. A. Wareham, 'The Transformation of Kinship and the Family in Late Anglo-Saxon England', *Early Medieval Europe*, 10 (2001), pp. 375–99; Green, 'Aristocratic Women', pp. 59–60.

29. J. C. Holt, 'Feudal Society and the Family in Early Medieval England, iv, The Heiress and the Alien', *Transactions of the Royal Historical Society*, 5th series, 35 (1985), p. 5.

30. British Library, London, Cotton MS. Claudius D xiii, fol. 49; F. M. Stenton, *The First Century of English Feudalism, 1066–1166* (2nd edn, Oxford, 1961), pp. 38–41, 260–61; Ward, ed., *Women of the English Nobility and Gentry*, pp. 97–99; S. F. C. Milsom, 'Inheritance by Women in the Twelfth and Early Thirteenth Centuries', in M. S. Arnold, T. A. Green, S. A. Scully and S. D. White, eds, *On the Laws and Customs of England: Essays in Honor of Samuel E. Thorne* (Chapel Hill, North Carolina, 1981), pp. 69, 77–79; Holt, 'The Heiress and the Alien', pp. 2, 9–12; J. Hudson, *Land, Law and Lordship in Anglo-Norman England* (Oxford, 1994), pp. 111–13. Green, 'Aristocratic Women', pp. 72–76, 79–82, questions Holt's view that the 'statutum decretum' was a deliberate act of royal policy.

31. G. Duby, trans. E. Forster, *Medieval Marriage: Two Models from Twelfth-Century France* (Baltimore, 1978), pp. 9–18.

32. J. Scammell, 'Freedom and Marriage in Medieval England', *Economic History Review*, 27 (1974), pp. 531–35; P. A. Brand and P. R. Hyams, 'Debate: Seigneurial Control of Women's Marriage', *Past and Present*, 99 (1983), pp. 127–30; M. M. Sheehan, 'Theory and Practice: Marriage of the Unfree and the Poor in Medieval Society', *Mediaeval Studies*, 50 (1988), pp. 473–77, 482–86.

33. J. D. Mansi, *Sacrorum conciliorum nova et amplissima collectio*, xxii (Graz, 1961), col. 251; C. N. L. Brooke, *The Medieval Idea of Marriage* (Oxford, 1989), pp. 126–43; J. A. Brundage, *Law, Sex and Christian Society in Medieval Europe* (Chicago, Illinois, 1987), pp. 229–416; M. M. Sheehan, 'Marriage, Theory and Practice in the Conciliar Legislation and Diocesan

Statutes of Medieval England', *Mediaeval Studies*, 40 (1978), p. 413; M. M. Sheehan, 'Choice of Marriage Partner in the Middle Ages: Development and Mode of Application of a Theory of Marriage', *Studies in Medieval and Renaissance History*, new series, 1 (1978), pp. 1–33.

34. N. Adams and C. Donahue Jr, eds, *Select Cases from the Ecclesiastical Courts of the Province of Canterbury, c. 1200–1301* (Selden Society, 95, 1978–9), pp. 127–37.

35. Mansi, *Sacrorum conciliorum*, xxii, col. 1035–39. Marriage within seven degrees of consanguinity was forbidden at the Council of London in 1074–75; Clover and Gibson, eds, *Letters of Lanfranc*, pp. 76–77. In England, Hardwicke's Marriage Act of 1753 attempted to put an end to the clandestine marriage.

36. For an example of a dispensation, see Ward, ed., *Women of the English Nobility and Gentry*, pp. 35–37.

37. P. J. P. Goldberg, *Women, Work and Life Cycle in a Medieval Economy: Women in York and Yorkshire, c. 1300–1520* (Oxford, 1992), pp. 234–43.

38. C. H. Talbot, ed., *The Life of Christina of Markyate: A Twelfth-Century Recluse* (Oxford, 1959), pp. 44–55; N. Davis, ed., *Paston Letters and Papers*, 2 vols, (Oxford, 1971), pp. 341–44.

39. F. Broomfield, ed., *Thomas of Chobham, Summa confessorum*, Analecta Mediaevalia Namurcensia, 25 (Louvain and Paris, 1968).

40. D. Whitelock, M. Brett and C. N. L. Brooke, eds, *Councils and Synods with Other Documents Relating to the English Church, 871–1204*, 2 vols (Oxford, 1981), i, pp. 1067–68; F. M. Powicke and C. R. Cheney, eds, *Councils and Synods, 1205–1313*, 2 vols (Oxford, 1964–81), i, pp. 25, 34, 62–63, 86–90; Sheehan, 'Marriage Theory and Practice', pp. 408–60.

41. D. L. d'Avray, *Medieval Marriage Sermons: Mass Communication in a Culture without Print* (Oxford, 2001), pp. 1–10, 14–20, 228ff, 274ff; N. Bériou and D. L. d'Avray, *Modern Questions about Medieval Sermons: Essays on Marriage, Death, History and Sanctity* (Spoleto, 1974), pp. 33–36, 118–21, 135–53.

42. C. R. Cheney and B. E. A. Jones, eds, *English Episcopal Acta*, ii, *Canterbury, 1162–90* (British Academy, 1986), p. 29; M. G. Cheney, *Roger Bishop of Worcester, 1164–79* (Oxford, 1980), p. 318.

43. Cheney and Jones, eds, *English Episcopal Acta*, ii, pp. 28–29; J. Dauvillier, *Le mariage dans le droit classique de l'église* (Paris, 1933), pp. 23–25.

44. P. M. Barnes, ed., 'The Anstey Case', in P. M. Barnes and C. F. Slade, eds, *A Medieval Miscellany for D. M. Stenton*, Pipe Roll Society, new series, 36 (1960), pp. 1–24; L. Voss, *Heinrich von Blois Bischof von Winchester, 1129–71* (Berlin, 1932), pp. 141–44, 166–68; M. J. Franklin, ed., *English Episcopal*

Acta, viii, *Winchester, 1070–1204* (British Academy, 1993), pp. 66–67; Millor and Butler, eds, *Letters of John of Salisbury,* i, pp. 227–37, 267–71; Brooke, *Medieval Idea of Marriage,* pp. 148–52; P. A. Brand, 'New Light on the Anstey Case', *Essex Archaeology and History,* 15 (1983), pp. 68–83.

45. F. Pedersen, *Marriage Disputes in Medieval England* (London, 2000), pp. 177–89; P. J. P. Goldberg, 'Fiction in the Archives: The York Cause Papers as a Source for Later Medieval Social History', *Continuity and Change,* 12 (1997), pp. 426–30.

46. R. H. Helmholz, *Marriage Litigation in Medieval England* (Cambridge, 1974), pp. 58–59.

47. M. T. Clanchy, *From Memory to Written Record: England, 1066–1307* (London, 1979), pp. 29–59.

48. Male wards came of age at twenty-one, female at fourteen if married and sixteen if single. S. S. Walker, 'Proof of Age of Feudal Heirs in Medieval England', *Mediaeval Studies,* 35 (1973), p. 307.

49. W. Stubbs and H. W. C. Davis, eds, *Select Charters* (Oxford, 1921), pp. 117–19; D. C. Douglas and G. W. Greenaway, eds, *English Historical Documents, 1042–1189* (2nd edn, London, 1981), p. 433.

50. The National Archives: Public Record Office, DL10/6; J. H. Round ed., *Ancient Charters Royal and Private Prior to AD 1200,* Pipe Roll Society, 10 (1888), pp. 8–10; C. Johnson and H. A. Cronne, eds, *Regesta Regum Anglo-Normannorum, 1100–1135* (Oxford, 1956), p. 162; J. S. Brewer, J. F. Dimock and G. F. Warner, *Giraldi Cambrensis Opera,* 8 vols, Rolls Series (London, 1861–91), vi, p. 29; Ward, ed., *Women of the English Nobility and Gentry,* pp. 26–27; Green, 'Aristocratic Women', pp. 69–70.

51. British Library, Sloane Roll xxxi 4, m. 5; Stenton, *First Century,* pp. 34–36, 259–60; Green, 'Aristocratic Women', p. 73; J. H. Round, ed., *Calendar of Documents Preserved in France, 918–1206* (London, 1899), p. 507; R. B. Patterson, ed., *Earldom of Gloucester Charters: The Charters and Scribes of the Earls and Countesses of Gloucester to AD 1217* (Oxford, 1973), p. 32. Further examples are given in R. C. DeAragon, 'In Pursuit of Aristocratic Women: A Key to Success in Norman England', *Albion,* 14 (1982), pp. 258–67.

52. J. H. Round, ed., *Rotuli de dominabus et pueris et puellis de xii comitatibus,* Pipe Roll Society, 35 (1913). A recent discussion of the rolls from the point of view of women is given in S. M. Johns, *Noblewomen, Aristocracy and Power in the Twelfth-Century Anglo-Norman Realm* (Manchester, 2003), pp. 165–88.

53. Round, ed., *Rotuli,* pp. 29–30, 76–77.

54. W. Stubbs, ed., *Gesta Regis Henrici Secundi Benedicti Abbatis*, 2 vols, Rolls Series (London, 1867), ii, p. 73. The lordship of Striguil was in south Wales, centred on Chepstow.

55. J. C. Holt, *Magna Carta* (2nd edn, Cambridge, 1992), pp. 208–10; M. Altschul, *A Baronial Family in Medieval England: The Clares, 1217–1314* (Baltimore, Maryland, 1965), pp. 25–26.

56. S. L. Waugh, 'Marriage, Class and Royal Lordship in England under Henry III', *Viator*, 16 (1985), pp. 181–207; P. Coss, *The Lady in Medieval England, 1000–1500* (Stroud, 1998), pp. 121–23; K. B. McFarlane, 'Had Edward I a "Policy" towards the Earls?', *History*, 50 (1965), pp. 145–59, and reprinted in idem, *The Nobility of Later Medieval England* (Oxford, 1973), pp. 248–67; J. C. Ward, *English Noblewomen in the Later Middle Ages* (London, 1992), pp. 19–20, 42.

57. Holt, *Magna Carta*, pp. 450–53.

58. S. S. Walker, 'Free Consent and the Marriage of Feudal Wards in Medieval England', *Journal of Medieval History*, 8 (1982), pp. 123–34.

59. D. E. Greenway, ed., *Charters of the Honour of Mowbray, 1107–91*, British Academy Records of Social and Economic History, new series, i (1972), pp. xxxix, lxii–iii; L. F. Salzmann, ed., *The Chartulary of the Priory of St Pancras of Lewes*, Sussex Record Society, 38 (1932), pp. 118–19. Alured held land of the Clares in Surrey and Essex, and was associated with them in Ceredigion and Gwent.

60. W. O. Ault, ed., *Court Rolls of the Abbey of Ramsey and of the Honor of Clare* (New Haven, Conneticut, 1928), p. 96.

61. Davis, *Paston Letters and Papers*, i, pp. 341–44.

62. J. S. Roskell, L. Clark and C. Rawcliffe, eds, *The History of Parliament: The House of Commons, 1386–1421*, 4 vols (Stroud, 1992), iv, pp. 39–44.

63. Davis, *Paston Letters and Papers*, i, pp. 286–87.

64. J. Nichols, *A Collection of All the Wills of the Kings and Queens of England* (London, 1780), pp. 133–34; C. Carpenter, ed., *Kingsford's Stonor Letters and Papers, 1290–1483* (Cambridge, 1996), pp. 135–37. Thomas Stonor had two sons, Thomas, said to have been aged seven in 1431, and John. There is no record of John after 1432.

65. Ward, *English Noblewomen*, pp. 16–24; S. J. Payling, 'The Economics of Marriage in Late Medieval England: The Marriage of Heiresses', *Economic History Review*, 54 (2001), pp. 413–29.

66. C. D. Ross, 'The Household Accounts of Elizabeth Berkeley, Countess of Warwick, 1420–21', *Transactions of the Bristol and Gloucestershire Archaeological Society*, 70 (1951), pp. 81–82; J. H. Cooke, 'On the Great Berkeley Lawsuit of the Fifteenth and Sixteenth Centuries: A Chapter of

Gloucestershire History', *Transactions of the Bristol and Gloucestershire Archaeological Society*, 3 (1878–79), pp. 305–24.

67. W. H. Bliss, ed., *Calendar of Entries in the Papal Registers Relating to Great Britain and Ireland: Papal Letters, 1305–42* (London, 1895), pp. 527–28.

68. A. J. Pollard, *North-Eastern England during the Wars of the Roses: Lay Society, War and Politics, 1450–1500* (Oxford, 1990), pp. 90, 110; W. R. Childs, *Anglo-Castilian Trade in the Later Middle Ages* (Manchester, 1978), p. 208; A. D. Carr, 'Sir Lewis John: A Medieval London Welshman', *Bulletin of the Board of Celtic Studies*, 22 (1967), pp. 260–70; Roskell, Clark and Rawcliffe, eds, *The House of Commons, 1386–1421*, ii, pp. 616–18, and iii, pp. 494–98; E. W. Ives, *The Common Lawyers of Pre-Reformation England: Thomas Kebell. A Case Study* (Cambridge, 1983), pp. 23–30, 368–69.

69. Davis, *Paston Letters and Papers*, i, pp. 662–63.

70. The National Archives: Public Record Office, DL27/93; G. W. Watson, 'Marriage Settlements', *Genealogist*, 34 (1918), pp. 30–31; H. Rothwell, ed., *English Historical Documents, 1189–1327* (London, 1975), pp. 333, 342.

71. British Library, London, Harley MS 1240, fol. 37v; *Calendar of Charter Rolls, 1257–1300* (London, 1906), pp. 89–91; G. W. Watson, 'Marriage Settlements', *Genealogist*, 33 (1917), pp. 134–36.

72. J. R. Lander, 'Marriage and Politics in the Fifteenth Century: The Nevilles and the Wydevilles', *Bulletin of the Institute of Historical Research*, 36 (1963), pp. 119–52.

73. Davis, *Paston Letters and Papers*, i, p. 26.

74. T. North, 'Legerwite in the Thirteenth and Fourteenth Centuries', *Past and Present*, 111 (1986), pp. 7–15.

75. J. M. Bennett, *Women in the Medieval English Countryside: Gender and Household in Brigstock before the Plague* (Oxford, 1987), pp. 93–94; E. Clark, 'The Decision to Marry in Thirteenth- and Early Fourteenth-Century Norfolk', *Mediaeval Studies*, 49 (1987), pp. 504–7.

76. Bennett, *Brigstock*, pp. 71–73; Z. Razi, *Life, Marriage and Death in a Medieval Parish: Economy, Society and Demography in Halesowen, 1270–1400* (Cambridge, 1980), pp. 60–64; R. M. Smith, 'Some Reflections on the Evidence for the Origins of the "European Marriage Pattern" in England', in C. Harris, ed., *The Sociology of the Family: New Directions for Britain*, Sociological Review Monograph, 28 (1979), pp. 74–112; Goldberg, *Women, Work and Life Cycle*, pp. 204–11, 222–32.

77. Clark, 'Decision to Marry', pp. 500–2; R. Faith, 'Debate: Seigneurial Control of Women's Marriage', *Past and Present*, 99 (1983), p. 145.

78. Scammell, 'Freedom and Marriage in Medieval England', pp. 487–90; E. Searle, 'Freedom and Marriage in Medieval England: An Alternative

Hypothesis', *Economic History Review*, 29 (1976), pp. 482–86; E. Searle, 'Seigneurial Control of Women's Marriage: The Antecedents and Function of Merchet in England', *Past and Present*, 82 (1979), pp. 5–7, 17–24, 29–30; Brand, Hyams and Faith, 'Debate: Seigneurial Control of Women's Marriage', pp. 127, 131–35; R. M. Smith, 'Women's Property Rights under Customary Law: Some Developments in the Thirteenth and Fourteenth Centuries', *Transactions of the Royal Historical Society*, 5th series, 36 (1986), pp. 168–72.

79. Faith, Debate: 'Seigneurial Control of Women's Marriage', pp. 142–44, 146–48.

80. M. Muller, 'The Function and Evasion of Marriage Fines on a Fourteenth-Century English Manor', *Continuity and Change*, 14 (1999), pp. 178–83.

81. J. M. Bennett, 'Medieval Peasant Marriage: An Examination of Marriage Licence Fines in *Liber Gersumarum*', in J. A. Raftis, ed., *Pathways to Medieval Peasants* (Toronto, 1981), pp. 195–96. This source has been published: E. B. DeWindt, ed., *The Liber Gersumarum of Ramsey Abbey* (Toronto, 1976).

82. Muller, 'The Function and Evasion of Marriage Fines', pp. 171–73; Bennett, 'Medieval Peasant Marriage', pp. 195–205.

83. Bennett, 'Medieval Peasant Marriage', pp. 219–21.

84. D. Postles, 'Migration and Mobility in a Less Mature Economy: English Internal Migration, c. 1200–1350', *Social History*, 25 (2000), pp. 285–99; A. R. DeWindt, 'Redefining the Peasant Community in Medieval England: The Regional Perspective', *Journal of British Studies*, 26 (1987), pp. 163–207; S. Penn, 'The Origins of Bristol Migrants in the Early Fourteenth Century: The Surname Evidence', *Transactions of the Bristol and Gloucestershire Archaeological Society*, 101 (1983), pp. 123–30; Goldberg, *Women, Work and Life Cycle*, pp. 284–87.

85. Douglas and Greenaway, eds, *English Historical Documents, 1042–1189*, pp. 1013–14, 1032–34, 1040–41.

86. N. Adams and C. Donahue Jr, eds, *Select Cases from the Ecclesiastical Courts of the Province of Canterbury c. 1200–1301*, pp. 25–28.

87. L. C. Hector and B. F. Harvey, eds, *The Westminster Chronicle, 1381–94* (Oxford, 1982), pp. 88–89; E. C. Lodge and R. Somerville, eds, *John of Gaunt's Register, 1379–83*, 2 vols, Camden Society, 3rd series, 56–7 (1937), i, pp. 178–80. Because of Mary's youth, she continued to live with her mother at the beginning of her marriage.

Notes to Chapter 3: Wives and Mothers

1. M. J. Bennett, 'Provincial Gentlefolk and Legal Education in the Reign of Edward II', *Bulletin of the Institute of Historical Research*, 57 (1984), pp. 203–8.

2. B. Yorke, *Wessex in the Early Middle Ages* (Leicester, 1995), pp. 276–77; Z. Razi, 'The Myth of the Immutable English Family', *Past and Present*, 140 (1993), pp. 3–44; Z. Razi, 'Intrafamilial Ties and Relationships in the Medieval Village: A Quantitative Approach Employing Manor Court Rolls', in Z. Razi and R. Smith, eds, *Medieval Society and the Manor Court* (Oxford, 1996), pp. 370–75.

3. W. H. Stevenson, ed., *Records of the Borough of Nottingham*, 4 vols (London, 1882–89), ii, pp. 48–49.

4. N. Saul, *Richard II* (New Haven, Connecticut, 1997), pp. 93–94, 455–57 and plate 20; N. Saul, *Death, Art and Memory in Medieval England: The Cobham Family and their Monuments, 1300–1500* (Oxford, 2001), pp. 193–99.

5. J. O. Halliwell, ed., *The Chronicle of William de Rishanger of the Barons' Wars: The Miracles of Simon de Montfort*, Camden Society, old series, 15 (London, 1840), p. 108; J. R. Maddicott, 'Follower, Leader, Pilgrim, Saint: Robert de Vere, Earl of Oxford, at the Shrine of Simon de Montfort, 1273', *English Historical Review*, 109 (1994), p. 649.

6. J. Ward, 'Letter-Writing by English Noblewomen in the Early Fifteenth Century', in J. Daybell, ed., *Early Modern Women's Letter Writing, 1450–1700* (Basingstoke, 2001), pp. 29–41; N. Davis, ed., *Paston Letters and Papers of the Fifteenth Century*, 2 vols (Oxford, 1971–6), i, pp. 664–66; C. Carpenter, ed., *Kingsford's Stonor Letters and Papers, 1290–1483* (Cambridge, 1996), no. 169; M. Jones, 'The Fortunes of War: The Military Career of John, Second Lord Bourchier (d. 1400)', *Essex Archaeology and History*, 26 (1995), pp. 148, 159.

7. Guildhall Library, London, MS 9171/1, fos 244r–45r, 344; 252r, 427.

8. A. Farley and H. Ellis, eds, *Liber Censualis vocatus Domesday Book* (4 vols, London, 1783–1816), i, fol. 373r.

9. A. W. B. Simpson, *An Introduction to the History of the Land Law* (Oxford, 1961), pp. 77–82; H. Rothwell, ed., *English Historical Documents, 1189–1327* (London, 1975), pp. 428–29; R. M. Smith, 'Women's Property Rights under Customary Law', *Transactions of the Royal Historical Society*, 5th series, 36 (1986), pp. 182–86; W. O. Ault, *Court Rolls of the Abbey of Ramsey and of the Honor of Clare* (New Haven, Connecticut, 1928), p. 93; Essex Record Office, D/Dby M2, m. 2d; R. M. Smith, 'Coping with Uncertainty: Women's Tenure of Customary Land in England, *c.* 1370–1430', in J. Ker-

mode, ed., *Enterprise and Individuals in Fifteenth-Century England* (Stroud, 1991), pp. 49–53.

10. J. S. Brewer, ed., *Monumenta Franciscana*, 2 vols, Rolls Series (London, 1858–82), pp. 112, 294–96; J. Ward, ed. and trans., *Women of the English Nobility and Gentry, 1066–1500* (Manchester, 1995), pp. 53–56.

11. R. F. Hunnisett, ed., *Bedfordshire Coroners' Rolls*, Bedfordshire Historical Record Society, 41 (1961), pp. 13–14; B. Cozens-Hardy, ed., *Norwich Consistory Court Depositions, 1499–1512 and 1518–30*, Norwich Record Society, 10 (1938), no. 11.

12. P. J. P. Goldberg, ed. and trans., *Women in England, c. 1275–1525* (Manchester, 1995), pp. 141–44; D. Webb, *Pilgrimage in Medieval England* (London, 2000), p. 157; N. Vincent, 'Simon of Atherfield (d. 1211): A Martyr to his Wife', *Analecta Bollandiana*, 113 (1995), pp. 349–61; P. Coss, *The Lady in Medieval England, 1000–1500* (Stroud, 1998), pp. 131–37; *Calendar of Patent Rolls, 1330–34* (London, 1893), p. 375. I would like to thank Dr Michael Ray for drawing my attention to the Pugeys case.

13. Razi, 'Intrafamilial Ties', pp. 369–70; L. R. Poos, ed., *Lower Ecclesiastical Jurisdiction in Late-Medieval England: The Courts of the Dean and Chapter of Lincoln, 1336–49, and the Deanery of Wisbech, 1458–84*, British Academy Records of Social and Economic History, new series, 32 (Oxford, 2001), p. 501; J. Kirby, ed., *The Plumpton Letters and Papers*, Camden Society, 5th series, 8 (1996), pp. 24–25; J. Ward, 'Elizabeth Beaumont, Countess of Oxford (d. 1537): Her Life and Connections', *Transactions of the Monumental Brass Society*, 17, part 1 (2003), p. 4; H. C. Maxwell Lyte, *Dunster and its Lords, 1066–1881* (Exeter, 1882), pp. 20–22, 44–46.

14. F. R. Fairbank, 'The Last Earl of Warenne and Surrey and the Distribution of his Possessions', *Yorkshire Archaeological Journal*, 19 (1907), pp. 193–264.

15. The National Archives: Public Record Office, C1/17/210; C1/25/83–90.

16. A. J. Finch, 'Sexual Morality and Canon Law: The Evidence of the Rochester Consistory Court', *Journal of Medieval History*, 20 (1994), pp. 261–75; S. L. Parker and L. R. Poos, 'A Consistory Court from the Diocese of Rochester, 1363–64', *English Historical Review*, 106 (1991), pp. 652–65; F. Pedersen, *Marriage Disputes in Medieval England* (London, 2000), pp. 59–69, 106–18; M. M. Sheehan, 'The Formation and Stability of Marriage in Fourteenth-Century England: Evidence of an Ely Register', *Mediaeval Studies*, 33 (1971), pp. 234–36, 249–51; C. Donahue Jr, 'Female Plaintiffs in Marriage Cases in the Court of York in the Later Middle Ages: What Can We Learn from the Numbers?', in S. S. Walker, ed., *Wife and Widow in Medieval England* (Ann Arbor, Michigan, 1993), p. 195.

17. R. H. Helmholz, *Marriage Litigation in Medieval England* (Cambridge,

1974), pp. 74–111; A. Finch, '*Repulsa Uxore Sua*: Marital Difficulties and Separation in the Later Middle Ages', *Continuity and Change*, 8 (1993), pp. 11–12, 21–25; J. Murray, 'On the Origins and Role of "Wise Women" in Causes of Annulment on the Grounds of Male Impotence', *Journal of Medieval History*, 16 (1990), pp. 235–49.

18. Helmholz, *Marriage Litigation*, p. 74; Donahue, 'Female Plaintiffs', pp. 185–88, 199.

19. D. M. Smith, ed., *English Episcopal Acta*, iv, *Lincoln, 1186–1206* (British Academy, 1986), pp. 32–33; W. Holtzmann and E. W. Kemp, eds, *Papal Decretals relating to the Diocese of Lincoln in the Twelfth Century*, Lincoln Record Society, 47 (1954), pp. 56–57, 60–61.

20. F. Pollock and F. W. Maitland, *The History of English Law before the Time of Edward I*, 2 vols (Cambridge, 1898), ii, pp. 395–96; *Rotuli Parliamentorum*, 6 vols (1783), i, pp. 146–47; Ward, ed. and trans., *Women of the English Nobility and Gentry*, pp. 61–63.

21. M. Prestwich, 'An Everyday Story of Knightly Folk', in M. Prestwich, R. Britnell and R. Frame, eds, *Thirteenth-Century England*, 9 (2003), pp. 151–62.

22. A. Morey and C. N. L. Brooke, eds, *The Letters and Charters of Gilbert Foliot* (Cambridge, 1967), pp. 214–18.

23. This English practice ran contrary to canon law, which provided for the legitimation of the children by the subsequent marriage of the parents. Sutton, Lincolnshire, however, followed canon law in the mid fourteenth century; G. Seabourne, 'A Local Rule on Legitimation by Subsequent Marriage', *Journal of Legal History*, 18 (1997), pp. 96–99.

24. Goldberg, ed. and trans., *Women in England*, pp. 169–70.

25. Z. Razi, *Life, Marriage and Death in a Medieval Parish: Economy, Society and Demography in Halesowen, 1270–1400* (Cambridge, 1980), pp. 84–85, 102–3, 124–25, 142–43.

26. S. Crawford, *Childhood in Anglo-Saxon England* (Stroud, 1999), p. 58.

27. S. Shahar, *Childhood in the Middle Ages* (London, 1990), pp. 149–50.

28. P. P. A. Biller, 'Birth-Control in the West in the Thirteenth and Early Fourteenth Centuries', *Past and Present*, 94 (1982), pp. 3–26; J. T. Noonan, *Contraception: A History of its Treatment by the Catholic Theologians and Canonists* (Cambridge, Massachusetts, 1966), pp. 212, 274; J. M. Riddle, 'Oral Contraceptives and Early-Term Abortifacients during Classical Antiquity and the Middle Ages', *Past and Present*, 132 (1991), pp. 3–32.

29. B. A. Kellum, 'Infanticide in England in the Later Middle Ages', *History of Childhood Quarterly*, 1 (1973–4), pp. 367–88; R. H. Helmholz, 'Infanticide in the Province of Canterbury during the Fifteenth Century', ibid., 2

(1974–5), pp. 379–90, and reprinted in Helmholz, *Canon Law and the Law of England* (London, 1987), pp. 157–68.

30. Ward, ed. and trans., *Women of the English Nobility and Gentry*, p. 70; *Calendar of Inquisitions Post Mortem*, vi (London, 1910), pp. 203–4.

31. O. Cockayne, ed., *Leechdoms, Wortcunning and Starcraft of Early England*, 3 vols, Rolls Series (London, 1864–66), i, pp. 339, 343–44; iii, p. 64.

32. Crawford, *Childhood in Anglo-Saxon England*, pp. 57–61.

33. C. Rawcliffe, *Medicine and Society in Later Medieval England* (Stroud, 1995), pp. 178–79; A. Crawford, ed., *Letters of Medieval Women* (Stroud, 2002), pp. 233–35; The National Archives: Public Record Office, E101/365/20, m. 8; Ward, ed. and trans., *Women of the English Nobility and Gentry*, p. 68; Halliwell, ed., *Rishanger: The Miracles of Simon de Montfort*, p. 76.

34. W. A. Pantin, *The English Church in the Fourteenth Century* (Cambridge, 1955), pp. 195–202.

35. M. H. Green, ed. and trans., *The Trotula: A Medieval Compendium of Women's Medicine* (Philadelphia, Pennsylvania, 2001), pp. 37, 44–51; M. H. Green, 'Women's Medical Practice and Health Care in Medieval Europe', *Signs*, 14 (1988–89), pp. 442, 453, 460–66; J. F. Benton, 'Trotula, Women's Problems and the Professionalization of Medicine in the Middle Ages', *Bulletin of the History of Medicine*, 59 (1985), pp. 30–49; A. Barratt, ed., *The Knowing of Woman's Kind in Childing: A Middle English Version of Material Derived from the Trotula and Other Sources* (Turnhout, Belgium, 2001), pp. 2, 42–43.

36. Barratt, *The Knowing of Woman's Kind in Childing*; B. Rowland, *Medieval Woman's Guide to Health: The First English Gynaecological Handbook* (London, 1981); M.-R. Hallaert, ed., *The 'Sekenesse of Wymmen': A Middle English Treatise on Diseases in Women* (Brussels, 1982).

37. *Calendar of Inquisitions Post Mortem*, ii (London, 1906), p. 401; ibid., vii (London, 1909), p. 187; S. B. Meech and H. E. Allen, eds, *The Book of Margery Kempe*, Early English Text Society, original series, 212 (London, 1940), pp. 6–7.

38. G. Kristensson, ed., *John Mirk's Instructions for Parish Priests* (Lund, 1974), pp. 71–75.

39. Rawcliffe, *Medicine and Society*, pp. 198–203; The National Archives: Public Record Office, DL28/1/2, fol. 17r; J. Gairdner, ed., *The Paston Letters, 1422–1509*, 4 vols (Edinburgh, 1910), p. 215.

40. *Calendar of Inquisitions Post Mortem*, ii (London, 1906), p. 29; ibid., v (London, 1908), p. 84.

41. N. Orme, *Medieval Children* (New Haven, Connecticut, 2001), pp. 23–24.

42. *Calendar of Inquisitions Post Mortem*, ii (London, 1906), p. 500; ibid., v (London, 1908), pp. 36, 50, 168.

43. B. Hamilton, *Religion in the Medieval West* (London, 1986), p. 113; G. M. Gibson, 'Blessing from Sun and Moon: Churching as Women's Theater', in B. A. Hanawalt and D. Wallace, eds, *Bodies and Disciplines: Intersections of Literature and History in Fifteenth-Century England* (Minneapolis, Minnesota, 1996), pp. 139–54. A small fee was paid by the woman, as recorded in the churchwardens' accounts of Saffron Walden church, Essex; L. R. Poos, *A Rural Society after the Black Death: Essex, 1350–1525* (Cambridge, 1991), pp. 121–27.

44. *Calendar of Inquisitions Post Mortem*, v (London, 1908), p. 50; ibid., vi (London, 1910), pp. 205–6.

45. The debate was sparked off by Philippe Ariès, who argued that effective family relationships dated from the modern period and medieval children were treated as miniature adults. In contrast, Shahar has argued vigorously for a strong bond between parent and child. P. Ariès, *L'enfant et la vie familiale sous l'ancien régime* (Paris, 1960), pp. 23–28; Shahar, *Childhood in the Middle Ages*, pp. 1–5; Crawford, *Childhood in Anglo-Saxon England*, pp. 1–6, 114–18; Orme, *Medieval Children*, pp. 5–7.

46. Crawford, *Childhood in Anglo-Saxon England*, pp. 92–96.

47. J. C. Robertson, ed., *Materials for the History of Thomas Becket*, 7 vols, Rolls Series (London, 1875–85), ii, pp. 255–57; Ward, ed. and trans., *Women of the English Nobility and Gentry*, pp. 71–73; The National Archives: Public Record Office, SC1/22/156; M. S. Serjeantson, ed., *Osbern Bokenham, Legendys of Hooly Wummen*, Early English Text Society, original series, 206 (London, 1938), pp. xx–xxi, 136–39.

48. Crawford, *Childhood in Anglo-Saxon England*, p. 47; The National Archives: Public Record Office, E101/365/17, m. 1, 2; Guildhall Library, London, MS 9171/1, fol. 244r.

49. Crawford, *Childhood in Anglo-Saxon England*, p. xiv.

50. J. Swanson, 'Childhood and Childrearing in *Ad Status* Sermons by Later Thirteenth Century Friars', *Journal of Medieval History*, 16 (1990), p. 309.

51. Ibid., pp. 315–16; A. L. Gabriel, *The Educational Ideas of Vincent of Beauvais* (Notre Dame, Indiana, 1962), pp. 17–20; Shahar, *Childhood in the Middle Ages*, pp. 22–31.

52. Crawford, *Childhood in Anglo-Saxon England*, pp. 70–74; S. D. Michalove, 'The Education of Aristocratic Women in Fifteenth-Century England', in S. D. Michalove and A. C. Reeves, eds, *Estrangement, Enterprise and Education in Fifteenth-Century England* (Stroud, 1998), p. 123; P. Chaplais, 'Some Private Letters of Edward I', *English Historical Review*, 77 (1962), pp. 81, 86.

53. The National Archives: Public Record Office, DL28/1/1, fos 19v, 20v, 21r, 23r; *Calendar of Inquisitions Post Mortem*, ii (London, 1906), p. 401; ibid., v (London, 1908), p. 128; British Library, London, Egerton Roll 8776, m. 5.

54. Crawford, *Childhood in Anglo-Saxon England*, p. 143; G. Egan, *The Medieval Household: Daily Living, c. 1150–c. 1450* (London, 1998), pp. 7, 281–84; N. Orme, 'The Culture of Children in Medieval England', *Past and Present*, 148 (1995), pp. 51–60.

55. K. M. Phillips, *Medieval Maidens: Young Women and Gender in England, 1270–1540* (Manchester, 2003), p. 64; W. H. Stevenson, ed., *Asser's Life of Alfred* (Oxford, 1904), p. 20; J. C. Parsons, ed., *The Court and Household of Eleanor of Castile in 1290*, Pontifical Institute of Medieval Studies, Studies and Texts, 37 (Toronto, 1977), pp. 63–64; R. J. Mitchell, *John Tiptoft, 1427–1470* (London, 1938), p. 12.

56. A. Steiner, ed., *Vincent of Beauvais, De Eruditione Filiorum Nobilium* (Cambridge, Massachusetts, 1938), pp. 172–202; Gabriel, *The Educational Ideas of Vincent of Beauvais*, pp. 40–44; R. B. Tobin, 'Vincent of Beauvais on the Education of Women', *Journal of the History of Ideas*, 35 (1974), pp. 485–89.

57. M. Y. Offord, ed., *W. Caxton, The Book of the Knight of the Tower*, Early English Text Society, supplementary series, 2 (Oxford, 1971), pp. xviii–xix, 3–4, 11–13; S. Lawson, trans., *Christine de Pisan, The Treasure of the City of Ladies or The Book of the Three Virtues* (Harmondsworth, 1985), pp. 160–62.

58. T. F. Mustanoja, ed., *The Good Wife Taught her Daughter; The Good Wyfe Wold a Pylgremage; The Thewis of Gud Women* (Helsinki, 1948), pp. 158–72; Goldberg, ed. and trans., *Women in England*, pp. 97–103; F. Riddy, 'Mother Knows Best: Reading Social Change in a Courtesy Text', *Speculum*, 71 (1996), pp. 66–86.

59. G. E. Brereton and J. M. Ferrier, eds, *Le Ménagier de Paris* (Oxford, 1981), pp. 125–36; E. Power, trans., *The Goodman of Paris* (London, 1928), pp. 205–20.

60. Crawford, *Childhood in Anglo-Saxon England*, p. 143.

61. J. M. Bennett, 'Writing Fornication: Medieval Leyrwite and its Historians', *Transactions of the Royal Historical Society*, 6th series, 13 (2003), pp. 131–58.

62. K. M. Phillips, 'Written on the Body: Reading Rape from the Twelfth to Fifteenth Centuries', in N. J. Menuge, ed., *Medieval Women and the Law* (Woodbridge, 2000), pp. 128–38; Phillips, *Medieval Maidens*, pp. 83, 146–52.

63. J. C. Parsons, 'Mothers, Daughters, Marriage, Power: Some Plantagenet

Evidence, 1150–1500', in J. C. Parsons, ed., *Medieval Queenship* (Stroud, 1994), p. 63; Phillips, *Medieval Maidens*, pp. 30–42.

64. Offord, ed., *Caxton, The Book of the Knight of the Tower*, pp. 16–17, 121–22, 158–60.

65. K. J. Lewis, 'Model Girls? Virgin-Martyrs and the Training of Young Women in Late Medieval England', in K. J. Lewis, N. J. Menuge and K. M. Phillips, eds, *Young Medieval Women* (Stroud, 1999), pp. 25–46; K. J. Lewis, *The Cult of St Katherine of Alexandria in Late Medieval England* (Woodbridge, 2000), pp. 175–226; K. J. Lewis, 'The Life of St Margaret of Antioch in Late Medieval England: A Gendered Reading', in R. N. Swanson, ed., *Gender and Christian Religion*, Studies in Church History, 34 (Woodbridge, 1998), pp. 129–42; Serjeantson, ed., *Bokenham's Legendys of Hooly Wummen*, pp. xx–xxi, 136–39, 259, 288; C. M. Meale, '"... alle the bokes that I haue of latyn, englisch and frensch": Laywomen and their Books in Late Medieval England', in C. M. Meale, ed., *Women and Literature in Britain, 1150–1500* (Cambridge, 1993), p. 138.

66. C. E. Moreton, *The Townshends and their World: Gentry, Law and Land in Norfolk, c. 1450–1551* (Oxford, 1992), p. 144.

67. A. Owen, ed., *Le traité de Walter de Bibbesworth sur la langue française* (Paris, 1929), p. 43; C. M. Barron, 'The Education and Training of Girls in Fifteenth-Century London', in D. E. S. Dunn, ed., *Courts, Counties and the Capital in the Later Middle Ages* (Stroud, 1996), pp. 139, 142, 147–48; British Library, London, Egerton Roll 8776, m. 5.

68. Crawford, *Childhood in Anglo-Saxon England*, pp. 122–23; D. Whitelock, ed., *Anglo-Saxon Wills* (Cambridge, 1930), pp. 56–63, 167–70.

69. E. C. Lodge and R. Somerville, eds, *John of Gaunt's Register, 1379–83*, 2 vols, Camden Society, 3rd series, 56–57 (London, 1937), i, pp. 106–7; T. H. Turner, ed., *Manners and Household Expenses of England in the Thirteenth and Fifteenth Centuries*, Roxburghe Club (London, 1841), p. 338.

70. Davis, ed., *Paston Letters and Papers*, i, p. 388.

Notes to Chapter 4: Widows

1. R. F. Hunnisett, ed., *Bedfordshire Coroners' Rolls*, Bedfordshire Historical Record Society, 41 (1961), p. 4.

2. C. Dyer, *Standards of Living in the Later Middle Ages* (Cambridge, 1989), pp. 109–18, 151–60.

3. J. Kermode, *Medieval Merchants: York, Beverley and Hull in the Later Middle Ages* (Cambridge, 1998), pp. 86–87.

4. F. Pollock and F. W. Maitland, *History of English Law before the Time of*

Edward I, 2 vols (Cambridge, 1898), ii, pp. 414–20. The custom of curtesy of England could also apply to villein holdings; L. R. Poos and L. Bonfield, eds, *Select Cases in Manorial Courts, 1250–1550: Property and Family Law*, Selden Society, 114 (1997), p. 102.

5. *Calendar of Inquisitions Post Mortem*, ii (London, 1906), p. 449.

6. D. L. Douie and H. Farmer, eds, *The Life of St Hugh of Lincoln*, 2 vols (London, 1961), ii, p. 136; M. D. Legge, ed., *Anglo-Norman Letters and Petitions from All Souls MS 182*, Anglo-Norman Text Society, 3 (Oxford, 1941), pp. 110–12; J. Ward, 'Letter-Writing by English Noblewomen in the Early Fifteenth Century', in J. Daybell, ed., *Early Modern Women's Letter Writing, 1450–1700* (Basingstoke, 2001), p. 32.

7. R. E. Archer and B. E. Ferme, 'Testamentary Procedure with Special Reference to the Executrix', in *Medieval Women in Southern England*, Reading Medieval Studies, 15 (1989), pp. 3–34; D. Whitelock, ed., *Anglo-Saxon Wills* (Cambridge, 1930), pp. 22–25, 121; P. Maddern, 'Friends of the Dead: Executors, Wills and Family Strategy in Fifteenth-Century Norfolk', in R. E. Archer and S. Walker, eds, *Rulers and Ruled in Late Medieval England: Essays Presented to Gerald Harriss* (London, 1995), p. 171; L. R. Poos, ed., *Lower Ecclesiastical Jurisdiction in Late-Medieval England: The Courts of the Dean and Chapter of Lincoln, 1336–49, and the Deanery of Wisbech, 1458–84*, British Academy Records of Social and Economic History, new series, 32 (Oxford, 2001), pp. 437–38; F. R. H. Du Boulay, ed., *Registrum Thome Bourgchier Cantuariensis Archiepiscopi*, Canterbury and York Society, 54 (1957), p. 209.

8. J. Nichols, *A Collection of All the Wills of the Kings and Queens of England* (London, 1780), pp. 83–87, 92. The earl of Pembroke left at least £300 to pay for his funeral.

9. Guildhall Library, London, MS 9531/3, fos 433v–34v; P. Northeast, ed., *Wills of the Archdeaconry of Sudbury, 1439–74*, part 1, *1439–61*, Suffolk Records Society, 44 (Woodbridge, 2001), p. 135.

10. The procedure for obtaining probate was clarified by Archbishop Chichele in 1416; E. F. Jacob, ed., *The Register of Henry Chichele, Archbishop of Canterbury*, 4 vols, Canterbury and York Society (1937–47), iii, pp. 16–18; J. Horn, ed., *The Register of Robert Hallum, Bishop of Salisbury, 1407–17*, Canterbury and York Society, 72 (1982), pp. 131–32.

11. J. W. Willis Bund, ed., *The Register of the Diocese of Worcester during the Vacancy of the See, 1301–1435*, Worcestershire Historical Society, 8 (1897), pp. lxxiii–iv, 95; R. N. Swanson, ed., *A Calendar of the Register of Richard Scrope, Archbishop of York, 1398–1405*, 2 vols, Borthwick Texts and Calendars: Records of the Northern Province (1981–85), p. 27; R. L. Storey, ed.,

The Register of Thomas Langley, Bishop of Durham, 1406–37, 6 vols, Surtees Society (1949–67), iv, pp. 97–98.

12. G. M. Benton, 'Essex Wills at Canterbury', *Transactions of the Essex Archaeological Society*, new series, 21 (1933–37), p. 264. The bowls were bequeathed to her son and heir, Thomas.

13. S. S. Walker, ed., *The Court Rolls of the Manor of Wakefield, 1331–33*, Yorkshire Archaeological Society (Leeds, 1983), pp. 12, 41, 47–48, 52, 61, 85. Juliana and her brother, Robert, paid their father's heriot the previous year and Juliana paid merchet earlier in 1332.

14. The National Archives: Public Record Office, E101/25/19; E101/28/4.

15. J. M. Bennett, *Women in the Medieval English Countryside: Gender and Household in Brigstock before the Plague* (Oxford, 1989), p. 144; R. Lock, ed., *The Court Rolls of Walsham le Willows, 1303–50*, Suffolk Records Society, 41 (1998), p. 113; Pollock and Maitland, *History of English Law*, ii, pp. 418–19; Poos and Bonfield, eds, *Select Cases in Manorial Courts*, p. 148.

16. B. A. Hanawalt, *Growing Up in Medieval London: The Experience of Childhood in History* (Oxford, 1993), pp. 89–101.

17. D. C. Douglas and G. W. Greenaway, eds, *English Historical Documents, 1042–1189* (2nd edn, London, 1981), p. 433; J. A. Green, 'Aristocratic Women in Early Twelfth-Century England', in C. W. Hollister, ed., *Anglo-Norman Political Culture and the Twelfth-Century Renaissance* (Woodbridge, 1997), pp. 62, 68.

18. M. Altschul, *A Baronial Family in Medieval England: The Clares, 1217–1314* (Baltimore, Maryland, 1965), p. 160.

19. N. J. Menuge, 'A Few Home Truths: The Medieval Mother as Guardian in Romance and Law', in N. J. Menuge, ed., *Medieval Women and the Law* (Woodbridge, 2000), pp. 77–103.

20. M. Cherry, 'The Struggle for Power in Mid Fifteenth-Century Devonshire', in R. A. Griffiths, ed., *Patronage, the Crown and the Provinces in Later Medieval England* (Gloucester, 1981), p. 125.

21. J. C. Holt, *Magna Carta* (2nd edn, Cambridge, 1992), pp. 450–53; H. Rothwell, ed., *English Historical Documents, 1189–1327* (London, 1975), pp. 317–18; F. W. Maitland, ed., *Bracton's Note Book*, 3 vols (London, 1887), ii, pp. 381, 550–51; iii, pp. 85–87, 178–79, 577–78.

22. P. Brand, '"Deserving" and "Undeserving" Wives: Earning and Forfeiting Dower in Medieval England', *Journal of Legal History*, 22 (2001), pp. 1–20.

23. P. Stafford, *Unification and Conquest: A Political and Social History of England in the Tenth and Eleventh Centuries* (London, 1989), p. 166; *DB*, i, fol. 280v; Green, 'Aristocratic Women', pp. 62, 64–65. The widow was also entitled to a share of her husband's goods, Glanvill envisaging a threefold

division between heir, widow and goods left at the husband's choice; J. S. Loengard, 'Rationabilis Dos: Magna Carta and the Widow's "Fair Share" in the Earlier Thirteenth Century', in S. S. Walker, ed., *Wife and Widow in Medieval England* (Ann Arbor, Michigan, 1993), p. 62.

24. F. M. Stenton, ed., *Facsimiles of Early Charters from Northamptonshire Collections*, Northamptonshire Record Society, 4 (1927), pp. 82–83; British Library, Harley Charters 76 F 35; J. Ward, ed. and trans., *Women of the English Nobility and Gentry, 1066–1500* (Manchester, 1995), pp. 63–64.

25. Holt, *Magna Carta*, pp. 452–53, 503–4; Douglas and Greenaway, eds, *English Historical Documents, 1042–1189*, p. 433; Rothwell, ed., *English Historical Documents, 1189–1327*, pp. 318, 333, 342; Loengard, 'Rationabilis Dos', pp. 59–71; J. S. Loengard, '"Of the Gift of her Husband": English Dower and its Consequences in the Year 1200', in J. Kirshner and S. F. Wemple, eds, *Women of the Medieval World* (Oxford, 1985), pp. 215–55. A freewoman was entitled to a half share of her husband's land.

26. Whitelock, ed., *Anglo-Saxon Wills*, pp. 70–71.

27. S. S. Walker, 'Introduction', in Walker, ed., *Wife and Widow*, p. 6.

28. E. Mason, ed., *The Beauchamp Cartulary: Charters, 1100–1268*, Pipe Roll Society, new series, 43 (1971–73), pp. xxiii, 8. Matilda's son also quitclaimed land there to James, in return for ten marks to pay a debt to the Jews.

29. The widow had to bring a writ of dower against the occupant of each holding where she claimed dower; S. S. Walker, 'Litigation as Personal Quest: Suing for Dower in the Royal Courts, c. 1272–1350', in Walker, ed., *Wife and Widow*, p. 85.

30. N. Vincent, ed., *English Episcopal Acta, ix, Winchester, 1205–38*, p. 10; C. Harper-Bill, ed., *English Episcopal Acta, xxi, Norwich, 1215–43*, p. 18; Maitland, ed., *Bracton's Note Book*, iii, p. 503; *Curia Regis Rolls*, ix (London, 1952), p. 367; *Curia Regis Rolls*, xi (London, 1955), p. 209.

31. W. T. Reedy, ed., *Basset Charters, c. 1120–1250*, Pipe Roll Society, new series, 50 (1989–91), p. 53.

32. Brand, '"Deserving" and "Undeserving" Wives', p. 15; S. Payling, 'The Politics of Family: Late Medieval Marriage Contracts', in R. H. Britnell and A. J. Pollard, eds, *The McFarlane Legacy* (Stroud, 1995), pp. 31–38. R. E. Archer, 'Rich Old Ladies: The Problem of Late Medieval Dowagers', in A. Pollard, ed., *Property and Politics: Essays in Later Medieval English History* (Stroud, 1984), pp. 28–31, argues that the Mowbray dowagers in the fifteenth century prevented the family from achieving its full potential.

33. Loengard, 'Rationabilis Dos', p. 62; C. M. Barron, 'The "Golden Age" of Women in Medieval London', in *Medieval Women in Southern England*, pp. 41–43; C. M. Barron, 'Introduction', in C. M. Barron and A. F. Sutton,

eds, *Medieval London Widows, 1300–1500* (London, 1994), pp. xvii–xxi; The National Archives: Public Record Office, Prob 11, 40 Milles (8); *Testamenta Eboracensia*, iv, Surtees Society, 53 (1869), p. 24; M. T. Clanchy, ed., *Civil Pleas of the Wiltshire Eyre, 1249*, Wiltshire Record Society, 26 (1970), pp. 63–64; A. M. Hopkinson and D. Crook, eds, *The Rolls of the 1281 Derbyshire Eyre*, Derbyshire Record Society, 27 (2000), pp. 4–5. Widows in provincial towns normally received one-third or one-half of their husband's property. *Legitim* was still found in London and York in the fifteenth century but not in other English towns.

34. Manorial customs may have been similar earlier but not necessarily so.

35. Bennett, *Women in the Medieval English Countryside*, pp. 144, 163–68; Lock, ed., *Court Rolls of Walsham le Willows*, i, pp. 54, 60, 113; Walker, ed., *Court Rolls of the Manor of Wakefield*, iii, pp. 39, 159, 185; H. M. Jewell, 'Women at the Courts of the Manor of Wakefield, 1348–50', *Northern History*, 26 (1990), pp. 69–73; Poos and Bonfield, eds, *Select Cases in Manorial Courts*, p. 98.

36. Stafford, *Unification and Conquest*, p. 160; P. Stafford, *Queens, Concubines and Dowagers: The King's Wife in the Early Middle Ages* (Leicester, 1998), pp. 148–49; Whitelock, ed., *Anglo-Saxon Wills*, pp. 54–57.

37. G. E. Woodbine, ed., S. E. Thorne, trans., *Bracton, De legibus et consuetudinibus Angliae*, 4 vols (Cambridge, Massachusetts, 1968–77), ii, pp. 334–37; Rothwell, ed., *English Historical Documents, 1189–1327*, pp. 382–83; *Close Rolls, 1264–68* (London, 1937), p. 130; Ward, ed. and trans., *Women of the English Nobility and Gentry*, p. 116; C. H. Knowles, 'Provision for the Families of the Montfortians Disinherited after the Battle of Evesham', in P. R. Coss and S. D. Lloyd, eds, *Thirteenth Century England*, i (Woodbridge, 1986), pp. 124–27.

38. C. D. Ross, 'Forfeiture for Treason in the Reign of Richard II', *English Historical Review*, 71 (1956), pp. 560–75; J. R. Lander, 'Attainder and Forfeiture, 1453–1509', *Historical Journal*, 4 (1961), pp. 119–51.

39. *Rotuli Parliamentorum*, 6 vols (London, 1783), iii, p. 245; Ward, ed. and trans., *Women of the English Nobility and Gentry*, p. 120.

40. C. J. Neville, 'Widows of War: Edward I and the Widows of Scotland during the War of Independence', in Walker, ed., *Wife and Widow*, pp. 109–13.

41. J. R. S. Phillips, *Aymer de Valence, Earl of Pembroke, 1307–24* (Oxford, 1972), pp. 233–39; British Library, London, Harley MS 1240, fos 86v–87r; Ward, ed. and trans., *Women of the English Nobility and Gentry*, pp. 116–19.

42. *Rotuli Parliamentorum*, vi, p. 282; A. Crawford, 'Victims of Attainder: The Howard and De Vere Women in the Late Fifteenth Century', *Medieval Women in Southern England*, pp. 59–74; M. A. Hicks, 'The Last Days of

Elizabeth Countess of Oxford', *English Historical Review*, 103 (1988), pp. 76–95.

43. M. C. Erler, 'Three Fifteenth-Century Vowesses', in Barron and Sutton, eds, *Medieval London Widows*, pp. 167–68.

44. D. Whitelock, ed., *English Historical Documents, 500–1042* (2nd edn, London, 1979), pp. 445, 465–66; A. J. Robertson, ed., *The Laws of the Kings of England from Edmund to Henry I* (Cambridge, 1925), pp. 84–85, 210–13.

45. J. A. Brundage, 'Widows and Remarriage: Moral Conflicts and their Resolution in Classical Canon Law', in Walker, ed., *Wife and Widow*, pp. 17–31.

46. Walker, ed., *Court Rolls of the Manor of Wakefield*, iii, p. 96; E. Clark, 'The Decision to Marry in Thirteenth- and Early Fourteenth-Century Norfolk', *Mediaeval Studies*, 49 (1987), pp. 501, 508–9; J. Ravensdale, 'Population Changes and Transfer of Customary Land on a Cambridgeshire Manor in the Fourteenth Century', in R. M. Smith, ed., *Land, Kinship and Life-Cycle* (Cambridge, 1984), pp. 203, 206–9, 217–18.

47. Z. Razi, *Life, Marriage and Death in a Medieval Parish: Economy, Society and Demography in Halesowen, 1270–1400* (Cambridge, 1980), pp. 63, 138; Bennett, *Women in the Medieval English Countryside*, p. 146; P. Franklin, 'Peasant Widows' "Liberation" and Remarriage before the Black Death', *Economic History Review*, 39 (1986), pp. 188–96.

48. W. O. Ault, *Court Rolls of the Abbey of Ramsey and of the Honor of Clare* (New Haven, Connecticut, 1928), p. 271. A similar case arose at Great Waltham and High Easter in 1327; Poos and Bonfield, eds, *Select Cases in Manorial Courts*, pp. 100–1.

49. Ravensdale, 'Population Changes', p. 218; Poos and Bonfield, eds, *Select Cases in Manorial Courts*, pp. 116–17.

50. Poos and Bonfield, eds, *Select Cases in Manorial Courts*, p. 63; E. Clark, 'Some Aspects of Social Security in Medieval England', *Journal of Family History*, 7 (1982), p. 319. A curtilage denoted a yard attached to the dwelling house.

51. Hanawalt, *Growing Up in Medieval London*, pp. 91, 96; D. Keene, 'Tanners' Widows', in Barron and Sutton, eds, *Medieval London Widows*, pp. 7–8, 22–25; M. Davies, 'Thomasyne Percyvale, "The Maid of Week" (d. 1512)', in ibid., pp. 185–207.

52. W. G. Benham, ed. and trans., *The Oath Book or Red Parchment Book of Colchester* (Colchester, 1907), p. 136; The National Archives: Public Record Office, C1/58/143; Kermode, *Medieval Merchants*, pp. 80–81, 86–87.

53. Stafford, *Queens, Concubines and Dowagers*, pp. 49–51, 143–46; Whitelock, ed., *Anglo-Saxon Wills*, pp. 6–9, 34–43, 138–39.

54. Douglas and Greenaway, eds, *English Historical Documents, 1042–1189*, p. 433; J. Hunter, ed., *Magnum Rotulum Scaccarii, 31 Henry I*, Record Commission (London, 1833), p. 110; Green, 'Aristocratic Women', pp. 65–67; S. M. Johns, *Noblewomen, Aristocracy and Power in the Twelfth-Century Anglo-Norman Realm* (Manchester, 2003), pp. 55, 59–61; R. C. DeAragon, 'Dowager Countesses, 1069–1230', in C. Harper-Bill, ed., *Anglo-Norman Studies*, 17 (1995), p. 95.

55. DeAragon, 'Dowager Countesses', p. 89.

56. Ibid., p. 87; P. M. Barnes, ed., *The Great Roll of the Pipe, 14 John*, Pipe Roll Society, 30 (1954), p. 37; T. D. Hardy, ed., *Rotuli chartarum in Turri Londinensi asservati, 1199–1216*, Record Commission (London, 1837), p. 189; J. Gillingham, *Richard I* (New Haven, Connecticut, 1999), p. 293.

57. Holt, *Magna Carta*, pp. 452–53; Rothwell, ed., *English Historical Documents, 1189–1327*, p. 318.

58. Altschul, *A Baronial Family in Medieval England*, pp. 157–58; *Calendar of Patent Rolls, 1405–8* (London, 1907), p. 97.

59. A. J. Robertson, ed., *Anglo-Saxon Charters* (Cambridge, 1956), pp. 128–31; N. J. Menuge, 'A Few Home Truths', pp. 77–103.

60. Guildhall Library, London, MS 2171/5, fol. 382r.

61. *Testamenta Eboracensia*, iv, Surtees Society, 53 (1868), pp. 94–97, 149–54; B. J. Harris, *Aristocratic Women, 1450–1550* (Oxford, 2002), p. 123.

62. Davis, ed., *Paston Letters and Papers*, i, pp. 380, 575–77.

63. M. S. Guiseppi, 'On the Testament of Sir Hugh de Nevill, Written at Acre, 1267', *Archaeologia*, 56, part 2 (1899), pp. 351–70; S. Lloyd, *English Society and the Crusade, 1216–1307* (Oxford, 1988), pp. 150, 168–69; C. Tyerman, *England and the Crusades, 1095–1588* (Chicago, Illinois, 1988), p. 194.

64. Lambeth Palace Library, London, Register of William de Whittlesey, fos 124v–125r; Nichols, *Royal Wills*, p. 86.

65. Harris, *Aristocratic Women*, pp. 173–74; H. W. Lewer, 'The Testament and Last Will of Elizabeth, Widow of John de Veer, Thirteenth Earl of Oxford', *Transactions of the Essex Archaeological Society*, new series, 20 (1933), pp. 7–16; J. Ward, 'Elizabeth Beaumont, Countess of Oxford (d. 1537): Her Life and Connections', *Transactions of the Monumental Brass Society*, 17, part 1 (2003), pp. 10–12.

66. Whitelock, ed., *Anglo-Saxon Wills*, p. 63.

67. Davis, ed., *Paston Letters and Papers*, i, pp. 341–42, 350, 538; J. T. Rosenthal, 'Looking for Grandmother: The Pastons and their Counterparts in Late Medieval England', in J. C. Parsons and B. Wheeler, eds, *Medieval Mothering* (New York, 1996), pp. 262–65.

68. N. H. Nicolas, *Testamenta Vetusta*, 2 vols (London, 1826), i, pp. 357–62;

J. Ward, *English Noblewomen in the Later Middle Ages* (London, 1992), pp. 18, 48, 99–100.

69. Jacob, ed., *The Register of Henry Chichele*, ii, pp. 534–39.

70. Nichols, *Royal Wills*, pp. 177–86.

71. Whitelock, ed., *Anglo-Saxon Wills*, pp. 10–15, 108–9.

72. Ward, 'Elizabeth Beaumont', p. 10.

73. Nichols, *Royal Wills*, p. 215.

74. *A Collection of the Ordinances and Regulations for the Government of the Royal Household*, Society of Antiquaries (London, 1790), pp. 37–39; Ward, ed. and trans., *Women of the English Nobility and Gentry*, pp. 217–18; C. A. J. Armstrong, 'The Piety of Cicely, Duchess of York: A Study in Late Medieval Culture', in C. A. J. Armstrong, *England, France and Burgundy in the Fifteenth Century* (London, 1983), pp. 135–56.

75. M. K. Jones and M. G. Underwood, *The King's Mother: Lady Margaret Beaufort Countess of Richmond and Derby* (Cambridge, 1992), pp. 187–88; M. C. Erler, 'English Vowed Women at the End of the Middle Ages', *Mediaeval Studies*, 57 (1995), pp. 168–69, 174–75, 183–203; P. H. Cullum, 'Vowesses and Female Lay Piety in the Province of York, 1300–1530', *Northern History*, 32 (1996), p. 30. Joan Gedney took the vow of chastity after the death of her third husband, Robert Large, but broke it to marry John Gedney; Erler, 'Three Fifteenth-Century Vowesses', pp. 171–73.

76. Erler, 'Three Fifteenth-Century Vowesses', pp. 167–69; Erler, 'English Vowed Women', p. 180.

77. E.g. Guildhall Library, London, MS 9171/6, fol. 218; Margaret Cappes of Havering, Essex, died in London in 1477. Three of her four daughters married away from Havering: one was in Maldon, one in Stondon Massey, and one in London.

Notes to Chapter 5: Work

1. M. Kowaleski, 'Singlewomen in Medieval and Early Modern Europe: The Demographic Perspective', in J. M. Bennett and A. M. Froide, eds, *Singlewomen in the European Past, 1250–1800* (Philadelphia, Pennsylvania, 1999), pp. 38–51.

2. M. K. McIntosh, *Autonomy and Community: The Royal Manor of Havering, 1200–1500* (Cambridge, 1986), pp. 157–59, 174.

3. E. Miller and J. Hatcher, *Medieval England: Towns, Commerce and Crafts, 1086–1348* (London, 1995), pp. 98–127, 264–74; C. Dyer, *Standards of Living in the Later Middle Ages* (Cambridge, 1989), pp. 188–202, 212–33; R. Britnell, 'Boroughs, Markets and Trade in Northern England, 1000–1216', in

R. Britnell and J. Hatcher, eds, *Progress and Problems in Medieval England: Essays in Honour of Edward Miller* (Cambridge, 1996), pp. 46–67; J. Hatcher, 'The Great Slump of the Mid Fifteenth Century', in ibid., pp. 237–72. The importance of taking the economic background into account is stressed by M. E. Mate, *Daughters, Wives and Widows after the Black Death: Women in Sussex, 1350–1535* (Woodbridge, 1998), p. 20.

4. F. L. Attenborough, ed., *The Laws of the Earliest English Kings* (Cambridge, 1922), pp. 56–57; D. Whitelock, ed., *English Historical Documents, 500–1042* (2nd edn, London, 1979), p. 406; D. Whitelock, ed., *Anglo-Saxon Wills* (Cambridge, 1930), pp. 10–11, 64–65, 110.

5. P. J. P. Goldberg, *Women, Work and Life-Cycle in a Medieval Economy: Women in York and Yorkshire, c. 1300–1520* (Oxford, 1992), pp. 370–71. The figure for Rutland does not include Oakham.

6. C. M. Woolgar, *The Great Household in Late Medieval England* (New Haven, Connecticut, 1999), p. 34; L. R. Poos, *A Rural Society after the Black Death: Essex, 1350–1525* (Cambridge, 1991), pp. 192–99.

7. P. Brand, '"Deserving" and "Undeserving" Wives: Earning and Forfeiting Dower in Medieval England', *Journal of Legal History*, 22 (2001), pp. 12–13.

8. *Testamenta Eboracensia*, i, Surtees Society, 4 (1836), pp. 335–37; ibid., iv, Surtees Society, 53 (1868), p. 60.

9. B. Stone, ed., *Medieval English Verse* (Harmondsworth, 1964), pp. 104–5.

10. M. Bailey, 'Demographic Decline in Late Medieval England: Some Thoughts on Recent Research', *Economic History Review*, 49 (1996), pp. 7–8; C. Phythian-Adams, *Desolation of a City: Coventry and the Urban Crisis of the Late Middle Ages* (Cambridge, 1979), pp. 204–5.

11. A. J. Kettle, 'Ruined Maids: Prostitutes and Servant Girls in Later Medieval England', in R. R. Edwards and V. Ziegler, eds, *Matrons and Marginal Women in Medieval Society* (Woodbridge, 1995), p. 27.

12. K. M. Phillips, *Medieval Maidens: Young Women and Gender in England, 1270–1540* (Manchester, 2003), p. 131; Poos, *A Rural Society after the Black Death*, pp. 205–6; Mate, *Women in Sussex*, p. 46; A. R. Myers, ed., *English Historical Documents, 1327–1485* (London, 1969), p. 1004.

13. S. A. C. Penn, 'Female Wage-Earners in Late Fourteenth-Century England', *Agricultural History Review*, 35 (1987), p. 2; Mate, *Women in Sussex*, p. 73; R. H. Hilton, *The English Peasantry in the Later Middle Ages* (Oxford, 1975), p. 102.

14. R. B. Pugh, ed., *Court Rolls of the Wiltshire Manors of Adam de Stratton*, Wiltshire Record Society, 24 (1968), p. 80; W. O. Ault, ed., *Court Rolls of the Abbey of Ramsey and of the Honor of Clare* (New Haven, Connecticut, 1928), p. 196; W. O. Ault, 'Open-Field Husbandry and the Village

Community: A Study of Agrarian By-Laws in Medieval England', *Transactions of the American Philosophical Society*, new series, 55, part 7 (1965), pp. 12–14, 33–35.

15. D. Oschinsky, ed., *Walter of Henley and Other Treatises on Estate Management and Accounting* (Oxford, 1971), pp. 444–45; Myers, ed., *English Historical Documents, 1327–1485*, p. 994; Ault, 'Open-Field Husbandry', p. 15; S. A. C. Penn and C. Dyer, 'Wages and Earnings in Late Medieval England: Evidence from the Enforcement of the Labour Laws', *Economic History Review*, 43 (1990), pp. 364–65.

16. E. C. Furber, ed., *Essex Sessions of the Peace, 1351, 1377–79*, Essex Archaeological Society, Occasional Publications, 3 (Colchester, 1953), pp. 158, 166; Penn, 'Female Wage-Earners', pp. 7–14; Hilton, *English Peasantry in the Later Middle Ages*, pp. 102–3; Mate, *Women in Sussex*, p. 72; S. Bardsley, 'Women's Work Reconsidered: Gender and Wage Differentiation in Late Medieval England', *Past and Present*, 165 (1999), pp. 3–29.

17. K. E. Lacey, 'Women and Work in Fourteenth and Fifteenth Century London', in L. Charles and L. Duffin, eds, *Women and Work in Pre-Industrial England* (London, 1985), p. 44.

18. R. F. Hunnisett, ed., *Bedfordshire Coroners' Rolls*, Bedfordshire Historical Record Society, 41 (1961), p. 13; J. M. Bennett, *Ale, Beer and Brewsters* (Oxford, 1996), p. 10.

19. J. M. Bennett, 'The Village Ale-Wife: Women and Brewing in Fourteenth-Century England', in B. A. Hanawalt, ed., *Women and Work in Preindustrial Europe* (Bloomington, Indiana, 1986), pp. 22–26; J. M. Bennett, *Women in the Medieval English Countryside: Gender and Household in Brigstock before the Plague* (Oxford, 1987), pp. 120–29, 190–91, 212–13.

20. Bennett, 'Village Ale-Wife', pp. 23, 26–27; Bennett, *Women in the Medieval English Countryside*, pp. 121, 124–25; H. Graham, '"A Woman's Work ...": Labour and Gender in the Late Medieval Countryside', in P. J. P. Goldberg, ed., *Women in Medieval English Society* (Stroud, 1997), pp. 136–44. Few women were presented for brewing offences on Devon manors; D. Postles, 'Brewing and the Peasant Economy: Some Manors in Late Medieval Devon', *Rural History*, 3 (1992), pp. 140–41.

21. D. Hutton, 'Women in Fourteenth Century Shrewsbury', in Charles and Duffin, eds, *Women and Work in Pre-Industrial England*, p. 95; W. Hudson, ed., *Leet Jurisdiction in the City of Norwich during the Thirteenth and Fourteenth Centuries*, Selden Society, 5 (1891), pp. 26–31. *Ultra Aquam* was the city ward across the river. R. H. Britnell, *Growth and Decline in Colchester, 1300–1525* (Cambridge, 1986), pp. 21, 89–91, 269–71 points out that the assize of ale was not enforced in the town; instead, there was a

licensing system under which most brewers were charged 3*d.* by the court. The two bailiffs headed the borough government.

22. Bennett, *Ale, Beer and Brewsters*, pp. 37–59; Mate, *Women in Sussex*, pp. 59–64; M. K. McIntosh, *Working Women in English Society, 1300–1620* (Cambridge, 2005), pp. 145–51.

23. Britnell, *Growth and Decline in Colchester*, pp. 64, 195–97; McIntosh, *Working Women*, pp. 163–64.

24. Bennett, *Women in the Medieval English Countryside*, pp. 190–91; Hutton, 'Women in Fourteenth-Century Shrewsbury', p. 95; H. Swanson, *Medieval Artisans: An Urban Class in Late Medieval England* (Oxford, 1989), p. 14.

25. Hutton, 'Women in Fourteenth-Century Shrewsbury', p. 94; R. H. Hilton, 'Lords, Burgesses and Hucksters', *Past and Present*, 97 (1982), p. 11, and reprinted in R. H. Hilton, *Class Conflict and the Crisis of Feudalism: Essays in Medieval Social History* (London, 1985), p. 201.

26. M. Kowaleski, 'Women's Work in a Market Town: Exeter in the Late Fourteenth Century', in Hanawalt, ed., *Women and Work in Preindustrial Europe*, pp. 147–49; R. H. Hilton, 'Women Traders in Medieval England', in Hilton, *Class Conflict*, p. 213; Hudson, ed., *Leet Jurisdiction in Norwich*, pp. 60, 72.

27. F. Collins, ed., *Register of the Freemen of the City of York, 1272–1558*, Surtees Society, 96 (1896), pp. 182, 186, 194–95; Hudson, ed., *Leet Jurisdiction in Norwich*, p. 66.

28. E. W. W. Veale, ed., *The Great Red Book of Bristol*, Bristol Record Society, 5 vols (1931–53), i, p. 133; iii, p. 90.

29. J. Laughton, 'Women in Court: Some Evidence from Fifteenth-Century Chester', in N. Rogers, ed., *England in the Fifteenth Century: Proceedings of the 1992 Harlaxton Symposium*, Harlaxton Medieval Studies, 4 (Stamford, Conneticut, 1994), pp. 93–94; M. Bonney, *Lordship and the Urban Community: Durham and its Overlords, 1250–1540* (Cambridge, 1990), p. 222; W. H. Stevenson, ed., *Records of the Borough of Nottingham* (4 vols, London, 1882–89), ii, pp. 268–69, 274.

30. H. Grieve, *The Sleepers and the Shadows: Chelmsford: a Town, its People and its Past*, 2 vols, Essex Record Office Publications, 100 and 128 (Chelmsford, 1988–94), i, pp. 60–61.

31. Mate, *Women in Sussex*, p. 60; Hilton, 'Lords, Burgesses and Hucksters', in Hilton, *Class Conflict*, p. 204; McIntosh, *Working Women*, p. 158.

32. M. Gervers, 'The Textile Industry in Essex in the Late Twelfth and Thirteenth Centuries: A Study based on Occupational Names in Charter Sources', *Essex Archaeology and History*, 20 (1989), pp. 34–73; A. F. Sutton, 'The Early Linen and Worsted Industry of Norfolk and the Evolution of

the London Mercers' Company', *Norfolk Archaeology*, 40 (1987–89), pp. 201–25; B. M. S. Campbell, 'Population Pressure, Inheritance and the Land Market in a Fourteenth-Century Peasant Community', in R. M. Smith, ed., *Land, Kinship and Life-Cycle* (Cambridge, 1984), pp. 87–94.

33. I. Blanchard, 'Industrial Employment and the Rural Land Market, 1380–1520', in Smith, ed., *Land, Kinship and Life-Cycle*, pp. 229–31.

34. M. Kowaleski, 'Women's Work in a Market Town', pp. 152–53; Swanson, *Medieval Artisans*, p. 42.

35. Sutton, 'The Early Linen and Worsted Industry', pp. 209–12; L. R. Poos, ed., *Lower Ecclesiastical Jurisdiction in Late-Medieval England: The Courts of the Dean and Chapter of Lincoln, 1336–49, and the Deanery of Wisbech, 1458–84*, British Academy Records of Social and Economic History, new series, 32 (Oxford, 2001), pp. 358–59. Judging by her household goods, Isabella Wylson of Wisbech carded and spun: ibid., pp. 353–54.

36. Sutton, 'The Early Linen and Worsted Industry', p. 214; Swanson, *Medieval Artisans*, p. 30; B. McClenaghan, *The Springs of Lavenham and the Suffolk Cloth Trade in the Fifteenth and Sixteenth Centuries* (Ipswich, 1924), pp. 14, 64; Myers, ed., *English Historical Documents, 1327–1485*, p. 1025.

37. Sutton, 'The Early Linen and Worsted Industry', p. 213; Poos, ed., *Lower Ecclesiastical Jurisdiction*, p. 385; Swanson, *Medieval Artisans*, p. 35.

38. F. B. Bickley, ed., *The Little Red Book of Bristol*, 2 vols (Bristol, 1900), ii, pp. 127–28; Myers, ed., *English Historical Documents, 1327–1485*, p. 1094; W. Hudson and J. C. Tingey, eds, *The Records of the City of Norwich*, 2 vols (Norwich, 1906–10), ii, pp. 379–80.

39. A. F. Sutton, 'The Shop-Floor of the London Mercery Trade, c. 1200–c. 1500: The Marginalisation of the Artisan, the Itinerant Mercer and the Shopholder', *Nottingham Medieval Studies*, 45 (2001), pp. 33–34; A. F. Sutton, 'Alice Claver, Silkwoman (d. 1489)', in C. M Barron and A. F. Sutton, eds, *Medieval London Widows, 1300–1500* (London, 1994), p. 137; Phillips, *Medieval Maidens*, pp. 133–34; K. Lacey, 'The Production of "Narrow Ware" by Silkwomen in Fourteenth and Fifteenth-Century England', *Textile History*, 18 (1987), p. 193. Corses were woven or plaited silk ribbons. The throwster converted raw silk into yarn.

40. Sutton, 'Shop-Floor of the London Mercery Trade', p. 33; Sutton, 'Alice Claver', pp. 136–37; Phillips, *Medieval Maidens*, pp. 132–33.

41. Sutton, 'Shop-Floor of the London Mercery Trade', pp. 43–45; Sutton, 'Alice Claver', p. 135.

42. L. Fox, 'The Coventry Guilds and Trading Companies with Special

Reference to the Position of Women', *Birmingham Archaeological Society Transactions and Proceedings*, 78 (1962), p. 21; P. J. P. Goldberg, ed. and trans., *Women in England, c. 1275–1525* (Manchester, 1995), pp. 197–98.

43. A. Farley and H. Ellis, eds, *Liber Censualis vocatus Domesday Book,*, i, fol. 74r; J. Alexander and P. Binski, eds, *Age of Chivalry: Art in Plantagenet England, 1200–1400* (London, 1987), pp. 45, 159.

44. H. Swanson, 'The Illusion of Economic Structure: Craft Gilds in Late Medieval English Towns', *Past and Present*, 121 (1988), pp. 29–36; Fox, 'The Coventry Guilds', p. 19; M. Kowaleski and J. M. Bennett, 'Crafts, Gilds and Women in the Middle Ages: Fifty Years after Marian K. Dale', *Signs*, 14 (1988–89), p. 478.

45. Goldberg, *Women, Work and Life-Cycle*, p. 130; J. H. Harvey, *English Medieval Architects* (Gloucester, 1984), pp. 243–44; E. Veale, 'Matilda Penne, Skinner (d. 1392/3)', in Barron and Sutton, eds, *Medieval London Widows*, pp. 47–54; C. M. Barron, 'Johanna Hill (d. 1441) and Johanna Sturdy (d. c. 1460), Bell-Founders', in ibid., pp. 104–6, 109–11.

46. S. Bartlet, 'Women in the Medieval Anglo-Jewish Community', in P. Skinner, ed., *The Jews in Medieval Britain: Historical, Literary and Archaeological Perspectives* (Woodbridge, 2003), pp. 113–27; R. B. Dobson, 'The Medieval York Jewry Reconsidered', in ibid., pp. 145–56.

47. Goldberg, *Women, Work and Life-Cycle*, pp. 125–27; Kowaleski, 'Women's Work in a Market Town', p. 152.

48. Lacey, 'Women and Work in Fourteenth- and Fifteenth-Century London', pp. 53–54; K. Lacey, 'Margaret Croke (d. 1491)', in Barron and Sutton, eds, *Medieval London Widows*, pp. 156–57.

49. E. M. Carus-Wilson, ed., *The Overseas Trade of Bristol in the Later Middle Ages*, Bristol Record Society, 7 (1937), pp. 154, 225, 227, 233; T. P. Wadley, *Notes or Abstracts of Wills in the Great Orphan Book and Book of Wills in the Council House at Bristol* (Bristol, 1886), pp. 164–65; W. R. Childs, ed., *The Customs Accounts of Hull, 1453–90*, Yorkshire Archaeological Society Record Series, 144 (1984), pp. 94, 116–19, 128, 132–33, 142, 148, 154, 158–61, 167, 170–72, 179; M. Sellers, ed., *The York Mercers and Merchant Adventurers, 1356–1917*, Surtees Society, 129 (1918), pp. 64, 67; Goldberg, *Women, Work and Life-Cycle*, p. 125.

50. C. M. Barron, 'The "Golden Age" of Women in Medieval London', in *Medieval Women in Southern England*, Reading Medieval Studies, 15 (1989), pp. 38–49.

51. Mate, *Women in Sussex*, pp. 16, 18. The wages of agricultural labourers were cut and employers began to provide food; this did not help families at home.

52. Sutton, 'Shop-Floor of the London Mercery Trade', pp. 12–13, 40–42. Shepsters cut out and made linen garments.

53. J. W. Percy, ed., *York Memorandum Book BY*, Surtees Society, 186 (1973), pp. 194–96, 216–18.

54. Veale, 'Matilda Penne, Skinner', p. 49; V. Sekules, 'Women's Piety and Patronage', in N. Saul, ed., *Age of Chivalry: Art and Society in Late Medieval England* (London, 1992), p. 131.

55. N. Davis, ed., *Paston Letters and Papers of the Fifteenth Century*, 2 vols (Oxford, 1971–76), i, p. 628.

56. C. Rawcliffe, *Medicine and Society in Later Medieval England* (Stroud, 1995), pp. 178, 186–89, 198–99. Nurses will be discussed in Chapter 9, below, in connection with hospitals and charity.

57. R. M. Karras, 'The Regulation of Brothels in Later Medieval England', *Signs*, 14 (1988–89), pp. 408–10; R. M. Karras, *Common Women: Prostitution and Sexuality in Medieval England* (Oxford, 1996), pp. 22–23; J. B. Post, 'A Fifteenth-Century Customary of the Southwark Stews', *Journal of the Society of Archivists*, 5 (1974–77), p. 418; M. Prestwich, ed., *York Civic Ordinances, 1301*, Borthwick Papers, 49 (1976), pp. 16–17; P. J. P. Goldberg, 'Pigs and Prostitutes: Streetwalking in Comparative Perspective', in K. J. Lewis, N. J. Menuge and K. M. Phillips, eds, *Young Medieval Women* (Stroud, 1999), pp. 172–74; Goldberg, ed. and trans., *Women in England*, pp. 210–13.

58. Goldberg, 'Pigs and Prostitutes', pp. 174–80; G. Rosser, *Medieval Westminster, 1200–1450* (Oxford, 1989), pp. 143–44; Kettle, 'Ruined Maids', pp. 28–29.

59. Karras, *Common Women*, pp. 35–43.

60. Goldberg, 'Pigs and Prostitutes', pp. 180–83.

61. Post, 'A Fifteenth-Century Customary of the Southwark Stews', pp. 422–28; M. Carlin, *Medieval Southwark* (London, 1996), pp. 213–17; Karras, 'The Regulation of Brothels', pp. 410–12, 418–21, 427–33.

62. M. Bateson, ed., *Records of the Borough of Leicester, 1103–1603*, 3 vols (Cambridge, 1899–1905), ii, p. 291; L. C. Attreed, ed., *The York House Books, 1461–90*, 2 vols (Stroud, 1991), i, p. 261; M. D. Harris, ed., *The Coventry Leet Book*, 4 vols, Early English Text Society (1907–13), ii, p. 545.

Notes to Chapter 6: Noblewomen

1. D. Whitelock, ed., *English Historical Documents, c. 500–1042* (2nd edn, London, 1979), pp. 391–94, 468; F. L. Attenborough, ed., *The Laws of the Earliest English Kings* (Cambridge, 1922), pp. 4–17.

2. D. Whitelock, ed., *Anglo-Saxon Wills* (Cambridge, 1930), pp. 6–9, 22–29,

34–43, 94–97; K. A. Lowe, 'The Nature and Effect of the Anglo-Saxon Vernacular Will', *Journal of Legal History*, 19 (1998), pp. 41–47; J. Crick, 'Women, Posthumous Benefaction and Family Strategy in Pre-Conquest England', *Journal of British Studies*, 38 (1999), pp. 401–2.

3. J. G. Nichols and J. Bruce, eds, *Wills from Doctors' Commons*, Camden Society, old series, 83 (1863), p. 1; J. Nichols, *A Collection of All the Wills of the Kings and Queens of England* (London, 1780), pp. 98–103; Borthwick Institute of Historical Research, York Archiepiscopal Register 14, fos 47v–48r. Mary Roos' mother was the daughter and heiress of Sir John de Orreby.

4. F. J. Furnivall, *The Fifty Earliest English Wills*, Early English Text Society, original series, 78 (1882), pp. 116–17; N. Davis, ed., *The Paston Letters and Papers of the Fifteenth Century* (2 vols, Oxford, 1971–76), i, pp. 382–89; H. Jenkinson, 'Mary de Sancto Paulo, Foundress of Pembroke College, Cambridge', *Archaeologia*, 66 (1915), pp. 432–35; A. M. Morganstern, *Gothic Tombs of Kinship in France, the Low Countries and England* (Philadelphia, Pennsylvania, 2000), pp. 73–80; L. L. Gee, *Women, Art and Patronage from Henry III to Edward III, 1216–1377* (Woodbridge, 2002), pp. 114–15.

5. C. H. Hunter Blair, 'Armorials on English Seals from the Twelfth to the Sixteenth Centuries', *Archaeologia*, 2nd series, 39 (1943), pp. 19–21; B. Bedos-Rezak, *Form and Order in Medieval France: Studies in Social and Quantitative Sigillography* (Aldershot, 1993), pp. 61–82; A. Ailes, 'Armorial Portrait Seals of Medieval Noblewomen: Examples in the Public Record Office', in J. Campbell-Kease, ed., *Tribute to an Armorist* (London, 2000), pp. 218–20; S. M. Johns, *Noblewomen, Aristocracy and Power in the Twelfth-Century Anglo-Norman Realm* (Manchester, 2003), pp. 122–31. The emblems of a lily and a hawk are ambivalent. The lily was the emblem of the Virgin Mary and stood for fertility and purity. The hawk reflected the noblewoman's social standing, but it also stood for evil and cruelty. The noblewoman in control of the bird may represent a woman who has overcome these sins.

6. Ailes, 'Armorial Portrait Seals', p. 219; Johns, *Noblewomen, Aristocracy and Power*, pp. 131, 212–13, 221; a catalogue of seals of the twelfth and early thirteenth centuries is given in ibid., pp. 203–30.

7. Ailes, 'Armorial Portrait Seals', pp. 220–21, 223, 225, 228; Hunter Blair, 'Armorials on English Seals', p. 21.

8. British Library, London, Harley Charter 47 E 39; L. C. Loyd and D. M. Stenton, eds, *Sir Christopher Hatton's Book of Seals* (Oxford, 1950), p. 53. Elizabeth's three husbands were John de Burgh, son and heir of

Richard de Burgh, earl of Ulster; Theobald de Verdun; and Roger Damory. She took her surname from her first husband.

9. W. S. Mackie, ed., *The Exeter Book*, part 2, Early English Text Society, original series, 194 (1934), pp. 38–39, 120–27, 202–3.

10. C. M. Woolgar, *The Great Household in Late Medieval England* (New Haven, Connecticut, 1999), pp. 34–36.

11. D. Whitelock, ed., *The Will of Æthelgifu*, Roxburghe Club (Oxford, 1968), pp. 12–15; Johns, *Noblewomen, Aristocracy and Power*, pp. 159–60; C. W. Foster, ed., *The Registrum Antiquissimum of the Cathedral Church of Lincoln*, Lincoln Record Society, 4 vols, (1931–37), i, pp. 293–95.

12. Davis, ed., *Paston Letters and Papers*, i, pp. 382–89; Borthwick Institute of Historical Research, Probate Register 3, fol. 61v; E. F. Jacob, ed., *The Register of Henry Chichele, Archbishop of Canterbury, 1414–43*, Canterbury and York Society, 4 vols (1937–47), ii, pp. 14–18; J. Ward, ed. and trans., *Women of the English Nobility and Gentry, 1066–1500* (Manchester, 1995), pp. 189–90.

13. D. Oschinsky, ed., *Walter of Henley and other Treatises on Estate Management and Accounting* (Oxford, 1971), pp. 394–407.

14. F. Heal, *Hospitality in Early Modern England* (Oxford, 1990), pp. 40–42.

15. *A Collection of Ordinances and Regulations for the Government of the Royal Household*, Society of Antiquaries (London, 1790), pp. 37–39; P. Payne and C. Barron, 'The Letters and Life of Elizabeth Despenser, Lady Zouche (d. 1408)', *Nottingham Medieval Studies*, 41 (1997), pp. 148–52; The National Archives: Public Record Office, C47/37/7, fol., 19v.

16. J. C. Ward, *English Noblewomen in the Later Middle Ages* (London, 1992), pp. 50–53; K. Mertes, *The English Noble Household, 1250–1600: Good Governance and Politic Rule* (Oxford, 1988), pp. 17–51; V. B. Redstone and M. K. Dale, ed. and trans., *The Household Book of Dame Alice de Bryene*, Suffolk Institute of Archaeology and Natural History (Ipswich, 1931), p. 124; C. D. Ross, 'The Household Accounts of Elizabeth Berkeley, Countess of Warwick, 1420–21', *Transactions of the Bristol and Gloucestershire Archaeological Society*, 70 (1951), p. 84. Early divisions within the household are described in 'The Establishment of the King's Household' of *c.* 1135; D. C. Douglas and G. W. Greenaway, eds, *English Historical Documents, 1042–1189* (2nd edn, London, 1981), pp. 454–60.

17. M. M. Crow and C. C. Olson, eds, *Chaucer Life-Records* (Oxford, 1966), pp. 13–22.

18. Ward, *English Noblewomen*, pp. 54–57; Nichols, *Royal Wills*, pp. 24–29; The National Archives: Public Record Office, E101/92/23; E101/93/12, m. 1–3.

19. Oschinsky, ed., *Walter of Henley*, pp. 388–93, 395–99.

20. C. D. Ross, *The Estates and Finances of Richard Beauchamp, Earl of Warwick*, Dugdale Society, Occasional Papers, 12 (1956), pp. 6–7; British Library, London, Egerton Roll 2210, and Additional MS 29608.

21. P. Stafford, *Unification and Conquest: A Political and Social History of England in the Tenth and Eleventh Centuries* (London, 1989), p. 176.

22. Johns, *Noblewomen, Aristocracy and Power*, pp. 84–86, 89–95; R. B. Patterson, ed., *Earldom of Gloucester Charters: The Charters and Scribes of the Earls and Countesses pf Gloucester to AD 1217* (Oxford, 1973), pp. 73–74, 87–89, 95–97, 114, 146–47, 152, 155–56, 177.

23. Patterson, ed., *Earldom of Gloucester Charters*, pp. 25–33, 35, 53–56, 59, 62–74, 78, 82–83, 89–91, 99–103, 105, 109, 113, 115, 117–25, 148–49, 153, 162–68, 178.

24. G. E. Cockayne, ed., revised and ed., V. Gibbs et al., *Complete Peerage* (12 vols, London, 1910–59), vi, pp. 451–58; D. Walker, ed., *Charters of the Earldom of Hereford*, Camden Society, 4th series, i (1964), pp. 1–10, 52–53, 67–68. Her grandson, Henry, inherited her lands in 1197 and was created earl of Hereford in 1200.

25. Walker, ed., *Hereford Charters*, p. 52; H. Hall, ed., *The Red Book of the Exchequer*, 3 vols, Rolls Series (London, 1896), i, pp. 293–94; T. Hearne, ed., *Liber Niger Scaccarii*, (2 vols, London, 1774), i, pp. 167–68. The fees of the old enfeoffment were created before 1135 and of the new between 1135 and 1166.

26. *Pipe Roll, 14 Henry II*, Pipe Roll Society, 12 (1890), pp. 122–23; ibid., *16 Henry II*, Pipe Roll Society, 15 (1892), p. 76; ibid., *33 Henry II*, Pipe Roll Society, 37 (1915), p. 140; ibid. *6 Richard I*, Pipe Roll Society, 43 (1928), pp. 234, 239.

27. Walker, ed., *Hereford Charters*, pp. 54–55, 58–59, 61–62, 66, 70–74; W. H. Hart, ed., *Historia et cartularium monasterii Sancti Petri Gloucestriae*, 3 vols, Rolls Series (London, 1863–67), ii, pp. 32, 80–81; D. Walker, 'Some Charters relating to St Peter's Abbey, Gloucester', in P. M. Barnes and C. F. Slade, eds, *A Medieval Miscellany for Doris Mary Stenton*, Pipe Roll Society, new series, 36 (1960), pp. 250, 263–64.

28. Walker, ed., *Hereford Charters*, pp. 53–68.

29. The National Archives: Public Record Office, C115/K2/6682, fol. 180r; Nichols, *Royal Wills*, pp. 278–81.

30. Oschinsky, ed., *Walter of Henley*, pp. 388–99.

31. J. C. Ward, 'Joan de Bohun, Countess of Hereford, Essex and Northampton, *c.* 1370–1419: Family, Land and Social Networks', *Essex Archaeology and History*, 32 (2001), pp. 146–53. Her daughter, Eleanor, married Thomas of Woodstock, duke of Gloucester, and Mary married Henry Bolingbroke.

32. Essex Record Office, D/DBy M1, m. 3d, 13d; M2, m. 11d, 14d, 48.

33. W. Dugdale, J. Caley, H. Ellis and B. Bandinel, eds, *Monasticon Anglicanum*, (6 vols, London, 1817–30), iv, pp. 134, 140.

34. H. Castor, *Blood and Roses: The Paston Family in the Fifteenth Century* (London, 2004), pp. 38–56, 124–71; Davis, ed., *Paston Letters and Papers*, i, pp. 91–98, 125–45, 220–30, 243, 246–47, 251–52, 255–61, 295–308, 323–24, 329–32.

35. Jenkinson, 'Mary de Sancto Paulo', pp. 409–10.

36. Johns, *Noblewomen, Aristocracy and Power*, pp. 92, 115, 117, 169.

37. *List of Sheriffs of England and Wales, from the Earliest Times to AD 1831*, PRO Lists and Indexes, 9 (London, 1898), p. 152; F. W. Maitland, ed., *Bracton's Note Book* (3 vols, London, 1887), iii, pp. 248–49; H. R. Luard, ed., *Annales Monastici*, 5 vols, Rolls Series (London, 1864–69), i, pp. 65–66; W. H. Rich Jones, ed., *The Register of St Osmund*, 2 vols, Rolls Series (London, 1883–84), ii, p. 13.

38. H. R. Luard, ed., *Matthaei Parisiensis, monachi Sancti Albani, Chronica Majora*, 7 vols, Rolls Series (London, 1872–83), v, pp. 235–36.

39. B. J. Harris, *English Aristocratic Women, 1450–1550* (Oxford, 2002), pp. 216–19, 221–24; A. R. Myers, 'The Household of Queen Elizabeth Woodville, 1466–67', in A. R. Myers and C. H. Clough, eds, *Crown, Household and Parliament in Fifteenth Century England* (London, 1985), pp. 288–89.

40. H. Nicolas, ed., *Proceedings and Ordinances of the Privy Council of England*, 7 vols, Record Commission (London, 1834–37), ii, pp. 287, 289, 295; Ross, 'Household Accounts of Elizabeth Berkeley', pp. 81–84; J. H. Cooke, 'On the Great Berkeley Law-Suit of the Fifteenth and Sixteenth Centuries', *Transactions of the Bristol and Gloucestershire Archaeological Society*, 3 (1878–79), pp. 305–24.

41. J. T. Appleby, ed., *The Chronicle of Richard of Devizes of the Time of King Richard I* (London, 1963), pp. 30–31; H. O. Coxe, ed., *Rogeri de Wendover Chronica sive flores historiarum*, 4 vols, English Historical Society (London, 1841–44), iv, pp. 18–24; Johns, *Noblewomen, Aristocracy and Power*, pp. 160–61; M. Prestwich, 'Isabella de Vescy and the Custody of Bamburgh Castle', *Bulletin of the Institute of Historical Research*, 44 (1971), pp. 148–52.

42. Luard, ed., *Paris, Chronica Majora*, v, pp. 336–37; British Library, Harley MS 1240, fos 86v–87r; G. A. Holmes, 'A Protest against the Despensers, 1326', *Speculum*, 30 (1955), pp. 207–12; Ward, ed. and trans., *Women of the English Nobility and Gentry*, pp. 116–19.

43. D. Whitelock, with D. C. Douglas and S. I. Tucker, eds, *The Anglo-Saxon Chronicle* (London, 1961), p. 148, sub anno 1067; R. R. Darlington and

P. McGurk, eds, *The Chronicle of John of Worcester* (3 vols, Oxford, 1995–98), iii, pp. 6–7; M. Chibnall, ed., *The Ecclesiastical History of Orderic Vitalis* (6 vols, Oxford, 1969–80), ii, pp. 224–25.

44. R. Howlett, ed., *Chronicles of the Reigns of Stephen, Henry II and Richard I*, 4 vols, Rolls Series (London, 1884–90), i, p. 179; Chibnall, ed., *Ecclesiastical History of Orderic Vitalis*, vi, pp. 538–41; R. C. Johnston, ed., *Jordan Fantosme's Chronicle* (Oxford, 1981), pp. 72–73, 78–79; Johns, *Noblewomen, Aristocracy and Power*, pp. 13–25, comments on the element of misogyny often apparent in chronicle accounts of women's active roles.

45. T. H. Turner, ed., *Manners and Household Expenses of England in the Thirteenth and Fifteenth Centuries*, Roxburghe Club (London, 1841), pp. 33–84; M. K. Jones and M. G. Underwood, *The King's Mother: Lady Margaret Beaufort, Countess of Richmond and Derby* (Cambridge, 1992), pp. 51–65.

46. Ward, *English Noblewomen*, pp. 104–7; J. C. Ward, 'Letter-Writing by English Noblewomen in the Early Fifteenth Century', in J. Daybell, ed., *Early Modern Women's Letter Writing, 1450–1700* (Basingstoke, 2001), pp. 30–33; M. D. Legge, ed., *Anglo-Norman Letters and Petitions from All Souls MS 182*, Anglo-Norman Text Society, 3 (Oxford, 1941), pp. 347–48, 360–62, 372–73; E. Rickert, 'A Leaf from a Fourteenth-Century Letter Book', *Modern Philology*, 25 (1927–28), pp. 253–54; The National Archives: Public Record Office, E101/93/4.

47. British Library, London, Sloane Roll xxxi 4, m. 5; F. M. Stenton, *The First Century of English Feudalism* (2nd edn, Oxford, 1961), pp. 34–36, 259–60. Witnesses do not necessarily give a completely accurate picture of a gathering, as lists were sometimes truncated or more names were added.

48. The National Archives: Public Record Office, E101/91/14, m. 4.

49. Redstone and Dale, ed. and trans., *The Household Book of Dame Alice de Bryene*, pp. 1, 28, 35, 87.

50. J. C. Ward, 'Elizabeth de Burgh, Lady of Clare (d. 1360)', in C. M. Barron and A. F. Sutton, eds, *Medieval London Widows, 1300–1500* (London, 1994), pp. 37–40; British Library, London, Egerton Roll 8347; D. D. Andrews, 'Richard Lord Rich's Mansion at Rochford Hall', *Essex Archaeology and History*, 34 (2004), pp. 69–73, 88–90.

51. The National Archives: Public Record Office, E101/91/27, m. 4; E101/91/30; E101/92/2, m. 1, 2, 14; E101/92/9, m. 10; DL28/1/2, fos 21r, 24r, 25r. Miniver was the fur from the belly of the Baltic squirrel; the term 'miniver pured' was used for the white belly skins with all the grey trimmed off; E. M. Veale, *The English Fur Trade in the Later Middle Ages* (Oxford, 1966), p. 228.

52. Jacob, ed., *Register of Henry Chichele*, ii, p. 536.

53. I. Short, 'Patrons and Polyglots: French Literature in Twelfth-Century England', in M. Chibnall, ed., *Anglo-Norman Studies*, 14 (1991), pp. 235–37, 243–44; M. S. Serjeantson, ed., *Osbern Bokenham, Legendys of Hooly Wummen*, Early English Text Society, original series, 206 (1938), pp. xx–xxi, 57–58, 136–39, 174, 227, 259, 288; J. Alexander and P. Binski, eds, *Age of Chivalry* (London, 1987), pp. 155–56, 501–4; L. F. Sandler, 'A Note on the Illuminators of the Bohun Manuscripts', *Speculum*, 60 (1985), pp. 364–72.

54. J. Summit, 'William Caxton, Margaret Beaufort and the Romance of Female Patronage', in L. Smith and J. H. M. Taylor, eds, *Women, the Book and the Worldly* (Woodbridge, 1995), pp. 151–65; A. Barratt, 'Dame Eleanor Hull: A Fifteenth-Century Translator', in R. Ellis, ed., *The Medieval Translator* (Woodbridge, 1989), pp. 87–101.

55. A. M. Dutton, 'Passing the Book: Testamentary Transmission of Religious Literature to and by Women in England, 1350–1500', in L. Smith and J. H. M. Taylor, eds, *Women, the Book and the Godly* (Woodbridge, 1995), pp. 44–51.

56. *Testamenta Eboracensia*, iv, Surtees Society, 53 (1868), p. 153; C. M. Meale, ' " ... Alle the Bokes that I Haue of Latyn, Englisch, and Frensch": Laywomen and their Books in Late Medieval England', in C. M. Meale, ed., *Women and Literature in Britain, 1150–1500* (Cambridge, 1993), pp. 134–35.

57. M. C. Erler, *Women, Reading and Piety in Late Medieval England* (Cambridge, 2002), pp. 48–67.

58. This form of patronage will be discussed, below, in Chapters 8 and 9.

59. J. I. Catto, *The Early Oxford Schools* (Oxford, 1984), pp. 205, 240, 244–45, 283, 292–93; H. E. Salter, ed., *The Oxford Deeds of Balliol College*, Oxford Historical Society, 64 (1913), pp. 1–14, 277–83.

60. A. C. Chibnall, *Richard de Badew and the University of Cambridge, 1315–40* (Cambridge, 1963), pp. 16–17, 37–41; D. R. Leader, *A History of the University of Cambridge*, i, *The University to 1546* (Cambridge, 1988), pp. 82–84; Jenkinson, 'Mary de Sancto Paulo', pp. 422–24, 433; *Calendar of Patent Rolls, 1334–38* (London, 1895), p. 237; ibid., *1345–48* (London, 1903), pp. 61, 135–36, 444; ibid., *1350–54* (London, 1907), p. 510; *Entries in Papal Registers Relating to Great Britain and Ireland, Petitions to the Pope, 1342–1419* (London, 1897), pp. 155–56, 410, 533; ibid., *Papal Letters, 1342–62* (London, 1897), pp. 253, 269, 306; ibid., *1362–1404* (London, 1902), pp. 58, 88–89, 167, 171–72.

61. Jones and Underwood, *The King's Mother*, pp. 202–31; J. P. C. Roach, ed., *The Victoria History of the County of Cambridgeshire and the Isle of Ely*, iii (Oxford, 1959), pp. 429–31, 437–38.

Notes to Chapter 7: Queens

1. B. Colgrave and R. A. B. Mynors, eds, *Bede's Ecclesiastical History of the English People*, Oxford Medieval Texts (1969), pp. 72–79, 162–67, 174–83, 294–309.

2. D. Whitelock, with D. C. Douglas and S. I. Tucker, eds, *The Anglo-Saxon Chronicle* (London, 1961), p. 22.

3. W. H. Stevenson, ed., *Asser, Life of King Alfred* (Oxford, 1904), c. 13–15, 17; P. Stafford, 'The King's Wife in Wessex, 800–1066', *Past and Present*, 91 (1981), pp. 3–4; the story of poisoning may well stem from the long-standing struggles between Wessex and Mercia.

4. J. L. Nelson, ed. and trans., *The Annals of St Bertin* (Manchester, 1991), p. 83; J. L. Nelson, 'Early Medieval Rites of Queen-Making and the Shaping of Medieval Queenship', in A. J. Duggan, ed., *Queens and Queenship in Medieval Europe* (Woodbridge, 1997), pp. 301–8, 313–14; J. L. Nelson, 'Inauguration Rituals', in P. H. Sawyer and I. N. Wood, *Early Medieval Kingship* (Leeds, 1977), p. 63.

5. Stafford, 'King's Wife in Wessex', p. 17.

6. L. G. Wickham Legg, ed., *English Coronation Records* (London, 1901), pp. 100–4, 108–12; W. Ullmann, ed., *Liber Regie Capelle*, Henry Bradshaw Society, 92 (1959), pp. 18, 22–24, 96–110.

7. J. Gairdner, ed., *Three Fifteenth-Century Chronicles*, Camden Society, new series, 28 (1880), p. 57.

8. J. L. Chamberlayne, 'Crowns and Virgins: Queenmaking during the Wars of the Roses', in K. J. Lewis, N. J. Menuge and K. M. Phillips, eds, *Young Medieval Women* (Stroud, 1999), pp. 47–68; J. L. Laynesmith, *The Last Medieval Queens: English Queenship, 1445–1503* (Oxford, 2004), pp. 87–89, 102–9.

9. The image is discussed by P. Stafford, 'Emma: The Powers of the Queen in the Eleventh Century', in Duggan, ed., *Queens and Queenship*, pp. 3–4, and plate 1.

10. M. Rule, ed., *Eadmeri Historia novorum in Anglia*, Rolls Series (London, 1884), pp. 121–26; M. Chibnall, ed., *The Ecclesiastical History of Orderic Vitalis*, 6 vols, Oxford Medieval Texts (1969–80), iv, pp. 272–75; W. Fröhlich, trans., *The Letters of St Anselm of Canterbury* (3 vols, Kalamazoo, Michigan, 1990–94), ii, pp. 191–92. The marriage can be compared to that of Henry VII to Elizabeth of York which strengthened the Tudor dynasty. Henry had no intention of relying on Elizabeth's claim as Yorkist heir but she added legitimacy to Tudor rule.

11. J. Gairdner, ed., *The Historical Collections of a Citizen of London in the Fifteenth Century*, Camden Society, new series, 17 (1876), pp. 226–27.

12. *Calendar of State Papers, Spanish*, i (London, 1862), p. 176; M. K. Jones and M. G. Underwood, *The King's Mother: Lady Margaret Beaufort, Countess of Richmond and Derby* (Cambridge, 1992), p. 40.

13. N. Saul, *Richard II* (New Haven, Connecticut, 1997), pp. 90–91; B. Wolffe, *Henry VI* (London, 1981), p. 182; Gairdner, ed., *Three Fifteenth-Century Chronicles*, p. 385.

14. P. Stafford, *Queen Emma and Queen Edith: Queenship and Women's Power in Eleventh-Century England* (Oxford, 1997), pp. 123–39.

15. L. L. Huneycutt, *Matilda of Scotland: A Study in Medieval Queenship* (Woodbridge, 2003), pp. 55–72.

16. D. Carpenter, *The Struggle for Mastery: Britain, 1066–1284* (London, 2003), pp. 193, 341; M. Howell, 'The Resources of Eleanor of Provence as Queen Consort', *English Historical Review*, 102 (1987), pp. 372–93. Queen's gold (which was also a valuable resource for Eleanor of Castile) was a customary payment dating from the twelfth century, comprising a surcharge on any voluntary fine of ten marks or more, paid to the king. It is still found in the fifteenth century but by then was less lucrative.

17. A. Crawford, ed., *Letters of the Queens of England, 1100–1547* (Stroud, 1994), pp. 70–72; A. R. Myers, 'The Household of Queen Margaret of Anjou, 1452–53', in A. R. Myers and C. H. Clough, eds, *Crown, Household and Parliament in Fifteenth-Century England* (London, 1985), pp. 137–47; A. R. Myers, 'The Household of Queen Elizabeth Woodville, 1466–67', in ibid., pp. 252–57; H. Johnstone, 'The Queen's Household', in T. F. Tout, *Chapters in the Administrative History of Medieval England* (6 vols, Manchester, 1920–33), v, pp. 251–58.

18. Crawford, ed., *Letters of the Queens of England*, pp. 8–10; A. R. Myers, 'The Captivity of a Royal Witch: The Household Accounts of Queen Joan of Navarre, 1419–21', in Myers and Clough, eds, *Crown, Household and Parliament*, pp. 93–94; B. P. Wolffe, *The Royal Demesne in English History* (London, 1971), pp. 54–55; Johnstone, 'The Queen's Household', pp. 231–89.

19. A customary payment of £7 a day was made when Margaret of Anjou and her servants resided in the king's household; Myers, 'Household of Margaret of Anjou', p. 154.

20. Stafford, *Queen Emma and Queen Edith*, pp. 107–12; Howell, 'Resources of Eleanor of Provence as Queen Consort', p. 372; Crawford, ed., *Letters of the Queens of England*, pp. 69–70, 82–83; J. C. Parsons, ed., *The Court and Household of Eleanor of Castile in 1290*, Pontifical Institute of Medieval

Studies, Studies and Texts, 37 (Toronto, 1977), pp. 28–40; F. D. Blackley and G. Hermansen, eds, *The Household Book of Queen Isabella of England, 1311–12* (Edmonton, Alberta, 1971), pp. xi–xviii, 2–237; Myers, 'Household of Margaret of Anjou', pp. 152–53.

21. H. R. Luard, ed., *Matthaei Parisiensis Chronica Majora*, 7 vols, Rolls Series (London, 1872–84), v, pp. 513–14.

22. Gairdner, ed., *Three Fifteenth-Century Chronicles*, pp. 65, 384–85; Gairdner, ed., *The Historical Collections of a Citizen of London*, pp. 185–86.

23. Edith was particularly at risk, not for childlessness but for political reasons, when her father and family were outlawed in 1051. She was not divorced but dispatched to a nunnery, probably Wilton but possibly Wherwell. She was restored to her position at court on Godwine's reinstatement in 1052. Whitelock, with Douglas and Tucker, eds, *Anglo-Saxon Chronicle*, pp. 120–21, 126; R. R. Darlington and P. McGurk, eds, *The Chronicle of John of Worcester*, 3 vols, Oxford Medieval Texts (1995–98), ii, pp. 563, 571; F. Barlow, ed., *The Life of King Edward Who Rests at Westminster* (2nd edn, Oxford, 1992), p. 36.

24. J. C. Parsons, 'The Year of Eleanor of Castile's Birth and her Children by Edward I', *Mediaeval Studies*, 46 (1984), pp. 249–65. It is not known if the baby born in 1278 was a boy or a girl, and there may have been two further children.

25. Chibnall, ed., *The Ecclesiastical History of Orderic Vitalis*, iii, pp. 102–9; R. Howlett, ed., *Chronicles of the Reigns of Stephen, Henry II and Richard I*, 4 vols, Rolls Series (London, 1884–89), i, pp. 170–72; ibid., iv, p. 256; W. Stubbs, ed., *The Historical Works of Master Ralph de Diceto*, 2 vols, Rolls Series (London, 1876), i, p. 355; J. C. Parsons, 'Mothers, Daughters, Marriage, Power: Some Plantagenet Evidence', in J. C. Parsons, ed., *Medieval Queenship* (Stroud, 1994), pp. 70–75.

26. Ullmann, ed., *Liber Regie Capelle*, pp. 72–73; K. Staniland, 'Royal Entry into the World', in D. Williams, ed., *England in the Fifteenth Century: Proceedings of the 1986 Harlaxton Symposium* (Woodbridge, 1987), pp. 297–313. By the fifteenth century, ceremonies had fossilised, and this form of the queen's churching can be traced back to the early fourteenth century.

27. M. D. Harris, ed., *The Coventry Leet Book*, 4 vols, Early English Text Society (1903–13, reprinted in two vols, 1971), ii, p. 300; H. Harrod, 'Queen Elizabeth Woodville's Visit to Norwich in 1469', *Norfolk Archaeology*, 5 (1859), pp. 32–37; A. Raine, ed., *York Civic Records*, i, Yorkshire Archaeological Society Record Series, 98 (1938), p. 156; M. James, 'Ritual, Drama and the Social Body in the Late Medieval English Town', *Past and Present*, 98 (1983), pp. 3–29.

28. W. Stubbs, ed., *Chronicles of the Reigns of Edward I and Edward II*, 2 vols, Rolls Series (London, 1882–83), i, pp. 354–55; C. L. Kingsford, ed., *A Survey of London by John Stow* (2 vols, Oxford, 1908), ii, pp. 29–30; R. Barber and J. Barker, *Tournaments, Jousts, Chivalry and Pageants in the Middle Ages* (Woodbridge, 1989), pp. 32, 206–7; C. Barron, 'Chivalry, Pageantry and Merchant Culture in Medieval London', in P. Coss and M. Keen, eds, *Heraldry, Pageantry and Social Display in Medieval England* (Woodbridge, 2002), pp. 220–23; J. Vale, *Edward III and Chivalry: Chivalric Society and its Context, 1270–1350* (Woodbridge, 1982), pp. 172–74; M. Vale, *The Princely Court. Medieval Courts and Culture in North-West Europe, 1270–1380* (Oxford, 2001), p. 217.

29. R. Bentley, *Excerpta Historica* (London, 1833), pp. 171–222; C. L. Scofield, *The Life and Reign of Edward IV* (2 vols, London, 1923), i, pp. 374–75, 417–20; H. E. L. Collins, *The Order of the Garter, 1348–1461: Chivalry and Politics in Late Medieval England* (Oxford, 2000), pp. 301–3.

30. Christine de Pisan, S. Lawson, trans., *The Treasure of the City of Ladies or the Book of the Three Virtues* (Harmondsworth, 1985), pp. 62–65; T. Johnes, trans., *Chronicles of England, France and Spain by Sir John Froissart* (2 vols, London, 1857), i, p. 188; J. C. Parsons, 'The Pregnant Queen as Counsellor and the Medieval Construction of Motherhood', in J. C. Parsons and B. Wheeler, eds, *Medieval Mothering* (New York, 1996), pp. 39–61.

31. C. Monro, ed., *Letters of Queen Margaret of Anjou and Bishop Beckington and Others*, Camden Society, old series, 86 (1863), pp. 90–91, 96–98, 103, 111–12, 115, 119–20, 122–23, 126–28, 135–36, 140–41, 148, 163–64; D. Dunn, 'Margaret of Anjou, Queen Consort of Henry VI: A Reassessment of her Role, 1445–53', in R. E. Archer, ed., *Crown, Government and People in the Fifteenth Century* (Stroud, 1995), pp. 115–40.

32. A. R. Myers, 'The Jewels of Queen Margaret of Anjou', in Myers and Clough, eds, *Crown, Household and Parliament*, pp. 212–13.

33. M. Howell, *Eleanor of Provence: Queenship in Thirteenth-Century England* (Oxford, 1998), pp. 24–54.

34. C. Ross, *Edward IV* (London, 1974), pp. 92–97; J. R. Lander, 'Marriage and Politics in the Fifteenth Century: The Nevilles and the Wydevilles', *Bulletin of the Institute of Historical Research*, 36 (1963), pp. 129–45; M. Hicks, 'The Changing Role of the Wydevilles in Yorkist Politics to 1483', in C. Ross, ed., *Patronage, Pedigree and Power in Later Medieval England* (Gloucester, 1979), pp. 60–71; A. R. Myers, ed., *English Historical Documents, 1327–1485* (London, 1969), p. 300.

35. Stafford, 'The King's Wife in Wessex', pp. 3–5, 24–26; P. Stafford, *Queens,*

Concubines and Dowagers: The King's Wife in the Early Middle Ages (Leicester, 1998), pp. 133, 148–49, 160–61.

36. Whitelock, with Douglas and Tucker, eds, *The Anglo-Saxon Chronicle*, pp. 61–67; A. Campbell, ed., *The Chronicle of Æthelweard* (London, 1962), p. 49, describes Æthelred as king; F. T. Wainwright, 'Æthelflaed, Lady of the Mercians', in F. T. Wainwright and H. P. R. Finberg, eds, *Scandinavian England* (Chichester, 1975), pp. 305–24.

37. Stafford, *Queen Emma and Queen Edith*, pp. 62, 174–78.

38. Ibid., pp. 209–74; Whitelock, with Douglas and Tucker, eds, *The Anglo-Saxon Chronicle*, pp. 97, 102–4, 107; A. Campbell, ed., *Encomium Emmae Reginae*, Camden Society, 3rd series, 72 (1949), pp. 39–53; Barlow, ed., *Life of King Edward*, pp. 22–24, 26–28, 62–64.

39. Chibnall, ed., *The Ecclesiastical History of Orderic Vitalis*, ii, pp. 208–11, 222–23; D. Bates, ed., *Regesta Regum Anglo-Normannorum: The Acta of William I* (Oxford, 1998), pp. 92–94, 183–85, 287–88, 530–33, 634–35, 722–23, 869; *DB*, i, fol. 238v. Baldwin was, in fact, count of Flanders.

40. C. Johnson and H. A. Cronne, eds, *Regesta Regum Anglo-Normannorum, 1100–35* (Oxford, 1956), pp. xvii, 28–30, 81, 84–85, 104, 124, 129, 132, 143–44; R. A. B. Mynors, R. M. Thomson and M. Winterbottom, eds, *William of Malmesbury, Gesta Regum Anglorum*, Oxford Medieval Texts (1998–99), i, pp. 718–19.

41. L. Wertheimer, 'Adeliza of Louvain and Anglo-Norman Queenship', *Haskins Society Journal*, 7 (1995), pp. 102–6.

42. K. R. Potter, ed., R. H. C. Davis, introd., *Gesta Stephani*, Oxford Medieval Texts (1976), pp. 122–37; E. King, ed., K. R. Potter, trans., *William of Malmesbury, Historia Novella*, Oxford Medieval Texts (1998), pp. 98–109.

43. M. Chibnall, *The Empress Matilda: Queen Consort, Queen Mother and Lady of the English* (Oxford, 1991), pp. 51–115.

44. W. L. Warren, *Henry II* (London, 1973), pp. 99, 101, 118–21, 138, 601–2; J. Gillingham, *Richard I* (New Haven, Connecticut, 1999), pp. 37, 79–80, 105; J. Martindale, 'Eleanor of Aquitaine, c. 1122–1204', *Oxford Dictionary of National Biography*, 18 (2004), p. 15.

45. Howell, *Eleanor of Provence*, pp. 112–17, 208–21.

46. Martindale, 'Eleanor of Aquitaine', pp. 16–17; J. Gillingham, *Richard I* (New Haven, Connecticut, 1999), pp. 42–43, 79–80, 105, 118, 125–26, 140–41, 229, 334, 336; N. Fryde, *The Tyranny and Fall of Edward II, 1321–26* (Cambridge, 1979), pp. 176–227; J. C. Parsons, 'Isabella of France', *Oxford Dictionary of National Biography*, 29 (2004), pp. 420–22.

47. H. E. Maurer, *Margaret of Anjou: Queenship and Power in Late Medieval England* (Woodbridge, 2003), pp. 77–208.

48. N. H. Nicolas, ed., *Privy Purse Expenses of Elizabeth of York* (London, 1830), pp. 1–2, 37, 56–57, 83–84, 97.

49. Stafford, 'The King's Wife in Wessex', pp. 23–24; Stafford, *Queens, Concubines and Dowagers*, pp. 125–27.

50. Fröhlich, trans., *Letters of St Anselm*, ii, pp. 221–30, 301–2, 313–14; iii, pp. 22–24, 28–31, 34–36, 46–48, 75–78, 87–88, 139–41, 155, 163–64.

51. Ibid., iii, pp. 139–41; T. Symons, ed., *Regularis Concordia* (London, 1953), p. 2; Mynors, Thomson and Winterbottom, eds, *William of Malmesbury, Gesta Regum Anglorum*, ii, pp. 9–10; Howell, *Eleanor of Provence*, p. 282.

52. Stafford, 'The King's Wife in Wessex', pp. 13, 23; F. Barlow, *Edward the Confessor* (New Haven, Connecticut, 1997), pp. 230–33; Barlow, ed., *Life of King Edward*, pp. 70–75.

53. Bates, ed., *Acta of William I*, pp. 270–96; E. M. C. Van Houts, ed., *The Gesta Normannorum Ducum of William of Jumièges, Orderic Vitalis and Robert of Torigni*, 2 vols, Oxford Medieval Texts (1992–95), ii, pp. 148–49, 260–61; Chibnall, ed., *The Ecclesiastical History of Orderic Vitalis*, iv, pp. 44–47; L. Musset, ed., *Les actes de Guillaume le Conquérant et de la reine Mathilde pour les abbayes caennaises*, Mémoires de la Société des Antiquaires de Normandie, 37 (1967), pp. 52–57, 77–90, 92–98, 111–13. Papal reluctance to approve the marriage was due to William and Matilda being within the prohibited degrees of consanguinity. Their daughter, Cecilia, was given to the abbey as a child and brought up as a nun, ruling the house as abbess between 1113 and 1127.

54. Mynors, Thomson and Winterbottom, eds, *William of Malmesbury, Gesta Regum Anglorum*, i, pp. 754–59; Johnson and Cronne, eds, *Regesta, 1100–35*, pp. 83, 85, 211, 214; H. A. Cronne and R. H. C. Davis, eds, *Regesta Regum Anglo-Normannorum, 1135–54* (Oxford, 1968), pp. 187–88, 190, 192; Huneycutt, *Matilda of Scotland*, pp. 109–10.

55. Cronne and Davis, eds, *Regesta, 1135–54*, pp. 76, 310–11. The Savignac order merged with the Cistercians in 1147.

56. C. L. Kingsford, *The Grey Friars of London*, British Society of Franciscan Studies, 6 (1915), pp. 17–18, 32, 35–36, 70–71, 74, 163–65.

57. W. Hinnebusch, *The Early English Friars Preachers* (Rome, 1951), pp. 34–37, 44–45, 73–79; Parsons, ed., *The Court and Household of Eleanor of Castile*, pp. 16–17, 88, 96–97, 100; Howell, *Eleanor of Provence*, p. 282.

58. *Calendar of Entries in the Papal Registers Relating to Great Britain and Ireland, Papal Petitions, 1342–1419* (London, 1897), p. 122; ibid., *Papal Letters, 1342–62* (London, 1897), p. 87; J. I. Catto, ed., *History of the University of Oxford*, i, *The Early Oxford Schools* (Oxford, 1984), pp. 238–40, 276, 278, 304–7.

59. This free lecture was provided for in the will of Alice Wyche in 1472. D. R. Leader, ed., *A History of the University of Cambridge*, i, *The University to 1546* (Cambridge, 1988), pp. 229, 261–62; Jones and Underwood, *The King's Mother*, p. 214.

60. Barlow, ed., *Life of King Edward*, pp. 22–23.

61. T. Tolley, 'Eleanor of Castile and the "Spanish" Style in England', in W. M. Ormrod, ed., *England in the Thirteenth Century: Proceedings of the 1989 Harlaxton Symposium* (Stamford, 1991), pp. 167–92; N. Saul, *Richard II*, pp. 308, 324, 456; W. Scase, 'St Anne and the Education of the Virgin: Literary and Artistic Traditions and their Implications', in N. Rogers, ed., *England in the Fourteenth Century: Proceedings of the 1991 Harlaxton Symposium* (Stamford, 1993), pp. 81–96.

62. Campbell, ed., *Encomium Emmae Reginae*; Barlow, ed., *Life of King Edward*; Stafford, *Queen Emma and Queen Edith*, pp. 28–49; F. Lifshitz, 'The *Encomium Emmae Reginae*: A "Political Pamphlet" of the Eleventh Century?', *Haskins Society Journal*, I (1989), pp. 39–50.

63. L. L. Huneycutt, 'The Idea of the Perfect Princess: The *Life of St Margaret* in the Reign of Matilda II (1100–18)', in M. Chibnall, ed., *Anglo-Norman Studies: Proceedings of the Battle Conference, 1989*, 12 (Woodbridge, 1990), pp. 81–97; L. L. Huneycutt, '"Proclaiming her Dignity Abroad": The Literary and Artistic Network of Matilda of Scotland, Queen of England, 1100–1118', in J. H. McCash, ed., *The Cultural Patronage of Medieval Women* (Athens, Georgia, 1996), pp. 157–66; Huneycutt, *Matilda of Scotland*, pp. 131–34, 138–42; Mynors, Thomson and Winterbottom, eds, *William of Malmesbury, Gesta Regum Anglorum*, i, pp. 2–9; I. Short, 'Patrons and Polyglots: French Literature in Twelfth-Century England', in M. Chibnall, ed., *Anglo-Norman Studies: Proceedings of the Battle Conference, 1991* (Woodbridge, 1992), p. 237.

64. Wertheimer, 'Adeliza of Louvain', pp. 107–8.

65. J. Martindale, 'Eleanor of Aquitaine', *Oxford Dictionary of National Biography*, 18 (2004), p. 19; K. M. Broadhurst, 'Henry II of England and Eleanor of Aquitaine: Patrons of Literature in French?', *Viator*, 27 (1996), pp. 53–84.

66. Howell, *Eleanor of Provence*, pp. 83–84, 88–91; Parsons, ed., *The Court and Household of Eleanor of Castile*, pp. 13–14; J. C. Parsons, 'Of Queens, Courts and Books: Reflections on the Literary Patronage of Thirteenth-Century Plantagenet Queens', in McCash, ed., *Cultural Patronage of Medieval Women*, pp. 176–88; Tolley, 'Eleanor of Castile and the "Spanish" Style in England', pp. 170–71; Tout, *Chapters in Medieval Administrative History*, v, p. 249.

67. Stafford, 'The King's Wife in Wessex', p. 16; Stafford, *Queens, Concubines and Dowagers*, p. 166.

68. A. R. Myers, 'The Captivity of a Royal Witch: The Household Accounts of Queen Joan of Navarre, 1419–21', in Myers and Clough, eds, *Crown, Household and Parliament*, pp. 93–133; M. Jones, 'Entre la France et l'Angleterre: Jeanne de Navarre, duchesse de Bretagne et reine d'Angleterre (1368–1437)', in G. Contamine and P. Contamine, eds, *Autour de Marguerite d'Ecosse: reines, princesses et dames du XVe siècle* (Paris, 1999), pp. 67–68. I would like to thank Dr Maureen Jurkowski for drawing my attention to this article.

69. Howell, *Eleanor of Provence*, pp. 300–7; M. Hicks, 'Elizabeth Woodville', *Oxford Dictionary of National Biography*, 18 (2004), p. 82.

70. King, ed., Potter, trans., *William of Malmesbury, Historia Novella*, pp. 60–63; Potter, ed., Davis, introd., *Gesta Stephani*, pp. 86–87; Darlington and McGurk, eds, *Chronicle of John of Worcester*, iii, pp. 268–69; W. W. Shirley, ed., *Royal and Other Historical Letters Illustrative of the Reign of Henry III*, 2 vols, Rolls Series (London, 1862–66), i, pp. 114–15; Wolffe, *Henry VI*, pp. 45, 90.

71. J. C. Parsons, '"Never was a Body Buried in England with Such Solemnity and Honour": the Burials and Posthumous Commemorations of English Queens to 1500', in Duggan, ed., *Queens and Queenship*, pp. 323, 325–27.

Notes to Chapter 8: Religious Women

1. B. Colgrave and R. A. B. Mynors, eds, *Bede's Ecclesiastical History of the English People*, Oxford Medieval Texts (1969), pp. 164–67, 202–5; M. A. Meyer, 'Queens, Convents and Conversion in Early Anglo-Saxon England', *Revue Bénédictine*, 109 (1999), pp. 110–11.

2. Colgrave and Mynors, eds, *Bede's Ecclesiastical History*, pp. 236–41.

3. D. Farmer, *The Oxford Dictionary of Saints* (Oxford, 1997), p. 238; D. Whitelock, ed., *English Historical Documents, c. 500–1042* (2nd edn, London, 1979), p. 710; S. Hollis, *Anglo-Saxon Women and the Church* (Woodbridge, 1992), pp. 75–112.

4. B. Yorke, *Nunneries and Anglo-Saxon Royal Houses* (London, 2003), pp. 2–3; a list of royal nunneries founded by c. 735 is given in ibid., pp. 197–98.

5. G. Waitz, ed., *Vita Leobae Abbatissae Biscofesheimensis auctore Rudolfo Fuldensi*, Monumenta Germaniae Historica, Scriptores, 15, part 1 (Hanover, 1887), p. 123; Whitelock, ed., *English Historical Documents, c. 500–1042*, pp. 782–83.

6. Colgrave and Mynors, eds, *Bede's Ecclesiastical History*, pp. 288–93, 294–309, 404–21, 428–31; Whitelock, ed., *English Historical Documents, c. 500–1042*, pp. 747–51. Ælfflaed was dedicated as a nun by her father, Oswiu, in thanksgiving for his victory over Penda of Mercia at the battle of Winwaed; she and her mother, Eanflaed, were later in charge of the monastery.

7. Farmer, *The Oxford Dictionary of Saints*, pp. 237, 349–50, 445, 511; Colgrave and Mynors, eds, *Bede's Ecclesiastical History*, pp. 390–97; Meyer, 'Queens, Convents and Conversion', p. 105. Æthelthryth is more commonly called Etheldreda or Audrey.

8. Whitelock, ed., *English Historical Documents, c. 500–1042*, pp. 689–90; Colgrave and Mynors, eds, *Bede's Ecclesiastical History*, pp. 292–93; Yorke, *Nunneries and Anglo-Saxon Royal Houses*, pp. 162–65.

9. M. Tangl, ed., *Die Briefe des Heiligen Bonifatius und Lullus*, Monumenta Germaniae Historica, Epistolae Selectae, 1 (Berlin, 1955), pp. 47–49, 54, 60, 229–31; Whitelock, ed., *English Historical Documents, c. 500–1042*, pp. 811–12. Bucge, who was the daughter of Centwine of Wessex, met Boniface in Rome in 738.

10. Waitz, ed., *Vita Leobae*, pp. 122–31; Tangl, ed., *Die Briefe*, pp. 52–53, 139–40, 216–17, 223; F. M. Stenton, *Anglo-Saxon England* (2nd edn, Oxford, 1947), p. 173; Hollis, *Anglo-Saxon Women and the Church*, pp. 271–300. Excerpts of the *Life* and Leofgyth's letter dated soon after 732 are printed in Whitelock, ed., *English Historical Documents, c. 500–1042*, pp. 782–87, 798–99.

11. Farmer, *The Oxford Dictionary of Saints*, pp. 461, 497.

12. Colgrave and Mynors, eds, *Bede's Ecclesiastical History*, pp. 420–23; Whitelock, ed., *English Historical Documents, c. 500–1042*, pp. 804–6; S. Foot, *Veiled Women* (2 vols, Aldershot, 2000), i, pp. 53–55.

13. D. Whitelock, with D. C. Douglas and S. I. Tucker, eds, *The Anglo-Saxon Chronicle* (London, 1961), pp. 41–43; Foot, *Veiled Women*, i, pp. 75–77.

14. Yorke, *Nunneries and Anglo-Saxon Royal Houses*, pp. 2–4, 191; J. Crick, 'Church, Land and Local Nobility in Early Ninth-Century Kent: The Case of Ealdorman Oswulf ', *Historical Research*, 61 (1988), pp. 251–69; Whitelock, with Douglas and Tucker, eds, *The Anglo-Saxon Chronicle*, pp. 58–59.

15. Yorke, *Nunneries and Anglo-Saxon Royal Houses*, p. 194; J. Crick, 'The Wealth, Patronage and Connections of Women's Houses in Late Anglo-Saxon England', *Revue Bénédictine*, 109 (1999), p. 180; P. Stafford, 'Queens, Nunneries and Reforming Churchmen: Gender, Religious Status and Reform in Tenth- and Eleventh-Century England', *Past and Present*, 163 (1999), pp. 33–34.

16. T. Symons, ed., *Regularis Concordia* (London, 1953), pp. 2–3. Not all nunneries benefited from the queen's protection; Ælfthryth founded the West

Saxon nunneries of Amesbury and Wherwell, but Barking suffered from her desire to extend royal influence; P. Halpin, 'Women Religious in Late Anglo-Saxon England', *Haskins Society Journal*, 6 (1994), p. 99.

17. Foot, *Veiled Women*, ii, pp. 165–77, 221–31; B. Yorke, 'The Legitimacy of St Edith', *Haskins Society Journal*, 11 (1998), pp. 107–10.

18. Foot, *Veiled Women*, i, pp. 127–34; Halpin, 'Women Religious in Late Anglo-Saxon England', pp. 103–6.

19. D. Whitelock, ed., *Anglo-Saxon Wills* (Cambridge, 1930), pp. 10–15, 108–9; G. R. Owen, 'Wynflaed's Wardrobe', *Anglo-Saxon England*, 8 (1979), pp. 195–222.

20. D. Whitelock, ed., *The Will of Æthelgifu*, Roxburghe Club (Oxford, 1968), pp. 6–17. Foot, *Veiled Women*, ii, pp. 183–86, suggests that her short-lived community may have been at Standon, Hertfordshire.

21. A. Farley and H. Ellis, eds, *Liber Censualis vocatus Domesday Book* (4 vols, London, 1783–1816), i, fol. 238r; ii, fol. 372r; W. Fröhlich, trans., *The Letters of St Anselm of Canterbury* (3 vols, Kalamazoo, Michigan, 1990–94), ii, pp. 199–200; iii, pp. 184–87.

22. H. Clover and M. Gibson, eds, *The Letters of Lanfranc Archbishop of Canterbury*, Oxford Medieval Texts (1979), pp. 166–67; M. Chibnall, ed., *The Ecclesiastical History of Orderic Vitalis*, 6 vols, Oxford Medieval Texts (1969–80), ii, pp. 268–69.

23. K. Cooke, 'Donors and Daughters: Shaftesbury Abbey's Benefactors, Endowments and Nuns, *c.* 1086–1130', in M. Chibnall, ed., *Anglo-Norman Studies*, 12, *Proceedings of the Battle Conference for 1989* (Woodbridge, 1990), pp. 29–45.

24. Yorke, 'The Legitimacy of St Edith', pp. 97–113; P. A. Hayward, 'Translation-Narratives in Post-Conquest Hagiography and English Resistance to the Norman Conquest', in C. Harper-Bill, ed., *Anglo-Norman Studies*, 21, *Proceedings of the Battle Conference, 1998* (Woodbridge, 1999), pp. 73–85; F. Barlow, 'Goscelin', *Oxford Dictionary of National Biography*, 22 (2004), pp. 1020–21.

25. Fröhlich, trans., *The Letters of St Anselm of Canterbury*, ii, pp. 102–3, 105–7, 212–14; iii, pp. 63–65, 167–68. Earl Waltheof, who had been put to death for rebellion in 1075, was buried at Crowland. Anselm also insisted that Waltheof's so-called son was to be expelled from the nunnery.

26. A. F. C. Bourdillon, *The Order of Minoresses in England*, British Society of Franciscan Studies, 12 (Manchester, 1926), pp. 25–26.

27. R. Gilchrist, *Gender and Material Culture: The Archaeology of Religious Women* (London, 1994), pp. 128–49; C. Rawcliffe, *Medicine and Society in Later Medieval England* (Stroud, 1995), pp. 33–34.

28. B. Millett and J. Wogan-Browne, *Medieval English Prose for Women* (Oxford, 1990), pp. xiv–xx, 2–43.

29. S. Thompson, 'The Problem of the Cistercian Nuns in the Twelfth and Early Thirteenth Centuries', in D. Baker, ed., *Medieval Women* (Oxford, 1978), pp. 227–28, 238, 242–43.

30. J. A. Gribbin, *The Premonstratensian Order in Late Medieval England* (Woodbridge, 2001), pp. 5–8; three nunneries are known but only two (at Irford, Lincolnshire, and Broadholme, Nottinghamshire) survived until the Dissolution.

31. B. Golding, *Gilbert of Sempringham and the Gilbertine Order, c. 1130–c. 1300* (Oxford, 1995), pp. 17–33; S. Thompson, *Women Religious: The Founding of English Nunneries after the Norman Conquest* (Oxford, 1991), pp. 73–79; S. Elkins, *Holy Women of Twelfth-Century England* (Chapel Hill, North Carolina, 1988), pp. 78–84, 134–38.

32. Golding, *Gilbert of Sempringham*, pp. 33–38; G. Constable, 'Aelred of Rievaulx and the Nun of Watton: An Episode in the Early History of the Gilbertine Order', in Baker, ed., *Medieval Women*, pp. 205–26; Elkins, *Holy Women*, pp. 106–11.

33. Golding, *Gilbert of Sempringham*, pp. 40–51; S. Elkins, *Holy Women*, pp. 111–17. All but one of the double houses were founded by 1160, the exception being Shouldham, Norfolk, founded in the 1190s.

34. S. P. Thompson, 'Mary, Countess of Boulogne', *Oxford Dictionary of National Biography*, 37 (2004), p. 66; Thompson, *Women Religious*, pp. 121–23, 166–69, 173–74, 193, 206; S. Johns, *Noblewomen, Aristocracy and Power in the Twelfth-Century Anglo-Norman Realm* (Manchester, 2003), pp. 60–61; M. Oliva, *The Convent and the Community in Late Medieval England* (Woodbridge, 1998), pp. 12–13; J. E. Burton, *The Yorkshire Nunneries in the Twelfth and Thirteenth Centuries*, Borthwick Paper 56 (York, 1979), pp. 1–27; J. H. Tillotson, *Marrick Priory: A Nunnery in Late Medieval Yorkshire*, Borthwick Paper, 75 (York, 1989), p. 4; M. J. Harrison, *The Nunnery of Nun Appleton*, Borthwick Paper 98 (York, 2001), pp. 1–3.

35. Thompson, *Women Religious*, pp. 25, 64–67; Oliva, *Convent and Community*, pp. 25–26.

36. K. H. Rogers, ed., *Lacock Abbey Charters*, Wiltshire Record Society, 34 (1979), pp. 1–2, 10–16; W. H. Rich-Jones, ed., *The Register of St Osmund*, 2 vols, Rolls Series (London, 1883–84), ii, pp. 13, 118–19.

37. W. Dugdale, J. Caley, H. Ellis and B. Bandinel, eds, *Monasticon Anglicanum* (6 vols, London, 1817–30), v, pp. 743–44; *Annales de Waverleia*, in H. R. Luard, ed., *Annales Monastici*, 5 vols, Rolls Series (London, 1864–69),

ii, pp. 344–45. Only two Cistercian nunneries were styled as abbeys, Marham and Tarrant in Dorset.

38. V. C. M. London, ed., *The Cartulary of Canonsleigh Abbey*, Devon and Cornwall Record Society, new series, 8 (1965), pp. ix–xviii, 77–81, 90–99.

39. The Isabella Rule was sanctioned by Pope Urban IV in 1263 for the nunnery of Longchamp near Paris, founded by Isabella, sister of Louis IX; Bourdillon, *The Order of Monoresses*, pp. 6–8.

40. Ibid., pp. 13–25; H. Jenkinson, 'Mary de Sancto Paulo, Foundress of Pembroke College, Cambridge', *Archaeologia*, 66 (1915), pp. 421–22; J. C. Ward, *English Noblewomen in the Later Middle Ages* (London, 1992), pp. 154–56.

41. The National Archives: Public Record Office, E101/394/19; E101/93/12; *Calendar of Entries in the Papal Registers Relating to Great Britain and Ireland, Papal Letters, 1362–1404* (London, 1902), pp. 37–38; *Rotuli Parliamentorum* (6 vols, London, 1783), iv, p. 145a; Bourdillon, *The Order of Minoresses*, p. 66; J. Ward, 'Elizabeth de Burgh, Lady of Clare (d. 1360)', in C. M. Barron and A. F. Sutton, eds, *Medieval London Widows, 1300–1500* (London, 1994), pp. 37–40.

42. D. Knowles and R. N. Hadcock, *Medieval Religious Houses: England and Wales* (London, 1971), p. 285; P. Lee, *Nunneries, Learning and Spirituality in Late Medieval English Society* (Woodbridge, 2001), pp. 15–16, 22.

43. C. Allmand, *Henry V* (London, 1992), pp. 274–76; J. S. Cockburn, H. P. F. King and K. G. T. McDonnell, eds, *Victoria History of the County of Middlesex*, i (Oxford, 1969), pp. 182–91.

44. J. A. Brundage and E. M. Makowski, 'Enclosure of Nuns: The Decretal *Periculoso* and its Commentators', *Journal of Medieval History*, 20 (1994), pp. 143–55; C. T. Martin, ed., *Registrum Epistolarum Johannis Peckham Archiepiscopi Cantuariensis*, 3 vols, Rolls Series (London, 1882–86), i, pp. 81–86; J. Ward, ed. and trans., *Women of the English Nobility and Gentry, 1066–1500* (Manchester, 1995), pp. 209–13.

45. Cooke, 'Donors and Daughters', p. 44.

46. B. M. Kerr, *Religious Life for Women, c. 1100–c. 1350: Fontevraud and England* (Oxford, 1999), pp. 102–3; Oliva, *Convent and Community*, pp. 48–51.

47. W. Brown and A. H. Thompson, eds, *The Register of William Greenfield, Lord Archbishop of York, 1306–15*, 5 vols, Surtees Society (1931–38), ii, p. 206.

48. Kerr, *Religious Life for Women*, p. 109; Oliva, *Convent and Community*, pp. 40–41; A. H. Thompson, ed., *Visitations of Religious Houses in the Diocese of Lincoln*, 3 vols, Canterbury and York Society (1915–27), p. 53.

49. F. D. Logan, *Runaway Religious in Medieval England, c. 1240–1540* (Cambridge, 1996), p. 259; J. Raine, ed., *Historical Papers and Letters from Northern Registers*, Rolls Series (London, 1873), pp. 196–98, 319–23.

50. R. B. Pugh, 'Fragment of an Account of Isabel of Lancaster, Nun of Ames-bury, 1333–34', in L. Santifallen, ed., *Festschrift zur Feier des Zweihundert Jährigen Bestandes des Haus-, Hof- und Staatsarchivs* (2 vols, Vienna, 1949), i, pp. 487–98. I would like to thank Dr Nigel Ramsay for this information.

51. County gentry were involved in county affairs and were wealthier than the parish gentry, who had a more local focus. Oliva, *Convent and Community*, pp. 52–61; N. Vickers, 'The Social Class of Yorkshire Medieval Nuns', *Yorkshire Archaeological Journal*, 67 (1995), p. 128; Tillotson, *Marrick Priory*, p. 6; Harrison, *The Nunnery of Nun Appleton*, p. 5; Bourdillon, *The Order of Minoresses*, pp. 51–52; Lee, *Nunneries, Learning and Spirituality*, pp. 59–67.

52. Agricultural and domestic work are occasionally mentioned in visitations; J. H. Tillotson, 'Visitation and Reform of the Yorkshire Nunneries in the Fourteenth Century', *Northern History*, 30 (1994), p. 12; Thompson, ed., *Visitations of Religious Houses*, i, p. 49.

53. Kerr, *Religious Life for Women*, pp. 125–26; Thompson, ed., *Visitations of Religious Houses*, i, pp. 50–51; Martin, ed., *Registrum Epistolarum Johannis Peckham*, i, p. 82; Ward, ed. and trans., *Women of the English Nobility and Gentry*, pp. 210–11.

54. J. Wogan-Browne, ' "Clerc u Lai, Muïne u Dame": Women and Anglo-Norman Hagiography in the Twelfth and Thirteenth Centuries', in C. M. Meale, ed., *Women and Literature in Britain, 1150–1500* (Cambridge, 1993), pp. 61–62, 65–74; J. Boffey, 'Women Authors and Women's Literacy in Fourteenth- and Fifteenth-Century England', in ibid., p. 160; D. K. Coldicott, *Hampshire Nunneries* (Chichester, 1989), p. 30.

55. N. R. Ker, ed., *Medieval Libraries of Great Britain* (2nd edn, London, 1964), p. 28; A. G. Watson, ed., *Medieval Libraries of Great Britain: Supplement to the Second Edition* (London, 1987), pp. 15, 56; J. Wogan-Browne, *Saints' Lives and Women's Literary Culture, c. 1150–1300* (Oxford, 2001), pp. 6–12, 151–75.

56. J. W. Clay, ed., *North Country Wills*, Surtees Society, 116 (1908), pp. 48–49; F. Riddy, ' "Women talking about the things of God": A Late Medieval Sub-Culture', in Meale, ed., *Women and Literature*, pp. 107–11; A. M. Dutton, 'Passing the Book: Testamentary Transmission of Religious Literature to and by Women in England, 1350–1500', in L. Smith and J. H. M. Taylor, eds, *Women, the Book and the Godly* (Woodbridge, 1995), pp. 41–54; Oliva, *Convent and Community*, p. 69.

57. Kerr, *Religious Life for Women*, p. 125.

58. R. Voaden, 'The Company She Keeps: Mechtild of Hackeborn in Late-Medieval Devotional Compilations', in R. Voaden, ed., *Prophets Abroad:*

The Reception of Continental Holy Women in Late-Medieval England (Woodbridge, 1996), pp. 65–68; J. G. Nichols and J. Bruce, eds, *Wills from Doctors' Commons*, Camden Society, old series, 83 (1863), p. 3; C. A. J. Armstrong, 'The Piety of Cicely, Duchess of York: A Study in Late Medieval Culture', in C. A. J. Armstrong, *England, France and Burgundy in the Fifteenth Century* (London, 1983), pp. 141–42, 144–51; Lee, *Nunneries, Learning and Spirituality*, pp. 135, 141; A. M. Hutchison, 'What the Nuns Read: Literary Evidence from the English Bridgettine House, Syon Abbey', *Mediaeval Studies*, 57 (1995), pp. 208–13.

59. Kerr, *Religious Life for Women*, p. 110; Thompson, ed., *Visitations of Religious Houses*, i, pp. 24, 45, 53, 67–68.

60. Thompson, ed., *Visitations of Religious Houses*, i, pp. 51, 67.

61. Brown and Thompson, eds, *The Register of William Greenfield*, ii, p. 206; iii, pp. 7–8, 9–10, 40, 42, 85–86; Tillotson, 'Visitation and Reform', pp. 7–10, 12–13, 19; Tillotson, *Marrick Priory*, pp. 23–24.

62. Nuns normally carried out their business responsibilities, only sometimes handing them over to men.

63. E. Crittall, ed., 'Fragment of an Account of the Cellaress of Wilton Abbey, 1299', *Wiltshire Archaeological and Natural History Society, Records Branch*, 7 (1956), pp. 143, 145, 154.

64. Oliva, *Convent and Community*, pp. 76, 85, 105–10; M. Oliva, 'Aristocracy or Meritocracy? Office-Holding Patterns in Late Medieval English Nunneries', in W. J. Sheils and D. Wood, eds, *Women in the Church* (Oxford, 1990), pp. 197–208.

65. H. A. Doubleday and W. Page, eds, *Victoria History of the County of Hampshire* (London, 1903), ii, pp. 132–33.

66. Thompson, ed., *Visitations of Religious Houses*, i, pp. 49–50; ii, pp. 1–4.

67. Tillotson, *Marrick Priory*, pp. 8–16.

68. C. M. Woolgar, ed., *Household Accounts from Medieval England*, 2 vols, British Academy Records of Social and Economic History, new series, 17 (Oxford, 1992), ii, pp. 604, 671–73; Thompson, ed., *Visitations of Religious Houses*, i, p. 24; Brown and Thompson, eds, *The Register of William Greenfield*, ii, p. 8.

69. Thompson, ed., *Visitations of Religious Houses*, ii, pp. 175–76; Oliva, *Convent and Community*, p. 117.

70. *Testamenta Eboracensia*, iv, Surtees Society, 53 (1868), p. 151; Guildhall Library, London, MS. 9171/3, fol. 246v; Borthwick Institute, York, Probate Register 4, fol. 110r.

71. N. H. Nicolas, *Testamenta Vetusta* (2 vols, London, 1826), i, p. 79; Essex Record Office, CR2, fol. 98r; Rogers, ed., *Lacock Abbey Charters*, p. 48.

72. M. Bateson, 'The Register of Crabhouse Nunnery', *Norfolk Archaeology*, 11 (1892), pp. 57–63.

73. J. Ward, *Women in Medieval Europe* (London, 2002), pp. 191–208.

74. A hermit lived on his or her own or in small groups; an anchoress was sealed in her cell, usually attached to a monastery or a parish church.

75. Thompson, ed., *Visitations of Religious Houses*, i, pp. 113–15.

76. R. Gilchrist and M. Oliva, *Religious Women in Medieval East Anglia: History and Archaeology, c. 1100–1540*, Studies in East Anglian History, 1 (Norwich, 1993), p. 75; A. K. Warren, *Anchorites and their Patrons in Medieval England* (Berkeley, California, 1985), pp. 127–279.

77. Farmer, *The Oxford Dictionary of Saints*, p. 227; S. B. Meech and H. E. Allen, eds, *The Book of Margery Kempe*, Early English Text Society, original series, 212 (1940), pp. 42–43; M. Archer, ed., *The Register of Bishop Philip Repingdon, 1405–19*, 2 vols, Lincoln Record Society (1963), i, p. 266; Borthwick Institute, York Archiepiscopal Register 18, fol. 358r; Ward, ed. and trans., *Women of the English Nobility and Gentry*, p. 228.

78. F. Barlow, 'Goscelin', *Oxford Dictionary of National Biography*, 22 (Oxford, 2004), pp. 1020–21; S. Hollis, ed., *Writing the Wilton Women: Goscelin's Legend of Edith and Liber Confortarius* (Turnhout, Belgium, 2004), pp. 97–338; G. Roy, ' "Sharpen your Mind with the Whetstone of Books": The Female Recluse as Reader in Goscelin's *Liber Confortarius*, Aelred of Rievaulx's *De Institutione Inclusarum* and the *Ancrene Wisse*', in Smith and Taylor, eds, *Women, the Book and the Godly*, pp. 113–22; Millett and Wogan–Browne, eds, *Medieval English Prose for Women*, pp. xxix–xxxiv, 110–49; M. B. Salu, trans., *The Ancrene Riwle* (Exeter, 1990), pp. 21–22, 182–92; Warren, *Anchorites and their Patrons*, pp. 294–98.

79. F. Beer, *Women and Mystical Experience* (Woodbridge, 1992), pp. 109–64.

80. Ibid., pp. 109–29

81. C. H. Talbot, ed., *The Life of Christina of Markyate*, Oxford Medieval Texts (1959), pp. 34–193.

82. Beer, *Women and Mystical Experience*, pp. 130–57; Julian of Norwich, C. Wolters, ed., *Revelations of Divine Love* (Harmondsworth, 1966), pp. 13–14, 63–66, 87–90, 92–93, 151–73.

83. Meech and Allen, eds, *The Book of Margery Kempe*, pp. 60–111, 198–209, 223–43; J. Wilson, 'Communities of Dissent: The Secular and Ecclesiastical Communities of Margery Kempe's *Book*', in D. Watt, ed., *Medieval Women in their Communities* (Cardiff, 1997), pp. 155–77.

Notes to Chapter 9: Charity and Lay Religion

1. B. Colgrave and R. A. B. Mynors, eds, *Bede's Ecclesiastical History of the English People*, Oxford Medieval Texts (1969), pp. 106–7, 236–37; A. Thacker, 'Monks, Preaching and Pastoral Care in Early Anglo-Saxon England', in J. Blair and R. Sharpe, eds, *Pastoral Care before the Parish* (Leicester, 1992), pp. 156–57.

2. St Luke, c. 10, v. 27–28.

3. J. M. Bennett, 'Writing Fornication: Medieval Leyrwite and its Historians', *Transactions of the Royal Historical Society*, 6th series, 13 (2003), pp. 143, 153–55; M. K. McIntosh, *Autonomy and Community: The Royal Manor of Havering, 1200–1500* (Cambridge, 1986), pp. 238–40; M. K. McIntosh, 'Local Responses to the Poor in Late Medieval and Tudor England', *Continuity and Change*, 3 (1988), pp. 210–25; M. K. McIntosh, *Controlling Misbehaviour in England, 1370–1600* (Cambridge, 1998), pp. 81–107, 195–200.

4. The common decision to relieve thirteen people stemmed from Jesus and his apostles numbering thirteen. C. Jamison, *The History of the Royal Hospital of St Katherine by the Tower of London* (Oxford, 1952), pp. 1–12, 19–22; C. Rawcliffe, 'The Hospitals of Later Medieval London', *Medical History*, 28 (1984), p. 20.

5. P. H. Cullum, *Cremetts and Corrodies: Care of the Poor and Sick at St Leonard's Hospital, York, in the Middle Ages*, Borthwick Paper, 79 (York, 1991), p. 7; C. Rawcliffe, *Medicine for the Soul: The Life, Death and Resurrection of an English Medieval Hospital. St Giles's, Norwich, c. 1249–1550* (Stroud, 1999), pp. 242–43.

6. Rawcliffe, 'Hospitals of Later Medieval London', pp. 9, 20–21.

7. Cullum, *Cremetts and Corrodies*, p. 13; C. Rawcliffe, 'Hospital Nurses and their Work', in R. Britnell, ed., *Daily Life in the Late Middle Ages* (Stroud, 1998), p. 59; Rawcliffe, *Medicine for the Soul*, pp. 242–45.

8. Rawcliffe, 'The Hospitals of Later Medieval London', pp. 13–14; Cullum, *Cremetts and Corrodies*, pp. 16–18.

9. Rawcliffe, 'Hospital Nurses and their Work', pp. 62–63; Cullum, *Cremetts and Corrodies*, p. 7.

10. Rawcliffe, 'The Hospitals of Later Medieval London', p. 2; N. Orme and M. Webster, *The English Hospital, 1070–1570* (New Haven, Connecticut, 1995), pp. 109–11; Cullum, *Cremetts and Corrodies*, p. 6.

11. Cullum, *Cremetts and Corrodies*, pp. 8–9, 18–27; *Calendar of Patent Rolls, 1396–99* (London, 1909), pp. 383–84.

12. Lambeth Palace Library, London, Register of Simon Sudbury, fos 90r-v;

J. Ward, ed. and trans., *Women of the English Nobility and Gentry, 1066–1500* (Manchester, 1995), p. 225.

13. P. H. Cullum, ' "And Hir Name was Charite": Charitable Giving by and for Women in Late Medieval Yorkshire', in P. J. P. Goldberg, ed., *Women in Medieval English Society* (Stroud, 1997), pp. 193–94; Cullum, *Cremetts and Corrodies*, p. 6.

14. J. A. A. Goodall, *God's House at Ewelme: Life, Devotion and Architecture in a Fifteenth-Century Almshouse* (Aldershot, 2001), p. 1; *Calendar of Patent Rolls, 1436–41* (London, 1907), p. 80; W. Dugdale, J. Caley, H. Ellis and B. Bandinel, eds, *Monasticon Anglicanum* (6 vols, London, 1817–30), vi, pp. 725–26; Ward, ed. and trans., *Women of the English Nobility and Gentry*, pp. 204–6; M. A. Hicks, 'Chantries, Obits and Almshouses: The Hungerford Foundations, 1325–1478', in C. M. Barron and C. Harper-Bill, eds, *The Church in Pre-Reformation Society* (Woodbridge, 1985), pp. 130–34.

15. St Matthew, c. 25, v. 31–46. The works of mercy were sometimes depicted in fresco or stained glass in the parish church, as at Potter Heigham, Norfolk, and All Saints', North Street, York.

16. J. M. Bennett, 'Conviviality and Charity in Medieval and Early Modern England', *Past and Present*, 134 (1992), pp. 19–41; M. Moisa and J. M. Bennett, 'Debate: Conviviality and Charity in Medieval and Early Modern England', *Past and Present*, 154 (1997), pp. 223–42.

17. P. Northeast, ed., *Wills of the Archdeaconry of Sudbury, 1439–74*, part 1, *1439–61*, Suffolk Records Society, 44 (2001), pp. 54, 115–16, 238, 247–48, 271.

18. J. Catto, 'Religion and the English Nobility in the Later Fourteenth Century', in H. Lloyd-Jones, V. Pearl and B. Worden, eds, *History and Imagination: Essays in Honour of H.R. Trevor-Roper* (London, 1981), p. 50.

19. D. Whitelock, ed., *The Will of Æthelgifu*, Roxburghe Club (Oxford, 1968), pp. 6–15.

20. C. Burgess, ed., *The Pre-Reformation Records of All Saints', Bristol*, 3 vols, Bristol Record Society (1995–2004), iii, pp. 9–10.

21. Borthwick Institute of Historical Research, York, Archiepiscopal Register 18, fos 357v–358v; Ward, ed. and trans., *Women of the English Nobility and Gentry*, pp. 227–30; E. F. Jacob, ed., *The Register of Henry Chichele, Archbishop of Canterbury, 1414–43*, 4 vols, Canterbury and York Society (1937–47), ii, pp. 535–36; J. Nichols, *A Collection of All the Wills of the Kings and Queens of England* (London, 1780), pp. 40–41.

22. T. H. Turner, ed., *Manners and Household Expenses of England in the Thirteenth and Fifteenth Centuries*, Roxburghe Club (London, 1841), p. 20; British Library, London, Additional Roll 63207; The National Archives:

Public Record Office, E101/93/4, m. 14; E101/93/12, m. 1–4, 4d; E101/93/18, m. 2.

23. The doctrine of the seven sacraments was finalised in the twelfth century and at the Fourth Lateran Council of 1215. The seventh sacrament comprised the ordination of the priest.

24. A. Thacker, 'Monks, Preaching and Pastoral Care', pp. 154–58, 164–65; S. Foot, '"By Water in the Spirit": The Administration of Baptism in Early Anglo-Saxon England', in Blair and Sharpe, eds, *Pastoral Care before the Parish*, pp. 171–92; C. Cubitt, 'Pastoral Care and Conciliar Canons: The Provisions of the 747 Council of *Clofesho*', in ibid., p. 194; G. Rosser, 'The Cure of Souls in English Towns before 1000', in ibid., pp. 279–80; A. W. Haddon and W. Stubbs, eds, *Councils and Ecclesiastical Documents Relating to Great Britain and Ireland* (3 vols, Oxford, 1869–73), iii, pp. 370–71; D. Whitelock, M. Brett and C. N. L. Brooke, eds, *Councils and Synods*, i, part 1, *871–1066* (Oxford, 1981), pp. 313–38; F. L. Attenborough, ed., *The Laws of the Earliest English Kings* (Cambridge, 1922), pp. 36–37.

25. Blair and Sharpe, eds, *Pastoral Care before the Parish*, p. 8; J. Blair, ed., *Minsters and Parish Churches: The Local Church in Transition, 950–1200*, Oxford University Committee for Archaeology, Monograph 17 (1988), pp. 1–19.

26. D. Whitelock, ed., *Anglo-Saxon Wills* (Cambridge, 1930), pp. 92–95, 206; P. Halpin, 'Women Religious in Late Anglo-Saxon England', *Haskins Society Journal*, 6 (1994), pp. 100–2.

27. M. Gibbs, ed., *Early Charters of the Cathedral Church of St Paul, London*, Camden Society, 3rd series, 58 (1939), pp. 233–34.

28. The National Archives: Public Record Office, E101/93/12, m. 4, 4d; SC6/1110/12, m. 1, 1d.

29. F. M. Powicke and C. R. Cheney, eds, *Councils and Synods*, ii, part 1, *1205–65* (Oxford, 1964), pp. 57–96.

30. S. Farmer, 'Persuasive Voices: Clerical Images of Medieval Wives', *Speculum*, 61 (1986), pp. 517–43.

31. A. E. Nichols, *Seeable Signs: The Iconography of the Seven Sacraments, 1350–1544* (Woodbridge, 1994), pp. 90–92. In addition to its religious content, the decoration of the church also included folklore elements, such as the Green Man.

32. M. Aston, 'Segregation in Church', in W. J. Sheils and D. Wood, eds, *Women in the Church*, Studies in Church History, 27 (Oxford, 1990), pp. 241, 252–59, 264–69; N. Orme, 'Children and the Church in Medieval England', *Journal of Ecclesiastical History*, 45 (1994), pp. 569–70; C. N. L. Brooke, 'Religious Sentiment and Church Design in the Later

Middle Ages', in C. N. L. Brooke, *Medieval Church and Society* (London, 1971), pp. 162–82; N. Tanner, ed., *Heresy Trials in the Diocese of Norwich, 1428–31*, Camden Society, 4th series, 20 (1977), pp. 43–44.

33. The pax was a small decorated board which was passed round the congregation and kissed to signify peace in the community. T. F. Simmons, ed., *The Lay Folks Mass Book*, Early English Text Society, original series, 71 (1879), pp. 2–60; R. N. Swanson, ed. and trans., *Catholic England: Faith, Religion and Observance before the Reformation* (Manchester, 1993), pp. 83–91; E. Duffy, *The Stripping of the Altars: Traditional Religion in England, 1400–1580* (New Haven, Connecticut, 1992), pp. 92–102, 109–14, 124–25; J. Bossy, 'The Mass as a Social Institution', *Past and Present*, 100 (1983), pp. 32–43, 51–56; L. R. Poos, ed., *Lower Ecclesiastical Jurisdiction in Late-Medieval England: The Courts of the Dean and Chapter of Lincoln, 1336–49, and the Deanery of Wisbech, 1458–84*, British Academy Records of Social and Economic History, new series, 32 (Oxford, 2001), p. 381.

34. Northeast, ed., *Wills of the Archdeaconry of Sudbury*, pp. 7, 487; A. Watkin, ed., *Archdeaconry of Norwich: Inventory of Church Goods temp. Edward III*, 2 vols, Norfolk Record Society, 19 (1947–48), i, pp. 52–53; Goodall, *God's House at Ewelme*, pp. 269–72.

35. Burgess, ed., *The Pre-Reformation Records of All Saints', Bristol*, i, pp. xxii, 5, 15–17; iii, pp. 9–10, 21–24.

36. Poos, ed., *Lower Ecclesiastical Jurisdiction*, p. 202.

37. K. L. Wood-Legh, *Perpetual Chantries in Britain* (Cambridge, 1965), pp. 8–29.

38. Nichols, *Royal Wills*, pp. 98–99; Goodall, *God's House at Ewelme*, pp. 1, 11–12; G. R. Dunstan, ed., *The Register of Edmund Lacy, Bishop of Exeter, 1420–55*, 4 vols, Canterbury and York Society (1963–71), pp. 387–93.

39. Borthwick Institute of Historical Research, York, Archiepiscopal Register 14, fol. 47v; Guildhall Library, London, MS 9171/6, fol. 178r; ibid. MS 9171/1, fol. 181v; Northeast, ed., *Wills of the Archdeaconry of Sudbury*, p. 326. Margaret also bequeathed a missal and a tabernacle over the pyx at the high altar to Long Melford church.

40. J. Catto, 'Religion and the English Nobility in the Later Fourteenth Century', pp. 49–53; J. C. Ward, *English Noblewomen in the Later Middle Ages* (London, 1992), p. 145; J. Hughes, *Pastors and Visionaries: Religion and Secular Life in Late Medieval Yorkshire* (Woodbridge, 1988), pp. 93, 107.

41. Guildhall Library, London, MS9171/1, fos 66r, 438r; MS 9171/5, fos 129r, 205v, 284v, 306v.

42. Craft guilds in the towns also made religious and charitable provision.

43. K. Farnhill, *Guilds and the Parish Community in Late Medieval East Anglia, c. 1470–1550* (Woodbridge, 2001), pp. 48–49; V. Bainbridge, *Gilds in the Medieval Countryside: Social and Religious Change in Cambridgeshire, c. 1350–1558* (Woodbridge, 1996), pp. 44–45.

44. P. Basing, ed., *Parish Fraternity Register: The Fraternity of the Holy Trinity and Saints Fabian and Sebastian in the Parish of St Botolph without Aldersgate*, London Record Society, 18 (1982), pp. xi, xvii, xxi–xxv, 4–9, 15–17.

45. Ibid., pp. xiii–xv, 54–55.

46. Bainbridge, *Gilds in the Medieval Countryside*, pp. 47–49; Farnhill, *Guilds and the Parish Community*, p. 52; J. Mattingly, 'The Medieval Parish Guilds of Cornwall', *Journal of the Royal Institution of Cornwall*, new series, 10, part 3 (1989), pp. 296–97.

47. Basing, ed., *Parish Fraternity Register*, pp. xxi–xxv, 14–16.

48. M. D. Harris, ed., *The Register of the Guild of Holy Trinity, St Mary, St John the Baptist and St Katherine of Coventry*, Dugdale Society, 13 (1935), p. 28; R. H. Skaife, ed., *The Register of the Guild of Corpus Christi in the City of York*, Surtees Society, 57 (1871), pp. vi–vii, 63, 69, 86, 89, 97, 121.

49. Mattingly, 'The Medieval Parish Guilds of Cornwall', pp. 310–17; K. L. French, 'Maidens' Lights and Wives' Stores: Women's Parish Guilds in Late Medieval England', *Sixteenth Century Journal*, 29 (1998), pp. 399–425.

50. H. F. Westlake, *The Parish Gilds of Medieval England* (London, 1919), pp. 151, 162.

51. Mattingly, 'The Medieval Parish Guilds of Cornwall', pp. 301–2; D. J. F. Crouch, *Piety, Fraternity and Power: Religious Gilds in Late Medieval Yorkshire, 1389–1547* (Woodbridge, 2000), p. 105.

52. W. A. Mepham, 'Medieval Drama in Essex: Dunmow', *Essex Review*, 55 (1946), pp. 129–36; D. Dymond and C. Paine, eds, *The Spoil of Melford Church* (Ipswich, 1989), pp. 5–9.

53. J. Sumption, *Pilgrimage: An Image of Mediaeval Religion* (London, 1975), p. 263; Swanson, ed. and trans., *Catholic England*, pp. 158–59.

54. E. A. Bond, ed., *Chronica Monasterii de Melsa*, 3 vols, Rolls Series (London, 1866–68), iii, pp. 35–36.

55. R. C. Fowler, ed., *Registrum Radulphi Baldock, Gilberti Segrave, Ricardi Newport et Stephani Gravesend, Episcoporum Londoniensium, 1304–38*, Canterbury and York Society, 7 (1911), pp. 25–26; F. C. Hingeston-Randolph, ed., *The Register of John de Grandisson, Bishop of Exeter, 1327–69* (3 vols, London, 1894–99), iii, pp. 1231–34; D. Webb, *Pilgrimage in Medieval England* (London, 2000), pp. 148, 154–57.

56. Bainbridge, *Gilds in the Medieval Countryside*, pp. 33–34, 61–62; Swanson,

ed. and trans., *Catholic England*, pp. 186–88; A. D. Brown, *Popular Piety in Late Medieval England* (Oxford, 1995), p. 85.

57. N. H. Nicolas, ed., *The Privy Purse Expenses of Elizabeth of York: Wardrobe Accounts of Edward IV* (London, 1830), pp. 3–4; Northeast, ed., *Wills of the Archdeaconry of Sudbury*, pp. 65–66; Jacob, ed., *The Register of Henry Chichele*, ii, pp. 385, 539; *Testamenta Eboracensia*, iv, Surtees Society, 53 (1869), p. 153.

58. D. Whitelock, with D. C. Douglas and S. I. Tucker, eds, *The Anglo-Saxon Chronicle* (London, 1961), p. 53; Whitelock, ed., *Anglo-Saxon Wills*, pp. 94–97; D. J. Birch, *Pilgrimage to Rome in the Middle Ages* (Woodbridge, 1998), p. 161; E. Mullins, *The Pilgrimage to Santiago* (Oxford, 2001), p. 66.

59. *Calendar of Patent Rolls, 1307–13* (London, 1894), p. 233; *Calendar of Entries in the Papal Registers Relating to Great Britain and Ireland, Papal Letters, 1342–62* (London, 1897), p. 112; *Papal Petitions, 1342–1419* (London, 1897), pp. 22–23.

60. S. B. Meech and H. E. Allen, eds, *The Book of Margery Kempe*, Early English Text Society, original series, 212 (1940), pp. 60–111, 223–43; Webb, *Pilgrimage in Medieval England*, pp. 204–7.

61. J. A. F. Thomson, 'Orthodox Religion and the Origins of Lollardy', *History*, 74 (1989), pp. 39–55; N. H. Nicolas, *Testamenta Vetusta* (2 vols, London, 1826), i, pp. 127–28.

62. Thomson, 'Orthodox Religion', p. 48; K. B. McFarlane, *Lancastrian Kings and Lollard Knights* (Oxford, 1972), pp. 195–96; G.H., 'Four Ancient Wills', *The Ancestor*, 10 (1904), p. 21.

63. F. J. Furnivall, ed., *The Fifty Earliest English Wills*, Early English Text Society, original series, 78 (1882), pp. 49–51; Jacob, ed., *The Register of Henry Chichele*, ii, pp. 7–10; *Calendar of Patent Rolls, 1405–8* (London, 1907), p. 343; ibid., *1408–13* (London, 1909), p. 450; *Calendar of Papal Letters, 1417–31* (London, 1906), p. 330; J. A. F. Thomson, 'Knightly Piety and the Margins of Lollardy', in M. Aston and C. Richmond, eds, *Lollardy and the Gentry in the Later Middle Ages* (Stroud, 1997), pp. 101–5.

64. S. McSheffrey, *Gender and Heresy: Women and Men in Lollard Communities, 1420–1530* (Philadelphia, Pennsylvania, 1995), pp. 2–4.

65. M. Aston, 'Lollard Women Priests?', *Journal of Ecclesiastical History*, 31 (1980), pp. 444–52, 459–61, and reprinted in M. Aston, *Lollards and Reformers* (London, 1984), pp. 52–59, 62–65; Tanner, ed., *Heresy Trials in the Diocese of Norwich*, pp. 61, 67.

66. S. McSheffrey and N. Tanner, eds, *Lollards of Coventry, 1486–1522*, Camden Society, 5th series, 23 (2003), pp. 127, 153–54; N. Tanner, ed., *Kent Heresy Proceedings, 1511–12*, Kent Archaeological Society, Kent Records, 26 (1997),

pp. 11–32; Tanner, ed., *Heresy Trials in the Diocese of Norwich*, pp. 59–62, 66–68.

67. Tanner, ed., *Heresy Trials in the Diocese of Norwich*, pp. 43–49. Falsyngham was Margery's name for Walsingham.

68. Ibid., pp. 28, 41–42, 47–48.

69. McSheffrey and Tanner, eds, *Lollards of Coventry*, pp. 122–23. Presumably, Henry Locock did not approve of Lollardy; the bishop did not require Margery to make a solemn abjuration of heresy, as he feared that she might be repudiated by her husband.

70. Ibid., pp. 9, 25–28, 116–21, 130–32, 155–61, 217–18; McSheffrey, *Gender and Heresy*, pp. 21, 29–36, 123–24.

Notes to Chapter 10: Death

1. W. Dugdale, J. Caley, H. Ellis and B. Bandinel, eds, *Monasticon Anglicanum* (6 vols, London, 1817–30), iv, pp. 134, 140; J. C. Ward, 'Joan de Bohun, Countess of Hereford, Essex and Northampton, *c.* 1370–1419: Family, Land and Social Networks', *Essex Archaeology and History*, 32 (2001), pp. 146–53. The biblical reference comes from St Luke, 2. 36–38.

2. Guildhall Library, London, MS 9171/6, fol. 218r-v; M. K. McIntosh, *Autonomy and Community: The Royal Manor of Havering, 1200–1500* (Cambridge, 1986), pp. 174, 218.

3. C. Burgess, ed., *The Pre-Reformation Records of All Saints Church, Bristol*, 3 vols, Bristol Record Society (1995–2004), i, pp. 7, 10; ii, pp. 60, 82; iii, pp. 15–17.

4. P. Northeast, ed., *Wills of the Archdeaconry of Sudbury, 1439–74*, part 1, *1439–61*, Suffolk Records Society, 44 (2001), p. 57. Maslin is a mixture of wheat and rye.

5. Guildhall Library, London, MS 9171/3, fos 429v–430v; MS 9171/4, fos 2v–3r.

6. Borthwick Institute of Historical Research, York, Probate Register 3, fol. 347r-v.

7. J. Nichols, *A Collection of All the Wills of the Kings and Queens of England* (London, 1780), p. 178.

8. Guildhall Library, London, MS 9171/6, fol. 178r.

Glossary

Affinity:
Marital kin; or a group of retainers who received fees and liveries from a lord or lady.

Agnatic Kinship:
Descent in the male line of the conjugal family.

Attainder:
Fifteenth-century acts of attainder, passed by parliament, condemned rebels against the crown and provided for their lands to be forfeited to the king.

Bookland:
Land granted by charter in the Anglo-Saxon period.

Childwite:
A fine paid by a father whose daughter gave birth to an illegitimate child.

Consanguinity:
Relationships between kindred. A marriage between related parties was forbidden without an episcopal or papal dispensation. For much of the middle ages, marriage was forbidden within four degrees of relationship (consanguinity).

Consent:
The medieval church distinguished between consent *de praesenti*, consent expressed in the present tense by the bride and bridegroom at the wedding ceremony, and consent *de futuro*, denoting conditional or future consent, which took place at betrothal.

Curiales:
Courtiers.

Dower:
The land to which a woman was entitled after the death of her husband. It was normally settled on her by the bridegroom's family at the time of the marriage.

Dowry:
The gift of land or money made by the bride's father to the bridegroom at the time of the marriage.

Endogamy:
Marriage within the community.

Enfeoffment to Use: The grant of estates to feoffees who held them to the use of a named beneficiary.

Exogamy: Marriage outside the community.

Free Bench: A widow's share in her husband's dwelling house.

Gavelkind: A form of land tenure found in Kent.

Heriot: A payment to the king or lord at death. In the Anglo-Saxon period, lords, ladies and burgesses paid their heriot to the king in horses, arms and money. In the later middle ages, the term was mainly used in connection with the death of a villein, when his best beast had to be rendered to his lord.

Honour: A lordship held by a lord or lady, centred on the chief castle, where vassals who held land of the lord by knight service attended the honour court.

Jointure: Land settled jointly on husband and wife, often at the time of their marriage, which the wife continued to hold after the death of her husband.

Leet Court: The lord's court which held the view of frankpledge and dealt with petty offences, including the assize of bread and ale. The view of frankpledge checked the tithings to which all men over the age of twelve had to belong and which were responsible for their members' good behaviour.

Leyrwite: The fine paid by women for a sexual relationship before marriage.

Maritagium: A term used under the Norman and Angevin kings to denote the dowry in the form of land provided by the bride's family. It reverted to her family if the marriage was childless.

Merchet: The purchase from the lord of a licence for a woman to marry. This usually applied to unfree peasants and in the later middle ages merchet was regarded as a mark of serfdom.

Primogeniture: Inheritance by the eldest son.

Scutage: A payment, mostly found in the twelfth and thir-
                    teenth centuries, when the lord and his vassals did
                    not perform their military service to the crown in
                    person.

Serf or Villein: An unfree peasant.

Bibliography

This is a selective bibliography of secondary works on medieval women. Many of the books have bibliographies which provide further information. Full references to primary sources are given in the notes.

R. E. Archer, '"How Ladies ... Who Live on their Manors Ought to Manage Their Households and Estates": Women as Landholders and Administrators in the Later Middle Ages', in P. J. P. Goldberg, ed., *Women in Medieval English Society* (Stroud, 1997), pp. 149–81.

R. E. Archer, 'Rich Old Ladies: The Problem of Late Medieval Dowagers', in A. Pollard, ed., *Property and Politics: Essays in Later Medieval English History* (Gloucester, 1984), pp. 15–35.

R. E. Archer, 'The Estates and Finances of Margaret of Brotherton, *c.* 1320–1399', *Historical Research*, 60 (1987), pp. 264–80.

M. Aston and C. Richmond, eds, *Lollardy and the Gentry in the Later Middle Ages*, (Stroud, 1997).

M. Bailey, 'Demographic Decline in Late Medieval England: Some Thoughts on Recent Research', *Economic History Review*, 49 (1996), pp. 1–19.

V. Bainbridge, *Gilds in the Medieval Countryside: Social and Religious Change in Cambridgeshire, c. 1350–1558* (Woodbridge, 1996).

D. Baker, ed., *Medieval Women*, Studies in Church History, Subsidia 1 (Oxford, 1978).

D. Baldwin, *Elizabeth Woodville, Mother of the Princes in the Tower* (Stroud, 2002).

R. Barber and J. Barker, *Tournaments: Jousts, Chivalry and Pageants in the Middle Ages* (Woodbridge, 1989).

S. Bardsley, 'Women's Work Reconsidered: Gender and Wage Differentiation in Late Medieval England', *Past and Present*, 165 (1999), pp. 3–29.

F. Barlow, *Edward the Confessor* (New Haven, Connecticut, 1997).

P. S. Barnwell, C. Cross and A. Rycraft, eds, *Mass and Parish in Late Medieval England: The Use of York* (Reading, 2005).

C. M. Barron, *London in the Later Middle Ages: Government and People, 1200–1500* (Oxford, 2004).

C. M. Barron, 'The Education and Training of Girls in Fifteenth-Century London', in D. E. S. Dunn, ed., *Courts, Counties and the Capital in the Later Middle Ages* (Stroud, 1996), pp. 139–53.

C. M. Barron, 'The Parish Fraternities of Medieval London', in C. M. Barron and C. Harper-Bill, ed., *The Church in Pre-Reformation Society: Essays in Honour of F.R.H. Du Boulay* (Woodbridge, 1985), pp. 13–37.

C. M. Barron and A. F. Sutton, eds, *Medieval London Widows, 1300–1500* (London, 1994).

F. Beer, *Women and Mystical Experience in the Middle Ages* (Woodbridge, 1992).

J. M. Bennett, *Ale, Beer and Brewsters in England* (Oxford, 1996).

J. M. Bennett, 'Conviviality and Charity in Medieval and Early Modern England', *Past and Present*, 134 (1992), pp. 19–41.

J. M. Bennett, 'Medieval Peasant Marriage: An Examination of Marriage Licence Fines in *Liber Gersumarum*', in J. A. Raftis, ed., *Pathways to Medieval Peasants*, Pontifical Institute of Medieval Studies, Papers in Medieval Studies, 2 (Toronto, 1981), pp. 193–246.

J. M. Bennett, *Women in the Medieval English Countryside: Gender and Household in Brigstock before the Plague* (Oxford, 1987).

J. M. Bennett, 'Writing Fornication: Medieval Leyrwite and its Historians', *Transactions of the Royal Historical Society*, 6th series, 13 (2003), pp. 131–62.

J. M. Bennett and A. M. Froide, eds, *Singlewomen in the European Past, 1250–1800* (Philadelphia, Pennsylvania, 1999).

J. Blair, ed., *Minsters and Parish Churches: The Local Church in Transition, 950–1200*, Oxford University Committee for Archaeology, Monograph 17 (1988).

J. Blair and R. Sharpe, eds, *Pastoral Care before the Parish* (Leicester, 1992).

J. Bossy, 'The Mass as a Social Institution, 1200–1700', *Past and Present*, 100 (1983), pp. 29–61.

J. Bothwell, P. J. P. Goldberg and W. M. Ormrod, eds, *The Problem of Labour in Fourteenth-Century England* (Woodbridge, 2000).

A. F. C. Bourdillon, *The Order of Minoresses in England*, British Society of Franciscan Studies, 12 (Manchester, 1926).

R. Britnell, ed., *Daily Life in the Late Middle Ages* (Stroud, 1998).

C. N. L. Brooke, *The Medieval Idea of Marriage* (Oxford, 1989).

A. D. Brown, *Popular Piety in Late Medieval England* (Oxford, 1995).

J. A. Brundage, *Law, Sex and Christian Society in Medieval Europe* (Chicago, Illinois. 1987).

J. A. Brundage, *Medieval Canon Law* (London, 1995).

J. A. Brundage and E. M. Makowski, 'Enclosure of Nuns: The Decretal *Periculoso* and its Commentators', *Journal of Medieval History*, 20 (1994), pp. 143–55.

C. Burgess, '"By Quick and by Dead": Wills and Pious Provision in Late Medieval Bristol', *English Historical Review*, 102 (1987), pp. 837–58.

C. Burgess, '"For the Increase of Divine Service": Chantries in the Parish in Late Medieval Bristol', *Journal of Ecclesiastical History*, 36 (1985), pp. 46–65.

J. E. Burton, *The Yorkshire Nunneries in the Twelfth and Thirteenth Centuries*, Borthwick Paper, 56 (York, 1979).

J. E. Burton, 'Yorkshire Nunneries in the Middle Ages: Recruitment and Resources', in J. C. Appleby and P. Dalton, eds, *Government, Religion and Society in Northern England, 1000–1700* (Stroud, 1997), pp. 104–16.

H. Castor, *Blood and Roses: The Paston Family in the Fifteenth Century* (London, 2004).

J. Catto, 'Religion and the English Nobility in the Later Fourteenth Century', in H. Lloyd-Jones, V. Pearl and B. Worden, eds, *History and Imagination: Essays in Honour of H.R. Trevor-Roper* (London, 1981), pp. 43–55.

L. Charles and L. Duffin, eds, *Women and Work in Pre-Industrial England* (London, 1985).

M. Chibnall, *The Empress Matilda: Queen Consort, Queen Mother and Lady of the English* (Oxford, 1991).

M. Chibnall, 'Women in Orderic Vitalis', *Haskins Society Journal*, 2 (1990), pp. 105–21.

E. Clark, 'Some Aspects of Social Security in Medieval England', *Journal of Family History*, 7 (1982), pp. 307–20.

E. Clark, 'The Decision to Marry in Thirteenth- and Early Fourteenth-Century Norfolk', *Mediaeval Studies*, 49 (1987), pp. 496–516.

D. K. Coldicott, *Hampshire Nunneries* (Chichester, 1989).

K. Cooke, 'Donors and Daughters: Shaftesbury Abbey's Benefactors, Endowments and Nuns, c. 1086–1130', in M. Chibnall, ed., *Anglo-Norman Studies: Proceedings of the Battle Conference, 1989*, 12 (Woodbridge, 1990), pp. 29–45.

P. Coss, *The Lady in Medieval England, 1000–1500* (Stroud, 1998).

P. Coss and M. Keen, eds, *Heraldry, Pageantry and Social Display in Medieval England* (Woodbridge, 2002).

S. Crawford, *Childhood in Anglo-Saxon England* (Stroud, 1999).

J. Crick, 'The Wealth, Patronage and Connections of Women's Houses in Late Anglo-Saxon England', *Revue Bénédictine*, 109 (1999), pp. 154–85.

J. Crick, 'Women, Posthumous Benefaction and Family Strategy in Pre-Conquest England', *Journal of British Studies*, 38 (1999), pp. 399–422.

D. J. F. Crouch, *Piety, Fraternity and Power: Religious Gilds in Late Medieval Yorkshire, 1389–1547* (Woodbridge, 2000).

P. H. Cullum, '"And Hir Name was Charite": Charitable Giving by and for Women in Late Medieval Yorkshire', in P. J. P. Goldberg, ed., *Women in Medieval English Society* (Stroud, 1997), pp. 182–211.

P. H. Cullum, *Cremetts and Corrodies: Care of the Poor and Sick at St Leonard's Hospital, York, in the Middle Ages*, Borthwick Paper, 79 (York, 1991).

P. H. Cullum, 'Vowesses and Female Lay Piety in the Province of York, 1300–1530', *Northern History*, 32 (1996), pp. 21–41.

P. H. Cullum and P. J. P. Goldberg, 'Charitable Provision in Late Medieval York: "To the Praise of God and the Use of the Poor"', *Northern History*, 29 (1993), pp. 24–39.

D. L. D'Avray, *Medieval Marriage Sermons: Mass Communication in a Culture without Print* (Oxford, 2001).

R. C. DeAragon, 'Dowager Countesses, 1069–1230', in C. Harper-Bill, ed., *Anglo-Norman Studies*, 17 (1994), pp. 87–100.

R. C. DeAragon, 'In Pursuit of Aristocratic Women: A Key to Success in Norman England', *Albion*, 14 (1982), pp. 258–67.

A. J. Duggan, ed., *Nobles and Nobility in Medieval Europe* (Woodbridge, 2000).

A. J. Duggan, ed., *Queens and Queenship in Medieval Europe* (Woodbridge, 1997).

D. Dunn, 'Margaret of Anjou, Queen Consort of Henry VI: A Reassessment of her Role, 1445–1453', in R. E. Archer, ed., *Crown, Government and People in the Fifteenth Century* (Stroud, 1995), pp. 107–43.

C. Dyer, *Standards of Living in the Later Middle Ages: Social Change in England, c. 1200–1520* (Cambridge, 1989).

S. K. Elkins, *Holy Women of Twelfth-Century England* (Chapel Hill, North Carolina, 1988).

M. C. Erler, 'English Vowed Women at the End of the Middle Ages', *Mediaeval Studies*, 57 (1995), pp. 155–203.

M. C. Erler, *Women, Reading and Piety in Late Medieval England* (Cambridge, 2002).

K. Farnhill, *Guilds and the Parish Community in Late Medieval East Anglia, c. 1470–1550* (Woodbridge, 2001).

C. Fell, *Women in Anglo-Saxon England* (London, 1984).

P. Fleming, 'Charity, Faith and the Gentry of Kent, 1422–1529', in A. Pollard, ed., *Property and Politics: Essays in Later Medieval English History* (Gloucester, 1984), pp. 36–58.

P. Fleming, *Family and Household in Medieval England* (Basingstoke, 2001).

S. Foot, *Veiled Women* (2 vols, Aldershot, 2000).

L. O. Fradenburg, ed., *Women and Sovereignty* (Edinburgh, 1992).

P. Franklin, 'Peasant Widows' "Liberation" and Remarriage before the Black Death', *Economic History Review*, 39 (1986), pp. 186–204.

K. L. French, 'Maidens' Lights and Wives' Stores: Women's Parish Guilds in Late Medieval England', *Sixteenth Century Journal*, 29 (1998), pp. 399–425.

R. L. Friedrichs, 'Marriage Strategies and Younger Sons in Fifteenth-Century England', *Medieval Prosopography*, 14 (1993), pp. 53–69.

L. A. Gates, 'Widows, Property and Remarriage: Lessons from Glastonbury's Deverill Manors', *Albion*, 28 (1996), pp. 19–35.

L. L. Gee, *Women, Art and Patronage from Henry III to Edward III, 1216–1377* (Woodbridge, 2002).

R. Gilchrist, *Gender and Material Culture: The Archaeology of Religious Women* (London, 1994).

P. S. Gold, *The Lady and the Virgin: Image, Attitude and Experience in Twelfth-Century France* (Chicago, Illinois, 1985).

P. J. P. Goldberg, 'The Public and the Private: Women in the Pre-Plague Economy', *Thirteenth Century England*, 3 (Woodbridge, 1991), pp. 75–89.

P. J. P. Goldberg, ed., *Women in Medieval English Society* (Stroud, 1997).

P. J. P. Goldberg, *Women, Work and Life Cycle in a Medieval Economy: Women in York and Yorkshire, c. 1300–1520* (Oxford, 1992).

P. J. P. Goldberg and F. Riddy, eds, *Youth in the Middle Ages* (Woodbridge, 2004).

B. Golding, *Gilbert of Sempringham and the Gilbertine Order, c. 1130-c. 1300* (Oxford, 1995).

J. A. A. Goodall, *God's House at Ewelme: Life, Devotion and Architecture in a Fifteenth-Century Almshouse* (Aldershot, 2001).

L. Granshaw and R. Porter, eds, *The Hospital in History* (London, 1989).

K. Gravdal, *Ravishing Maidens: Writing Rape in Medieval French Literature and Law* (Philadelphia, Pennsylvania, 1991).

J. A. Green, 'Aristocratic Women in Early Twelfth-Century England', in C. W. Hollister, ed., *Anglo-Norman Political Culture and the Twelfth-Century Renaissance* (Woodbridge, 1997), pp. 59–82.

M. Green, 'Women's Medical Practice and Health Care in Medieval Europe', *Signs*, 14 (1988–89), pp. 434–73.

P. A. Halpin, 'Anglo-Saxon Women and Pilgrimage', in C. Harper-Bill, ed., *Anglo-Norman Studies*, 19 (1996), pp. 97–122.

P. A. Halpin, 'Women Religious in Late Anglo-Saxon England', *Haskins Society Journal*, 6 (1994), pp. 97–110.

B. A. Hanawalt, *Growing Up in Medieval London: The Experience of Childhood in History* (Oxford, 1993).

B. A. Hanawalt, ed., *'Of Good and Ill Repute': Gender and Social Control in Medieval England* (Oxford, 1998).

B. A. Hanawalt, *The Ties that Bound: Peasant Families in Medieval England* (Oxford, 1986).

B. A. Hanawalt, ed., *Women and Work in Preindustrial Europe* (Bloomington, Indiana, 1986).

B. J. Harris, *English Aristocratic Women, 1450–1550* (Oxford, 2002).

M. J. Harrison, *The Nunnery of Nun Appleton*, Borthwick Paper, 98 (York, 2001).

F. Heal, *Hospitality in Early Modern England* (Oxford, 1990).

R. H. Helmholz, *Canon Law and the Law of England* (London, 1987).

R. H. Helmholz, *Marriage Litigation in Medieval England* (Cambridge, 1974).

R. H. Hilton, *Class Conflict and the Crisis of Feudalism* (London, 1985).

R. H. Hilton, *The English Peasantry in the Later Middle Ages* (Oxford, 1975).

S. Hollis, *Anglo-Saxon Women and the Church* (Woodbridge, 1992).

M. Howell, *Eleanor of Provence: Queenship in Thirteenth-Century England* (Oxford, 1998).

J. Hughes, *Pastors and Visionaries: Religion and Secular Life in Late Medieval Yorkshire* (Woodbridge, 1988).

L. L. Huneycutt, *Matilda of Scotland: A Study in Medieval Queenship* (Woodbridge, 2003).

H. Jenkinson, 'Mary de Sancto Paulo, Foundress of Pembroke College, Cambridge', *Archaeologia*, 66 (1915), pp. 401–46.

H. M. Jewell, *Women in Medieval England* (Manchester, 1996).

S. M. Johns, *Noblewomen, Aristocracy and Power in the Twelfth-Century Anglo-Norman Realm* (Manchester, 2003).

H.Johnstone, 'The Queen's Household', in T.F.Tout, *Chapters in the Administrative History of Medieval England*, v (Manchester, 1930), pp. 231–89.

M. K. Jones and M. G. Underwood, *The King's Mother: Lady Margaret Beaufort, Countess of Richmond and Derby* (Cambridge, 1992).

R. M. Karras, *Common Women: Prostitution and Sexuality in Medieval England* (Oxford, 1996).

R. M. Karras, 'The Regulation of Brothels in Later Medieval England', *Signs*, 14 (1988–89), pp. 399–433.

B. A. Kellum, 'Infanticide in England in the Later Middle Ages', *History of Childhood Quarterly*, 1 (1973–74), pp. 367–88.

B. M. Kerr, *Religious Life for Women, c. 1100–c. 1350: Fontevraud in England* (Oxford, 1999).

A. J. Kettle, 'Ruined Maids: Prostitutes and Servant Girls in Later Medieval England', in R. R. Edwards and V. Ziegler, eds, *Matrons and Marginal Women in Medieval Society* (Woodbridge, 1995), pp. 19–31.

M. Kowaleski and J. M. Bennett, 'Crafts, Gilds and Women in the Middle Ages: Fifty Years after Marian K. Dale', *Signs*, 14 (1988–89), pp. 474–501.

J. R. Lander, 'Marriage and Politics in the Fifteenth Century: The Nevilles and the Wydevilles', *Bulletin of the Institute of Historical Research*, 36 (1963), pp. 119–52.

J. Laughton, 'Women in Court: Some Evidence from Fifteenth-Century Chester', in N. Rogers, ed., *England in the Fifteenth Century: Proceedings of the 1992 Harlaxton Symposium* (Stamford, Conneticut, 1994), pp. 89–99.

J. L. Laynesmith, *The Last Medieval Queens: English Queenship, 1445–1503* (Oxford, 2004).

P. Lee, *Nunneries, Learning and Spirituality in Late Medieval English Society* (Woodbridge, 2001).

K. J. Lewis, N. J. Menuge and K. M. Phillips, eds, *Young Medieval Women* (Stroud, 1999).

H. Leyser, *Medieval Women: A History of Women in England, 450–1500* (London, 1995).

D. Logan, *Runaway Religious in England, c. 1240–1540* (Cambridge, 1996).

M. E. Mate, *Daughters, Wives and Widows after the Black Death: Women in Sussex, 1350–1535* (Woodbridge, 1998).

M. E. Mate, *Women in Medieval English Society* (Cambridge, 1999).

J. Mattingly, 'The Medieval Parish Guilds of Cornwall', *Journal of the Royal Institution of Cornwall*, new series, 10, part 3 (1989), pp. 290–329.

H. E. Maurer, *Margaret of Anjou: Queenship and Power in Late Medieval England* (Woodbridge, 2003).

J. H. McCash, ed., *The Cultural Patronage of Medieval Women* (Athens, Georgia, 1996).

K. B. McFarlane, *The Nobility of Later Medieval England* (Oxford, 1973).

M. K. McIntosh, 'Local Responses to the Poor in Late Medieval and Tudor England', *Continuity and Change*, 3 (1988), pp. 209–45.

M.K.McIntosh, *Working Women in English Society, 1300–1620* (Cambridge, 2005).

S. McSheffrey, *Gender and Heresy: Women and Men in Lollard Communities, 1420–1530* (Philadelphia, Pennsylvania, 1995).

C. M. Meale, ed., *Women and Literature in Britain, 1150–1500* (Cambridge, 1993).

Medieval Women in Southern England, Reading Medieval Studies, 15 (1989).

N. J. Menuge, ed., *Medieval Women and the Law* (Woodbridge, 2000).

M. A. Meyer, 'Early Anglo-Saxon Penitentials and the Position of Women', *Haskins Society Journal*, 2 (1990), pp. 47–61.

M. A. Meyer, 'Queens, Convents and Conversion in Early Anglo-Saxon England', *Revue Bénédictine*, 109 (1999), pp. 90–116.

M. A. Meyer, 'Women's Estates in Later Anglo-Saxon England: The Politics of Possession', *Haskins Society Journal*, 3 (1991), pp. 111–29.

S. D. Michalove, 'The Education of Aristocratic Women in Fifteenth-Century England', in S. D. Michalove and A. C. Reeves, eds, *Estrangement, Enterprise and Education in Fifteenth-Century England* (Stroud, 1998), pp. 117–39.

C. E. Moreton, *The Townshends and their World: Gentry, Law and Land in Norfolk, c. 1450–1551* (Oxford, 1992).

A. M. Morganstern, *Gothic Tombs of Kinship in France, the Low Countries and England* (Philadelphia, Pennsylvania, 2000).

M. Müller, 'The Function and Evasion of Marriage Fines on a Fourteenth-Century English Manor', *Continuity and Change*, 14 (1999), pp. 169–90.

A. R. Myers and C. H. Clough, eds, *Crown, Household and Parliament in Fifteenth Century England* (London, 1985).

M. Oliva, 'Counting Nuns: A Prosopography of Late Medieval English Nuns in the Diocese of Norwich', *Medieval Prosopography*, 16 (1995), pp. 27–55.

M. Oliva, *The Convent and the Community in Late Medieval England: Female Monasteries in the Diocese of Norwich, 1350–1540* (Woodbridge, 1998).

N. Orme, 'Children and the Church in Medieval England', *Journal of Ecclesiastical History*, 45 (1994), pp. 563–87.

N. Orme, *From Childhood to Chivalry: The Education of the English Kings and Aristocracy, 1066–1530* (London, 1984).

N. Orme, *Medieval Children* (New Haven, Connecticut, 2001).

N. Orme, 'The Culture of Children in Medieval England', *Past and Present*, 148 (1995), pp. 48–88.

N. Orme and M. Webster, *The English Hospital, 1070–1570* (New Haven, Connecticut, 1995).

J. C. Parsons, ed., *Medieval Queenship* (Stroud, 1994).

J. C. Parsons, ed., *The Court and Household of Eleanor of Castile in 1290*, Pontifical Institute of Medieval Studies, Studies and Texts, 37 (Toronto, 1977).

J. C. Parsons and B. Wheeler, eds, *Medieval Mothering* (New York, 1996).

S. J. Payling, 'The Economics of Marriage in Late Medieval England: the Marriage of Heiresses', *Economic History Review*, 54 (2001), pp. 413–29.

S. J. Payling, 'The Politics of Family: Late Medieval Marriage Contracts', in R. H. Britnell and A. J. Pollard, eds, *The McFarlane Legacy* (Stroud, 1995), pp. 21–47.

F. Pedersen, *Marriage Disputes in Medieval England* (London, 2000).

S. A. C. Penn, 'Female Wage-Earners in Late Fourteenth-Century England', *Agricultural History Review*, 35 (1987), pp. 1–14.

S. A. C. Penn and C. Dyer, 'Wages and Earnings in Late Medieval England: Evidence from the Enforcement of the Labour Laws', *Economic History Review*, 43 (1990), pp. 356–76.

K. M. Phillips, *Medieval Maidens: Young Women and Gender in England, 1270–1540* (Manchester, 2003).

L. R. Poos, 'Sex, Lies and the Church Courts of Pre-Reformation England', *Journal of Interdisciplinary History*, 25 (1994–95), pp. 585–607.

J. B. Post, 'A Fifteenth-Century Customary of the Southwark Stews', *Journal of the Society of Archivists*, 5 (1974–77), pp. 418–28.

J. B. Post, 'Ravishment of Women and the Statutes of Westminster', in J. H. Baker, ed., *Legal Records and the Historian* (London, 1978), pp. 150–64.

J. B. Post, 'Sir Thomas West and the Statute of Rapes, 1382', *Bulletin of the Institute of Historical Research*, 53 (1980), pp. 24–30.

D. Postles, 'Brewing and the Peasant Economy: Some Manors in Late Medieval Devon', *Rural History*, 3 (1992), pp. 133–44.

D. Postles, 'Migration and Mobility in a Less Mature Economy: English Internal Migration, c. 1200–1350', *Social History*, 25 (2000), pp. 285–99.

C. Rawcliffe, *Medicine and Society in Later Medieval England* (Stroud, 1995).

C. Rawcliffe, *Medicine for the Soul: The Life, Death and Resurrection of an English Medieval Hospital. St Giles's, Norwich, c. 1249–1550* (Stroud, 1999).

C. Rawcliffe, 'The Hospitals of Later Medieval London', *Medical History*, 28 (1984), pp. 1–21.

Z. Razi, *Life, Marriage and Death in a Medieval Parish: Economy, Society and Demography in Halesowen, 1270–1400* (Cambridge, 1980).

Z. Razi, 'The Myth of the Immutable English Family', *Past and Present*, 140 (1993), pp. 3–44.

Z. Razi and M. Smith, eds, *Medieval Society and the Manor Court* (Oxford, 1996).

F. Riddy, 'Mother Knows Best: Reading Social Change in a Courtesy Text', *Speculum*, 71 (1996), pp. 66–86.

J. T. Rosenthal, 'Aristocratic Marriage and the English Peerage, 1350–1500: Social Institution and Personal Bond', *Journal of Medieval History*, 10 (1984), pp. 181–94.

J. T. Rosenthal, 'Other Victims: Peeresses as War Widows, 1450–1500', *History*, 72 (1987), pp. 213–30.

M. C. Ross, 'Concubinage in Anglo-Saxon England', *Past and Present*, 108 (1985), pp. 3–34.

G. Rosser, *Medieval Westminster, 1200–1450* (Oxford, 1989).

J. Scammell, 'Freedom and Marriage in Medieval England', *Economic History Review*, 27 (1974), pp. 523–37.

E. Searle, 'Seigneurial Control of Women's Marriage: The Antecedents and Function of Merchet in England', *Past and Present*, 82 (1979), pp. 3–43.

E. Searle, 'Women and the Legitimization of Succession at the Norman Conquest', R. A. Brown, ed., *Anglo-Norman Studies*, 3 (1981), pp. 159–70.

E. Searle, P. A. Brand, P. R. Hyams and R. Faith, 'Debate: Seigneurial Control of Women's Marriage', *Past and Present*, 99 (1983), pp. 123–60.

S. Shahar, *Childhood in the Middle Ages* (London, 1990).

S. Shahar, *Growing Old in the Middle Ages* (London, 1997).

S. Shahar, *The Fourth Estate: A History of Women in the Middle Ages* (London, 1983).

M. M. Sheehan, *Marriage, Family and Law in Medieval Europe. Collected Studies* (Toronto, 1996).

M. M. Sheehan, *The Will in Medieval England: From the Conversion of the Anglo-Saxons to the End of the Thirteenth Century*, Pontifical Institute of Medieval Studies, Studies and Texts, 6 (Toronto, 1963).

W. J. Sheils and D. Wood, eds, *Women in the Church*, Studies in Church History, 27 (Oxford, 1990).

I. Short, 'Patrons and Polyglots: French Literature in Twelfth-Century England', in M. Chibnall, ed., *Anglo-Norman Studies*, 14 (1991), pp. 29–49.

P. Skinner, ed., *The Jews in Medieval Britain: Historical, Literary and Archaeological Perspectives* (Woodbridge, 2003).

L. Smith and J. H. M. Taylor, *Women, the Book and the Godly* (Woodbridge, 1995).

L. Smith and J. H. M. Taylor, *Women, the Book and the Worldly* (Woodbridge, 1995).

R. M. Smith, 'Coping with Uncertainty: Women's Tenure of Customary Land in England, c. 1370–1430', in J. Kermode, ed., *Enterprise and Individuals in Fifteenth-Century England* (Stroud, 1991), pp. 43–67.

R. M. Smith, ed., *Land, Kinship and Life-Cycle* (Cambridge, 1984).

R. M. Smith, 'Women's Property Rights under Customary Law: Some Developments in the Thirteenth and Fourteenth Centuries', *Transactions of the Royal Historical Society*, 5th series, 36 (1986), pp. 165–94.

P. Stafford, *Queens, Concubines and Dowagers: The King's Wife in the Early Middle Ages* (Leicester, 1998).

P. Stafford, *Queen Emma and Queen Edith: Queenship and Women's Power in Eleventh-Century England* (Oxford, 1997).

P. Stafford, 'Queens, Nunneries and Reforming Churchmen: Gender, Religious Status and Reform in Tenth- and Eleventh-Century England', *Past and Present*, 163 (1999), pp. 3–35.

P. Stafford, 'The King's Wife in Wessex, 800–1066', *Past and Present*, 91 (1981), pp. 3–27.

P. Stafford, *Unification and Conquest: A Political and Social History of England in the Tenth and Eleventh Centuries* (London, 1989).

P. Stafford, 'Women and the Norman Conquest', *Transactions of the Royal Historical Society*, 6th series, 4 (1994), pp. 221–49.

F. H. Stoertz, 'Young Women in France and England, 1050–1300', *Journal of Women's History*, 12 (2001), pp. 22–46.

R. N. Swanson, *Religion and Devotion in Europe, c. 1215–c. 1515* (Cambridge, 1995).

A. F. Sutton, 'The Early Linen and Worsted Industry of Norfolk and the Evolution of the London Mercers' Company', *Norfolk Archaeology*, 40 (1987–89), pp. 201–25.

A. F. Sutton, 'The Shop-Floor of the London Mercery Trade, c. 1200-c. 1500: The Marginalisation of the Artisan, the Itinerant Mercer and the Shopholder', *Nottingham Medieval Studies*, 45 (2001), pp. 12–50.

F. Swabey, *Medieval Gentlewoman: Life in a Widow's Household in the Later Middle Ages* (Stroud, 1999).

H. Swanson, *Medieval Artisans: An Urban Class in Late Medieval England* (Oxford, 1989).

J. Swanson, 'Childhood and Childrearing in *Ad Status* Sermons by Later Thirteenth-Century Friars', *Journal of Medieval History*, 16 (1990), pp. 309–31.

J. A. F. Thomson, 'Orthodox Religion and the Origins of Lollardy', *History*, 74 (1989), pp. 39–55.

J. A. F. Thomson, 'Piety and Charity in Late Medieval London', *Journal of Ecclesiastical History*, 16 (1965), pp. 178–95.

S. Thompson, *Women Religious: The Founding of English Nunneries after the Norman Conquest* (Oxford, 1991).

J. H. Tillotson, *Marrick Priory: A Nunnery in Late Medieval Yorkshire*, Borthwick Paper 75 (York, 1989).

J. H. Tillotson, 'Visitation and Reform of the Yorkshire Nunneries in the Fourteenth Century', *Northern History*, 30 (1994), pp. 1–21.

M. Vale, *The Princely Court: Medieval Courts and Culture in North-West Europe, 1270–1380* (Oxford, 2001).

E. Van Houts, *Memory and Gender in Medieval Europe, 900–1200* (Basingstoke, 1999).

N. Vickers, 'The Social Class of Yorkshire Medieval Nuns', *Yorkshire Archaeological Journal*, 67 (1995), pp. 127–32.

R. Voaden, ed., *Prophets Abroad: The Reception of Continental Holy Women in Late-Medieval England* (Woodbridge, 1996).

S. S. Walker, ed., *Wife and Widow in Medieval England* (Ann Arbor, Michigan, 1993).

J. C. Ward, *English Noblewomen in the Later Middle Ages* (London, 1992).

J. C. Ward, *Women in Medieval Europe, 1200–1500* (London, 2002).

A. K. Warren, *Anchorites and their Patrons in Medieval England* (Berkeley, California, 1985).

D. Watt, ed., *Medieval Women in their Communities* (Cardiff, 1997).

D. Watt, *Secretaries of God: Women Prophets in Late Medieval and Early Modern England* (Woodbridge, 1997).

S. L. Waugh, 'Marriage, Class and Royal Lordship in England under Henry III', *Viator*, 16 (1985), pp. 181–207.

D. Webb, *Pilgrimage in Medieval England* (London, 2000).

J. Whittle, 'Inheritance, Marriage, Widowhood and Re-Marriage: A Comparative Perspective on Women and Landholding in North-East Norfolk, 1440–1580', *Continuity and Change*, 13 (1998), pp. 33–72.

A. Williams, *The English and the Norman Conquest* (Woodbridge, 1995).

J. Wogan-Browne, *Saints' Lives and Women's Literary Culture, c. 1150–1300* (Oxford, 2001).

K. L. Wood-Legh, *Perpetual Chantries in Britain* (Cambridge, 1965).

C. M. Woolgar, *The Great Household in Late Medieval England* (New Haven, Connecticut, 1999).

B. Yorke, *Nunneries and the Anglo-Saxon Royal Houses* (London, 2003).

B. Yorke, *Wessex in the Early Middle Ages* (Leicester, 1995).

Index